STUDIES IN WELSH H

Editors

RALPH A. GRIFFITHS   CHRIS WILLIAMS
ERYN M. WHITE

37

THE COMMUNIST PARTY OF GREAT BRITAIN
AND THE NATIONAL QUESTION IN WALES, 1920–1991

THE COMMUNIST PARTY OF GREAT BRITAIN AND THE NATIONAL QUESTION IN WALES, 1920–1991

by

DOUGLAS JONES

CARDIFF
UNIVERSITY OF WALES PRESS
2017

www.uwp.co.uk

British Library CIP Data
A catalogue record for this book is available from the British Library

ISBN 978-1-78683-131-6 (hardback)
ISBN 978-1-78683-130-9 (paperback)
eISBN: 978-1-78683-132-3

The right of Douglas Jones to be identified as author of this work has been asserted in accordance with sections 77 and 79 of the Copyright, Designs and Patents Act 1988.

The University of Wales Press acknowledges funding by the Welsh Books Council in publication of this volume.

Typeset by Mark Heslington Ltd, Scarborough, North Yorkshire
Printed by CPI Antony Rowe, Melksham

SERIES EDITORS' FOREWORD

Since the foundation of the series in 1977, the study of Wales's history has attracted growing attention among historians internationally and continues to enjoy a vigorous popularity. Not only are approaches, both traditional and new, to the study of history in general being successfully applied in a Welsh context, but Wales's historical experience is increasingly appreciated by writers on British, European and world history. These advances have been especially marked in the university institutions in Wales itself.

In order to make more widely available the conclusions of original research, much of it of limited accessibility in postgraduate dissertations and theses, in 1977 the History and Law Committee of the Board of Celtic Studies inaugurated this series of monographs, *Studies in Welsh History*. It was anticipated that many of the volumes would originate in research conducted in the University of Wales or under the auspices of the Board of Celtic Studies, and so it proved. Although the Board of Celtic Studies no longer exists, the University of Wales continues to sponsor the series. It seeks to publish significant contributions made by researchers in Wales and elsewhere. Its primary aim is to serve historical scholarship and to encourage the study of Welsh history.

CONTENTS

SERIES EDITORS' FOREWORD   V

LIST OF ACRONYMS AND ABBREVIATIONS   ix

Introduction   1

1   Conspicuous by its Absence, 1920–1932   6

2   The Awakening of a National Consciousness within the Communist Party in Wales, 1933–1950   50

3   Praxis, Neglect and Renewal, 1950–1969   120

4   Devolution, Defeat and Dissolution, 1970–1991   199

Conclusion   285

BIBLIOGRAPHY   306

INDEX   329

LIST OF ACRONYMS AND ABBREVIATIONS

AEU	Amalgamated Engineering Union
ARJAC	Anglo-Russian Joint Advisory Council
BDA	Broad Democratic Alliance
BRS	*The British Road to Socialism*
BSP	British Socialist Party
BUF	British Union of Fascists
CC	Central Committee
CCG	Communist Campaign Group
CLC	Central Labour College
CLP	Communist Labour Party
CND	Campaign for Nuclear Disarmament
Comintern	Communist (Third) International
CPB	Communist Party of Britain
CPGB	Communist Party of Great Britain
CPI	Communist Party of Ireland
CYIG	Welsh Language Society
DPC	District Party Committee
EC	Executive Committee
ECCI	Executive Committee of the Communist International
GFTC	Glamorgan Federation of Trades Councils
ILP	Independent Labour Party
ILS	International Lenin School
KSČ	Communist Party of Czechoslovakia
LCDTU	Liaison Committee for the Defence of Trade Unions
MFGB	Mineworkers' Federation of Great Britain
MMM	Miners' Minority Movement
NCB	National Coal Board
NCC	National Cultural Committee
NCP	New Communist Party
NMM	National Minority Movement
NUM	National Union of Mineworkers

NUT	National Union of Teachers
NUWM	National Unemployed Workers' (Committee) Movement
OB	Organisational Bureau
PB	Political Bureau
PC	Political Committee
PCE	Spanish Communist Party
PCF	French Communist Party
PCI	Italian Communist Party
PWC	Parliament for Wales Campaign
RILU	Red International of Labour Unions
RSS	Rhondda Socialist Society
RWG	Revolutionary Workers' Groups
SDF	Social Democratic Federation
SLP	Socialist Labour Party
SNP	Scottish National Party
SWCC	South Wales Communist Committee
SWMF	South Wales Miners' Federation
SWSS	South Wales Socialist Society
TGWU	Transport and General Workers' Union
TUC	Trades Union Congress
URC	Unofficial Reform Committee
USC	United Socialist Council
WAC	Wales for the Assembly Campaign
WCSMC	Wales Congress in Support of Mining Communities
WEC	Welsh Executive Committee
WRCL	Welsh Regional Council of Labour
WSF	Workers' Socialist Federation
YCL	Young Communist League

INTRODUCTION

The establishment of the National Assembly for Wales in 1999 marked the culmination of another stage of the debate on Welsh self-government which, commencing in 1886 with the formation of Cymru Fydd, had spanned a 'long twentieth century' in Welsh politics. A central component of this debate was the nature of the relationship between socialism and nationalism, one of the most divisive and complex issues in twentieth-century Welsh politics. The role played by Plaid Cymru and the Labour Party on the road to the National Assembly has, understandably, formed the basis for most of the academic work related to the devolution debate. A small, but growing body of work has begun to focus on Labour's relationship with nationalism and the national question and on the role of socialism within Plaid Cymru.[1] In contrast, the Communist Party of Great Britain's (CPGB) relationship with the national question remains a neglected part of the story of Welsh devolution, and yet from the mid-1930s onwards the party was supportive of Welsh self-government, offered progressive policies on the Welsh language and played an active role in both the Parliament for Wales Campaign of the 1950s and the Wales for the Assembly Campaign during the 1979 devolution referendum campaign. The CPGB's absence from this debate reflects its

---

[1] On the Labour Party's attitude to Welsh nationalism and the national question, see Carwyn Fowler, 'Nationalism and the Labour Party in Wales', *Llafur*, 8 (4), 2003, pp. 97–105; John Gilbert Evans, *Devolution in Wales: Claims and Responses 1931–1979* (Cardiff, 2006); R. Merfyn Jones and Ioan Rhys Jones, 'Labour and the Nation' in Duncan Tanner, Chris Williams and Deian Hopkin (eds), *The Labour Party in Wales 1900–2000* (Cardiff, 2000), pp. 241–63; John Graham Jones, 'Y Blaid Lafur, Datganoli a Chymru, 1900–1979', *Cof Cenedl VII*, 1992, pp. 167–200; on Plaid Cymru and socialism, see Richard Wyn Jones, *Rhoi Cymru'n Gyntaf: Syniadaeth Plaid Cymru Cyfrol 1* (Cardiff, 2007); Laura McAllister, *Plaid Cymru: The Emergence of a Political Party* (Bridgend, 2001); John Davies, *The Green and the Red: Nationalism and Ideology in 20th Century Wales* (Aberystwyth, 1985).

absence from the broader field of Welsh political studies, which, by focusing on the two main Welsh parties, Labour and Plaid, has left the CPGB's role in Welsh politics relatively unexplored – a surprising omission since despite its electoral insignificance the party had influence in excess of its small size, playing a prominent role within the Welsh labour movement and within a number of extra-parliamentary political movements. The party therefore deserves serious attention when discussing Welsh politics and it offers an interesting contrast to both the Labour Party and Plaid Cymru's approach to the national question, and thus an original perspective from which to approach the relationship between socialists and the national question in Wales.

The history of the CPGB has undergone a significant transformation since the late 1980s, a transformation which can largely be attributed to the opening of the party's archives in Manchester to the public in 1994 along with those of the Communist International in Moscow, both of which have provided a new impetus for research.[2] From being a relatively under-researched party, it now boasts a number of well-researched histories, both general and thematic.[3] Unfortunately, the history of the party in Wales remains an under-researched area. There is no specific work on the party in Wales and where the party's history in Wales has been studied in any detail it has tended to be in the context of other subjects – its often-prominent role in relation to the South Wales Miners' Federation has been covered in Hywel Francis and Dai Smith's history of that organisation; both Hywel Francis and Robert Stradling have studied the party's involvement in the Spanish Civil War and the International Brigades; Stuart Macintyre's volume on working-class militancy during the inter-war period focuses partly on the communists of the village of Maerdy or 'Little Moscow'; while, most recently, Kevin Morgan, Andrew Flinn and Gidon Cohen have partly focused on Wales in relation to discussion

---

[2]   See Kevin Morgan, 'The Archives of the British Communist Party: An Historical Overview', *Twentieth Century History,* 7 (3), 1996, pp. 404–21; and Kevin Morgan, 'The CPGB and the Comintern Archives', *Socialist History* 2, 1993, pp. 9–29.

[3]   For an extensive bibliography of works about and by the CPGB, see Dave Cope, *Bibliography of the Communist Party of Great Britain* (London, 2016).

3

on issues such as migration and ethnicity and their effects on the party and on the nature of party membership.[4] There is also a small number of biographies and autobiographies of leading figures in the Welsh party, the most recent of which is Nina Fishman's outstanding biography of Arthur Horner.[5] The literature on the party's relationship with the national question in Wales and the devolution debate is even sparser, amounting to all of two articles.[6] To an extent historians of the party in Wales, as in the rest of Britain, were restricted by the lack of access to the party's archives and, despite the opening of the party's archives, those of the Welsh party remained inaccessible until 2002, when they were deposited at the National Library of Wales, having resided in the garage of the former secretary of the Welsh party, Bert Pearce, since the party's dissolution. This development has, for the first time, offered historians the chance to research the history of the Welsh party more fully than ever before.

This study seeks to answer three key questions. First, what was the nature of the relationship between the CPGB and the national question in Wales between 1920 and 1991? While the national question in Wales was only fleetingly a major concern for the British party, following the nationalist resurgence of the mid- to late 1960s and in the run-up to the 1979 devolution referendum, from the late 1930s onwards, and especially during the post-war period, the national question and specifically support for a Welsh parliament gained increasing prominence in the Welsh party's policy programme. In exploring the party's relationship to the national question, the present study adopts a broader

---

[4] Hywel Francis and Dai Smith, *The Fed: A History of the South Wales Miners in the Twentieth Century* (Cardiff, 1998); Hywel Francis, *Miners Against Fascism: Wales and the Spanish Civil War* (London, 1984); Robert Stradling, *Wales and the Spanish Civil War: The Dragon's Dearest Cause?* (Cardiff, 2004); Stuart Macintyre, *Little Moscows: Communism and Working Class Militancy in Inter-War Britain* (London, 1980); Kevin Morgan, Andrew Flinn and Gidon Cohen, *Communists and British Society, 1920–91* (London, 2007).

[5] Nina Fishman, *Arthur Horner: A Political Biography*, 2 vols. (London, 2010); Arthur Horner, *Incorrigible Rebel* (London, 1960); Will Paynter, *My Generation* (London, 1972).

[6] Brian Davies, 'Heading for the Rocks', *Arcade*, 5 February 1982; Lyndon White, 'The CPGB and the National Question in Post-War Wales: The Case of Idris Cox', *Communist History Network Newsletter* 12, Spring 2002.

framework for examining the national question not only tracing the development of the party's policy on the issue of self-government, but also examining its broader policy programme for Wales, especially in fields such as language and education, where the Welsh party was granted significant leeway in developing polices that were specific to Wales. It will also examine the party's attitude to Welsh culture and the Welsh language; how the party viewed Wales' relationship to England, Britain and Britishness; its relationship with Welsh nationalism; and the discourse offered by the party in relation to Welsh history.

Secondly, we examine the organisational structure of the party, primarily in relation to the Welsh party and its relationship with the party centre. In examining this relationship, a central issue is the measure of autonomy the party had in developing policy for Wales. Theoretically, the role of the party's District Committee was to gauge local conditions and offer guidance and suggestions to the party centre on polices that suited these specific conditions within the broader policy framework developed at the British level. Clearly, the specific needs of Wales as a nation, especially in areas such as language, culture and self-government, gave the Welsh District more leeway in developing policy, than it did to English districts without these important national characteristics. The present study will seek to trace the extent to which the party had autonomy in developing policy in these areas, whilst also identifying points of consensus and points of conflict between the party centre and the Welsh District.

Finally, we will ask what the CPGB's attitude to the national question tells us about the broader relationship between the left and the national question in Wales. One aim of the study is to offer a new perspective to the left's attitude to the national question by showing that there were alternatives to the Labour Party's 'slow and unwilling' path to self-government.[7] Unlike much of the labour movement in Wales, rather than rejecting self-government per se, the CPGB, finding the middle ground between the Labour Party and Plaid Cymru on the issue, sought to develop a policy on the national

---

[7] Jones, 'Y Blaid Lafur, Datganoli a Chymru, 1900–1979', p. 199. My translation.

question that could accommodate Wales' right to self-determination while maintaining the unity of the British working-class movement, which was viewed as the only viable means by which capitalism could be defeated in Britain. In more specific terms the study will also seek to explore the question of why the CPGB was more engaged with the national question than the Labour Party in Wales, arguing in general terms that in line with other communist parties, the party came to the realisation that in order to counter its public perception as an alien import into the domestic political scene and to broaden its popular appeal, it had to associate itself with domestic traditions and national culture, while arguing for progressive polices on self-determination with their roots in Marxist theory. In addition, the study will illustrate how from the 1950s onwards the party's policy on Welsh self-government complemented the increasingly reformist policy programme adopted by the party during the post-war era in the form of successive versions of its party programme, *The British Road to Socialism*, central to which was the radical reform of the British state and constitution as well as a focus on the devolving of democratic power.

The book comprises four chapters and is structured chronologically to provide narrative cohesion. The first chapter examines the period between the party's formation in 1920 and the beginning of the end of the Third Period in 1932, and, looking at the situation in Ireland and Scotland, seeks to answer why the national question in Wales was absent from the party's policy during this early period. The second chapter examines the period between 1933 and 1950 from the party's initial engagement with the national question at the beginning of the Popular Front period, through to the further development of its policy on the issue in the post-war period, noting the influence of international and domestic factors, both British and Welsh. The third chapter examines the period from 1950 to 1969, beginning with the party's involvement in the Parliament for Wales Campaign, the period of relative inactivity on the issue that followed, the party's re-engagement with the issue during the early 1960s and the major reassessment of party policy that followed the re-emergence of Welsh nationalism as a major force in Welsh politics from the mid-1960s onwards. The fourth and final chapter examines the period from 1970 through to the party's dissolution in 1991 and looks at the party's role in the extended devolution debate in Wales during the 1970s, its role in the Wales for the Assembly Campaign and its response to the 1979 referendum defeat, its role in the establishment of the Wales TUC, its pursuit of alliances with the nationalist movement in the context of the CPGB's turn to Eurocommunism from the late 1970s onwards, and the party's dissolution in 1991.

1

CONSPICUOUS BY ITS ABSENCE, 1920–1932

The first twelve years of the CPGB's existence were characterised by crisis, struggle and disappointment. Despite the
optimism expressed at its foundation, the party was soon
struggling to make an impact, the adoption of the united
front in 1921 and the Bolshevisation of the party organisation in 1922 failing to deliver the mass party that both
the party leadership and the Communist International
(Comintern) desired. While the party made some progress
within the trade union movement during this period, its
influence was largely restricted to a small, but significant
number of industries, most notably mining and engineering.
Similarly, although the party was able to find some allies on
the left, attempts to affiliate with the Labour Party came to
nothing, relations between the two parties becoming increasingly hostile over the decade with communists proscribed
from membership of the Labour Party by 1924. It was not
until the General Strike and miners' lockout that the CPGB
was to make significant gains, but the party proved unable to
retain these new members as mass unemployment took its
toll on the militancy of an increasingly demoralised working
class and the party came under concerted attack from both
the Labour Party and the Trades Union Congress (TUC).
These problems were compounded by the adoption of a new,
extreme left-wing line in 1928, that of 'class against class',
characterised by bitter attacks on both social democrats and
the trade unions, with the CPGB's natural allies on the left of
the labour movement particular targets. The new line's vision
of an increasingly militant working class moving towards the
CPGB proved a complete misreading of British conditions at
the time, its goal of bringing the British working class under
the CPGB's independent leadership only leading the party
down a blind alley of self-imposed isolation.

South Wales was to provide the CPGB with one of its strongest bases of support, where the party was able to build on a tradition of militancy dating back to the pre-war Cambrian Combine strikes and the publication of the syndicalist *The Miners' Next Step*, as well as on the organic links in the coalfield between the workplace, the lodge and the community which allowed for greater political penetration. The Welsh party proved relatively successful during this early period, becoming increasingly influential within the coalfield's main political organisation, the South Wales Miners' Federation (SWMF), through the careful cultivation of alliances with leading left-wingers within the union and the growing influence of leading communist miners such as Arthur Horner. By 1924 the CPGB was a significant force within the SWMF and party members also held important positions in local Labour parties in areas such as the Rhondda and Maesteg, while communist influence in certain mining villages such as Maerdy and Bedlinog attested to the possibilities available to the CPGB in the coalfield. As at the British level it was during the General Strike and the seven-month miners' lockout that the CPGB, as the only consistent supporter of a militant line during the lockout, was to reach the peak of its powers. For the CPGB in Wales the adoption of class against class proved particularly damaging, pushing the Welsh party to the brink of collapse. A turn away from working within the trade unions and the sectarian nature of the new line saw support for the CPGB dwindle to almost nothing in south Wales, while attacks on the party's leading industrial militant in the coalfield, Arthur Horner, saw the party almost lose its most valuable asset. Only the abandonment of the new line in 1932 allowed the party to begin the slow road to recovery.

The national question was conspicuous by its absence during this period; the party in south Wales focused on its industrial work. However, a tradition of local autonomy evident among the syndicalists of south Wales was also evident amongst south Wales communists at the party's foundation, a tradition that found some room for manoeuvre during its early years due to the federal structure initially adopted by the party. From 1922, however, the party became increasingly centralised, as it went through the process of Bolshevisation, thus diminishing the Welsh party's autonomy. By the Third Period the weakness of the CPGB in Wales was raising serious concerns at the party centre on which the Welsh party leadership was increasingly dependent, to the extent that some of the more experienced party members were accusing them of been the party centre's 'yes-men'.

CELTIC COMMUNISM? COMMUNISM AND THE NATIONAL QUESTION IN THE CELTIC NATIONS, 1920–1932

The available evidence shows that the CPGB showed no interest in the Welsh national question between 1920 and 1932. As a means of assessing the CPGB's lack of interest in the national question in Wales during this period, we must therefore begin by looking at how communists in other Celtic nations viewed the national question. The cases of Ireland and Scotland provide two contrasting examples of situations where Irish communists, on the one hand, lent their active support to the national struggle for independence, and, on the other, in Scotland where the party showed a distinct lack of interest in the national question and resisted the formation of a separate Scottish communist party, despite the efforts of the country's leading Marxist activist to put independence firmly on the political agenda of the radical left. Both cases offer some tentative answers as to why the CPGB failed to engage with the Welsh national question during this period.

From its establishment in October 1921 the national question was a central focus for the Communist Party of Ireland's (CPI) activities and policy.[1] The CPI's ultimate aim was the establishment of a Workers' Republic, although for much of the period in question it viewed the creation of an Irish

---

[1] For the history of Communism in Ireland, see Emmet O'Connor, *Reds and the Green: Ireland, Russia and the Communist Internationals* (Dublin, 2004); Mike Milotte, *Communism in Modern Ireland: The Pursuit of the Workers' Republic since 1916* (Dublin, 1984). For biographies of leading figures in the Irish communist movement, see Charlie McGuire, *Roddy Connolly and the Struggle for Socialism in Ireland* (Cork, 2008); Emmet O'Connor, *James Larkin* (Cork, 2002); Seán Byers, *Seán Murray: Marxist-Leninist and Irish Socialist Republican* (Sallins, 2015).

Republic as a necessary stage in the pursual of that goal. Established just prior to its signing, the Anglo-Irish Treaty was to prove a turning point for the CPI, the party being the first organisation to declare its opposition to the treaty whilst declaring its support for an Irish Republic, arguing that the Free State was promoting the interests of British imperialism.[2] Despite some involvement in organising the unemployed and in disputes involving agricultural workers, the CPI's overriding focus, especially with the outbreak of the Civil War, was on pursuing alliances with republicans, party leader Roddy Connolly believing that the CPI was too weak and ill-equipped to make any inroads into the labour movement.[3] Both the CPI and the Comintern viewed the republican movement, especially the IRA, as the group in Irish society with the most revolutionary potential and it was winning this movement for communism where the CPI's hopes lay. As Emmett O'Connor notes, 'Whatever influence the tiny CPI might exert on a few soviets was small beer compared with the prize of shaping the republican revolution.'[4] Initially, communists had sought to curry favour with the republicans by facilitating arms deals with the Soviet Union. From July 1922 onwards the focus was placed on getting the IRA and the republican movement to adopt a social policy developed in conjunction with the Comintern representative Mikhail Borodin.[5] Seeking an alliance with the republicans was to remain the main focus for the CPI until its dissolution in early 1924, indeed the CPI would pursue this policy in contradiction to the Comintern directives in December 1921 to pursue united fronts with reformist socialists. Rejecting forming alliances with the Labour Party due to its support for the Anglo-Irish Treaty, the CPI was to ignore this directive until the Fourth Comintern Congress held a year later, where the CPI was brought in line with Comintern policy.[6] This decision went some way to fostering the demise of the party with Milotte noting that two factions

---

[2] Milotte, *Communism in Modern Ireland,* p. 52.
[3] O'Connor, *Reds and the Green,* pp. 55–6, 58–61.
[4] O'Connor, *Reds and the Green,* p. 61.
[5] O'Connor, *Reds and the Green,* pp. 66–7; McGuire, *Roddy Connolly,* pp. 58–62.
[6] O'Connor, *Reds and the Green,* pp. 57–8, p. 77.

were discernible; one that saw the national question as the starting point for party activity and another that saw economic issues as the party's main focus.[7]

Following an unsuccessful attempt to establish a new party under Jim Larkin's leadership, the Comintern were eventually to establish a new party based around former International Lenin School (ILS) students, notably Seán Murray and Jim Larkin Jr., and members of various communist front groups such as the Labour Defence League and the League Against Imperialism. The domination of these front groups by republicans attested to the increasing links between communist and left republicans during this period, as did the high number of republicans involved in the preparations for the establishment of the new party.[8] The Comintern's desire to foster relations with republicans and to win them over to communism was also reflected in the decision to exclude republicans from attacks under the new Third Period line emanating from the Comintern from 1927 onwards.[9] However, much of this goodwill was lost in the summer of 1930, following the establishment of a new party, the Revolutionary Workers' Party, when this decision was reversed, leading to the withdrawal of support from a large number of left republicans, most notably Peadar O'Donnell.[10] While the party subsequently toned down its criticism of republicans, largely ignoring them in the party press, this proved a disastrous change of line for the Irish communists for, as O'Connor notes, 'at a time when the IRA was moving left and borrowing ideas and techniques from communism, the [communists] complied with a policy that isolated them from the IRA dominated Comintern fronts, intensified their marginality, and conflicted with the visceral sympathies of most of their members'.[11] The new line sought to place the new party, in June 1933 re-established as the CPI, at the head of the national movement, with Murray declaring in a speech

---

[7] Milotte, *Communism in Modern Ireland,* p. 69.

[8] Milotte, *Communism in Modern Ireland,* p. 98; O'Connor, *Red and the Green,* p. 153.

[9] O'Connor, *Red and the Green,* p. 140.

[10] O'Connor, *Red and the Green,* p. 155.

[11] O'Connor, *Reds and the Green,* p. 160.

to the 1932 CPGB Congress that 'The Communist Party must be the party of national independence.'[12] To secure this aim the CPI on its re-establishment declared its intention to form communist fractions within the IRA with the aim of splitting the organisation.[13]

A number of the key left republican figures who were close to the communists, including O'Donnell, had in March 1931 received approval by the IRA's General Army Convention to establish a new radical political group, Saor Éire. While this can be viewed as a reaction to the Third Period line emanating from the communists on behalf of these left republicans, it also reflected the IRA's own realisation that it needed to engage in political activity in order to regain political relevance as it lost members to Fianna Fáil, and to make its political positon clear in the face of attacks from both the left and right of the political spectrum.[14] The Saor Éire programme owed much to the links that had developed between communists and left republicans, its content having a distinct communist influence. Indeed, Seán Murray, by now the leading figure amongst the Communists, had been consulted on the Saor Éire programme and had assisted in setting up some of its branches, while Communist delegates were among those who attended its inaugural conference in September 1931. However, the Irish communists and Comintern opposed the formation of a political party, and while the Communists remained publically neutral in regards to Saor Éire its fraction within the organisation, applying the Third Period line, argued that the IRA left should join the communists.[15]

Saor Éire was soon cut adrift by the IRA following the enactment of a Public Safety Bill that led to the proscription of a large number of left-leaning political organisations, including Saor Éire and the IRA. By 1933 relations between the communists and the IRA leadership had worsened significantly, with the IRA prohibiting members from engaging in

[12] Milotte, *Communism in Modern Ireland*, p. 113.
[13] Milotte, *Communism in Modern Ireland*, p. 143.
[14] Adrian Grant, *Irish Socialist Republicanism 1909–36* (Dublin, 2012), pp. 175–6.
[15] Grant, *Irish Socialist Republicanism 1909–36*, pp. 181–2; O'Connor, *Red and the Green*, pp. 170–3.

independent political activity, and, following the establishment of the CPI, publishing a statement definitively
distancing the IRA from the CPI. Issued at the height of one
of a series of red scares in Ireland, as Adrian Grant argues,
the IRA statement was as much motivated by the IRA
'attempting to protect itself from anti-communism' as it was
in trying to 'prevent its members from joining a party that
aimed at supplanting the IRA as the main revolutionary force
in the country'.[16] The prohibition on independent political
activity had, by March 1934, led to a split within the IRA, with
leading left republicans such as O'Donnell, George Gilmore
and Frank Ryan leaving the IRA to form the Republican
Congress. While it was active in establishing the Congress,
the CPI was also to play a decisive role in its demise. Its opposition to the Congress becoming a political party and its
support for the Congress seeking a Republic rather than a
Workers' Republic, as a result of misinformation given to the
party by the CPGB regarding the Comintern's preferred line,
contributed to a damaging split at its inaugural conference
that left the Congress moribund at its inception.[17] This was to
be the last serious attempt to build a united front between
communists and republicans in the pre-war period, notwithstanding the CPI's mobilisation alongside left republicans
over the Spanish Civil War. By 1941 the party in Éire had
withdrawn from political activity, rather than argue the case
for Irish involvement in the Second World War, its Northern
Irish section remaining the only functioning part of the party
in Ireland. By 1949 the Northern Irish CPI had moved to a
position that increasingly accepted the reality of partition as
it sought to consolidate its predominately Protestant support
base.[18]

What factors made the CPI's approach to the national
question different to that of the CPGB in Scotland and Wales
during the united front and class against class periods? First,
the CPI's approach to the national question owed much to
the particular political environment, at a crucial point in

---

[16] Grant, *Irish Socialist Republicanism*, p. 206.
[17] O'Connor, *Red and the Green*, pp. 200–6.
[18] O'Connor, *Red and the Green*, p. 233.

Ireland's struggle for independence, in which it had been established in October 1921. Clearly, this was the most obvious factor in necessitating a meaningful engagement with the Irish national question. The CPI, if it was to pursue its aim of becoming a mass communist party, could hardly have not placed the national question at the core of its activity. Its failure to make inroads into the labour movement only heightened this focus on the national question and relations with republicans.

A second contributory factor was the CPI's links both to the pre-war socialist republican tradition that traced its ancestry back to James Connolly and Jim Larkin, and, more generally, to the broader republican movement.[19] All three of the communist movement's leaders during this period could trace their lineage back to this tradition. Roddy Connolly was not only James Connolly's son but also a veteran of the Easter Rising, while Seán Murray had been an active IRA member in Antrim and maintained a close friendship with Peader O'Donnell throughout his life.[20] The republican background of many of the CPI's members was, as O'Connor has noted, typical of communist parties established in colonial countries where most party members had been involved in the national liberation movements.[21] It was also key in making the national question and relations with the republican movement a central issue for the CPI. This republican make-up of the party was not always viewed a positive attribute, a highly critical 1934 article in *Communist International* arguing that 'The republican background of many of its members and their experience in clandestine guerrilla warfare "kept many of these comrades from active participation in economic and political struggles of the masses"'.[22]

---

[19] On the Irish socialist republican tradition, see Grant, *Irish Socialist Republicanism* and Emmett O'Connor, 'The Age of the Red Republic: The Irish Left and Nationalism, 1909–36', *Saothar* 30, 2005, pp. 73–82. Both Grant and O'Connor give prominence to Jim Larkin's contribution to the development of socialist republicanism through his key role in the establishment of the Irish Transport and General Workers' Union.

[20] On Connolly, see McGuire, *Roddy Connolly*, pp. 11–16; on Murray, see Byers, *Seán Murray*, pp. 12–18.

[21] O'Connor, *Red and the Green*, p. 51.

[22] Milotte, *Communism in Modern Ireland*, p. 143.

Crucially, it was in the socialist republican sphere that the CPI was to make its biggest impact. While the CPI failed to build a mass party and overcome its marginality in the industrial and political sphere, and while it had also failed to form an alliance with the IRA or to successfully supplant it as the major revolutionary force in Ireland, it did exert significant influence over the direction of socialist republicanism during this period, following its development of a social policy in 1922. That social policy had formed the basis of Liam Mellows' influential Notes from Mountjoy Jail, while we have seen above how the close collaboration between communists and left republicans influenced the Saor Éire programme.[23] In addition, most of the united front groups through which the 'relationships [that] would form the basis of socialist republican politics until 1936' were developed were 'started by Irish or British communists and joined by leftist republicans'.[24] As O'Connor argues, 'the history of the CPI provides further evidence that social republicanism during the Free State era was not due exclusively to an internal revision of IRA policy. Communists prompted the evolution at almost every step'.[25]

A third factor was the position of the Irish struggle for independence within Marxist theory and the role of the Comintern. Within Marxist debates on nationalism and the right of self-determination, the Irish national struggle had always been seen as the type of progressive national movement that should be supported. Marx would eventually come round to arguing that a successful independence struggle in Ireland would strike a decisive blow against British imperialism in its own backyard that would provide an example for British workers.[26] The Comintern also supported the struggle for Irish independence, sharing the view of most CPI members that Ireland was a colony with an unresolved

---

[23] Grant, *Irish Socialist Republicanism*, p. 139.

[24] Grant, *Irish Socialist Republicanism*, pp. 161–2.

[25] Emmett O'Connor, 'Communists, Russia and the IRA, 1920–1923', *The Historical Journal*, 46 (1) (2003), p. 131.

[26] For Marx's changing views on the Irish independence, see Erica Benner, *Really Existing Nationalisms: A Post-Communist View from Marx and Engels* (Oxford, 1995), pp. 186–97 and Kevin B. Anderson, *Marx at the Margins: On Nationalism, Ethnicity and Non-Western Societies* (Chicago, 2010), pp. 115–53.

national question.[27] Indeed at the Second Comintern Congress Lenin's thesis on the national and colonial question had been far in advance of a report prepared by the Irish delegation, which took an ambivalent view on nationalism, while calling for a federal workers' republic for Britain and Ireland, a point of view quickly shed as Congress progressed.[28] Comintern support for the national struggle in Ireland and its identification of the republican movement as one with revolutionary potential allowed the CPI to place the national question and its relationship with republicans at the heart of its strategy, to the extent that it effectively ignored the Comintern's directives regarding the united front for a year. The Comintern's willingness to initially adapt the Third Period line with regards to the republicans illustrates how important they felt the republican movement was to building a mass communist movement in Ireland. However, ultimately it was the Comintern's decision to fully implement the Third Period line, at a time when the IRA was shifting leftwards, that effectively killed off any hopes of a united communist and republican movement.

For Scottish communists debates regarding the national question during this period largely revolved around John Maclean's attempt to form a Scottish communist party and his support for Scottish independence. Following Maclean's failure to establish a separate Scottish communist party, with most Scottish communists entering the CPGB, the CPGB showed little interest in the Scottish national question, remaining aloof to the labour movement campaign for home rule in the early 1920s. Indeed, when the party did take up a position on devolution it was distinctly centralist.[29] This was particularly evident in calls by communist-linked trade unions for the unification of the Trades Union Congress (TUC) and the Scottish Trades Union Congress (STUC) following the general strike.[30] The emergence of the Scottish national movement in the early 1930s saw the CPGB begin to

[27] O'Connor, *Red and the Green*, p. 238.
[28] O'Connor, *Red and the Green*, pp. 43–4.
[29] Michael Keating and David Bleiman, *Labour and Scottish Nationalism* (London, 1979), p. 19.
[30] Keating and Bleiman, *Labour and Scottish Nationalism*, p. 100.

engage with the Scottish national question, especially following the 1932 Dumbarton by-election, where the Communist candidate had finished behind the Nationalist. However, it was not until the Popular Front period that the Scottish party would fully engage with the issue. Much of the CPGB's opposition to devolution during this period was based around a desire to maintain the unity of the British working class, an issue that would remain at the core of debates on devolution in both Scotland and Wales, and on Britishness, throughout the CPGB's history.[31]

John Maclean's support for Scottish independence came against a background in which support for Scottish devolution was relatively widespread in the Scottish labour movement with the ILP, in particular, active in campaigning for home rule.[32] While Maclean would dismiss home rule as a form of 'anaemic local government',[33] from 1919 until his death in 1923 Maclean's support for independence, specifically in the form of a communist republic, was to become a distinct feature of his political programme. By the end of 1919, Maclean had joined Ruaraidh Erskine's National Committee,[34] which was campaigning for Scottish independence, although he had refused to sign a memorial on independence for the Paris Peace Conference, arguing that a Scottish parliament should be established not by a 'quack Peace Conference ... but through the revolutionary efforts of the Scottish working class itself'.[35] Indeed, Maclean was in general highly critical of the post-war settlement for those small nations promised self-determination during the war, viewing the Bolsheviks not Woodrow Wilson as 'the real bene-factors of the home rule movement'.[36] Some leading nationalists, including Erskine, had also welcomed the Bolshevik Revolution due to the threat it presented to the

[31] Keating and Bleiman, *Labour and Scottish Nationalism,* pp. 19–20.
[32] William Kenefick, *Red Scotland: The Rise and Fall of the Radical Left c.1872–1932* (Edinburgh, 2007), pp. 185–6.
[33] Nan Milton, *John Maclean* (London, 1973), p. 248.
[34] Milton, *John Maclean,* pp. 216–17.
[35] Milton, *John Maclean,* p. 195.
[36] John Maclean, *In the Rapids of Revolution* (London, 1979), p. 165.

established political order and the Bolsheviks' support for the right of self-determination.[37]

To a large extent, Maclean's support for independence was rooted in his anti-imperialism and internationalism. Central to Maclean's support for Scottish independence was his belief that a 'Scottish break-away', specifically in the form of a communist republic, 'would bring the empire crashing to the ground and free the waiting workers of the world'. For Maclean, Scottish independence could act not only as a spur to the break-up of the British Empire, but also as both an example to English workers and a platform from which a contribution could be made to the further development of world communism.[38] Indeed, Maclean made a direct link between the end of British imperialism and the further development of both the Soviet Union and world communism, noting that 'The break-up of the British empire is necessary for the economic development of Russia and the releasing of revolutionary world forces held in check by that bloodiest of bloody brutes, John Bull.'[39] A final geopolitical influence on Maclean's support for independence was his belief that another inter-imperialist war was imminent, this time between Britain and the USA, with Maclean believing that only independence would be able to keep Scotland out of such a war, and ensure 'that the youths of Scotland will not be forced out to die for England's markets' as they had done during the First World War.[40]

Maclean's support for Scottish independence as a means of weakening British imperialism and furthering a global communist revolution can be directly linked to Marxist analyses of the Irish national struggle. The Easter Rising and the War of Independence were a significant influence on Maclean, who viewed the events in Ireland as 'the most revolutionary in British history'.[41] After visiting Ireland in 1919,

---

[37] David Howell, *A Lost Left: Three Studies in Socialism and Nationalism* (Manchester, 1986), p. 210.

[38] Maclean, *In the Rapids of Revolution*, p. 220.

[39] Maclean, *In the Rapids of Revolution*, p. 242

[40] Maclean, *In the Rapids of Revolution*, pp. 237–8.

[41] Maclean, *In the Rapids of Revolution*, p. 178; on Maclean's engagement with the Irish Revolution, see Gavin Foster, "Scotsmen, Stand by Ireland": John Maclean and the Irish Revolution', *History Ireland* 16 (1) (2008), pp. 32–7.

Maclean became a vocal supporter of the Irish republicans, campaigning for a general strike in support of the withdrawal of British troops during the War of Independence.[42] Maclean had initially argued that a successful Irish struggle 'depended on the revolt and success of British labour', but by June 1920 had reversed this view arguing that a successful outcome in Ireland could become an 'inciting influence to British labour'. Indeed, for Maclean, Irish independence was a necessary step in establishing communism in Ireland.[43] Maclean was also highly critical of the inaction of the British left during the crisis, especially the revolutionary left, who he argued had failed 'to see with sufficient clarity the tight corner the Irish are placing Britain in'. Again making links between national struggles and the struggle for communism Maclean argued that Sinn Féin 'who make no profession of socialism or communism, and who are at best non-socialists, are doing more to help Russia and the revolution than all we professed Marxian Bolsheviks in Britain'.[44]

There were also important domestic considerations that influenced Maclean's support for independence. Maclean's support for independence was inextricably linked his belief that Scotland held a better prospect for the establishment of communism than Britain as a whole. This was based on two assumptions, the first, which owed much to the heightened political agitation on the Clyde and elsewhere in Scotland in the immediate post-war period, was the belief that the Scottish working class were more advanced politically than their counterparts in England.[45] For Maclean, Scotland was 'firmer for Marxism than any other part of the British empire', and he was convinced that an independent Scottish parliament would return a socialist majority, which would pave the way for a social revolution: 'The social revolution is possible sooner in Scotland than in England.'[46] Maclean was not alone in believing that the Scottish workers were more advanced than those in England, it was a view

[42] Maclean, *In the Rapids of Revolution*, p. 175.
[43] Maclean, *In the Rapids of Revolution*, pp. 174–5.
[44] Maclean, *In the Rapids of Revolution*, p. 178.
[45] Milton, *John Maclean*, p. 217.
[46] Maclean, *In the Rapids of Revolution*, pp. 225 and 247.

expressed at different times by the Scottish Co-operative Movement, with whom Maclean had strong links, the Scottish Farm Servants' Union and by the Scottish Union of Dock Labourers, following the collapse of the Triple Alliance in 1921.[47] While Maclean clearly viewed independence as crucial to the advancement of socialism in Scotland, and by example to the rest of Britain and the world, his position was complicated by his support for industrial unionism and his belief that Scottish workers should 'be joined in one big industrial union with their British comrades against industrial capitalism'.[48]

Second, Maclean argued that the 'Celtic or communistic system' of the Highland clans had allowed them to avoid feudalism and the 'abominations of serfdom'.[49] While this distinctly romantic conception of a Celtic communism owed much to James Connolly, who made similar claims for the Irish clans, in Scotland these themes were developed by both Maclean and Erskine, who published a series of articles in Maclean's paper *The Vanguard* and also in *The Socialist.*[50] For Maclean these Highland traditions would need to be revived and used as a basis for building communism in Scotland, although Maclean insisted that these would need to 'adapted to modern conceptions and conditions'. As Maclean himself succinctly put it, 'back to communism and forward to communism'.[51]

Maclean's decision to form a separate Scottish communist party was linked to a number of these issues, notably his belief that conditions for socialist advance were riper in Scotland than in England, that the establishment of a Scottish Workers' Republic would strike a significant blow to British imperialism and that a separate Scottish communist party could play an important role in ensuring that Scotland was not drawn into another imperialist war.[52] Maclean was

---

[47] Keating and Bleiman, *Labour and Scottish Nationalism,* pp. 74–5 and p. 86; Kenefick, *Red Scotland,* pp. 186–7.
[48] Maclean, *In the Rapids of Revolution,* p. 237.
[49] Maclean, *In the Rapids of Revolution,* p. 221.
[50] Howell, *A Lost Left,* p. 32.
[51] Maclean, *In the Rapids of Revolution,* p. 218.
[52] B. J. Ripley and J. McHugh, *John Maclean* (Manchester, 1989), p. 114.

also insistent that in line with the Comintern's '21 points' Scotland, as a nation, had every right to establish its own communist party. For Maclean, any co-operation between revolutionary groups in the United Kingdom had to be based on the recognition of their right to organise based on their national units:

> We in Scotland must not let ourselves play second fiddle to any organisation with headquarters in London, no more than we would ask Dublin to bend to the will of London. Whatever co-operation may be established between the revolutionary forces in the countries at present composing the 'United' Kingdom, that co-operation must be based on the wills of the free national units.[53]

Unfortunately for Maclean, this was not a view held in Moscow, the Second Comintern Congress passing a resolution in favour of the amalgamation of all the communist groups and parties in Britain.[54] Shortly after its establishment both Scottish and South Wales Districts of the CPGB were established, but it would be some time until these were recognised as distinct national units of the CPGB. Although a committed supporter of the Bolsheviks, Maclean had also expressed some concern at the level of Russian influence on the formation of the CPGB, noting 'We stand for the Marxian method applied to British conditions. The less Russians interfere in the internal affairs of other countries at this juncture the better for the cause of revolution in those countries.'[55] While these issues were significant factors in Maclean's decision to attempt to establish a separate party, his animosity to the CPGB was also driven by his belief that the CPGB was not rigorously Marxist, especially from the perspective of some of the members it had attracted who had been fast-tracked into leadership positions, such as the former Liberal and anti-socialist campaigner Lieutenant-Colonel C. J. Malone.[56]

[53] Maclean, *In the Rapids of Revolution*, pp. 224–5.
[54] L. J. Macfarlane, *The British Communist Party: Its Origin and Development* (London, 1966), pp. 63–4.
[55] Maclean, *In the Rapids of Revolution*, p. 225.
[56] Milton, *John Maclean*, pp. 219–20; Ripley and McHugh, *John Maclean*, pp. 126–8.

Maclean, despite being the most recognised Scottish Marxist activist of the period, and despite his reputation amongst the Bolsheviks leading to his being made an honorary president of the Petrograd Soviet and the Soviet Consul for Scotland, was excluded from the unity negotiations that led to the establishment of the CPGB in January 1921. This was partly due to circumstance: in 1919 Maclean had broken with the British Socialist Party (BSP), the key driver of the unity negotiations, disillusioned with its overriding focus on these negotiations and the 'Hands Off Russia' campaign at the expense of its broader industrial and political strategy.[57] This left him on the outside from the very beginning, his firm belief in the need for a Scottish party only serving to further distance Maclean from the negotiations surrounding the establishment of the British party. A final contributory factor was the personal conflicts which had arisen between Maclean and other figures in the revolutionary movement, most notably with William Gallacher. Maclean, who viewed Gallacher as an anarchist rather than a Marxist, was particularly concerned that Gallacher was presenting Moscow with false information on British conditions, grossly exaggerating the extent of a revolutionary situation.[58] Indeed, Maclean's failure to visit Moscow to make his own case to Lenin probably put paid to any hopes he had of establishing a communist party recognised by the Comintern. Gallacher himself was to play a significant role in thwarting the establishment of Maclean's Scottish Communist Party, which Maclean had hoped to establish from the remnants of the Socialist Labour Party (SLP) in December 1920, Gallacher writing to the SLP Executive Committee accusing Maclean of being mentally unstable. While Gallacher's intervention points to significant concern within CPGB circles regarding the potentiality of Maclean's venture, the central factor in the failure to establish the party lay in the SLP's own refusal to 'support any nationalist initiative'.[59] Maclean would go on to establish the Scottish

---

[57] Ripley and McHugh, *John Maclean*, p. 124.
[58] Ripley and McHugh, *John Maclean*, p. 130; Milton, *John Maclean*, p. 255.
[59] Ripley and McHugh, *John Maclean*, p. 145.

Workers' Republican Party in 1923, by which time the CPGB had drawn most of the Scottish revolutionaries into its fold, with Scots taking up most of the key leadership positions. Increasingly isolated, Maclean's party failed to make any major impact.

The dispute between Maclean and the CPGB over the formation of a separate Scottish Party meant that the British Marxist whose opposition to the war can be most characterised as being close to a Leninist position was left outside the Communist Party.[60] As Keating and Bleiman note, it also 'deprived the Communist Party of its most nationalist elements'.[61] For the CPGB Maclean also presented the party with a problematic legacy – how was it to explain the fact that Maclean had not joined the CPGB and had instead sought to establish a separate party? While Soviet historians sought to explain this away by reference to an unidentified illness, to a withdrawal from politics or through simple omission, the line emanating from the CPGB linked it to Maclean's mental health.[62] Claims regarding Maclean's mental instability were given their first published airing in Gallacher's autobiography, *Revolt on the Clyde*.[63] However, links between his mental health and his political positions were made most explicitly in Tom Bell's short biography of Maclean, published by the CPGB's Scottish Committee in 1944, who lamented that due to the impact of prison on his mental health, during the post-war period Maclean had been unable 'to bring to bear upon the new tasks the same measure of sound judgment that characterised him in the pre-war years'.[64] While there is evidence to suggest that Maclean had suffered a nervous breakdown while in prison, linked to a delusion that his prison food was being poisoned, there is little ground for believing that this breakdown had effected the rest of his political career.[65] Indeed, Harry McShane would dismiss

[60] Ripley and McHugh, *John Maclean*, p. 114.
[61] Keating and Bleiman, *Labour and Scottish Nationalism*, p. 65.
[62] Ian D. Thatcher, 'John Maclean: Soviet Versions', *History*, 77 (251), 1992, 421–9.
[63] William Gallacher, *Revolt on the Clyde* (London, 1978), pp. 214–16.
[64] Tom Bell, *John Maclean: A Fighter for Freedom* (Glasgow, 1944), p. 151.
[65] Ripley and McHugh, *John Maclean*, pp. 99–103.

Gallacher's claims as a 'scurrilous accusation'.[66] In reality, the spin placed on this issue by the CPGB was a dishonest attempt to link dissension with mental instability.

When looking at the failure of Welsh communists to engage with the national question during this period through the prism of the Irish and Scottish cases, we can draw some tentative conclusions. The most obvious contrast was the lack of a revolutionary situation linked to the national question in either Wales or Scotland. This is significant not only in domestic terms but also in how the Comintern viewed the different national claims of the Celtic nations. This factor is also related to how the differing claims were viewed at the time within the Marxist tradition. Indeed, Trotsky would attack Scottish socialists for their support for a Scottish parliament, arguing that it was something for which they would have 'absolutely no use'.[67] A second contrast was the lack in Wales of a similar socialist republican tradition as existed in Ireland in which issues of national independence and the establishment of a workers' republic were inextricably linked. A third contrast, this time with Scotland, was the lack of a figure similar to John Maclean to emerge to at least place the issue on the political agenda of the revolutionary left in Wales.

There are also similarities. In both Wales and Scotland, the overriding concern of the CPGB was in maintaining the unity of the British working-class movement, a position that precluded any serious engagement with the national question; indeed in Scotland this led the party to centralist positions. The connection between Liberalism and the national question in both Wales and Scotland must also have played a role in turning communists away from the issue, especially as the party entered the Third Period. The onset of the depression and the industrial struggles that were to follow also played a major role in both Wales and Scotland in keeping the party's focus away from the more abstract question of the nation. Finally, as we shall see, in both Wales and Scotland, the emergence of the national movement in the

---

[66]   Harry McShane and Joan Smith, *No Mean Fighter* (London, 1978), p. 151.

[67]   Kenefick, *Red Scotland*, p. 185.

1930s, notwithstanding its relative weakness, was to play a key role in initiating the CPGB's engagement with the national question in both nations. While the party in Wales showed little interest in the national question during the period under discussion, we can identify some devolutionary possibilities in the politics of south Wales revolutionaries and a strong sense of the value of local autonomy. In what remains of the chapter we shall examine these dimensions of the political thought and organisation of the south Wales revolutionaries and how these were impacted by developments within the CPGB.

United Fronts, Bolshevisation and Local Autonomy, 1920–1927

The establishment of the CPGB in August 1920 marked the end of a period of torturous negotiations between various disparate Marxist parties and revolutionary groups in Britain. The CPGB had emerged from a number of 'squabbling small groups' that were on the periphery of the labour movement.[68] As Willie Thompson has noted, this put the nascent CPGB at a disadvantage from its inception in that it was denied the significant bases of support and influence that continental communist parties could, in theory, build from.[69] Of these disparate groupings the leading players in the negotiations were the BSP, the Communist Unity Group, which had split from the SLP over the negotiations, and Sylvia Pankhurst's Workers' Socialist Federation (WSF). The fourth main group involved and the Welsh representative at the negotiations was the South Wales Socialist Society (SWSS), although this group would go out of existence before the negotiations were finalised, subsumed for the most part into the SLP and WSF, and replaced at the negotiating table by the South Wales Communist Council (SWCC).[70] Most of the south Wales revolutionaries who entered the CPGB did so

---

[68] Eric Hobsbawm, *Revolutionaries* (London, 1999), p 15.

[69] Willie Thompson, *The Good Old Cause: British Communism 1920–1991* (London, 1993), pp. 7–8.

[70] James Klugmann, *History of Communist Party of Great Britain Vol. 1: Formation and Early Years 1919–1924* (London, 1976), p. 21.

from these Welsh bodies, which had themselves emerged out of the syndicalist Unofficial Reform Committee (URC), the body responsible for *The Miners' Next Step*. Indeed, the SWSS had been responsible for the publication of its sequel, *Industrial Democracy for Miners*.[71] While the number of members joining the party was relatively low, as MacFarlane notes, 'The importance of South Wales to the Communist Party lay in the fact that for thousands of miners the Communist Party was the natural heir to the tradition of militant rank-and-file struggle against the coal owners, weak federation leadership and capitalism.'[72]

Central to the debate surrounding the unity negotiations was the question of local autonomy, which, along with the issues of parliamentary action and affiliation to the Labour Party, formed the crux of the matters at hand. The question of local autonomy, epitomised by a tendency within south Wales to form independent organisations such as the SWSS, also evident in the decision to establish the Industrial Democracy League rather than join Tom Mann's Industrial Syndicalist Education League in 1912, was central to the development of revolutionary ideas in Wales in the pre-CPGB period and offers some insight into how those syndicalists who entered the CPGB in 1920 may have viewed the increasing moves towards centralisation of the party in the years from 1922 onwards. They also offer, with their focus on the decentralisation of power, an intriguing insight into aspects of the national question.

Largely focused on the specific need to reorganise the Mineworkers' Federation and the coal industry, the syndicalists of south Wales had little to say explicitly on the subject of the national question, remaining, as David Egan has noted in Ablett's case, 'tantalisingly silent on the matter'.[73] Their opposition to parliamentary action suggests they would not have viewed a Welsh parliament as a solution to the ills affecting south Wales. However, the centrality of both local autonomy and the decentralisation of power to both *The*

[71] MacFarlane, *British Communist Party*, pp. 44–6.
[72] MacFarlane, *British Communist Party*, p. 46.
[73] David Egan, 'Noah Ablett 1883–1935', *Llafur*, 4 (3), 1986, p. 24.

Miners' Next Step and *Industrial Democracy for Miners* reflected a brand of revolutionary politics that was specifically concerned with democratising the workplace through the devolution of political power. While *The Miners' Next Step* argues for a more effective centralised union structure based on the concept of industrial unionism, crucially, through its critique of leadership and its debilitating effects through both self-interest and incorporation into the trade union and political establishment, it argues that such a union can only truly be effective if power is at the same time devolved to the branches and democratic control of the union established from the bottom up.[74] The central body of the union is envisioned as an essentially administrative body, responsive to the needs of the branches, acting as an arbiter in internal disputes and capable of providing effective unified national leadership when industrial disputes cannot be resolved locally; as the pamphlet notes 'Decentralisation for Negotiation' and 'Centralisation for Fighting'.[75] At all times, however, the power is held by the local branches, a position echoed in *Industrial Democracy for Miners* when it argues, 'the only possible method of control is from the bottom upwards'.[76] Local autonomy was better at solving local problems, due to its intimate knowledge of local conditions, as Ablett noted with regards to those favouring the nationalisation of the mines, 'They are willing to let ignorance in Whitehall sit in judgment of knowledge in the Rhondda, to let the man who does not know govern the men who do.'[77] However, this attitude was able to transcend mere parochialism, as William Hay, joint author of both *The Miners' Next Step* and *Industrial Democracy for Miners*, was keen to point out. For while *The Miners' Next Step*, he noted, was a response to the 'advanced economic development of South Wales', its aim was to offer what *The Times* described as a 'distinct advance on Continental

---

[74] Unofficial Reform Committee, *The Miners' Next Step: Being a Suggested Scheme for the Reorganisation of the Federation* (London, 1973), pp. 18–20.

[75] Unofficial Reform Committee, *The Miners' Next Step*, p. 30.

[76] Unofficial Reform Committee, *Industrial Democracy for Miners* (Porth, 1919), p. 12.

[77] Kenneth O. Morgan, 'Socialism and Syndicalism: The Welsh Miners' Debate, 1912' in *Modern Wales: Politics, Places and People* (Cardiff, 1995), p. 139.

Syndicalism' from a distinctly Welsh perspective, noting that 'Wales is not content to produce only boxers, millionaires, footballers and Chancellors. She must also contribute to the intellectual uplifting of humanity. "Cymru yn y blaen"!'[78]

Despite the hopes held by members at its formation, the CPGB had soon entered its first period of crisis. By January 1921, party membership had dropped to around 2,500, however, the influx of new members following a Second Unity Conference meant that membership rose again to 4,838 by July 1921, with a further influx of members following the 1921 miners' lockout pushing the figure up to 5,116 by June 1922. By November, however, the party's membership had again plunged to around half this figure – 2,761.[79] In south Wales, party membership had dropped from 600 in June 1922 to 215 members by December,[80] although the district remained the fourth largest in terms of the distribution of party membership, accounting for some 12 per cent of the total membership in June 1922.[81] In addition, the party's finances were also in crisis, the party dependent on Soviet subsidies to keep it afloat, receiving £55,000 from the Comintern between August 1920 and December 1921.[82] To further exacerbate matters, the party had also failed to gain any real influence within the trade unions or the Labour Party, while the arrest and imprisonment of key personnel, including the party's national organiser Bob Stewart and its secretary Albert Inkpin, had added to its woes. This poor performance inevitably led to criticism from both the Comintern and from within the party, notably from William Gallacher, which focused on the need for the reorganisation of the party along Bolshevik lines. The drive for party

[78] 'Syndic', 'The Miners' Next Step', *The Rhondda Socialist*, 16 March 1912, p. 5.

[79] Andrew Thorpe, 'Membership of the Communist Party of Great Britain', *The Historical Journal* 43 (3), 2000, p. 781.

[80] CPGB Archive, Communist Party of Great Britain Archive, Report on Party Membership 12 June 1922, 495/100/63/63, Labour History Archive and Study Centre (LHASC); CPGB Archive, Analysis of Branch Reports December 1922, 495/100/63/73, LHASC.

[81] Thorpe, 'Membership of the CPGB', p. 790; CPGB Archive, Report on Party Membership 12 June 1922, 495/100/63/63, LHASC.

[82] Andrew Thorpe, *British Communist Party and Moscow, 1920–43* (Manchester, 2000), p. 44.

reorganisation came directly from the Comintern, part of its broader campaign for the Bolshevisation of all its national sections, and was backed by figures such as Gallacher who, reflecting the views of many younger party members, viewed the radical reform of the party as a means of breaking with what they viewed as the outmoded practices of the propagandist Marxist parties of the recent past. In response to these concerns, a three-man commission comprising Rajani Palme Dutt, Harry Pollitt and Harry Inkpin was established to look at all aspects of the party's work.

At its inception the CPGB had adopted a federalist structure based around the party branches, which were grouped into geographical divisions. Each branch chairman was a member of the Divisional Committee, which in turn elected a Divisional Council. The party's Executive Committee (EC), in turn, was comprised of two representatives from each division, elected by the Divisional Council. This organisational structure raised two main concerns, firstly, that it gave too much power to the divisions and meant that there was little central control over the direction of party policy, and secondly, that it had created an unwieldy top-heavy structure, with one party functionary to every thirty-three party members by May 1922.[83] Concerns regarding the federal structure and the lack of central direction had become evident during the miners' lockout of 1921. While party members had been active during the lockout, with over sixty communists arrested, a significant proportion of them in the Rhondda Valley, much of the party's activity had been organised by local party groups, with little or no guidance emanating from the party centre.[84] For Mikhail Borodin, the Comintern representative in Britain from February to August 1922, 'there was not one party but as many parties as there were districts',[85] while Tom Bell noted 'much difficulty was experienced in trying to educate the comrades to recognise the necessity for central direction and executive responsibility for political leadership'.[86]

[83] Kevin Morgan, *Labour Legends and Russian Gold* (London, 2006), p. 49.
[84] MacFarlane, *British Communist Party*, p. 119.
[85] Borodin quoted in Morgan, *Labour Legends*, p. 38.
[86] Tom Bell, *British Communist Party: A Short History* (London, 1937), p. 82.

For the party commission, it was the organisational structure of the party that was at the heart of its problems, an
organisational structure that it viewed as better suited to the
traditions of the old, propagandist socialist parties, rather
than to a new revolutionary party committed to the principles
of the Bolshevik Revolution. As a result, the party was stag-
nating, both in terms of the lack of effective leadership and
direction it provided, and in the quality of members it
created, with a significant proportion of the membership not
taking an active role in party work, largely due to the weakness of local organisation and party training.[87] In particular,
the party's structure meant 'Each branch directed its own
members so that there were in practice as many directions of
policy as there were branches.'[88] In response, the commission
called for a new centralised party structure based on a strong
Central Committee (CC). The CC was to have both a Political
Bureau (PB) and an Organisational Bureau (OB), made up
of CC members, while Leading Committees would also be set
up with responsibility for given areas of policy, to better coordinate party policy. The executive itself would be elected by
congress rather than the districts in order to ensure that the
strongest candidates were allowed to stand for election and
reduce the power of the districts vis-à-vis the executive.

At the regional level District Party Committees were to be
set up along the same lines, with the District Party Committee
(DPC) elected at the District Party Congress. The DPC's role
was to ensure that the EC's decisions were implemented,
coordinate the activities of the membership and advise the
EC as to the specific conditions within the district and put
forward policy proposals related to these conditions. At the
local level the branch was to be replaced by the Local Party
Committee, but the real focus of organisation was the Area
Group, a small unit of party members in each locality, each
engaged in specific party work and maintaining daily contact
with each other. Each group leader was to report to the Local
Party Committee, which in turn was answerable to the DPC.
In addition to this, party members were also expected to

[87] *Report on Organisation presented by the Party Commission to the Annual Conference of
the Communist Party of Great Britain, October 7, 1922* (London, 1922), pp. 11–13.
[88] *Report on Organisation presented by the Party Commission*, p. 12.

participate in 'special groups and committees' be they speakers' groups or working within the local Labour Party fraction or trade union nuclei, while increased emphasis was put on the need for better party training and education.[89] The Commission's proposals were adopted at the party's Fifth Congress in October 1922.[90] A South Wales DPC was established at the first District Congress, held that December in Cardiff, with Dutt in attendance on behalf of the EC, and Jock Wilson elected as its first district organiser.[91]

Despite the initial enthusiasm for the new party structure, criticism of the reorganisation soon emerged. In reality, the reorganisation was just as unwieldy as the federal structure, with a further increase in the number of party organisers. Many party members complained that the focus on organisational forms was to the detriment of the spirit and inner life of the party, accusing the reformers of organisational fetishism. Of particular note were complaints from party members that they were expected to join so many party organisations or organisations related to the party's work, and were thus forced to attend so many meetings, that they had little time for actual party work. In addition, the centralisation of the party's organisation in London and the professionalisation of the party centre helped alienate some of the party's grass-roots activists in the industrial heartlands such as south Wales, whilst exciting the syndicalist sympathies of many within the CPGB who were already concerned at the profusion of party functionaries under the old party structure.[92] Reorganisation had also proved ineffective in solving the party's fundamental problems, with no significant rise in party membership and with the party still facing serious financial difficulties. The increased focus on party-based education and training had also led to a split between the party and the Plebs League.[93]

[89] *Report on Organisation presented by the Party Commission,* pp. 16–28.

[90] MacFarlane, *British Communist Party,* p. 83.

[91] CPGB Archive, Minutes of Organisation Bureau, 22 November, 6 December and 13 December 1922, CPGB 1995 Moscow Reel 1920s and 1930s (LHASC).

[92] Morgan, *Labour Legends,* pp. 206–17.

[93] Andy Miles, 'Workers' Education: The Communist Party and the Plebs League in the 1920s', *History Workshop* 18, 1984, pp. 102–14.

Most importantly, however, it had led to a diminution in the role of the districts, the party's Control Commission reporting to the Sixth Party Congress, held in May 1924, that the EC showed 'a tendency to underrate the importance of the District as a pivot of organisation', while the DPCs were failing to report adequately on their work, showing 'too much inclination to look to the Executive as the only source of inspiration and to forget that the DPC's in conjunction with the Executive constitute the Party lead'.[94] While the re-election of a number of the old leadership to an expanded CC at this congress and the removal of the main advocates of Bolshevisation from the OB led to a halt of the Bolshevisation process, no attempts were made to alter the new organisational structure of the party, a recognition of the Comintern's role in the process and its insistence that such measures be implemented. In addition, for many communists the centralisation and bureaucratisation associated with Bolshevisation was also seen as a feature of most modern political parties and as a natural part of the organisation of modern industrial society. However, while local autonomy within the party was diminished by the reorganisation, the stronger districts, such as south Wales, were still able to influence party policy to some degree. In addition, as in the case with the Comintern and the national sections, the general and often-confused nature of the lines emanating from the party centre meant that the districts had some leeway in how they interpreted party policy, a factor that would become particularly evident during the Third Period.

The Comintern's adoption of a united front strategy in December 1921 was a result of the end of the post-war revolutionary wave and a recognition that its thesis that world revolution was imminent was in need of reassessment. In the face of a resurgent capitalism, the aim of the united front was to consolidate gains made by the working class, to mount a unified defensive struggle to protect workers' interests and to act as a means of attracting workers to communism. Specifically, the thesis on the united front issued by the

---

[94] *Report of the Control Commission to the Party Congress, May 1924* (London, 1924), p. 7.

Executive Committee of the Communist International (ECCI) in December 1921, while insisting on the 'absolute independence of every communist party', called for a united front between these parties and all working-class organisations.[95] While the united front 'from above', through the collaboration of the leaderships of communist and other working-class organisations, was not discounted, the main emphasis of the united front was to be 'from below', by focusing their energies on influencing the rank and file, with the hope that they could eventually be won over to communism by the exposure of the inadequacies of their reformist leadership.

While the adoption of the united front had been unpopular with some continental parties, in the CPGB's case the new line was suited to its position as a small party with low membership in need of alliances to make a real impact.[96] At the British level, the party, despite some success within the trade unions, notably the Mineworkers' Federation of Great Britain (MFGB), on the whole struggled to make headway with the united front strategy prior to the General Strike in 1926. This was especially true of its relations with the Labour Party, which rejected all the CPGB's requests for affiliation and calls for a united front, the 1924 Labour Party Conference barring CPGB members from membership of the Labour Party.[97] In south Wales, however, the united front proved relatively successful, communists making significant progress within the ranks of the SWMF and the Labour Party. This can be attributed to the centrality of the miners' lodge to political organisation in south Wales, within which communists, many associated with the URC, were particularly active. Evidence from responses to a questionnaire on the united front, distributed to the districts by the EC in 1922 shows that the new line was broadly welcomed in south Wales, although concerns remained surrounding the level of cooperation

[95] 'Directives on the United Front of the Workers, Adopted by the ECCI, 18 December, 1921' in Jane Degras (ed.), *The Communist International 1919–1943: Documents Vol. 1, 1919–1922* (Oxford, 1956), pp. 307–16.

[96] McDermott and Agnew, *Comintern*, p. 32.

[97] Noreen Branson and Bill Moore, *Labour–Communist Relations, 1920–1951, Part 1- 1920–1935 (Our History Pamphlet 82)* (London, 1990), p. 18.

that should be pursued in particular in relation to the Labour Party.[98]

The Welsh party had gained some early success, most notably in its campaign in favour of the MFGB's affiliation to the Red International of Labour Unions (RILU), and in the serious consideration given to the idea of the SWMF itself affiliating to the same organisation, a proposal rejected following consultations with Borodin over fears that affiliation to the RILU would lead to the SWMF's expulsion from the MFGB.[99] For Lenin, this marked out the south Wales miners as a potential revolutionary vanguard amongst the British working class arguing that the SWMF's decision in favour of affiliation had the potential to create 'the beginning of the real proletarian mass movement in Great Britain', representing 'the beginning of a new era'.[100] While this was not to be the case the party, through the URC, was able to build on its success in south Wales, joining with the left-wing of the SWMF in the 100 per cent unionism campaign from June 1921 onwards and becoming a real force within the SWMF by 1924, playing a leading role in the election of A. J. Cook as leader of the MFGB. The party was to be given a further boost through the increasingly important role of Arthur Horner, who was becoming the most important communist militant within the SWMF, elected to its executive council in 1925.[101]

Despite its success, however, the south Wales party's focus on work within the SWMF led to concerns at the party centre that the South Wales DPC was becoming increasingly economistic in its outlook, focusing too much energy on industrial issues. This feeling was echoed by some in the south Wales party, including Mel Thomas, a leading communist from the Maesteg area, who had joined the party through his involvement with the Miners' Minority Movement (MMM). Thomas

---

[98]   CPGB Archive, J. R. Wilson to Albert Inkpin, undated [*c.*October 1922]; CPGB Archive, Jack Jones to EC, 15 October 1922; CPGB Archive, A. E. Cook to EC, undated [*c.*October 1922], CPGB 1995 Reel (LHASC).

[99]   MacFarlane, *British Communist Parry*, pp. 130–1.

[100]   V. I. Lenin, 'To Comrade Thomas Bell' in *On Britain* (Moscow, 1958), p. 562.

[101]   On Horner's rise to prominence within the SWMF, see Nina Fishman, *Arthur Horner: A Political Biography Vol. 1* (London, 2010), pp. 51–110.

notes that in the period after 1926 'there were big discussions [going] on in the Party ... and a lot of people felt that all we were becoming were left-wing trade unionists, and that not enough attention was given to building [a revolutionary party]'.[102] Like a number of other south Wales communists Thomas was also active in his local Labour Party at Caerau, becoming its secretary by 1926. CPGB members also retained a significant presence on Labour Party branches in Maesteg, Bedlinog and in the Rhondda.[103]

Despite a growing influence, it was not until the General Strike and the miners' lockout that the Welsh party grew substantially in terms of membership. In Britain as a whole party membership grew from some 6,000 in April 1926 to 12,000 by September; however, this figure had fallen to 5,000 by January 1928.[104] In Wales membership had grown to 1,500 by September 1926,[105] and by 1927 the South Wales District was the party's largest district with 2,300 members;[106] however, some 300 members had also left the party by February 1927.[107] Unlike Will Paynter, for whom the experience of 1926 was to lead to a lifelong commitment to the CPGB, the majority of the CPGB's new members had soon left the party, their experience of party membership proving transitory. Communists were particularly active during the General Strike and miners' lockout, with CPGB fractions in all the important councils of action,[108] and with much of the party's south Wales leadership arrested at the end of the General Strike in an attempt to decapitate the party.[109] However, the aftermath of the strike led to increasingly poisonous relations between the CPGB, the trade unions and Labour Party, especially after Comintern intervention led the CPGB to increase its criticism of the left-wing trade union leaders who had sat on the TUC General Council at the time of the

[102] Interview with Mel Thomas, 17 May 1973, AUD 283, SWML.
[103] MacFarlane, *British Communist Party*, pp. 190–1.
[104] Thorpe, 'Membership of the CPGB', p. 781.
[105] Smith and Francis, *The Fed*, p. 66.
[106] Kenneth Newton, *The Sociology of British Communism* (London, 1969), p. 176.
[107] Thorpe, *British Communist Party and Moscow*, p. 105.
[108] Roderick Martin, *Communism and the British Trade Unions 1924–1933: A Study of the National Minority Movement* (Oxford, 1969), p. 72.
[109] '1926 in Aberdare', *Llafur* 2 (2), 1977, p. 39.

General Strike. In consequence, the increasingly bitter and personal attacks on the trade union leadership, many of who were now former allies, led to the imposition of sanctions against the National Minority Movement (NMM), the CPGB's influential rank-and-file movement within the trade unions heralding the beginning of its decline. Relations with the Labour Party were no better, the decisions of the 1924 Labour Conference, implemented in south Wales for the first time, resulting in the disaffiliation of the Rhondda Borough Labour Party and the exclusion of communists from the Ogmore Divisional Labour Party in 1927. Increasingly, the CPGB was finding itself isolated from those working-class organisations that it was supposed to form a united front with. The groundwork for the emergence of the Third Period had been laid.

WALES AND THE THIRD PERIOD, 1928–1932

The period from 1928 to 1932 marked a significant left-turn for the international communist movement, leading to a period of unprecedented internal conflict within the CPGB as well as one of further decline after a period of relative progress between 1925 and 1926. The new direction was based on the work of Nikolai Bukharin who argued, as early as December 1926, that capitalism's advance since 1922 had created contradictions within the system that marked a significant heightening of class tensions and the possibility of the emergence of a new revolutionary wave, which Bukharin stressed, was a long way off. In addition, drawing on the recent experience of the General Strike in Britain, on the failure of united front policies in Germany and China, and on his own theories of state capitalism, Bukharin argued that the social democrats and the trade union movement were increasingly being incorporated into the administration of capitalism, thus decisively moving towards becoming a wing of the bourgeoisie rather than the working class, while the working class was becoming increasingly more militant.[110] Its adoption at the Sixth Comintern Congress marked the

---

[110] Nicholas N. Kozlov and Eric D. Weitz, 'Reflections on the Origins of the "Third

abandonment of the broader united front. The new communist strategy was to be based on its independent leadership of the working-class movement, focused on a policy of a united front from below aimed at drawing the rank and file away from the social democratic parties and the trade unions and into communist organisations, and for more open and vocal opposition to the established labour movement, while being aware of 'right deviations' among their own ranks. However, following its adoption the more sophisticated Bukharinist interpretation of the Third Period was, from July 1929, superseded by a cruder interpretation that stressed that revolution was now imminent, that the bourgeois state was undergoing a process of 'fascisation' and that social democrats were to be viewed as 'social fascists'. This was followed by a further revision in February 1930, this time emphasising the dangers of 'left deviation' as the failures of the second phase became apparent.[111]

Pressure on the CPGB leadership to adopt a change of line had been evident from late 1927 onwards, the party only formally adopting the new line at its Tenth Congress in January 1929 and only fully implementing the policy following Comintern intervention in February. Pressure for a change had come above all from the Comintern, but also from a group of 'Young Turks' within the party, notably William Rust, Walter Tapsell and Robin Page Arnot, as well as from other senior party figures such as Dutt and Pollitt. Further pressure had come from the districts, with the South Wales, London, Liverpool, Birmingham, Tyneside, Manchester and Sheffield conferences all voting in favour of a new electoral strategy based on outright opposition to the Labour Party.[112] However, the party's showing in the 1929 General Election, fought on a 'class against class' programme that identified the Labour Party as the 'third capitalist party' and called for a revolutionary workers' government, was a

Period": Bukharin, the Comintern, and the Political Economy of Weimar Germany', *Journal of Contemporary History* 24, 1989, pp. 387–410.

[111] Matthew Worley, 'Courting Disaster? The Communist International in the Third Period' in Matthew Worley (ed.), *In Serach of Revolution: International Communist Parties in the Third Period* (London, 2004, pp. 1–17.

[112] Thorpe, *British Communist Party and Moscow,* p. 129.

major setback, the party winning only 50,000 votes and losing its only MP, Shapurji Saklatvala.[113] A special congress, held at Leeds in November, saw the removal of much of the party leadership and the adoption of a line to the left of even that emanating from Moscow.[114] The victory of the left was to be short-lived, however. By December 1930 the Young Turks had lost the initiative, their own inadequacies in leadership exposed. The adoption of the new line failing to halt the decline in party membership, attempts to form new 'red unions' failed as had a communist-led textile strike in Bradford, while the CPGB's new daily newspaper, the *Daily Worker*, was failing under the editorship of Rust.

In September 1930, Pollitt, who had in line with the shift in Comintern policy recognised that left sectarianism was the greatest threat within the CPGB, was endorsed as party leader by the PB.[115] By February 1931 party membership had begun to grow again, given added impetus with the resurgence of the National Unemployed Workers' Movement (NUWM) and the collapse of the Labour Government in August and the election of a National Government. The CPGB's failure to capitalise on this at the 1931 General Election, in which it increased its vote to 75,000, led Pollitt, who had been opposed to the Comintern's policy of forming independent 'red unions', to argue that if the CPGB was to develop as a mass party it had to work through the trade unions and build up rank-and-file organisations, urging all CPGB members to join a trade union. The acceptance of these recommendations by the ECCI marked the first turn away from class against class and allowed the CPGB to begin to break out of the isolation it had placed itself.

The political impact of the Third Period on the CPGB was disastrous, isolating the party from its closest allies on the left as it relentlessly pursued the chimera of independent leadership. In the process the party lost its most effective instrument within the trade unions, the NMM. In terms of party

---

[113] *Class Against Class: The General Election Programme of the Communist Party of Great Britain 1929* (London, 1929), p. 10.

[114] Matthew Worley, *Class Against Class: The Communist Party in Britain Between the Wars* (London, 2002), pp. 141–3.

[115] Thorpe, *British Communist Party and Moscow*, pp. 168–9.

membership, it was during the Third Period that the party hit its lowest point, with membership dropping to 2,350 by August 1930,[116] although caution needs to be taken in ascribing this decline solely in terms of the impact of the Third Period. The decline had begun in 1927, before the adoption of the new line, reflecting a general trend towards reduced membership across the labour movement in this period, as demoralisation and unemployment took their toll. In addition, the party had mounted a significant recovery by January 1932, by which time membership had grown to 9,000.[117]

One district where the new line did have a negative effect on party membership was south Wales, which fell from 1,147 in February 1927 to only 264 in November 1930.[118] Throughout the Third Period the Welsh party was to be a constant concern, the leadership privately admitting that it was the only area where members had been lost due to the new line, identifying south Wales as 'the home of trade union legalism and denial of radicalism' and accusing the party of operating 'mainly as an opposition fraction within the South Wales Miners Federation'.[119] The strong tradition of working within the established trade unions and the unique position of the lodge within the community meant that the turn towards independent leadership, and especially the branding of fellow trade unionists as social fascists, led many workers to abandon the party altogether. The Welsh party leadership was also targeted as right wing following the Leeds conference, with Jock Wilson, the district organiser, and Dai Lloyd Davies removed along with Horner, to be replaced by supporters of the new line like Charlie Stead, Max Goldberg, Len Jefferies, Garfield Williams and Ben Francis. Significantly Stead, Jefferies, Williams and Goldberg were all to attend the ILS during this period.[120] In addition, the thesis that the

---

[116] Thorpe, 'Membership of the CPGB', p. 78.

[117] Mike Squires, 'CPGB Membership During the Class Against Class Years', *Socialist History* 3 (1993), pp. 4–13; Thorpe, 'Membership of the CPGB', pp. 781–2.

[118] Worley, *Class Against Class,* p. 37.

[119] Thorpe, 'Membership of the CPGB', p. 791; John McIlroy and Alan Campbell, 'The Heresy of Arthur Horner', *Llafur* 8 (2), 2001, p. 106.

[120] McIlroy and Campbell, 'The Heresy of Arthur Horner', p. 106.

workers were moving left as their leaders moved right, a central plank of the new line, found little resonance in south Wales. As Dai Lloyd Davies, a leading Maerdy communist, noted, 'When comrades speak of the radicalisation of the masses and the great wave of insurrection, I want to tell you that in my experience – which is not small – I have not seen a ripple of it.'[121]

The south Wales that had emerged from the seven-month miners' lockout was one that was bitter, demoralised, drained and defeated, reflected in the fall in membership of the SWMF to 75,480 by December 1930,[122] compared to a membership of 148,000 in 1924.[123] Those keen to maintain a sense of militancy faced almost insurmountable odds and the opprobrium of their fellow workers. As Oliver Powell, a Tredegar collier, noted,

> You never found so much hatred and bitterness amongst the workmen when we returned after 1926. They would hold us responsible for the state they were in … and they directed their venom directly at the strikers (i.e. the young militants) most unpleasant … But there you are we were supposed to be left-wing militants, and we had to put up with it.[124]

Both mass unemployment and emigration from the coal-field further weakened attempts to organise at the point of production, especially for communists who found themselves among the first to be victimised and denied work, migration from the coalfield a significant factor in the party's decline.[125] Increasingly, for those communists who stayed in south Wales the focus of political organisation moved from the lodge to the wider community, especially through the activities of the NUWM, revived following the organisation of a march of 300 unemployed miners from south Wales to London in November 1927.

---

[121] Branson, *History of the Communist Party of Great Britain 1927–1941* (London, 1985), p. 49.
[122] Francis and Smith, *The Fed*, p. 138.
[123] Francis and Smith, *The Fed*, p. 31.
[124] Francis and Smith, *The Fed*, p. 78.
[125] For the impact of migration on the Welsh party and the impact of Welsh migrants on other party districts, see Morgan, Cohen and Flinn, *Communists in British Society 1920–1991*, pp. 40–6.

These fundamental difficulties were exacerbated for the CPGB in south Wales by its increasingly fraught relationship with the Labour Party and the SWMF. Communists had been purged from local Labour parties in the Rhondda and Ogmore in 1927. Relations between the SWMF and the CPGB were also to deteriorate following the miners' lockout, the leadership of the MFGB keen to outlaw the MM from within its ranks, following bitter criticism from the NMM over the role of the SWMF leadership during the lockout. These tensions were further heightened following the adoption of the new line, with communists branding Federation officials as fascist and social fascist. In particular, the SWMF leadership was targeted with Tom Richards and Enoch Morrell attacked for their support of the Mond–Turner talks and S. O. Davies, along with A. J. Cook, targeted as 'fake lefts' by the party, the attack on Cook being particularly damaging for the party due to his exemplary role in the 1926 lockout.[126] Matters were to come to a head with the expulsion of the communist-controlled Maerdy Lodge in February 1930, for its support of Arthur Horner in the 1929 General Election, its continued attacks on the SWMF leadership as social fascists, and its links with the NUWM.

As membership dwindled from 546 in December 1929 to 264 by November 1930,[127] concerns for the district began emanating from the party centre, especially over the nature of its leadership. Increasingly, the party centre saw the South Wales DPC as holding the wrong line on a number of issues, and saw it as increasingly sectarian in its activities. A report by Garfield Williams provided evidence of this leftward drift among what remained of the party, noting that communists at pit meetings in Cardiff refused to sit with non-communists.[128] By April, the Maerdy branch was painting a bleak picture of the state of the party in south Wales, 'We may be termed despondent when we tell you that in our opinion the danger of disintegration of the Party in the District and locally in particular, is very real; working on the spot as we do,

[126] McIlroy and Campbell, 'The Heresy of Arthur Horner', p. 107.
[127] Worley, *Class Against Class*, p. 264, note 43.
[128] Worley, *Class Against Class*, p. 244.

we cannot fail to see this.'[129] A change of leadership was finally initiated in June following a call by the DPC for a coalfield strike in sympathy with Yorkshire woollen workers, a strike that in reality it had little hope of bringing off successfully, dismissed by the PB as 'a string of hopeless phrases'.[130]

The dispute that was to follow in 1931 between the CC and Arthur Horner over his alleged 'Hornerism' further highlighted the weakness of the party structure and organisation in south Wales, whilst also laying bare the tensions implicit in implementing a party line that was unsuited to local conditions. The dispute centred on Horner's opposition to the new line, especially the policy of establishing independent Communist-led trade unions, and was sparked by Horner's insistence that the party should not seek to extend a strike in the south Wales coalfield under communist leadership that had been called off by the SWMF.[131] Horner was immediately attacked by the PB for his failure to show independent leadership. For Horner, the party's insistence on pursuing independent leadership of the trade union movement was seriously damaging the party's prospects in Wales. He argued at a meeting of the PB in January that 'the tactics being applied in south Wales are responsible for reducing the district to the weakest place it has held in the last twenty years – these tactics of isolation will result in the party not being 240 strong but 100 strong'.[132]

By March, a campaign against Horner had begun in the *Daily Worker* orchestrated in particular by Rust, with Horner now accused of Hornerism, a difference over tactics elevated into an ideological heresy, with some members of the EC claiming that Hornerism was now prevalent within the party.[133] In April Horner lost the support of the DPC, with Idris Cox playing a leading role in swinging the vote against

[129] CPGB Archive, Central Committee minutes, 5 April 1930, CI Reel 1 (LHASC).

[130] Worley, *Class Against Class*, p. 267.

[131] For a detailed account of the affair, see Fishman, *Arthur Horner Vol. 1*, pp. 186–227.

[132] McIlroy and Campbell, 'The Heresy of Arthur Horner', p. 111; CPGB Archive, Central Committee minutes, 31 May 1931, CI Reel 2 (LHASC).

[133] CPGB Archive, Central Committee minutes, 15 March 1931, CI Reel 12 (LHASC).

him.[134] Horner, who had by now withdrawn from party work to all intents and purposes, agreed to appear in front of the EC in May, delivering an unrepentant defence of his position. With Horner, the party's leading industrial militant, on the brink of leaving the party, the Comintern intervened, Horner eventually agreeing to go to Moscow to recant. The Comintern's response to Horner's recantation was mixed for both the party centre and Horner himself. Significantly, Horner was not expelled from the CPGB by the Comintern and the issue of Hornerism was effectively dismissed as a figment of the ultra-left's imagination, with Horner found guilty of only tactical errors and not ideological deviation.[135]

However, Horner's partial vindication was in some sense a pyrrhic victory in that in order to remain within the party, he had been forced to abandon his principled stand on the issue and admit to mistakes he clearly felt he had not made in an agreed act of self-criticism published in the *Daily Worker* in November 1931. This though was to prove the end of the matter, with Horner in all likelihood viewing the *Daily Worker* article as a necessary sacrifice that kept him in the party. More significantly, the failure of the Young Turks to get their pound of flesh in the form of Horner's expulsion from the party marked a significant defeat for the hard-liners. Ultimately, for Horner loyalty to the revolutionary movement meant loyalty to the party, and though he had been pushed to the brink of leaving the CPGB, Horner could not bring himself to take that final step.[136] Horner was soon welcomed back into the party fold, a process eased by his arrest and imprisonment following an eviction dispute in Maerdy in late 1931. Later that year Horner stood as the CPGB's candidate in Rhondda East at the general election, with Cox as his agent, gaining 10,359 votes. However, Horner's relationship with the party had been damaged by the whole affair. By January 1932 the CPGB's industrial policy was drastically

[134] Nina Fishman, 'Horner and Hornerism' in John McIlroy, Alan Campbell and Kevin Morgan (eds), *Party People and Communist Lives: Explorations in Biography*, London, 2001, p. 136.
[135] Thorpe, *British Communist Party and Moscow*, p. 179.
[136] See Horner's statement to the Central Committee in May, CPGB Archive, Central Committee minutes, 31 May 1931, CI Reel 2 (LHASC).

altered, reverting to work within the trade unions and in essence backing Horner's stance of 12 months before. It was also to mark the beginning of the end of the Third Period.

In terms of the party in Wales, it's evident that the whole issue of Hornerism was partly used as an attempt to cover up deficiencies within the district itself. As Horner himself noted at the May EC meeting, there was clear failure on the DPC's behalf to organise itself adequately, 'During the whole of the strike except for these casual chats between Stead, Williams and myself there was not a single party meeting held in South Wales in the centre, never a single DPC called on the question … The Party was liquidated in practice.'[137] Horner also complained that the DPC was also too dependent on cues from the party centre acting like 'machines that only exist to say "yes" to everything that the centre does'.[138] Support for Horner within the Welsh party was sparse, with only a few individuals such as Mel Thomas and Will Paynter openly declaring their support for Horner's stance, the whole affair leaving Paynter 'a little sour for a time'.[139] More commonly, support for Horner was shown through abstention, rather than through open dissent. However, significant sections of the party were opposed to Horner with the Maesteg, Caerphilly, Dowlais, Aberdare and West Wales branches all calling for his expulsion. Only the Rhondda branches, notably Maerdy, Ferndale, Tylorstown, Ynyshir and Porth, backed Horner. While there was, according to Will Paynter, a tendency for 'stereotype decisions' to be taken over the country with branches 'supporting the official decision … without any knowledge of what the real issues were' it is evident that within Wales what remained of the party was firmly behind the new line.[140] Despite this, in opposing the imposition of the new line it was Horner that showed himself most aware of the specific local conditions in south Wales and not the DPC. In chasing the chimera of independent

[137] Horner's statement to the Central Committee in May, CPGB Archive, Central Committee minutes, 31 May 1931, CI Reel 2 (LHASC).

[138] Morgan, *Labour Legends*, p. 248.

[139] Fishman, 'Horner and Hornerism', p. 135; Will Paynter, *My Generation* (London, 1972), p. 48.

[140] Fishman, 'Horner and Hornerism', p. 136.

leadership, the Welsh party had brought itself to the brink of collapse, while its self-imposed isolation and commitment to a new line that was wholly unsuited to the political structure of the mining communities had left it bereft of influence by the end of 1931. Only the realignment of the party's industrial policy and the role of the NUWM in agitation over unemployment were to allow the party to reassert itself in south Wales from 1932 onwards.

CONCLUSION – THE NATIONAL QUESTION IN WALES: CONSPICUOUS BY ITS ABSENCE

By 1931 the Welsh party had reached its nadir, its membership dwindling, its influence within the SWMF curtailed, and its leadership involved in an acrimonious dispute with its leading industrial militant. A party that during the 1920s was among the CPGB's strongest assets had, by the beginning of the 1930s, become a focus for the national leadership's concerns. To a large extent, these problems were of the party's own making, the move away from work within the trade unions, the focus on independent leadership and the attacks on fellow trade unionists and socialists all worked against the CPGB within the tightly knit coalfield communities. The party's own mistakes were further compounded by the attacks on it by the SWMF and Labour Party, eager to punish the CPGB for helping lead the labour movement into the General Strike.

During this period the party in Wales had seen its autonomy of action diminished, a victim of the increasing centralisation of the party, put in motion by the Bolshevisation process begun in 1922. While this process had been halted by 1924, the organisational structure that it had brought into being remained, with the power of the districts diminished at the expense of the party centre. Increasingly, the districts were looked down upon by those at the party centre, a point noted by Horner in 1929: 'We are faced at headquarters with a conception among the leaders that work in the districts is a degradation if you have once occupied a position in the Central Committee.'[141] By the Third Period the Welsh party's

---

[141] Martin, *Communism and the British Trade Unions*, p. 52.

autonomy was further curtailed, with a series of leadership changes designed to bring the DPC closer to the line advocated by the party centre. However, the very fact that the party centre felt it necessary to implement these changes points to a degree of local autonomy within the Welsh party that made the leadership particularly uneasy to begin with. Despite this, the eagerness of the DPC and the Welsh party in general to turn on Horner suggests that the line from the party centre was generally accepted by those left within the CPGB in Wales, whilst reflecting the impact that the change of leadership forced by the Young Turks had had on the Welsh party. However, that Horner also maintained the support of some sections of the Welsh party also attests to the persistence of opposition to these changes. On a more general level the devolutionary possibilities of south Wales syndicalism had, by the Third Period, been largely lost to the now Bolshevised Welsh party, while the national question remained dormant as an issue for the time being.

Despite Kenneth Morgan's assertion that the CPGB was committed to self-government in Scotland and Wales from its inception, there is little evidence to support this.[142] By and large, the national question in Wales is absent from the CPGB's political discourse during this period, while it only breaks cover in discussions within the Scottish party in 1932. For the 1920s at least it was simply not an issue for most communists, despite the party being at the forefront of political agitation against the British Empire and for independence in the colonies.[143] And this is the crux of the matter: while Ireland, for instance, was seen as a country colonised by British imperialism, neither Wales nor Scotland were viewed in such a light. Indeed, when discussion on the national question in Scotland began in 1932, it was not a discussion as to whether Scotland as a nation should be given independence, but rather whether Scotland constituted a nation per se.[144]

[142] Kenneth Morgan, 'Leaders and Led in the Labour Movement', *Llafur* 6 (3), 1994, p. 110.

[143] John Callaghan, 'The Communists and the Colonies: Anti-Imperialism Between the Wars' in Andrews et al. (eds), *Opening the Books: Essays on the Social and Cultural History of the British Communist Party* (London, 1995), pp. 4–22.

[144] R. MacLennan, 'The National Question in Scotland', *The Communist Review* 4 (10), 1932.

Sympathies for the Irish struggle for independence were widespread throughout the CPGB, with a number of the party's leadership, notably Arthur MacManus, having had close links with James Connolly during their days in the SLP. The CPGB had also played a key role in the establishment of the CPI. Similar sympathies were also present in Wales, with a number of communists, notably Arthur Horner and George Phippen, joining the Citizens' Army, and others, like William Hewlett, helping facilitate their journey to Ireland.[145] In addition, there was a significant Irish contingent within the Welsh party, the Maesteg branch, for example, included a number of former IRA men.[146] Of course, the motives for those leaving for Ireland were mixed, with avoiding conscription a distinct motivation for some, while for others it was a genuine commitment to the Irish cause. For Horner, the perspective of the Welsh experience was also a contributory factor, noting, 'As a small nationality ourselves, we had watched with sympathy the Irish people's fight for independence long before the war broke out.'[147] While this sits uncomfortably with Horner's later negative attitude towards Welsh self-determination, it at least reflects an awareness of Irish problems linked explicitly to the problems of Wales as a small nation. More importantly, for the CPGB and the Comintern, the armed struggle in Ireland represented a potentially revolutionary situation at the heart of the British Empire, and nationalism was viewed as a useful rallying tool that had drawn a number of disparate class groups together, and could act as a precursor for class struggle given the right conditions.[148] Clearly, for the party, the national question in Wales and Scotland held no such immediate revolutionary potential; indeed for much of the period the national question, at least in Wales, was a dormant issue, the creation of the Irish Free State, having taken home rule off the political agenda in the early 1920s.

---

[145] Interview with Mel Thomas, 17 May 1973, AUD 283, SWML.
[146] Interview with Idris Cox, 9 June 1973, AUD 171, SWML.
[147] Horner, *Incorrigible Rebel,* p. 25.
[148] Fred Willis, 'Ireland and the Social Revolution', *The Communist Review* 1 (1), 1921, pp. 7–9.

The removal of the national question from the mainstream political agenda for much of the 1920s goes some way to explaining its absence as an issue within the CPGB while the association of the national question with Liberalism in Wales may also have led communists to view the issue as a bourgeois concern. The lack of an effective nationalist party during the 1920s also accounts for the lack of political discussion on the issue; the CPGB unthreatened by a resurgent nationalism had little need to confront the issue. It is significant that in Scotland it is the emergence of an effective national movement that leads to calls for the party to start taking the issue seriously.[149] Similarly, in Wales the increased profile of the Welsh Nationalist Party in the mid-1930s, following the arson attack on the bombing school at Penyberth, was a contributory factor in the party beginning to deal with the national question.[150] Of perhaps more significance for the period under discussion, however, was the fact that the party's energies were directed elsewhere to the more pressing issues at the point of production. As we have seen, the party's main focus in Wales was its work within the SWMF and within the coalfield in south Wales. The immediate issues related to economic decline, momentous industrial struggles and building a revolutionary party were far more pressing for communists than any abstract discussion regarding the national question, which had little potential in drawing recruits into a mass communist party. This situation was worsened due to the crisis the party in Wales entered into during the Third Period, which helped push the party to the brink of collapse and effectively neutered its influence within the SWMF and the Labour Party. In Scotland, however, the Third Period can be seen as a contributory factor to the emergence of the national question, with Helen Crawfurd's contribution reflecting a more positive aspect of the self-criticism then prevalent throughout the party when she notes that this was an area the party in Scotland had neglected to their own

---

[149] Helen Crawfurd, 'The Scottish National Movement', *The Communist Review,* 5 (2), 1933, pp. 84–7.
[150] *Draft Statement on Welsh Nationalism,* 1938, Bert Pearce Collection WN 1/1, NLW.

cost.[151] For the CPGB in Wales, it was to take the emergence of the Popular Front, the effective abandonment of whole coalfield communities as distressed areas, and the increased profile of the national movement, for it to engage meaningfully with the national question.

---

[151] Crawfurd, 'The Scottish National Movement'.

2

THE AWAKENING OF A NATIONAL CONSCIOUSNESS
WITHIN THE COMMUNIST PARTY IN WALES, 1933–1950

The period from the adoption of the Popular Front to the end of the Second World War was to be the most successful in the CPGB's history, The party played a leading role in a number of the day's leading campaigns, notably those against fascism both at home and abroad, playing a central role in the campaigns in support of Republican Spain and against Mosley's British Union of Fascists (BUF). While its anti-fascist credentials were dealt a temporary blow due to its decision, in line with Soviet policy, to oppose the war in 1939, by December 1942, buoyed by its association with the Soviet Union and now fully behind the war effort, party membership had reached its highest mark – at 56,000.[1] Within the trade unions the party, now fully committed to working within, rather than independently of, the established movement, had made important advances, with a number of communist trade unionists holding important positions within their own unions – the most notable being the election of Arthur Horner as president of the SWMF in 1936 and as general secretary of the National Union of Mineworkers (NUM) ten years later – and one communist, Bert Papworth, elected to the General Council of the TUC by 1945. Electorally, the party had one MP elected in 1935, William Gallacher for West Fife, followed by another, Phil Piratin, for the Mile End constituency, who joined Gallacher in the Commons following the 1945 General Election. In addition, the party had also succeeded in broadening its appeal during the 1930s with a number of intellectuals and professional workers now entering its ranks largely due to its campaigning over Spain and the establishment of the Left Book Club. Despite this progress, the party had singularly failed to

---

[1] Thorpe, 'Membership of the CPGB', p. 781.

achieve its stated goals of building a Popular Front during the 1930s, in the face of Labour Party and TUC opposition and the shadow of the terror in the USSR, or of building a mass party along the lines of the French Communist Party (PCF) or of the Italian Communist Party (PCI). In fact, the impact of the Cold War, and the party's own failure to capitalise on the leftward shift in Britain at the end of the war, meant that the immediate post-war years once again saw the party increasingly marginalised and the target of further anti-communist campaigns and purges within both the Labour Party and the trade unions.

In Wales, the new direction taken by the party following the abandonment of class against class was also fruitful, the party regaining respect in the coalfield through its key role in helping rebuild the SWMF and through the leadership shown by communist militants within the SWMF in the battle against company unionism, in which Arthur Horner was a leading figure. In addition, the party's campaign against the unemployment regulations in 1934 and 1935 was a rare example of successful, de facto, united front activity, while its agitation over Spain and against the BUF was central in cementing the party's reputation as an effective organiser of extra-parliamentary campaigns. In electoral terms, a series of contests in Rhondda East saw the party eat into the Labour Party incumbent's majority, and almost take the seat in the 1945 General Election, while the party could also point to some success in terms of its performance in local elections in south Wales, although it never came near to threatening the Labour Party's dominance of this arena. However, despite these signs of growing support, the party was unable to translate such support into increased membership, for while party membership was indeed on the up during this period, it failed to match the expectations of both the district or the party centre, with the South Wales, and later Welsh District viewed as a problem child in this regard, much to the frustration of the party leadership. The formation of a North Wales District Committee in January 1937 can be seen as further evidence of the party's broadening appeal, and was to prove significant in confronting the party with the issues revolving around the national question, while the formation of a Welsh

Committee in 1944 saw the party becoming one of the first sections of the working-class movement in Britain to organise on a national basis within Wales.

It was also during this period that the national question first began to be taken seriously by the party in Wales. The awakening of the party's national consciousness was a process that took place over two periods, from 1936 to 1939, and from around 1944 onwards, both influenced by a number of different factors. The first period, from 1936 to 1939, can be attributed to a number of factors, both international and domestic. At the international level, the turn towards the Popular Front, and especially its plea for communist parties to engage meaningfully with the national question, was to provide the decisive shift, while the example of the PCF prior to the Seventh Comintern Congress, was also a key factor. Within the British context a conscious effort by the party, led initially by the London District Committee, to broaden the appeal of its propaganda, coupled with an awareness that the CPGB was viewed as alien to British political life, led the party to adopt a much more nationalistic tone in its propaganda, explicitly linking the party to native radical-democratic traditions. At the Welsh level, the publicity given to the issues relating to the national question and to the Welsh Nationalist Party following the attempted arson at the Penyberth bombing school in 1936, contact between communist and nationalist students at Cardiff, and the formation of a North Wales District in 1937, saw the party for the first time having to confront the issue of Welsh self-government, as well as the fate of the Welsh language and culture, head-on. The second period from 1944 onwards can be attributed to the spirit of change engendered by post-war reconstruction, and an overriding commitment not to let Wales return to its desperate situation in the 1930s, of which Welsh self-government was seen as a crucial component. Internationally, Wales' right to self-government was viewed within the context of a new post-war world order based on a family of democratic nations and the contribution made by Wales during the war against fascism.

ACCLIMATISING PROLETARIAN INTERNATIONALISM
IN WALES, 1933–1939

The emergence of the national question in Wales as an issue for the Communist Party between 1936 and 1939 was due to a combination of international, British and Welsh factors. On the international level the increasing importance of the national question and the nation in communist discourse during this period was facilitated by the communist response to the rise of fascism, especially in Germany, and the adoption of the Popular Front in 1935. Recognising the need to broaden the general appeal of communism, alongside a need to reclaim national heritage for the anti-fascist movement, communist parties consciously began adopting patriotic positions and developing a historical discourse that emphasised both radical-democratic traditions and the centrality of working-class struggle to the historical development of the nation. In Britain, the party, drawing on the French experience, and keenly aware of the party's alien status and of the need to build a truly mass party, consciously began from 1936 onwards to project a more British image, both through organisational changes and through its propaganda. In Wales, the sudden focus given to national issues following Penyberth, contact with Welsh Nationalist Party members and the formation of a North Wales District presented a now rebuilt party with new challenges and issues to confront.

As McDermott and Agnew have noted, the adoption of the Popular Front, at the Seventh Comintern Congress of August 1935, was the result of a 'triple interaction' of pressures from below, specifically the call by a number of communist parties, including the CPGB, for a change of line, and the spontaneous formation of a united front in Austria and a Popular Front in France during 1934; from above, with a change in the Comintern leadership from a divided collective leadership, that had led to a paralysis in decision making within the higher echelons of the Comintern, to the leadership of Georgi Dimitrov, who, following his acquittal at the Reichstag Fire Trial, was able to use his influence as the new hero of the communist movement to push forward the new line; and

from the demands of Soviet foreign policy following the shift towards collective security and the non-aggression pact with France.[2] The Popular Front, as enunciated at the Seventh Comintern Congress, marked a sea change in communist strategy that was to have profound consequences for communist policy thenceforth. The main components of the new line were first, a call on the national sections to build a united front of all working-class organisations to fight fascism; second, the establishment of a 'anti-fascist peoples' front', which included alliances with bourgeois parties and organisations; and third, the defence of bourgeois democracy, and the gains made under it, against fascism.[3]

The fourth component of the Popular Front was the new emphasis placed on the importance of a positive communist attitude to the national question. Fascism, as Dimitrov noted in his report to Congress, had distinct national peculiarities, 'The development of fascism, and of fascist dictatorship itself, assumes different forms in different countries according to historical, social and economic conditions and to the national peculiarities and the international position of the given country.'[4] Thus, fascism called for a response that was not uniform like class against class, but was responsive to 'national peculiarities'. In his speech to Congress, Dimitrov was to go further, arguing that the failure of communists to take fascist ideology and techniques seriously, in particular in relation to the national question, had allowed the fascists free rein in expropriating national symbols as their own, leaving the impression that communists were anti-national, the fascists having been able to 'rummag[e] through the entire history of every nation so as to be able to pose as the heirs and continuers of all that was exalted and heroic in its past, while all that was degrading or offensive to the national sentiments of the people they make use of as weapons against the enemies of fascism'.[5] For Dimitrov, the time had come

[2] Kevin McDermott and Jeremy Agnew, *The Comintern: A History of International Communism from Lenin to Stalin* (Basingstoke, 1996), pp. 121–30.

[3] 'The Resolution of the Seventh Comintern Congress on Fascism, Working Class Unity, and the Tasks of the Comintern' in Jane Degras, *The Communist International 1919–1943: Documents Vol. 3, 1929–1943* (Oxford, 1965), p. 364.

[4] Georgi Dimitrov, *The Working Class Against Fascism* (London, 1935), p. 11.

[5] Dimitrov, *The Working Class Against Fascism,* p. 69.

for communists to make every effort to reclaim these national symbols for themselves and he was highly critical of those communists who rejected the need to engage with the national question and the nation.[6]

In distancing the communist stance on the issue from 'bourgeois nationalism', Dimitrov emphasised that the task of the communist parties was to place the national question within the context of internationalism, relating national struggles to the broader international context, to 'acclimatise' proletarian internationalism to national conditions.[7] Elaborating further on this theme, Dimitrov argued that there was no contradiction between the class struggle and the national struggle. While emphasising the primacy of class struggle for communists, Dimitrov argued that by the very act of aiming towards the setting up of a socialist society, communists were in fact at the same time fighting for a better future for the nation. For Dimitrov, only through the removal of capitalism and transition to a socialist society could true national freedom be achieved and national cultures flourish.[8]

Dimitrov's call for communists to engage more meaningfully with the national question was taken up by Maurice Thorez, the PCF leader, and Pollitt, in their speeches to Congress. Thorez, drawing on the experiences of the PCF, noted, 'We claim the intellectual and revolutionary heritage of the Encyclopaedists who paved the way for the great revolution of 1789 ... the Jacobins ... and the Commune. We present ourselves to the masses of the people as the champions of the liberty and independence of the country.'[9] Indeed, the PCF were pioneers in this regard, the turn towards the Popular Front in 1934–1935 having, for the first time, allowed the communists to embrace and reclaim their national symbols and heritage. In July 1935, Jacques Duclos, a leading party member, had called for an alliance of the tricolour and the red flag, each he argued representing past and future struggles, while much was made by the party of

---

[6] Dimitrov, *The Working Class Against Fascism*, p. 70.
[7] Dimitrov, *The Working Class Against Fascism*, p. 71.
[8] Dimitrov, *The Working Class Against Fascism*, p. 72.
[9] Degras, *Communist International Documents Vol. 3*, p. 358.

the need to 'reconcile' the *Marseillaise* and the *Internationale*.[10] For the 1936 election, the PCF adopted the slogan 'For a free, strong and happy France', by August was calling for a French Front aimed at uniting the forces of the left and right 'for the respect of the laws, the defence of the national economy and the freedom and independence of France', and later in 1936 was using the slogan 'France for the French', previously the preserve of the extreme right.[11]

Pollitt, in turn, emphasised the need for communists to engage with the national question as a way of combating the national chauvinism which fascism exploited, calling specifically for communists to use national history to their advantage in this struggle, while emphasising that class struggle was also a form of national struggle.

> Especially it is necessary to combat jingoism amongst the youth and to destroy the slanderous canard that 'the Communists are friends of every country but their own'. There is now more need than ever to popularise the history of our own country and recall all the great traditions and names that have been associated in the past with the fight for progress and for democratic rights. We must prove that we love our country so well, that our lives are dedicated to removing all the black spots on its name – to removing poverty, unemployment and the bloody oppression of the colonial peoples.[12]

The relevance of the national question to the fight against fascism was further emphasised in the Congress resolutions, the main resolution warning communists 'against adopting a disparaging attitude on the question of national independence and the national sentiments of the broad masses of the people' while arguing that 'it must be shown that the working class, which fights against every form of servitude and national oppression, is the only genuine protagonist of national freedom and the independence of the people'. Communists were further advised to 'in every way combat the fascist falsification of the history of the people, and do

[10] Edward Mortimer, *The Rise of the French Communist Party 1920–1947* (London, 1984), p. 257; M. Adereth, *The French Communist Party: A Critical History (1920–84) from Comintern to 'the Colours of France'* (Manchester, 1984), p. 63.

[11] Mortimer, *The Rise of the French Communist Party*, pp. 258–9.

[12] 'Speech at the Seventh World Congress of the Communist International' in Harry Pollitt, *Selected Articles and Speeches Vol. 1 1919–1936* (London, 1953), p. 156.

everything to enlighten the toiling masses on the past of their own people ... so as to link up their present struggle with the revolutionary traditions of the past'.[13]

Communist policy with regard to the national question was thus threefold. First, communists were now to break with previous bad habits and engage constructively with the national question, refrain from offering disparaging remarks regarding national sentiment and make it part of the armoury of class struggle. Secondly, communists were to make a concerted effort to provide a historical discourse that emphasised the role of class struggle and native radical-democratic traditions, as a means to both combat the fascist appropriation of national symbols and heritage, and as a means of broadening the communists' appeal to the mass of the population. Finally, engagement with the national question did not mean a reversion to 'bourgeois nationalism'; rather communists were to link the national struggle to the broader anti-fascist struggle while emphasising that only through the victory of socialism could true national freedom be achieved.

The CPGB's first responses to Dimitrov's call for a greater emphasis on the national question were evident in a change in both the party's organisational structure and in its propaganda. In organisational terms, a concerted effort was made to better adapt the party's organisation to the norms of British political party organisation, through a restructuring of the party's organisation from a cell-based structure to one based on branch organisation during 1936. The opening of branch meetings to non-party members reflected a desire to lose the party's conspiratorial associations, while the replacement of the terms such as cell with group further reflected a desire to anglicise the party's nomenclature. While the main reason behind changing the structure was to better co-ordinate the party's activities and bring the often-disparate workplace and street groups together in an expanded branch organisation, it also reflected a conscious effort to

---

[13] 'Resolution of the Seventh Comintern Congress on Fascism, Working Class Unity, and the Tasks of the Comintern' in Degras, *Communist International Documents Vol. 3*, p. 366.

make the party better suited to the British political scene, the party's national organiser, R. W. Robson, noting, 'We must be able to approach Labour Party organisations on an equal level and discuss questions in organisational terms common to both parties.'[14] This change in nomenclature was complemented by a change in the type of language used by party members, with references to soviet power and proletarian dictatorship in speeches and articles used more sparingly, replaced by references to a radical-democratic form of patriotism.[15]

It was this adoption of the rhetoric of radical-democratic patriotism that marked the CPGB's second significant response to the Comintern's call for a new approach to the national question. From 1935 onwards, the party's propaganda increasingly linked communism to the domestic radical-democratic traditions of the working class, emphasising the need for party members to relate the party's present-day struggles to those of their forefathers. Expounding on this theme, Ralph Fox, one of the party's leading intellectuals writing shortly after the Seventh Congress, noted 'We too have our revolutionary past, stretching back for hundreds of years. Marxist-Leninist dialectic applies to English history as much as to the French.'[16] Fox would later express support for a federated Soviet republic in Britain.[17] Similarly, Pollitt, responding to questions on his stance vis-à-vis the national question, urged party members to fully engage with the issue noting, that in his speech to the Seventh Congress, 'I was concerned with making of all that is best in national feeling a weapon in the hands of the workers for the overthrow of capitalism.' Defending his speech, Pollitt argued that there was no contradiction between it and Marx's call for the proletariat to constitute itself as a nation.[18]

[14] Branson, *History of the CPGB 1927–1941*, p. 190.
[15] Kevin Morgan, *Against Fascism and War: Ruptures and Continuities in British Communist Politics 1935–1941* (Manchester, 1989), pp. 40–1.
[16] *Daily Worker*, 11 September 1935, p. 4.
[17] Wade Matthews, *The New Left, National Identity and the Break-Up of Britain* (Chicago, 2013), pp. 39–40.
[18] *Daily Worker*, 13 September 1935, p. 4.

The first concrete expression of this new attitude to the nation and its radical-democratic heritage came in September 1936, with the organisation of a 'March of English History' by the London District Party. Announcing the march in the *Daily Worker*, the London District's propaganda leader, Ted Bramley, noted that the march was an opportunity to counter 'the false argument that Communism is a foreign idea imported from Russia after the war' and the notion that 'the English people advanced economically, socially and politically by other means than that of class struggle'. For Bramley, the march was an opportunity to show that 'The Communist Party and the millions of English people are the heirs of hundreds of years of mighty traditions of struggle against poverty and tyranny. Communism is not something foreign to Englishmen, but has grown out of the very soil of England. It is natural to England as the green grass and hedges.'[19] Held on 20 September 1936, the march attracted some 4–5,000 people, with 15–20,000 attending the rally that followed, and was viewed as a considerable success by the party, with Rust drawing attention to its success at the 1937 CPGB Congress noting that the party had 'a lot to learn from London, from the way in which they have taken up the question of mass agitation'.[20]

Despite its branding as The March of English History, the march itself had consisted of a tableau of banners depicting scenes from English, Scottish, Welsh and Irish history, from the Peasants' Revolt through to the setting up of the CPGB, the General Strike and the campaign for the Spanish Republic, with banners depicting the struggle against company unionism at Taff-Merthyr, the Easter Rising and Robert Burns. As Kevin Morgan has noted,[21] the pamphlet published to commemorate the march offered an almost *Boys Own*-style patriotism that recalled the derring-do of both English heroes and its people, and, curiously, with its depiction of soldiers 'stationed beneath burning desert skies' and English heroes using their 'endurance, skill and courage to

---

[19] *Daily Worker*, 14 September 1936, p. 4.
[20] *Daily Worker*, 21 September 1936, p. 1; *It Can Be Done: Report of the Fourteenth Congress of the Communist Party of Great Britain* (London, 1937), pp. 163–4.
[21] Morgan, *Against Fascism and War*, p. 42.

conquer nature and space for humanity' implicit intimations of Empire. This, however, was tempered by a less than rosy depiction of the state of the nation, with the lot of the majority of the population depicted as 'insecurity and doubt ... grey days of endless anxiety, the soul-destroying burden of unemployment, the hideous means test'. Whilst conforming to a self-image that would not have been out of place in any patriotic piece by any political party, depicting the English as 'A great nation ... A people proud of their instinct for fair play, for the rule of law and justice, who wish to be the veritable pillar of peace and democracy in this modern world', the pamphlet also noted that English history had been shaped by their 'arduous and stubborn struggle against tyranny and oppression', lauding the 'ceaseless effort of the common men and women to rise out of poverty and degradation into happiness and freedom, to make our country a Free and Merry England'.[22] These echoes of Blatchford were part and parcel of a depiction of the CPGB as the heir of these native traditions and as the defender of democracy in Britain, in the face of the onslaught of fascism and 'the black shapes of reaction'. The CPGB was depicted as the standard bearer of English freedom whilst fascism was equated with the worst aspects of the ancien régime in the form of the Inquisition, the Star Chamber and the use of torture.[23]

The historical discourse offered by this new communist approach to English history was further elaborated by Robin Page Arnot and Jack Lindsay. Writing in *Labour Monthly* the following month, Arnot argued that the march had shown that 'The Communists have claimed their rightful place in the great tradition, the heritage which is theirs',[24] whilst noting that 'the great figures of English historic struggle in arms are not the soldiers of the greedy oligarchy, like the boasted Clive or Wellington, but those who led the struggle against the class oppressors in their own country'.[25] The

[22] *The March of English History: A Message to you from the Communist Party* (London, 1936), p. 3.

[23] *The March of English History*, p. 10.

[24] Robin Page Arnot, 'The English Tradition', *Labour Monthly*, 18 (11), November 1936, p. 694.

[25] Arnot, 'The English Tradition', p. 695.

Australian-born Jack Lindsay, in a book that covered the history of the struggle of the English people from the Peasants' Revolt through to the struggle against the Means Test and for Republican Spain, came to the conclusion that 'Communism is English'[26] and that the 'Communist Party ... resumes the real tradition of the working class of England with renewed scientific insight'.[27] For Lindsay, his patriotism was intrinsically linked with the traditions of working-class struggle described in his book, 'We love England for reasons other than those that enable a small pack of landlords and investors and capitalists to live in comfort on the misery and disease of their fellows. What we love in England has nothing to do with profits and parasites. We love England, in short for reasons that involve everything in life except profits and parasites.'[28]

As with the March of History, however, Lindsay's book also blurred the differences between English and British history, including episodes from Welsh history such as the Merthyr Rising and Rebecca Riots.[29] This tendency to conflate British history as English history reflected the persistence of an Anglocentric view of history within the party and a distinct failure to engage with the 'national peculiarities' of the Welsh, Scots and Irish. In a later volume co-edited by Lindsay, the legacy of conquest on the history of the Celtic nations was acknowledged and 'the heroic resistance of Welsh, Scots and Irish to the encroachments of the English Crown' recognised along with 'National independence as an essential guarantee of social freedom'.[30] Ultimately, however, it was up to Welsh party members to adapt this style of historical discourse to Welsh history, the most notable contribution in this regard coming from Islwyn Nicholas who, in a series of books recounting Wales' radical-democratic traditions, explicitly linked historical figures such as the Chartists, Dr.

[26] Jack Lindsay, *England, My England: A Pageant of the English People* (London, 1939), p. 64.
[27] Lindsay, *England, My England*, pp. 62–3.
[28] Lindsay, *England, My England*, pp. 4–5.
[29] Lindsay, *England, My England*, pp. 53–4.
[30] Jack Lindsay and Edgell Rickword (eds), *A Handbook of Freedom: A Record of English Democracy through Twelve Centuries* (London, 1939), p. xvi.

William Price, Dic Penderyn, Iolo Morganwg and R. J. Derfel
to present-day struggles against fascism.[31]
The impact of the success of the London march was to
have broad consequences for party propaganda, leading to a
reassessment of its relation to the national question. In
August 1937, Bramley brought up the issue of party propaganda at a Central Committee meeting, arguing that its
content needed to be broadened in order to be more effective in drawing people into the party. Bramley argued that
the party had to engage with the British public in the same
way as the PCF if it was to see an improvement in recruiting
for the party. In particular, he called for a broadening of
party propaganda to cover matters that would appeal to
unorganised workers. Central to this was offering a more
positive approach with regards to patriotism, with Bramley
noting 'We have got to be able to give the conception that
the Communist Party has grown out of English struggle and
is going to make England what every Englishman wants it to
be. We give the impression that we are against the Union Jack
but we have got to make it clear that we are not against
England and against the positive things in the minds of the
workers when they think of their country.'[32] Similar sentiments were offered by Pollitt in a Central Committee meeting
the following month, where he argued that in response to
accusations of being 'the slave of Moscow' the party's propaganda should emphasise that 'We Communists are sons of
the British people, which has a magnificent record of struggle
against reaction and for a working-class programme.'
Elaborating further, Pollitt argued that this was a record that
the party was 'not only proud, but anxious to defend and
carry forward'.

> In the course of our propaganda, we must demonstrate our desire to
> retain and extend those traditions, to show that we are sons of the
> British Labour movement ... and we, being sons of the British Labour

[31] T. Islwyn Nicholas, *One Hundred Years Ago: The Story of the Montgomeryshire Chartists* (Aberystwyth, 1939); *A Welsh Heretic: Dr William Price, Llantrisant* (London, 1940); *Dic Penderyn: Welsh Rebel and Martyr* (London, 1944); *R. J. Derfel: Welsh Rebel Poet and Preacher* (London, 1945); *Iolo Morganwg: Bard of Liberty* (London, 1945).

[32] CPGB Archive, Central Committee (CC) minutes, 6 August 1937, CPGB CI Reel 8, (LHASC).

Movement, not only appreciate those traditions ... but want to defend them and carry them forward to a new point. Our Party is a British Party, whose only interest is to save the British people and the working class movement ... If we are going seriously to set out to convince the British people that we are a British Party, we should not always be appealing to them to join it because we are the Party of Stalin, Dimitrov and Thälmann.[33]

Bramley was to further elaborate on this in an article for the party's theoretical journal *Discussion*, arguing that much more focus needed to be placed on domestic issues and on appealing to national sentiment.

How often do we hear it said 'Communists love every country but their own'? I am afraid we do not fully appreciate how strong is the love of England among the workers in spite of poverty. We somehow present our Internationalism as though it is an alternative to a love of England. It is amazing to see some of the poorest people in East London aroused by Mosley proudly boasting of being English. We cannot carry the Union Jack, but we can certainly develop a more positive attitude to England. We must speak to and for the whole English people against the handful who are destroying England. We must show our pride in the good qualities of our people. The splendid working-class history and the ability to fight. The freedom we have won. The beauties of our countryside. The skill and efficiency of our craftsmen. The natural wealth and resources of our country. We must do as our French comrade said: 'Know and love our own people.'[34]

Responding to this article, Glyn Jones, the secretary of the South Wales District, noted that Wales had its own particular problems with regards to propaganda. Jones argued that the exodus of some 300,000 people from south Wales called for the party's propaganda in the District to be broadened in order to reach a wider audience by concentrating on day-to-day issues and focusing less propaganda on the mining areas. For Jones, echoing the sentiments expressed by Bramley but placing them firmly in a Welsh context, a key dimension to broadening the appeal of the party's propaganda in south Wales was to focus on the distinct national characteristics of Wales and to increase its propaganda efforts on issues related

[33] CPGB Archive, CC minutes, 10 September 1937, CPGB CI Reel 8 (LHASC).
[34] Ted Bramley, 'Our Propaganda', *Discussion* 2 (4), September 1937, pp. 7–8.

to the national question, whilst also increasing its production
of Welsh-language propaganda,

> We must pay attention to the national characteristics, prejudices and
> traditions of Wales. For without understanding these things, and
> sympathetically paying attention to them, we can never hope to win
> the Welsh people to our Party. In this respect our attitude to the
> National question in Wales is of utmost importance to the future
> success of our work.
>
> Our line should be that of convincing the Welsh people of the
> correctness of our policy for dealing with the present situation, by
> approaching them through definitely Welsh channels. Not half
> enough attention is paid to those things that have agitated the
> Welshman for centuries, such as the right, free from restriction, to
> develop the Welsh language and culture, and the right of Wales, at
> least to a greater degree of administrative autonomy. Forty per cent of
> the people of Wales speak Welsh. The remaining sixty per cent are
> mostly Welsh in sentiment and tradition, and though they cannot
> speak the language, they are not outside its sphere of influence. That
> is why the Welsh Nationalist Party, although not strong numerically,
> has been able to win influence among religious, professional and
> petty-bourgeois elements.[35]

By doing this Jones hoped that the party could win some
influence amongst the numerous Welsh Societies in south
Wales, whilst tapping into a previously untapped pool of
potential support for the party. In addition, the focus on the
nationalists' ability to 'win influence among the religious,
professional and petty-bourgeois elements' reflected the new
dimensions to communist politics created by the Popular
Front. If the party was serious about attracting these groups
into the CPGB it was now forced to engage meaningfully with
the issues that were of concern to them.

Significantly, Jones also called for a weekly Welsh column
in the *Daily Worker* – a request he reiterated at a Central
Committee meeting in February the following year, this time
calling for 'one or two columns of Welsh news in the Welsh
language each week'.[36] Despite winning support for this

[35] Glyn Jones, 'Problems of Propaganda in South Wales', *Discussion*, 2 (7),
December 1937, pp. 7–8.
[36] CPGB Archive, CC minutes, 5 February 1938, CI Reel 9 (LHASC).

proposal from both Dutt and Gallacher, with both arguing that it should be given serious consideration in the hope of reaching a wider audience in Wales, apart from Welsh-language reports from the National Eisteddfod, nothing was to come of this proposal, although it may have been that the party felt that T. E. Nicholas' weekly column in *Y Cymro* was a more effective way of putting over the communist perspective to the Welsh-speaking community. The Welsh-language reports on the National Eisteddfod that year did, however, win some praise from the *Daily Worker*'s Welsh-speaking readership and were to continue until the banning of the *Daily Worker* in 1941.[37] Dave Springhall, commenting on the coverage given to the Eisteddfod as part of his report on the *Daily Worker* at a Central Committee meeting in October 1938, noted that it was a 'very good and excellent thing' that emphasised that the Daily Worker 'should be a paper which expresses the life of the people and if it is a fact that the life of the people is made up not only of the time spent in factories, but of … all sorts and types of social and cultural events, which have a big importance to the whole of the people in different localities, even though they have no direct class content, then it is necessary that our paper deals with these and making provision for adequately treating with them.'[38]

Practical examples of the influence of this new trend in party propaganda were visible in Wales by early 1937. A south Wales 'March of History' was held in the Rhondda in March 1937, possibly organised with the assistance of Bramley, who had visited the District in the first half of the year.[39] Both a contribution to the Unity Campaign launched by the CPGB, ILP and Socialist League in January 1937, and a means of linking the CPGB to south Wales' radical-democratic heritage, the march through Tonypandy attracted 2,500 people, and made the front page of the *Daily Worker*, a reflection of the importance placed on this type of event by the party centre.[40] In contrast to the pamphlet for the London march, the commemorative pamphlet for the south Wales

[37] *Daily Worker*, 12 August 1938.
[38] CPGB Archive, CC minutes, 9 October 1938, CI Reel 9 (LHASC).
[39] CPGB Archive, CC minutes, 8 August 1937 CI Reel 8 (LHASC).
[40] *Daily Worker*, 22 March 1937, p. 1.

march focused less on the exploits of individual heroes and more on the community as an actor, a reflection of the success of community action against the unemployment regulations, the united front that had been built to combat them, and the District's aim of building on these gains. Gone were the references to conquering 'nature and space for humanity', replaced by references 'to a people whose skill in subduing the forces of nature has set examples for the industrial world, whose heroism in industry has written immortal pages of comradeship and self-sacrifice'.[41] Recounting the Merthyr Rising, Scotch Cattle, Rebecca Riots and the Chartists forward to the Cambrian Combine dispute, the General Strike, the 1935 demonstrations against the unemployment regulations and the election of Arthur Horner as president of the SWMF, the pamphlet directly linked the party to the history of working-class struggle in Wales.[42] Fascism, on the other hand, was viewed as representing 'everything that is alien and hated by the freedom-loving people of South Wales'.[43] However, although the 'early struggles against the tyranny of English oppressors' were mentioned 'as a struggle which has through the ages marked South Wales as a place whose people carry forward only the most noble traditions', no mention was made of the fight for national freedom elsewhere in the pamphlet, the Act of Union only mentioned in passing, and the rest of the specifically Welsh historic milestones beginning in 1799 and focusing exclusively on the Welsh working class.

An explicit attempt by the party to link itself to Welsh-language traditions and culture was to come a year later with the publication of the party's first National Eisteddfod pamphlet. A bilingual pamphlet, *Lore of the People*, was to sell some 10,000 copies, with 6,000 copies sold on the Eisteddfod field alone according to a party report.[44] *Lore of the People* was

---

[41] *South Wales in the March of History: A Message to you from the Communist Party* (Tonypandy, 1937), p. 2.

[42] *South Wales in the March of History: A Message to you from the Communist Party*, pp. 3–9.

[43] *South Wales in the March of History: A Message to you from the Communist Party*, p. 10.

[44] *South Wales Congress Report* (Cardiff, 1939), p. 8.

a joint venture between the North and South Wales District Committees, the pamphlet presenting the party's views on the nation's cultural heritage. The Eisteddfod was viewed as a democratic, progressive and, indeed, plebeian institution, a symbol of national unity and of the Welsh people's commitment to the preservation of their native language and culture, a goal to which, the pamphlet noted, the CPGB was now fully committed.

> The Eisteddfod is symbolic of the national unity of the Welsh people and their unconquerable determination to preserve their national consciousness, their language, and their native culture. And in that national consciousness there is nothing narrow or jingoistic; it is the legitimate pride of a people who feel that they have a language and a literature worth preserving, through which they will be best able to contribute to the common treasure-house of human culture. The Communist Party in Wales shares that pride, and is in the ranks of those who struggle to provide the conditions necessary for the safeguarding of the Welsh language and the development and enrichment of the national culture.[45]

Identifying the Eisteddfod as a key arena for the development of national movements, and going on to link the 'struggle to safeguard our cultural heritage, and to preserve our hard-won liberties and popular rights' with the 'great democratic figures of our nation's past' such as Iolo Morganwg, John Jones Glan-y-Gors, Robert Owen and Gwilym Hiraethog, the pamphlet argued that the fate of small nations and their language and culture was explicitly linked to the struggle against fascism.

> These forces are not a remote and distant peril, but an immediate threat to all those ideals of which the Welsh people are the proud inheritors. Durango and Guernica are symbolic of the attitude of Fascism towards small countries; it would destroy Welsh culture as it has destroyed that of the valiant Basque people, and prohibited their language.[46]

However, while noting that the long-term fate of the Welsh language would only be secure once the transition to socialism had been achieved, the pamphlet argued that in

[45] John Roose Williams, *The Lore of the People/Llên y Werin* (London, [1938]), p. 3.
[46] Williams, *The Lore of the People/Llên y Werin*, pp. 7–8.

the short term a Popular Front made up of all the political groupings in Wales was needed to turn the tide of economic ruin, which threatened not only the economic and social well-being of the country but its cultural heritage as well.

> In a Wales freed from capitalist exploitation, unemployment, and the haunting fear of war, an even brighter future awaits the Eisteddfod and the culture of which it is the expression and the rallying point. But these possibilities can only be realised if the material basis of culture is safeguarded. That is why the Communist Party calls for the same unity in defending the lives and happiness of the Welsh people as is already manifested in the National Eisteddfod, where Welshmen of all shades of opinion co-operate to foster and promote Welsh culture and literature. Surely the people of Wales, of all shades of political opinion, Labour and Communist, Liberal and Nationalist, who believe in the defence of democracy and peace, and wish to safeguard the future of the Welsh people, can find a common ground for carrying on the struggle against the common enemy.[47]

Despite this commitment to protecting the nation's cultural heritage no reference was made to self-government as a solution; rather, the party stuck to a safer, strictly cultural form of national consciousness, viewed here as a key component in broadening the anti-fascist struggle in Wales. As we shall see, both the party in Wales and the party centre were, in fact, engaged in serious discussions as to its stance on the Welsh self-government at this time, which helps explain this omission. Nevertheless, the impetus provided by the London District's propaganda department had, by 1938, clearly made an impact in Wales. However, the CPGB's engagement with the national question in Wales had begun in 1936, although the South Wales District's engagement was initially tentative. In contrast, it was communists from north Wales who, despite the lack of a district organisation and a small membership base, were the first to fully engage with the issue.

By 1936, the South Wales District had made significant progress in rebuilding the party following the debacle of the Third Period. The key role played by party members in the fight against the South Wales Miners Industrial Union (SWMIU) at the Emlyn Colliery and at Taff-Merthyr; in

---

[47] Williams, *The Lore of the People/Llên y Werin*, p. 9.

rebuilding the SWMF membership; and in the agitation over the Means Test and Part Two of the Unemployment Insurance Act, had put the party in good stead.[48] Despite being described as a 'graveyard' by Pollitt in June 1933, the party was viewed as making progress by May 1934, although a progress report still noted a failure to recruit and retain enough members and a tendency towards an economistic outlook within the district.[49] However, the unprecedented impetus provided by the party's agitation over the issue of unemployment, culminating in the mass protests against the second part of the Unemployed Insurance Act in January 1935, saw the party's influence increase dramatically, with a de facto united front created along the way, party membership rising to almost 3,000 members by 1935.[50] By April, the party was claiming that its membership had trebled in six months, with *The Rhondda Vanguard*, the Rhondda Communist Party organ, achieving a circulation of 8,000, and 352 communists active within the SWMF, many in responsible positions, with Horner elected president of the SWMF the following year.[51] In a series of electoral contests at Rhondda East, the CPGB was able to increase its share of the vote from 15 per cent in 1929 to 38 per cent by 1935, among only two seats contested by the party that year, the other being West Fife, where William Gallacher defeated the Labour incumbent.[52] Indeed, such was the communist advance in south Wales during this period that the Labour Party set up the South Wales Regional Council of Labour in 1937, with the express function of countering communist influence within the labour movement.[53]

By 1936, the South Wales District, hoping to further consolidate the popular movement built up since 1934, was

[48] Hywel Francis, *Miners Against Fascism: Wales and the Spanish Civil War* (London, 1984), pp. 61–83.

[49] CPGB Archive, PB minutes, 15 June 1933 CI Reel 14 (LHASC); *South Wales Report, May 1934*, CPGB Archive CP/IND/DUTT/31/01.

[50] Gwyn A. Williams, *When Was Wales?* (London, 1985), p. 270; for a contemporary assessment of the United Front tactics employed in south Wales, see Will Paynter, 'The United Front in South Wales', *Labour Monthly*, 17 (4), April 1935, pp. 227–31.

[51] Francis and Smith, *The Fed*, p. 269.

[52] Chris Williams, *Democratic Rhondda: Politics and Society 1885–1951* (Cardiff, 1996), pp. 158–61.

[53] Ian McAllister, 'The Labour Party in Wales: The Dynamics of One-Partyism', *Llafur*, 3(2), 1981, p. 80.

confident enough to publish a wide-ranging programme for the reconstruction of south Wales. Written by Idris Cox, *The People Can Save South Wales* is significant as the being the first Communist pamphlet to offer a policy programme that encompassed the whole of south Wales. At the heart of the pamphlet was a call to build a 'People's Movement' for the reconstruction of south Wales, in support of the party's proposals for the relief of south Wales, based on the development of new industry, the improvement of housing provision, the abolition of the Means Test and the improvement of transport links.[54] Significantly, Cox opened his pamphlet by placing the coming struggle within the context of the historical tradition of revolt linked to Welsh resistance to English rule, with English invaders now replaced by the encroachment of British capital on Welsh society.

> Centuries ago Welsh chieftains roused the people of Wales to arms against the English Kings and their invaders who set out to oppress the Welsh nation and to make them slaves of their English masters. The flag of revolt was hoisted on the Welsh mountains and our ancestors laid down their lives to fight for freedom and liberty.
>
> To-day it is not the military invaders who threaten the people of Wales. It is the profit-making system of capitalism which is sucking the life-blood of our people. It is not only the English masters who seek to enslave a proud Welsh nation, but the capitalist employers, bankers and landlords of Wales, England and Scotland, whose instrument of oppression is the National Government.[55]

Despite this appeal to national sentiment, the pamphlet itself did not mention the national question, its proposals for the salvation of south Wales' economy based on building up better economic and transport links with the west of England, rather than with the rest of Wales, notably through the building of a Severn Bridge.[56] While this was to be partly rectified by the inclusion of a call for the building of a North–South trunk road in a new version of the pamphlet, published in 1937, this was again not envisioned as a way of building economic ties, but more mundanely to 'provide easy access

[54] Idris Cox, *The People Can Save South Wales* (London, 1936), pp. 13–20.
[55] Cox, *The People Can Save South Wales*, pp. 5–6.
[56] Cox, *The People Can Save South Wales*, p. 17.

to some of the most beautiful spots in Wales, and help bring the people of Wales closer together'.[57] Nevertheless, Cox's pamphlet was important in providing, for the first time, a thoroughgoing policy programme for the whole of south Wales. A more direct engagement with the national question came in the form of contacts established between communist and nationalist students at Cardiff University during 1936 and 1937, where discussions between members of the party's student branch and Welsh Nationalist Party students led to a reconsideration of the party's position on the issue, not only amongst the students themselves, but also on the South Wales DPC.[58] By 1937, the district had begun moving towards a position that was more amenable to the national question, declaring its willingness to work with the Welsh Nationalist Party on campaigns against the National Government, whilst rejecting 'individual acts of terrorism'.[59]

Some movement on the issue was already evident by 1936, this time from north Wales, following the publication of the party's first Welsh-language pamphlet, *Llwybr Rhyddid y Werin*, written by the north Walian communist, John Roose Williams. Significantly, this pamphlet was both commissioned and funded by the party centre, attesting to the lack of a region-wide organised party structure in north Wales at that time, but also suggesting some indifference to the national question within the South Wales District.[60] Communism did not emerge in north Wales until the mid-1930s. Arriving in north Wales in 1931, the Bristol-born communist Douglas Hyde found no CPGB branches in the area; indeed, Hyde describes himself as 'the only communist between Chester and Holyhead' at this time and opted instead to join the ILP, using his position in that organisation to move the north Wales ILP towards the CPGB.[61] Hyde notes that while he had some limited success in drawing people towards party

[57] *A Programme of Life, Health and Work for South Wales* (Cardiff, [1937]), p. 12.
[58] Alistair Wilson, 'National Consciousness and Class Consciousness' [1979], p. 7, Bert Pearce Papers WN 1/5.
[59] *Daily Worker,* 23 February 1937, p. 6.
[60] 'Communist Policy' [1944], John Roose Williams Papers, Bangor University Archive.
[61] Douglas Hyde, *I Believed: The Autobiography of a Former British Communist* (London, 1951), p. 44.

positions, after two years in north Wales he still had not managed to set up a single branch of the CPGB, noting the intense difficulty he had in overcoming the influence of nonconformity when attempting to win recruits.[62] According to Hyde, it was the adoption of the Popular Front, agitation over the Spanish Civil War and the formation of branches of the Left Book Club that finally brought members into the party.[63]

However, the key figure in the development of communism in north Wales, and, along with Idris Cox, in moving the Welsh party towards engaging seriously with the national question, was Roose Williams. Williams' political trajectory is particularly significant in this regard, moving from early membership of the Welsh Nationalist Party in 1925, to membership of the CPGB by 1932.[64] Writing in 1925, Williams noted the 'absence in the [Welsh Nationalist] Party's outline of its aims and methods of the least vestiges of a social and economic programme', arguing,

> The Nationalist Party … can succeed only in so far as it is able to satisfy the demands of the workers, who form an overwhelming majority of the nation … A political party without a social policy is an anomaly, a survival from a past age, and out of touch with the needs of the present age. It is, however, equally true that a Nationalist Party, paying due attention to the needs and aspirations of the workers, and determined to make political independence a means by which economic emancipation could be won for the workers, would command the sympathy and allegiance of the Welsh working-class to an extent which no other party has ever succeeded in achieving.[65]

Disillusioned with the direction taken by the Nationalists, Williams left the Welsh Nationalist Party and moved increasingly to the left, joining the CPGB in October 1932.[66] Williams played a central role in building the party in north Wales, travelling from village to village on his bike and holding

---

[62] Hyde, *I Believed: The Autobiography of a Former British Communist,* pp. 45–8.

[63] Hyde, *I Believed: The Autobiography of a Former British Communist,* pp. 55–9.

[64] D. Hywel Davies, *The Welsh Nationalist Party: A Call to Nationhood* (Cardiff, 1983), p. 96.

[65] John Roose Williams, 'A Social Policy for the Welsh Nationalist Party', *The Welsh Outlook,* October 1925, pp. 269–70.

[66] Secretariat of the CPGB to John Roose Williams, 31 October 1932, John Roose Williams Papers, Bangor University Archive.

impromptu political meetings.[67] With the help of William Rust, Williams set up the first branch of the CPGB in north Wales, at Bangor in 1935, and became District Secretary for the North Wales District on its formation in January 1937, remaining in that post until its amalgamation into the Welsh Committee in 1944.[68] The North Wales District was to remain a small district throughout its existence, with a membership of 80 in September 1938, rising to 90 by February 1939 and to 200 by 1942, at which time it was the party's smallest district.[69]

From its inception, the North Wales District was keenly aware of the need to engage with the national question if they were to appeal to the Welsh-speaking population of north Wales and counter the challenge of the Welsh Nationalist Party. The main subject of discussion at its inaugural conference was the District's attitude to the national question,[70] while the Welsh-language by-line of the District Party journal, *Llais y Werin*, 'Through Socialism to National Freedom', as opposed to the English by-line 'Unite Against Fascism and War', hints at the different political priorities the north Wales party attributed to the two linguistic groups in the District.[71] For Williams, in particular, the desire to see the party engage fully with the national question was to become a central focus, noting in his diary in 1945, 'I remain a Communist, but I believe more and more that Communism must put on Welsh clothing and fight for Wales' interests. This, from now on, will be my main work, that is, to infuse the Communist Party with the best traditions of Wales.'[72]

A second key figure in disseminating the communist gospel amongst the Welsh-speaking community was T. E. Nicholas. A well-known poet and preacher, as well as a

[67] Keith Gildart, 'Thomas Jones (Tom) (1908–90)', *Dictionary of Labour Biography Vol. 11* (London, 2003), p. 160.

[68] John Roose Williams to the Central Committee of the CPGB, 2 September 1935, John Roose Williams Papers, Bangor University Archive; *Daily Worker*, 4 February 1937; *Y Cymro*, 13 February 1937.

[69] CPGB Archive, 'Party Membership, February 1939', CI Reel 17 (LHASC); Newton, *The Sociology of British Communism*, p. 177.

[70] *Daily Worker*, 4 February 1937.

[71] *Llais y Werin: Organ of the North Wales District of the Communist Party of Great Britain*, July 1937. Author's own translation.

[72] John Roose Williams Diary, 14 October 1945, John Roose Williams Papers, Bangor University Archive. Author's own translation.

part-time dentist, Nicholas was the most recognisable Welsh-speaking communist during this period, Pollitt describing him as 'Wales' greatest man'.[73] In contrast to the younger Williams, Nicholas had a long history within the labour movement in Wales, being particularly active in the anti-war movement during the First World War, an associate of Keir Hardie and a member of the ILP. Enthused by the Russian Revolution, Nicholas became a founder member of the CPGB in 1920.[74] Highly critical of Liberal nationalism, Nicholas had long advocated the need for socialism in Wales to be given a Welsh dimension and had been central to discussions to form a Welsh ILP in 1911.[75] Writing in 1912, Nicholas had called for a fusion of the Welsh Dragon with the Red Flag, arguing that the struggle for national freedom was synonymous with the struggle for socialism; however, it was the class struggle that was given primacy by Nicholas.[76] Nicholas could claim something of a propaganda coup for the CPGB in early 1937, beginning a weekly column, O Fyd y Werin, in the main Welsh-language newspaper Y Cymro, which he stopped writing following censorship of an article on the Nazi–Soviet Pact.[77] Writing in March 1938, Nicholas reiterated his earlier stance qualifying his support for self-government by arguing that without a transition to socialism such a move would be meaningless, as it was only to hand power to Welsh capitalists, noting that self-government in Ireland had done little to improve the lot of the Irish working class. Nicholas was also critical of the Welsh Nationalist Party for lacking a coherent economic policy and displaying tendencies towards parochialism. Unsurprisingly, for Nicholas, the only country to deal successfully with the national question was the Soviet Union, which he portrayed

[73] Alan B. Williams to T. E. Nicholas, 5 October 1946, Bangor MSS. 23361, Bangor University Archive.

[74] Sian Howys Williams, Bywyd a Gwaith Thomas Evan Nicholas 1879–1971, p. 28, MA Thesis, University of Wales, 1983.

[75] Dylan Morris, 'Sosialaeth i'r Cymru: Trafodaeth yr ILP', Llafur, 4 (2), 1985, pp. 51–63.

[76] T. E. Nicholas, 'Y Ddraig Goch a'r Faner Goch: Cenedlaetholdeb a Sosialaeth', Y Geninen, 30 (1), January 1912, pp. 10–16.

[77] Rowland Thomas to T. E. Nicholas, 29 August 1939, John Roose Williams Papers, Bangor University Archive.

as a model federal state where all national cultures were given the opportunity to flourish, and political, religious and economic freedoms were guaranteed.[78]

Llwybr Rhyddid y Werin marks the CPGB's first exposition of its attitude towards the national question in Wales. Intended as a Welsh-language introduction to both Marxism and CPGB policy, and identifying Wales as a nation both receptive to socialism and with a long-standing revolutionary tradition, the final section of the pamphlet outlined the communist attitude to the national question and towards the Welsh Nationalist Party. In a rare admission for a communist, Williams identified Wales as part of the empire and expressed the CPGB's support for Welsh self-government and for the development of its language and culture. This support was linked to a vision of the party as one that had grown out of the struggles of the Welsh people, while arguing that it was only through the removal of economic exploitation of the working class that Wales could achieve a meaningful national freedom.

> The Communist Party believes in self-government for Wales as it does for every other part of the Empire, and in nurturing our nation's language and culture, because its roots are deep in the life of the people and has grown out of their suffering and endeavours. But we must first secure a Wales that is owned by the people of Wales, its land, its minerals and all its riches used in the interests of the nation's workers and small farmers, with everybody contributing something of use to society.[79]

Reflecting the underdevelopment of the party's thought on the issue, at this stage the form of self-government supported was not intimated in the pamphlet.

Responding to criticism that the CPGB had not expressed enough support to the Welsh nationalist movement, Williams avoided a direct answer, instead choosing to attack as reactionary nationalist party policy. Reflecting his earlier reservations, Williams attacked the Welsh Nationalists' social and economic policies, describing them as a 'strange mixture of inconsistencies', arguing that their approach to issues

---

[78] *Y Cymro,* 19 March 1938, pp. 8, 15.
[79] John Roose Williams, *Llwybr Rhyddid y Werin* (London, [1936]), p. 18. Author's own translation.

such as unemployment were totally inadequate and reactionary, the Nationalists' Thursday Dinner Club, in particular, bearing a 'similarity to Hitler's methods'.[80] Similarly, Welsh Nationalist proposals for the de-industrialisation of south Wales exposed the backward-looking thinking of the party leadership and its failure to understand the nature of modern society and the laws that governed social progress.[81] For Williams, 'It is not the destruction of these marvellous machines that is needed, but to use them for society's advancement, in order to ensure a better world for the workers, and this cannot be achieved without Socialism.' More broadly, the Nationalist Party was portrayed as "anti-working class" for its rejection of class struggle and its self-portrayal as a bulwark against communism in Wales. Williams was, however, careful to differentiate between the rank and file and the party's leadership, arguing that it was the leadership's views that showed a danger of moving towards fascism. Despite this, Williams warned that good relations between the two parties were dependent on nationalist involvement in the popular front, 'If the Nationalist Party refuses to take its place side by side with the working class in the battle against starvation, Fascism and war, it must be considered an enemy. It is not possible to take a middle road in the big battle that faces the people today, a battle that is fundamental to the future of all mankind.'[82] Williams was to provide a straighter answer to the CPGB's failure to engage with the national question in a couple of later articles, noting that the party in south Wales had, to a large extent, been denationalised during its earlier years,[83] the areas where the party was strongest being heavily anglicised, while the party itself had been preoccupied in combating the more urgent needs of the population that had emerged with the depression and the aftermath of the 1926 lockout.[84]

---

[80] Williams, *Llwybr Rhyddid y Werin,* p. 17.
[81] Williams, *Llwybr Rhyddid y Werin,* pp. 17–18.
[82] Williams, *Llwybr Rhyddid y Werin,* p. 18.
[83] 'Communist Policy', p. 1, John Roose Williams Papers, Bangor University Archive
[84] John Roose Williams, 'Comiwnyddiaeth a Chymru', *Heddiw,* 2 (1), February 1937, p. 8.

While Williams does not mention the arson attack on the bombing school at Penyberth in *Llwybr Rhyddid y Werin*, suggesting that the pamphlet was commissioned before that event, the publication of the pamphlet in latter part of 1936 is significant, and can be seen partly as a response to the arson attack and its aftermath, in particular, the publicity given to Welsh nationalism and the Nationalist Party. That Penyberth had made some impact within British communist circles is evident from a review of Stalin's *Marxism and the National and Colonial Question* in *Left Review*, which noted that Penyberth 'must have opened many people's eyes to the existence of national problems not only in the colonial dependencies of the British Crown, but actually within the boundaries of the Mother Country herself', identifying a tendency of the English, and implicitly English communists, to belittle the national characteristics of Britain's smaller nations.[85] In Wales, the centrality of the party's attitude to nationalism at the North Wales District's inaugural conference in January 1937 must also have been influenced by Penyberth, while the specific call within policy documents that were to be drawn up by the party during 1938 for an independent Welsh judiciary, the right to trial in Welsh and the right to be tried within Wales, was as much a response to the trial of the three nationalists accused of the arson attack, as it was to the political nature of trials of communists in south Wales.[86] For Welsh communists, Penyberth was symptomatic of the wrong-headed approach of the Welsh Nationalists to the national question in general, a 'terrorist act' that would 'lend support for the idea that the Welsh people are uncivilised barbarians', the Nationalists condemned for not attempting to broaden the campaign against the bombing school into that of the Popular Front.[87] This was disingenuous, for, as an editorial in *Heddiw*

---

[85] Edgell Rickword, 'Stalin on the National Question', *Left Review* 2 (14), November 1936, p. 746.

[86] *Statement on the National Question in Wales* [1938], CPGB Archive, CP/IND/DUTT/15/8 (LHASC); John Roose Williams, 'Comiwnyddiaeth a Chymru', *Heddiw*, 2 (1), February 1937, p. 7.

[87] *Land of my Fathers*, 1938, p. 14, Bert Pearce (Welsh Communist Party) Papers WN 1/1, NLW; John Roose Williams, 'Comiwnyddiaeth a Chymru', p. 8.

responding to the publication of *Llwybr Rhyddid y Werin* pointed out, the CPGB had paid little attention to the building of the bombing school at the time.[88] A more sober assessment offered some time later by Williams saw the issue of the bombing school as an opportunity lost, and, while condemning 'the use of incendiarism as a political weapon', viewing the whole episode as an attempt by the Welsh Nationalists to make some political capital out of the issue, he was also critical of the failure of the labour movement to take the lead on the bombing school, 'with the result that the burning of the bombing school became for thousands of sincere peace-lovers, chapel people, students, and even many workmen, a symbol of the struggle for peace'.[89]

Indeed the growth in influence of the Welsh Nationalists in north Wales was viewed as a consequence of the labour movement's failure to give a lead on issues related to the national question, as well as due to its organisational weakness in the region – political space that the nationalists as the heirs of the Liberal nationalism of the late nineteenth century were able to occupy. By engaging with the national question, the CPGB hoped to claim this political space, and help build a stronger, unified working-class movement in the whole of Wales, but especially in the north. In this regard, the role of the North Wales District was viewed as crucial, the area seen by the party centre 'as one of greatest importance because of its liberal and democratic traditions'.[90] Taking this role seriously, it was a resolution put forward by the North Wales District at the 1937 CPGB Congress on the status of the Welsh language that initiated discussions between the North and South Wales Districts on both this issue and the issue of the national question. Responding to the District's resolution, the PB proposed the setting up of a joint commission between north and south to discuss the status of the Welsh language. By early 1938 these proposed discussions had

---

[88] 'Golygyddol – Comiwnyddiaeth a Chymru', *Heddiw*, 1(5), December 1936, p. 162.

[89] John Roose Williams, 'The Welsh Nationalist Movement: Its Aims and Political Significance', *Discussion* 3 (2), March 1938, p. 31.

[90] Williams, 'The Welsh Nationalist Movement', p. 32; *It Can Be Done*, p. 170.

metamorphosed into an attempt to tackle the national question as a whole.[91]

The PB had discussed the party's approach to the national question in Scotland in January 1938, supporting Scotland's right to self-determination, including the right to independence, the building of a mass movement in conjunction with the Nationalists and Labour Party on social and economic issues, and backing the establishment of a Scottish Grand Commission as a first step on the road to self-government. However, despite the call within the document by the Scottish District to the PB for support for a Scottish Parliament with tax-raising powers, the PB offered a more cautious approach to self-government, arguing that 'the question of [a] Scots Parliament can best be raised in connection with the development of the mass movement'.[92] The party in Scotland had, despite Helen Crawfurd's plea for the party to show more consideration to the national question in 1933, remained opposed to engagement with the national question.[93] Indeed as late as November 1936, James Barke, in an article in *Left Review*, while acknowledging distinct Scottish national traditions and characteristics argued that 'there is no real Scottish national question'.[94] It was only after intervention by the party centre, concerned at the failure of the Scottish District to formulate a specific policy programme for Scotland, and at its abandonment of the national question to the nationalists, that the Scottish DPC began to formulate policy on this issue.[95]

In Wales, discussions on the national question, held under the auspices of the South Wales DPC, but with substantial contributions from the North Wales District, began in early 1938, with a discussion document put before the PB in July that year, and a statement on the national question drafted just prior to the 15th CPGB Congress in September 1938, at

[91] John Roose Williams, 'Communist Policy', p. 2.
[92] CPGB Archive, PB minutes, 28 January 1938, CPGB Original Reel 7 (LHASC); 'Scottish Nationalism' pp. 11–12, CP/IND/DUTT/15/8 (LHASC).
[93] Ragnheiður Kristjánsdóttir, 'Communists and the National Question in Scotland and Iceland, c.1930 to c.1940', *The Historical Journal*, 45 (3), 2002, pp. 608–11.
[94] James Barke, 'The Scottish National Question', *Left Review*, 2 (14), November 1936, p. 741.
[95] Kristjánsdóttir, 'Communists and the National Question', pp. 615–16.

which the party declared its support for Welsh and Scottish self-determination. Following this, the party's intention was to draw up a comprehensive programme for Wales which included support for Welsh self-government, a task that was cut short by the outbreak of the Second World War.[96] At the outset it should be noted that only a few documents relating to these discussions are extant, and that the minutes for the crucial PB meetings on the issue are also unavailable. It is, therefore, impossible to offer an exhaustive account of these discussions; however, the documents that have survived give us some insight into the Welsh party's position at this time, as well as a hint of some dissension over the issue. All the documents, bar the final version of the statement presented to the party centre prior to the 15th Congress, support the call for a Secretary of State and National Administrative Council in the short term, and a Welsh Parliament within a federal system as a long-term policy goal.

Much of the focus of the early discussions was on the Welsh Nationalist Party and the nature of Welsh nationalism. Certainly, most of a discussion document on the national question, drafted in February 1938, focused on these issues, before turning to the issue of self-government. The Welsh Nationalist Party was identified as the heir of the radical traditions of Welsh nonconformity and Liberalism, although its nationalism was viewed as anti-capitalist, opposed to 'the big trusts and combines which it claims are controlled by English capitalists'.[97] Four factors were identified as contributing to the growth of Welsh nationalism – the decline of the Liberal Party; the impact of the economic depression, especially the mass migration from the south Wales coalfield; restrictions placed on Welsh language and culture, especially its lack of official and legal status and restrictions on Welsh-language education; and the weakness of the CPGB.[98] In addition, Penyberth and its aftermath, especially the refusal of a trial in Welsh to the three nationalist defendants, were viewed as the key to their recent upsurge in support.[99] Identifying the

---

[96] 'Communist Policy', p. 2.
[97] 'Draft Statement on Welsh Nationalism' 24 February 1938, p. 2, Bert Pearce (Welsh Communist Party) Papers WN 1/1, NLW.
[98] 'Draft Statement on Welsh Nationalism', pp. 2–4.
[99] 'Draft Statement on Welsh Nationalism', pp. 5–6.

Nationalist economic programme as its weak point, comparing it unfavourably with that of the Scottish nationalists, their politics were described as 'hazy', taking 'refuge in the most abstract references to the "ideal conditions" in Denmark, Holland and Sweden, as the "non-Imperialist countries" whose example Wales should follow', while offering little in the form of concrete proposals as to how to deal with south Wales's plight as a Distressed Area.[100]

Noting that communists and nationalists had worked together in united front activity, the party's own attitude to the Nationalists in south Wales was viewed as one of 'benevolent friendliness ... It would be true to say ... that they are on more friendly terms with the Communists than with the Labour Party'. However, the attitude of the CPGB rank and file was noted to be negative towards both the nationalists and the national question, party members showing indifference to both; 'There are strong tendencies within the Communist Party either to call them "Fascists" or to treat them as being of no consequence, arising from the conception that there is no national problem for the people of Wales.'[101] These accusations of fascism were downplayed, however, the document instead focusing on the 'splendid possibilities for friendly relations and joint activity with the Welsh Nationalists on a common programme', despite the 'Fascist tendencies' of 'certain elements in the Welsh nationalist movement'. Reflecting the new opportunities presented by the Popular Front, arriving at a consensus with the progressive wing of the Welsh Nationalist Party was seen as the main goal.

> The main aim must be to win the support of the best elements in the Welsh Nationalist movement in support of the economic programme of the Party for the salvation of South Wales, and to prepare a similar programme for North Wales. The most active Welsh Nationalists realise the need for an economic programme, and once they are won over, would fight for its adoption within the ranks of the Welsh Nationalist Party.[102]

---

[100] 'Draft Statement on Welsh Nationalism', p. 5.
[101] 'Draft Statement on Welsh Nationalism', pp. 6–7.
[102] 'Draft Statement on Welsh Nationalism', p. 7.

The final section dealt with the party's proposals for self-government in Wales, recommending support for a Welsh Secretary and the establishment of a National Administrative Council as immediate demands. These, it was made clear, were proposed as the first step towards a Welsh Parliament within a federal Britain. In addition, the party was urged to support equal status for Welsh in schools, and while not supporting the compulsory teaching of Welsh, it recommended support for making this optional. Equal legal status was also called for both in the courts – a direct response to the outcry following the Penyberth trial – and in official documents as well as for more time to be given to the Welsh news on the BBC.[103]

A similar attitude to the Welsh Nationalists was evident in an article written by Roose Williams the following month. While arguing that the 'Third Way' position taken by the Welsh Nationalist Party left it in danger of moving towards fascism, especially due to what Williams viewed as the reactionary, backward-looking positions taken by its leadership, the main focus was on the need to form a Popular Front with the left of the party. Indeed, Williams noted with encouragement the left-wing challenge to the Nationalist leadership on the issue of their attitude to fascism at the party's Summer School the previous August. In order to achieve this aim and counter the emergence of a more reactionary version of nationalism in Wales, Williams argued that the CPGB had to begin to make clear its position vis-à-vis the national question and develop a policy that was more receptive to the 'national and cultural aspirations of the Welsh people'.[104]

Despite evidence of some limited joint action at a local level, no formal unity was to be achieved between the Nationalist Party and the Communists during this period. While there was some support for the Popular Front on the left of the Nationalist Party, from figures such as Dafydd Jenkins and Cyril Cule, the leadership dismissed these calls out of hand.[105] For the Nationalist leadership their view of

---

    [103] 'Draft Statement on Welsh Nationalism', p. 8.
    [104] John Roose Williams, 'The Welsh Nationalist Movement: Its Aims and Political Significance', p. 32.
    [105] *The Welsh Nationalist,* July 1938, p. 2; *Y Ddraig Goch,* November 1936, p. 10; *Y Cymro,* 27 February 1937

their party as a bulwark against communism, their opposition to any form of totalitarianism, and their fear that the
national question would cease to be the main issue, precluded
any thought of a Popular Front with the CPGB. For James
Kitchener Davies, responding to an article by Williams, while
both parties took similar positions on a number of issues, the
fundamental difference between the parties' solutions to
these problems, especially in terms of economic theory, left
them poles apart. In particular, the communist insistence
that the national question was ultimately subordinate to the
overriding issue of class struggle was rejected, Davies insisting
that the national question was the main battle to be fought.[106]
On the Communist side, there is no evidence that apart from
declarations from the leadership that they were willing to
work with the Nationalist Party, that any formal approach was
made to the Nationalists on them joining a Popular Front.
Considering the attitudes of the party's membership
described above, it is perhaps no surprise that this call to
unity remained largely rhetorical.

By April 1938, a discussion document put before the South
Wales DPC's Secretariat (made up of Glyn Jones, Will Paynter,
Len Jefferies and Arthur Horner) had been circulated to all
branches and preparations were underway for an all-day
session of the DPC that would finalise the District's position
on the national question. In its report to the party centre that
month, the DPC proposed a further improvement in links
between the North and South Wales Districts, recommending
increasing the frequency of meetings between the North and
South Wales Committees, and a monthly meeting between
the South Wales District Organiser and the North Wales leadership; for the organisation of discussions in every branch on
the national question; for the organisation of party classes in
Welsh, and for a final document on the national question to
be released 'as soon as possible' and for it to form the basis of
a pamphlet.[107]

[106] J. Kitchener Davies, 'Cenedlaetholdeb Cymru a Chomiwnyddiaeth', *Heddiw*, 2
(3). April 1937, pp. 84–90.
[107] 'Communist Party of Great Britain South Wales District Report' [April 1938],
p. 10, CPGB Archive, CI Reel 17 (LHASC).

This period of consultation was over by July, the debate on the national question moving to the party centre. In a brief discussion document that covered the aspects of the national question to 'which a clear answer must be given before it is possible for the Party in Wales to issue a pamphlet on for the Welsh people', the South Wales DPC argued that the national question had to be addressed if the party was to appeal to the broader population and build an effective Popular Front in south Wales. 'Whilst we already have an economic programme in broad outline, we have succeeded only in bringing a small minority into motion, and have given no thought to the political demands of the people.' These political and cultural demands were seen as crucial as they 'concern the Welsh people as a whole and not only the working class movement'. Noting that there were more Welsh people active in the chapels, choirs, eisteddfodau and in cultural organisations than there were within the trade unions, the DPC argued that it was a necessity for the party to tap in to this potential pool of support by emphasising the links between the economic base and the development of language and culture. In addition, the DPC argued that tendencies towards centralisation in National Government policy, and its link to the erosion of cultural rights should also be emphasised to help furnish the building of a Popular Front.[108]

While locating Wales within Stalin's definition of a nation as 'a historically evolved, stable community of language, territory, economic life, and psychological make-up manifested in a community of culture',[109] the DPC nevertheless had some difficulty over the question of Wales as an economic unit. Recognising that Wales was not economically self-sufficient, 'community of economic life' was interpreted as meaning 'that people are bound together by economic ties' in order for it to be qualified in this category. Recognising the weakness of this interpretation, the DPC attempted to offer a more relativist argument declaring, 'It would be

---

[108] 'The National Problem in Wales', p. 1, CPGB Archive, CP/IND/DUTT/15/8 (LHASC)

[109] Joseph Stalin, *Marxism and the National and Colonial Question* (London, 1936), p. 8.

wrong to stick to rigid rules and definitions. The main thing is that the Welsh people regard themselves as a Nation, have a clearly defined territory, separate language, national sentiments and are bound together by economic ties.' Indeed, despite the difficulties over the economic issue, the DPC argued that Wales had a stronger claim to nationhood than 'most European nations'. In terms of concrete proposals, the DPC recognised Wales' right to self-determination and supported an unstated measure of autonomy with the long-term goal of a federal Welsh Parliament 'with wide powers of autonomy'. While an alliance with the Welsh Nationalist Party was rejected, and a commitment entered into to 'expose the Fascist tendencies' of the Welsh Nationalist leadership, the DPC also recommended that the party work to draw progressive nationalists into a Popular Front.[110]

While the PB's response to these proposals is unknown due to the unavailability of the relevant minutes, some evidence as to the nature of the PB's response can be gleaned from a further statement on the national question, written by John Roose Williams, which was put before the party centre prior to the 15th CPGB Congress in September 1938.[111] Firstly, the South Wales DPC's attempt to fit Wales into the category of a 'community of economic life' had failed, with Wales now declared not to be an economic unit.[112] While Williams was to note later that there was a reluctance on the party's behalf during this period to view Wales as an economic unit, so as not to give ground to the nationalists, considering the attempt by the South Wales DPC to portray it as such, it is reasonable to assume that the DPC's attempt to second-guess Stalin on the issue was not wholly appreciated by the party centre. Secondly, the statement was restricted to immediate demands, only calling for a Secretary of State.[113] Crucially, a reference to the appointment of a Secretary of State with extensive powers 'as a first step towards self-government', included in an earlier draft by Williams, was omitted in the

---

[110] 'The National Problem in Wales', p. 2.
[111] CPGB Archive, 'Statement on the National Question in Wales', 1938, CP/IND/DUTT/15/8 (LHASC).
[112] CPGB Archive, 'Statement on the National Question in Wales', pp. 3–4.
[113] CPGB Archive, 'Statement on the National Question in Wales', p. 7.

final version of the statement. Williams, responding to this omission, argued, 'But I should like to go further than that. I heartily agree with the demand for a Secretary of State for Wales but only as a first step towards something far more fundamental that is a measure of autonomy that will enable us by political means to plan the economic future of Wales and to create an economic unit out of the present welter of sectional interests.' Williams' plea for the scope of the party's statement on the issue to be broadened was ignored. Differences between the North Wales District and the South Wales District are also hinted at with the replacement of the *Llais y Werin* slogan 'Through Socialism to national freedom', included by Williams in the first draft, with a more orthodox, internationalist slogan, 'Through Socialism to real freedom for all peoples and the solidarity of the workers of all countries', the reference to national freedom dropped entirely.[114]

While it is fair to assume that the emendations to Williams' earlier draft were made following further discussion with the South Wales DPC, they sit uncomfortably with the consistent proposals put forward in previous policy papers in support of a Welsh parliament. Some conflict over the issue was inevitable, considering the different cultural backgrounds and political priorities of Welsh communists, especially between those from north and south. As we have seen, there was some indifference to the issue of the national question within the party in south Wales, and there is also evidence that among the party leadership Arthur Horner, for one, was opposed to Welsh self-government.[115] There is, therefore, some evidence to suggest that the emendations were the result of pressure from opponents to a Welsh Parliament in south Wales. However, the PB's response to the Scottish DPC's proposals in support of a Scottish Parliament had been less than enthusiastic, the PB withdrawing the statement from the Scottish DPC, and, while advocating closer ties with the Scottish Nationalists on social and economic issues, choosing to focus on immediate demands such as the establishment of a

[114] Untitled draft of statement and associated comments, Section 4 'Our Demands', pp. 1–2, John Roose Williams Papers, Bangor University Archive. My italics.

[115] Idris Cox, 'Story of a Welsh Rebel', pp. 74–5, Idris Cox Papers 1, NLW.

Scottish Grand Commission, relegating the issue of a Scottish Parliament to the status of one to be raised at a later date.[116] It is therefore possible that the same approach was taken by the PB to the issue of a Welsh Parliament, the south Wales DPC responding to pressure from the centre to focus, for the time being, on immediate demands. The issue of a Welsh Parliament, while not totally discarded, was thus avoided by changing the focus of the party statement. A definitive answer, however, cannot be reached until further evidence is uncovered.

Whatever the view of the party centre on a Welsh parliament, the immediate demands relating to the Welsh language were progressive, calling for its equality of status with English, for its legal status in court and the appointment of an independent judiciary, as well as the setting up of an independent Welsh Broadcasting Corporation for Wales.[117] Welsh-language culture was identified as inherently plebeian due to the anglicisation of the Welsh ruling class, a process begun in the Tudor era. Providing historical justification for the argument that the oppressors of Wales were British capitalists, rather than the English capitalists blamed by the Welsh Nationalists, the Welsh ruling class' incorporation into the British state during the Tudor era was viewed as making them complicit in imperialism and the building of Empire from the very beginning.[118] Thus, the comparison made by the Nationalists between the fate of the colonies and that of Wales was viewed as invalid, as 'the upper class in Wales have from the beginning been partners with their blood brothers of the English ruling class in the building up of this vast empire, and have always divided the spoils with them'.[119] Capitalism was identified as the greatest threat to Welsh cultural life, a culture which found its refuge in the homes of the Welsh working class, with whose fate it was ultimately bound.[120] However, the main focus of the statement in terms of political action was on uniting all progressive forces in

[116] CPGB Archive, PB minutes, 28 January 1938, Original Reel 7 (LHASC).
[117] 'Statement on the National Question in Wales', p. 7.
[118] 'Statement on the National Question in Wales', p. 1.
[119] 'Statement on the National Question in Wales', p. 4.
[120] 'Statement on the National Question in Wales', p. 5.

Wales against the National Government, thus, while rejecting much of the Nationalist Party's programme, and making a pointed reference to the fate of Basque culture under Franco, the statement nevertheless called on 'all democratic and liberal opinion, including the Nationalist Party' and the Nonconformist churches to join in a Popular Front against the National Government 'which is the forerunner of open and brutal Fascist dictatorship'.[121] The statement ended with the party, 'born out of the hopes and sufferings of the working class', declaring its support for 'the freedom of Wales' and, adopting a distinctly nationalist style of rhetoric, issuing a call for 'Wales for the Welsh', 'the Welsh' in this context identified as 'the workers ... the miners, quarrymen, farmers and agricultural workers ... small traders, teachers, and all who contribute to the welfare of the nation'.[122]

The 15th CPGB Congress was to prove a milestone in the party's attitude to the national question in both Wales and Scotland. In its report to Congress, the CC acknowledged 'That for many years the party has underestimated the importance of the Scottish Nationalist Movement and the Welsh Nationalists, and also the fact their influence is much greater than their numbers.' In a carefully worded statement, the CC expressed its support for Welsh and Scottish national rights and for their right to self-determination, 'Our Party stands for a policy which preserves the best traditions of the Scottish people and the Welsh people, resists every attempt to encroach upon their national rights, and demands the fullest opportunities for the development of self-government.' The details of this new policy were to be explained in a set of pamphlets to be published by the Welsh and Scottish parties before the year was out, but these pamphlets were not to emerge until after the war.[123] The CC statement again showed some trepidation over the issue, and no mention was made of this new approach to the national question in the official Congress Report.[124]

---

[121] 'Statement on the National Question in Wales', pp. 6–7.
[122] 'Statement on the National Question in Wales', p. 8.
[123] CPGB – *Report of the Central Committee to the 15th Party Congress* (London, 1938), https://www.marxists.org/history/international/comintern/sections/britain/central_committee/1938/09/report.htm. Accessed 28 January 2017.
[124] *For Peace and Plenty: Report of the Fifteenth Congress of the CPGB* (London, 1938).

While the discussions between the North and South Wales Districts on a new policy programme continued into 1939, the outbreak of the war meant that for the time being the policy programme was put on hold. At its 1939 Congress, the South Wales District's resolution on the national question, in line with the previous year's statement, supported the immediate demand for a Secretary of State. That there was some difficulty in getting the rank and file behind the issue is hinted at in the report, which, while placing the national question within the context of the National Government's tendency towards bureaucratic centralism and the restriction of democratic rights, pointedly emphasised 'that we do not by any means accept the policy of the Welsh Nationalists, many of whose leaders are confused and who only succeed in creating divisions among the people'.[125] While the only concrete result of the discussions on the national question was the Eisteddfod pamphlet *The Lore of the People*, another positive outcome was that the discussions had led to a greater level of co-operation between the two districts, laying the seeds for the formation of a national committee in 1944.[126]

On the whole, the outcome of this first period of engagement with the national question in Wales was mixed. The party had acknowledged the need to engage with the question, and had, in particular, put forward progressive policies in terms of the status of the Welsh language and culture, and begun to develop its policy on Welsh self-government. However, its stance on self-government remained confused with conflict between party members and possibly with the party centre over this issue. In addition, amongst the rank and file, what evidence there is suggests that, at least in south Wales, the issue was still viewed as inconsequential, the party having some difficulty putting over the view that Wales had a distinct national problem, exacerbated by a tendency to view any form of self-government as separatism or linked to the 'fascist demagogy' of the Welsh Nationalist Party. A second attempt to popularise a positive attitude to the national question within the party would emerge from the ruins of war and the hope that a new world could be built upon them.

[125] *South Wales Congress Report 1939,* pp. 7–8.
[126] 'Communist Policy', p. 3.

RECONSTRUCTION, THE CPGB AND THE
NATIONAL QUESTION, 1943–1950

The CPGB's engagement with the national question was rekindled during the final years of the Second World War, the party increasingly seeing self-government as the most effective way of ensuring successful post-war reconstruction in Wales. The CPGB did not begin turning its attention to the post-war period until the end of 1942, prior to which the party, following its reversion to a pro-war position after the invasion of the Soviet Union in June 1941, had viewed discussions on what would happen after the war as divisive, arguing that the whole of the party's focus should be on winning the war. The publication of the Beveridge Report in November 1942, however, called for a response, the party welcoming the report and also issuing a memorandum on *Guiding Lines on Post-war Construction* in December 1942, although this, for the time being, called on the party to restrict itself to general propaganda and to campaigning on day-to-day issues. At the 16th CPGB Congress in June 1943, a resolution on 'Britain Today and Tomorrow' was put before Congress, although it mainly dealt with 'Britain Today'. However, from this congress onwards, as victory in the war became more certain, the party began drawing up its post-war proposals culminating in the publication, in May 1944, of its suggestions for a post-war policy programme, *Britain for the People*, ready for the 17th Congress in October of that year.[127] Reflecting a shift in the party's thinking on democracy and a reassessment of the value of parliamentary politics, the party established a Parliamentary and Local Government Committee in 1943, which called for the introduction of proportional representation and the reform of parliament.[128] The party's deliberations over post-war policy were also boosted by the Moscow and Teheran Conferences, which raised hopes of post-war co-operation between the allies and a vision of a 'family of democratic nations' which was to prove a particular

[127] Geoffrey Roberts, 'The Limits of Popular Radicalism: British Communism and the People's War, 1941–1945', *Chronicon: an electronic history journal* 1, 1997, 3: 39–43. http://www.ucc.ie/chronicon/robfra.htm. Accessed 28 January 2017.
[128] Noreen Branson, *History of the Communist Party of Great Britain 1941–1951* (London, 1997), pp. 83–4.

feature on the party's thinking on the national question in Wales.

Initially, the Welsh national question was raised in the context of the war effort, the resolution on 'Victory over Fascism' at the 1943 South Wales District Congress arguing, in relation to the home front, that 'The refusal to grant measures of self-government is hampering the war effort in South Wales and encouraging unscrupulous elements to divert attention from the urgent need of defeating Fascism.' The granting of immediate measures such as appointing a Secretary of State, the better provision of Welsh-language education and help in developing Welsh culture were viewed as a crucial step in 'winning a greater response throughout Wales for the war effort',[129] while the 'unscrupulous elements' were clearly the Welsh Nationalists. Reiterating the demand for a Welsh Secretary, the District also moved closer to calling for a Welsh Parliament, noting that the implementation of these immediate legislative measures should be the first step to 'a system of self-government in association with the British Parliament'.[130] This carefully-worded statement suggests some indecision over the precise nature of the form of self-government that the party wished to see implemented post-war. Continued divisions over the importance of the national question were evident in a resolution on labour unity in south Wales, which, while condemning sectarian tendencies within the party towards Labour, also expressed frustration at similar attitudes, as well as a degree of economism, towards the national question, noting that sectarianism was 'also expressed in the neglect to take an interest in the national desires of the Welsh people; to think only in terms of narrow economic demands; to ignore the awakening interest in Welsh language and culture, and so leave a free field for unscrupulous elements to exploit the desires of the Welsh people to hinder the fight against Fascism'.[131] By linking the national question to the war effort and to questions of unity, the DPC clearly hoped that by placing the

[129] *The Way Forward for South Wales: Report of the South Wales Congress of the Communist Party* (Cardiff, 1943), p. 3.
[130] *The Way Forward for South Wales,* p. 11.
[131] *The Way Forward for South Wales,* p. 14.

national question within this new context that they could stimulate greater interest in the national question amongst the rank and file.

For Idris Cox, the whole experience of the war had given further impetus to the question of Welsh self-government. Writing in a follow-up pamphlet to *The People Can Save South Wales*, outlining the South Wales District's proposals for the post-war era, Cox argued that the Welsh could 'be proud of their share in the struggle for the salvation of humanity'. However, noting that Wales was also a nation and had 'the right to demand full rights of self-government', Cox also argued that 'It is not enough to fight for the freedom of all other nations, and refuse to fight for our own. In the new world after the war, Wales must take a positive part as a free country in building the new family of democratic nations.'[132] This was to become a major theme in the immediate post-war proposals for Welsh self-government, with a number of communist commentators noting the new perspectives offered by the experience of the war, which was viewed as having led to an upsurge of national feeling, as well as bringing the whole concept of nation-building into stark relief. Cyran Lloyd Humphreys, a Llanelli communist and member of the Welsh Committee, writing some months later, noted,

> The war is the most important fact today. Big and small nations are in the melting pot. On the one hand, strong and powerful countries were reduced to weak powers in a few weeks (France); and, on the other hand, peoples whose governments surrendered to fascism showed a surprising capacity to fight and to develop a national spirit (Denmark and Yugoslavia). Consciously or unconsciously all people will, in such circumstances, think about the birth and rebirth of nations. The future of countries, peoples and nations is being shaped. The war must inevitably alter the map of the world and the destiny of nations ... Today, the United Nations pride themselves that they are fighting against oppression, for the right of all peoples to 'live free lives.' This should apply to our own Wales. Since Wales is a nation one of its rights is to manage its own affairs. This does not mean withdrawing into isolation and ignoring world events, but it does mean giving conscious attention to Wales as an economic, political and social unit. A

[132] Idris Cox, *Forward to a New Life for South Wales* (Cardiff, 1944), p. 13.

consequence would be a great revival in national character and development.[133]

In terms of the party's proposals on the national question, Cox returned to the district's initial pre-war position, supporting a Secretary of State and a National Advisory Council, while calling for Wales to be given 'full rights of self-government' post-war. Arguing for self-government, Cox noted that by giving Wales the power to run its own affairs, devolution of governmental responsibility would better prevent Wales from slipping back to the dark days of the inter-war years. For Cox, while the abolition of capitalism remained the ultimate goal, in the short term the devolution of power 'hastened the process in which Wales will work out its own salvation',[134] and, reflecting a shift in communist thought towards building a national form of communism, Cox argued that 'Britain may not have to travel step by step along the same path as the Russian Revolution', noting that 'Every country will achieve socialism in its own way.'[135]

While the South Wales District, as Cox's call for 'full rights of self-government' shows, remained coy about calling by name for a Welsh Parliament, the publication of the party centre's post-war policy proposals in May 1944 held no such fear, calling for the establishment of both Welsh and Scottish parliaments as part of its programme of democratic reforms, along with proposals for the introduction of proportional representation and the reform of local government.[136] These proposals had been part of the remit of the Parliamentary and Local Government Committee, headed by William Gallacher, the proposals on self-government in Wales and Scotland, presumably arrived at in consultation with the Welsh and Scottish Districts. The policy document, entitled *Britain for the People*, was also significant in the emphasis it placed on parliamentary democracy, the party now arguing that socialism could be achieved through a mixture of participation in parliamentary politics, albeit through a reformed parliamentary system, and the nurturing of popular

[133] C. Lloyd Humphreys, 'Welsh National Rights', *Labour Monthly*, 26 (11), November 1944, pp. 346–7.
[134] *Forward to a New Life*, p. 13.
[135] *Forward to a New Life*, p. 10.
[136] *Britain For the People: Proposal for Post-war Policy* (London, 1944), p. 20.

extra-parliamentary movements – a far cry from the outright rejection of achieving socialism through parliamentary means contained in *For Soviet Britain* nine years earlier.[137]

The formation of a Welsh Committee of the CPGB in July 1944 marked another significant step in the party's relationship with the national question. Membership of both districts had grown significantly during the war, with 246 members in the North Wales District and 2,579 in the South Wales District by 1943; the amalgamated Welsh party claiming a membership of 2,724 in 1944.[138] Unfortunately, no record remains of the discussions that led to the formation of the Welsh Committee, so the exact motives of the participants remain elusive. However, co-operation between the two districts had increased following the discussions on the national question in 1938, while the formation of a Welsh Reconstruction Advisory Council and its definition of Wales as a single economic unit may also have led the party to think in terms of organising on a national basis. The small size of the North Wales District, by now the party's smallest district, must also have been a contributory factor, while Roose Williams notes that the war itself had also played a part in this process noting that 'the transformation of the war to a struggle for liberation opened a new perspective before the Welsh and the Communist Party in Wales'.[139] Whatever the reasons, the formation of a Welsh Committee meant new challenges for the party, not least in confirming the need for distinctive Welsh policies to answer Welsh problems. Writing to the CPGB's Central Organisation Department in July, Idris Cox noted that 'since becoming responsible for the whole of Wales we find from experience that our Party policy for Britain does not answer some of the main problems for Wales as a whole'.[140] For Roose Williams, the new task before the party was 'to integrate the struggle of the working class for economic emancipation with the fight to realise the national emancipation of the Welsh people'.[141]

[137] *For Soviet Britain*, pp. 20–1.
[138] Kenneth Newton, *The Sociology of British Communism* (London, 1969), p. 178.
[139] 'Communist Policy', p. 1.
[140] CPGB Archive, Idris Cox to CPGB Central Organisation Department, 19 July 1944, CP/CENT/ORG/01/01 (LHASC).
[141] 'Communist Policy', first draft, p. 2.

A renewed focus on the national question was evident from the outset with notes taken by Roose Williams at an early session of the Welsh Committee showing that the first issue discussed was Welsh national rights, noting that a start had already been made in 'getting the Party and [the] working class to face up to [the] national problem', a proposal to draw up a document on the issue leading to 'considerable discussion' on its content.[142] In more concrete terms, the party's focus on the national question was evident in the publication, within a month of its formation, of a statement on the national question and a second Eisteddfod pamphlet, which also dealt with the issue of self-government, both pamphlets declaring support for a Welsh Parliament within a federal system, as well as for equal status for the Welsh language and the greater provision of Welsh-language education.[143]

The party's statement, *Communists and Welsh Self-government*, can be seen as an attempt make its stance on self-government clear not only to the general public, but also to party members. As in the late 1930s, the Nationalist Party was portrayed as consisting of a largely progressive rank and file, 'sincere in its desire to win the recognition for Wales as a nation and to advance the interests of Wales', many of whom are 'responsive to socialist ideas', who were hampered by a reactionary leadership beholden to a 'blend of semi-Fascist ideology and Roman Catholicism'.[144] Turning to the Labour Party and the labour movement, the statement noted their failure to offer a definitive lead on these issues and argued that the labour movement should follow the Welsh Committee's example and organise on a national basis, while calling for the formation of a Welsh Regional Council of Labour based on the Welsh Labour Party, the Welsh Co-operative Movement and, most significantly, a Wales TUC, which would function as part of a British National

---

[142] Welsh Committee minutes, undated but prior to 10 August 1944, BTD Shorthand Notebook, John Roose Williams Papers, Bangor University Archive.
[143] *Communists and Welsh Self-Government* (Cardiff, 1944); *The Flame of Welsh Freedom/Fflam Rhyddid Cymru* (Cardiff, 1944).
[144] *Communists and Welsh Self-government*, p. 3.

Council of Labour.[145] In terms of Communist policy the statement called by name, for the first time, for the establishment of a Welsh Parliament as the party's long-term policy goal, while maintaining its support for a Secretary of State and National Administrative Council in the short term. On the Welsh language, the party called for greater provision of Welsh-language education, Welsh as a compulsory qualification for teachers, and the setting up of a Welsh Broadcasting Corporation.[146]

The Flame of Welsh Freedom, a bilingual pamphlet published for the 1944 National Eisteddfod at Llandybie, represented another attempt by the party to link itself to Welsh-language culture. This time the Eisteddfod was depicted as a symbol of progress and civilisation, 'In a world where the Nazi cult of brute force and racial arrogance have trampled underfoot the ideals of culture, freedom and the dignity of man.' Noting the experience of the war, which 'had witnessed the fate of one small nation after another, and seen their lands overrun, their industry destroyed, their people enslaved, their culture treated with contempt and their language prohibited', Roose Williams, the pamphlet's author, argued that in the new world following the war from which 'will arise a world family of independent nations ... The Welsh people will have a new birth of freedom and national consciousness.'[147] For Williams, the war had also meant that Wales was no longer viewed as a part of England, with its economic unity recognised by the Welsh Reconstruction Advisory Council along with a recognition of the special needs of Welsh-language education in the 1944 Education Act.[148] While self-government represented the 'age old dream [of] Welsh patriots from Owain Glyn Dŵr to Tom Ellis', Williams couched his argument for the establishment of a Welsh parliament in terms of the democratic reform of the British parliamentary system, noting both the Welsh people's democratic right 'to deal with their own specific problems and difficulties' as well as the establishment of the Welsh

---

[145] *Communists and Welsh Self-government*, pp. 3–4.
[146] *Communists and Welsh Self-government*, p. 4.
[147] *The Flame of Welsh Freedom*, pp. 5–6.
[148] *The Flame of Welsh Freedom*, p. 7.

Parliament as a means of relieving 'the pressure from the Federal Parliament in London'.[149]

The party's desire to portray itself as at the centre of Welsh cultural life was also evident in the publication of a symposium of tributes to T. Gwynn Jones, which, attesting to the party's new-found respectability, included contributions not only from communist authors such as Idris Cox, T. E. Nicholas, Dilys Cadwaladr and William Rees but also from figures such as Idris Bell, Keidrych Rhys, Gwenallt and D. Tecwyn Lloyd.[150] Apart from a call for the better provision of Welsh-language education by Idris Cox, the symposium is otherwise devoid of overt political content, instead concentrating on the merit of T. Gwynn Jones's literary work. However, the publication of the pamphlet reflected a desire amongst some of the party leadership in Wales, notably Roose Williams, that the party give itself a distinct Welsh identity and link itself to Welsh culture, a subtler variant of which can be seen in the adoption of Wales' national colours, red and green, on the Welsh Committee's letterhead. Roose Williams also sought to educate party members in Welsh history, writing a series on the 'Pioneers of Democracy in Wales' for the party's internal organ, *Party News*, which, reflecting his Christian Communism, were later published in the journal of the Welsh Congregational Union, *Y Dysgedydd*.[151]

August 1944 had also seen the publication of the party's policy proposals for the post-war era, *Wales in the New World*. Largely based on the South Wales District's presentation to the Welsh Reconstruction Advisory Council in February 1944, the party's policy proposals for the post-war period were based on the premise that the war economy, having transformed the economic life of Wales, had shown that it was not a poor country, rather one rich in mineral resources

---

[149] *The Flame of Welsh Freedom*, p. 10.

[150] *A Great Welshman* (Cardiff, 1944). D. Tecwyn Lloyd had, however, been a member of the party pre-war, leaving the party in 1939; information from Meredydd Evans.

[151] See *Party News*, 22 September 1945 for the first article in the series and *Y Dysgedydd*, 127 (7), July 1947, pp. 176–7, for its equivalent in the Congregationalists journal.

that had been held back and exploited by industrial monopolies and the big landowners.[152] To prevent a return to this
system of exploitation, and to Wales' pre-war condition, the
party proposed a programme for the nationalisation of
industry and the land,[153] along with a large-scale house-
building programme, government assistance for small
farmers, the development of new industries and the expansion of educational provision.[154] Much of the focus of the
party's programme was on building up Wales as a single
economic unit, with a diverse industrial base and improved
transport links between not only north and south, but also to
mid-Wales, viewed as vital in keeping Wales on its feet.
Reiterating the party's stance on self-government and the
language question, the party added a call for the establishment of both a national orchestra and theatre, while noting
that the Welsh Parliament, as an integral part of a federal
system, would 'not only enable Wales to develop as a nation,
but help improve the efficiency of the British Parliamentary
system and its democratic methods'.[155]

However, despite its support for a Welsh Parliament the
party maintained that the underlying causes of Wales' pre-war
misery, the vested interests of monopoly capital and the big
landowners, could only be solved through action at a British
level. Rejecting the policy of the Welsh Nationalists, characterised as breeding 'hostility between the people of England
and Wales and between the English-speaking and Welsh-
speaking people in Wales', the party argued that 'the future
of Wales as a nation is bound up with the interest of the
British people', noting that 'The menace which threatens
the interests of Welsh people comes from British monopoly
capital, which combines both Welsh and English capitalists.
The main enemy of the Welsh people is also the enemy of the
English.'[156] For the party, the national struggle was thus predicated on the success of the struggle of the British working
class, who, it was assumed, would be won over to the idea of

[152] *Wales in the New World* (Cardiff, 1944), p. 7.
[153] *Wales in the New World*, p. 9.
[154] *Wales in the New World*, pp. 12–25.
[155] *Wales in the New World*, pp. 26–7.
[156] *Wales in the New World*, p. 11.

devolving power. However, as we shall see, this was a dangerous assumption to make, as for many communist workers, even in Wales, there was a contradiction between the tendency towards centralisation of the trade unions and the call for devolution and federalism in the governmental sphere.

Arguing that 'Wales is not getting a square deal from the British government', campaigning for the party programme was to be concentrated on the building of a popular movement in preparation for the new Welsh Day in parliament, a campaign that met with only limited success. The Welsh Day had been welcomed by the party as a 'signal victory' for Wales, who viewed it as a potential first step on the road to a Welsh Parliament.[157] While the party also saw the campaign as a means of expressing its support for devolutionary measures, its enthusiasm for the Welsh Day was ridiculed by the Welsh Nationalist Party, with Idris Cox lampooned as the 'sprite of sudden patriotism' in *The Welsh Nationalist.*[158] The Nationalist Party's criticism was unfair, for while the party's hopes for the Welsh Day can be viewed as wildly optimistic, the party's enthusiasm for the Welsh Day is best viewed as an opportunity for the party to try and build up effective extra-parliamentary campaigns, and it is debatable whether the party viewed the value of the Welsh Day as anything other than that. Indeed, by 1947, the party's support for the Welsh Day had waned, a combination of the failure of the party's own Welsh Day campaigns and a realisation that one day in parliament a year was not enough to solve Wales' problems.[159]

In an article introducing the party's standpoint on the national question to the broader British communist readership, published to coincide with the Welsh Day, Cyran Lloyd Humphreys noted that Wales suffered from economic, political and cultural inequality in relation to the British state. Reflecting the new focus on Wales as an economic unit, Humphreys argued that cultural autonomy was not sufficient

---

[157] *'Welsh Day' in Parliament* (Cardiff, 1944), p. 1.
[158] *The Welsh Nationalist,* November 1944, p. 1.
[159] *Make 1947 a Real New Year in Wales: The Communist Plan to Save Young People and to Prevent Wales Becoming Derelict Again* (Cardiff, 1947), p. 1.

for Wales, noting, 'Is our future as a nation only to be in the world of culture? This cannot be. Cultural opportunity implies political responsibility.'[160] Explaining the inequalities between Wales and England, Humphreys put a distinct emphasis on issues such as capital flight to England, the ownership of key Welsh industries by English capitalists, the 'English monopoly of government administration', and the anglicisation of Welsh culture through the radio and cinema and the refusal of incomers to learn the Welsh language.[161] This focus on the anglicisation of Wales and the specific references to Wales' exploitation by England and specifically by English capitalists, rather than British capitalists, was something of a departure for communists commenting on the national question – indeed the party had condemned the Welsh Nationalist Party for singling out English capitalists.

Humphreys, in particular, related Wales' economic problems directly to the political relationship between Wales and England, 'Welsh people suffer economic inequality due to the political connections between Wales and England', whilst noting that 'In the appointment of government officials seldom is any reference made to any qualifications for dealing with Welsh affairs.'[162] Humphreys also noted that the Welsh industrial worker, and implicitly Welsh party members, while 'very conscious of his relation to the capitalist' and to imperialism, still failed to recognise 'that the struggle for Welsh National Rights is an essential part of, and of great assistance to, the fight against capitalism' and was often 'indifferent to the obstacles which prevent greater scope to the culture and language of his native Wales'.[163] For Humphreys, it was vital that the industrial worker 'learn to regard his country with pride and to participate in her development' and 'not oppose national rights' through a misguided internationalism. For Humphreys, only a solution to the national question would help overcome the relationship of superiority and inferiority between the two

[160] Humphreys 'Welsh National Rights', p. 347.
[161] Humphreys, 'Welsh National Rights', pp. 347–8.
[162] Humphreys, 'Welsh National Rights', p. 348.
[163] Humphreys, 'Welsh National Rights', p. 346.

nationalities, noting 'The Englishman no less than the indifferent Welshman must learn to respect nationality.'[164]

The party's position on the national question in Wales was given the rubber stamp by both the British and Welsh Congresses, albeit not without controversy. In October 1944, at the 17th CPGB Congress it was left to Dutt to move the resolution on 'Britain for the People' that included support for a Welsh Parliament, with Pollitt himself making no comment on the issue in his political report to Congress, leaving some commentators to argue that Pollitt was opposed to such a measure.[165] The policy programme contained in *Wales in the New World* was adopted at the First All-Wales Congress in January 1945, the national question given some prominence in Congress resolutions, forming part of the first resolution adopted by Congress.[166] However, the prominence given to the issue in the congress resolutions belied a split amongst leading party members over a Welsh Parliament, with Arthur Horner, Cox notes, taking 'the unprecedented step of attacking this concept in his opening remarks to Congress' having 'never been won over to this view'.[167] Much of Horner's opposition stemmed from the contradiction that he, along with other communists associated with the NUM, felt existed between, on the one hand, supporting a national, centralised miners' union at the British level, and the Welsh party's support for a federal system of government.[168] This dispute was to simmer until the next party congress held in September 1946.

The 1945 election was to be a disappointment for the CPGB, the party failing to capitalise on the leftward shift during the election following its decision to contest only 22 seats in an attempt to prevent splitting the anti-Tory vote. In the event, despite a strong showing for Communist candidates, only two were elected – William Gallacher and

[164] Humphreys, 'Welsh National Rights', p. 350.
[165] *Victory, Peace, Security: Report of the 17th Congress of the Communist Party* (London, 1944), p. 41; Brian Davies, 'Heading for the Rocks?', *Arcade*, 5 February 1982, p. 10.
[166] *Communist Policy for the People of Wales: Report of the First All-Wales Congress of the Communist Party* (Cardiff, 1945), pp. 21–2.
[167] 'Story of a Welsh Rebel', pp. 74–5, Idris Cox Papers 1, NLW.
[168] Lyndon White, 'The CPGB and the national question in post-war Wales: the case of Idris Cox', *Communist History Network Newsletter,* 12, Spring 2002, pp. 19–20.

Phil Piratin. For many party members the party's decision to campaign for a Labour Government had been the wrong one, many feeling the party should have gone it alone.[169] In Wales, Harry Pollitt came within 972 votes of defeating W. H. Mainwaring at Rhondda East, the Welsh Nationalist candidate, Kitchener Davies, coming third, polling 2,123 votes.[170] While the party blamed the defeat on a number of factors, for Idris Cox it had highlighted the need for the party to take the national question more seriously, Cox including the failure to adopt a more positive attitude to the national question amongst the factors that had led to the party's defeat.[171] Despite its disappointment at the election result, the CPGB remained committed to supporting the Labour Government. This support was unrequited, however, with the CPGB failing in its final attempt at affiliation to the Labour Party at the 1946 Labour Party Conference, losing the crucial support of the NUM despite south Wales voting narrowly in favour of affiliation, a further amendment adopted barring the affiliation of any organisation that had its own programme, principles and policies, ending all hopes of Communist affiliation to the Labour Party.[172]

In Wales, there was disappointment at the Labour Party's failure to plan for Wales as a single economic unit, the party growing increasingly critical of the Labour Party's response to unemployment and the building of new industries following demobilisation. For the Communists, an economic plan for Wales was a necessity if it was not going to return to its pre-war condition. Labour's failure to develop such a plan was seen as lying at the heart of Wales' lack of progress in the immediate post-war period, particularly in terms of increasing unemployment and the continued migration of Welsh workers.[173] There was also disappointment that a Secretary of State had been rejected by the Labour Party in its 1946 White Paper on Wales, with supporters of self-government within

[169] Branson, *History of the CPGB 1941–1951*, pp. 87–8, 97–9.
[170] Williams, *Democratic Rhondda*, p. 163.
[171] John Mahon, *Harry Pollitt: a Biography* (London, 1976), p. 309.
[172] Branson, *History of the CPGB 1941–1951*, pp. 115–17.
[173] See, in particular, *Make 1947 a Real New Year in Wales*, pp. 1–5 for a detailed attack on Labour's progress.

the CPGB arguing that it should adopt a demand for a Welsh Parliament as party policy, discarding the call for a Secretary of State. This was certainly the gist of an outline scheme presented by Justin Lewis to the Welsh Committee in 1946. Rejecting the government's proposal for a Welsh Advisory Council as 'totally inadequate to meet the needs of Wales', 'utterly undemocratic in character' and as a 'gross insult' to the people of Wales, Lewis argued that the proposal of an Advisory Council for Wales 'offered the shadow and denied the substance of Self-government'.[174] For Lewis, the limited nature of the government's proposals called for the party to provide a lead and decide between supporting the immediate proposals such as those for a National Administrative Council or instead opt to bite the bullet and support a Welsh Parliament. Lewis, opting for the latter option, argued that 'The fundamental issue of Self-Government for Wales should be faced now and public interest and discussion promoted to this end. A Parliament for Welsh Affairs is by far the most effective measure of Self-Government for Wales.' For Lewis, if the public imagination was to be aroused on the issue then it would take a bold plan like one for a Welsh parliament to generate support, rather than the limp proposals offered by the Labour Government.[175] Outlining his proposals for a Welsh Parliament, Lewis proposed a single-chamber legislature, with its own executive responsible for all services and basic industries, along with all existing national institutions.[176] Lewis' proposal for changing the party's policy to supporting a Welsh Parliament as an immediate aim is significant in that it prefigured its decision to take part in the Parliament for Wales Campaign in 1950, and would soon become an issue of discussion for the party following the Second Welsh Congress of September 1946.

At Congress, the Welsh Committee was instructed to clarify the party's position further, a request that attested to the confusion that still existed amongst the rank and file over the

---

[174] Justin Lewis, 'An Outline Scheme for Self-Government for Wales', p. 1, Bert Pearce Papers WN 1/1, NLW.

[175] Lewis, 'An Outline Scheme for Self-Government for Wales', p. 2.

[176] Lewis, 'An Outline Scheme for Self-Government for Wales', p. 2.

issue.[177] This set in motion a further round of debate on the Welsh Committee, during October and November, as to how to present the issue to the party. Little survives of this debate apart from the contribution of Len Jefferies. Jefferies, noting that the discussions over the issue had been complex, argued that the party must endeavour to offer the simplest explanation possible. For Jefferies, part of the problem was that the party had not started in the right place, engaging in too much abstract historical discussion, and not relating the issue to contemporary political problems. Like Lewis, Jefferies was critical of Labour's decision to reject a Secretary of State and like Lewis, also viewed Labour's decision as offering the party an opportunity.

> Shorn of its trimmings this reverence for the existing constitution suggests that even the mere granting of a Secretary of State would result in undermining the authority of the British State. Certain it is that it would result in giving Welsh claims more publicity, but more important still it would give Welsh claims more public backing. This fact has not gone unnoticed by the present Cabinet. Inasmuch as the problems of Wales demand pressure on the existing state machine for a solution and that the Labour Cabinet is pledged to defend at all costs the existing State, the stand of the Cabinet against granting the Secretary of State for Wales is understandable.

For Jefferies, this decision called for the party membership to offer its support for Welsh self-government, arguing that any transformation to a socialist society would also entail drastic constitutional changes, and, thus, that any weakening of the present constitution was to be welcomed and supported by the party.

> It should be clear to Communists, however, that a weakening of the State in this respect must mean the strengthening of the fight for a Socialist State and that no real socialist state is possible without very big changes in the present State apparatus. Thus the opposition of the Labour Cabinet to a Secretary of State on constitutional grounds should be an added incentive to Welsh Communists to throw their full weight for Welsh demands as contained in the Party resolutions.

---

[177] *Report and Resolutions of the Second Welsh Congress September 28/29, 1946* (Cardiff, 1946), p. 2; C. Lloyd Humphreys to Welsh Committee, 23 October 1946, Bert Pearce Papers WN 1/1, NLW.

Jefferies also viewed the party's support for self-govern-ment as crucial if the party was to tap into what he perceived as the growing post-war national sentiment in Wales, or in combating a more reactionary type of national sentiment, which Jefferies associated with a rise in anti-Semitism in south Wales.

Turning to opponents of self-government, Jefferies argued that the contradiction seen by party members within the NUM was a false one.

> Reluctance to accept the policy of fighting for Welsh demands comes from comrades who profess to see a contradiction between fighting for these demands and supporting, for example, one Union for Mineworkers. The fact that there is a NMU [sic] is an excellent thing for all miners. But Welsh miners as well as being part of the NMU are also part of a Miners International and a part of the WFTU. This unifi-cation does not prevent Welsh Miners giving support to struggling peoples in any country in the world. At Conference after Conference this is done. Despite the establishment of the NMU the problems facing the Welsh nation remain and membership of the NMU far from precluding support for Welsh demands should be effectively used to further the aims of the Welsh people. Mining comrades should be won to see the value of winning support in the NMU for Welsh and Scottish demands as one of the means for achieving a Socialist Britain and thus improvements in conditions for all mineworkers.[178]

The discussion statement released by the Welsh Committee in November followed Lewis's lead and argued that the party had to decide whether to back a two-stage approach to the question of the devolution of power or to back the call for a Welsh Parliament as an immediate demand, the Welsh Committee backing the latter option arguing that having both immediate and long-term demands 'can only lead to confusion'. Commenting on the inadequacy of previous debate on the issue, the discussion statement, reflecting Jefferies' concerns, noted a previous 'tendency to engage in abstract discussions, and to delve into past Welsh history, and to draw mechanical conclusions from the treatment of the national problem by Engels, Lenin and Stalin'. While main-taining that an understanding of Marxist theory on the

---

[178] Len Jefferies to the Welsh Committee, [October 1946], Bert Pearce Papers WN 1/1, NLW.

national question remained vital, the statement noted that 'it would be a serious mistake to expect ready-made solutions which apply to the peculiar historical development of Wales'. Arguing that the need for a Welsh Parliament was based on three factors: Wales' status as a nation; the existence of specific economic and political problems in Wales; and a need to relieve the pressure at Westminster due to an 'overloading of the British legislative machine', the discussion statement, for the first time, defined the division of power between a Welsh and British parliament. The British Parliament was to retain power over foreign policy, defence, international relations, finance and economic and social planning for Britain, while the Welsh Parliament would be responsible for economic planning in Wales within the framework of a British economic plan, for housing, health, education, culture, local administration and broadcasting in Wales. By defining the areas of power to be devolved to the Welsh Parliament, the Welsh Committee argued that the immediate demands for a Secretary of State, Economic Planning Board and a National Administrative Council could be incorporated into the single demand for a Welsh Parliament. In arguing for this broader measure of self-government, the Welsh Committee, placed itself in between the Labour Party and the Welsh Nationalists, stressing that it was

> Important for the Communist Party to avoid trailing behind the Labour reformist conception that the solution of the Welsh national problem has nothing to do with the fight for Socialism, but also to avoid the other extreme narrow separatist outlook of the Welsh Nationalists whose political conceptions are directly opposed to Socialism.[179]

In the event, however, the Welsh Committee's recommendations were rejected, the party opting for the status quo, retaining its two-pronged approach to the national question.[180]

[179] 'Discussion Statement on Welsh Parliament', *Party News,* 16 November 1946.
[180] See, for example, the 1948 Welsh Congress Report, *Party News* special supplement, June 1948, p. 3, which calls for 'more effective measures of self-government for Wales in preparation for the formation of a Welsh Parliament'.

Whatever the outcome, the Welsh Committee's bold suggestions reflect the prevalence of supporters of a Welsh Parliament on the committee at this time, and also prefigure the party's support for the Parliament for Wales Campaign (PWC), showing that the decision to join the campaign was the culmination of a number of years debate on the issue. However, the Welsh Committee, as the response to its proposals shows, was to face both opposition and indifference from within the party. Most common it seems was indifference, a problem that had plagued the party's stance on the national question since it was first brought up in the mid-1930s. A report to the party centre in July 1947 noted that 'the general tendency in the Party is to ignore the existence of a national problem in Wales, and among prominent members in trade unions even to pour scorn on any efforts by the party to formulate a policy for Wales'.[181] The impression given then is that it was the Welsh Committee that was proactive on the issue, but was fighting a losing battle in the face of indifference from party members and outright opposition by some within the NUM.

An opponent to the Welsh Committee's proposals, in a series of articles intended for Party News, noted that opposition to self-government was based on four fundamental points. First, reflecting the views of a number of the communists associated with the NUM, an opposition to federalism, which was viewed as a 'dangerous tendency', with Cox, in particular, viewed as its main exponent within the party.[182] Second, that Wales was not an economic unit, its 'potential economic integrity' having been 'dismembered' by 'capitalist expediency' on 'the path of industrial progress' leaving any perception of Wales as an economic unit 'a monstrous illusion'. Third, noting that the 'Welsh language as a National heritage is no longer common to all Welshmen' and that political demands such as those for a Secretary of State had caused division within the ranks of Labour MPs, national consciousness was rejected as a unifying force: 'On the

---

[181] CPGB Archive, 'Report on Wales for the Political Committee on Tuesday, 10th July', p. 3, [1947], CP/CENT/ORG/11/1 (LHASC).
[182] Untitled fourth article for Party News, p. 2, [1946/47], Bert Pearce WN 1/3, NLW; 'Second Article', p. 1, [1946/47], Bert Pearce Papers WN 1/3, NLW.

contrary, if pressed, by overzealous partisans, it can become a mischievous disintegrating and disruptive element in the Labour Movement.'[183] Finally, the Welsh Committee's proposals were depicted as not fitting into the centralising dynamic of the 'historical trends of development'.[184] These arguments reflected an implicit assumption that any devolution of governmental responsibility would inevitably lead to separatism and would end up weakening the unity of the British working class. With the author only willing to concede a level of cultural autonomy, these arguments, which essentially meant the rejection of any form of Welsh self-government, offered no practical solution to the national question and did not succeed in winning favour on the Welsh Committee. However, opposition to the party's approach to the national question was growing on the Committee by 1950.

Despite these difficulties, the Welsh Committee continued to add an explicitly Welsh dimension to its politics. The centenary of the Communist Manifesto in 1948 provided further focus in this regard, with the publication of the first Welsh translation of the manifesto and a companion pamphlet by Idris Cox, *The Fight for Socialism in Wales*, which related the ideas expressed in the manifesto to Wales' development in those one hundred years. The publication of *Y Maniffesto Comiwnyddol* was viewed as particularly important by Cox who argued that it

> enables us to get in touch with nearly 200,000 people in Wales for whom Welsh is the first language and English the secondary language, and another half-million for whom English is the first language and Welsh the second. It is important because it gives us an entry into the Welsh-speaking rural areas, among the small farmers, and to combat the muddle-headed, but dangerous ideas of the Welsh Nationalists.[185]

While Wales was not mentioned explicitly in the introduction to the *Maniffesto*, its translator, William Rees, offering a general introduction to Marx and Marxism, devoted a whole

[183] 'Fourth Article', p. 1.
[184] 'Fourth Article', p. 2.
[185] Idris Cox's speech in *The Battle of Ideas: Six Speeches on the Centenary of the Communist Manifesto* (London, 1948), p. 11.

section to the communist attitude to the national question, noting that Communists supported the right to self-determination in oppressed nations, even where the national movement itself was essentially reactionary.[186] Cox, in the companion pamphlet, argued that the main stages of development described by Marx were also evident in Wales, noting in particular Wales' industrial development since 1848, the increased domination of town over country, the recurrence of cyclical crises and the prevalence of class struggle during the previous century. Reflecting on the national question, Cox argued that it was due to capitalist development that Wales initially became incorporated into Britain, with the Welsh ruling class, in particular, playing a key role through the elevation of their own needs over those of Wales and its culture. For Cox, only through the development of a socialist and federal Britain could the national question be solved, emphasising that this would only come about through the united action of the British workers.[187]

Following the debates of 1946 and 1947, something of an impasse had been reached on the national question, however, the debate was to be rekindled at the end of the period under discussion with the presentation of two significant reports during 1949 and 1950, the first written in May 1949 by George Thomson and commissioned by the party centre, the second by William Rees, presented to the Welsh Committee in October 1950. Thomson's report focused on the national question in both Wales and Scotland, and attributed the late emergence of the national question in Wales to uneven development, the late development of a Welsh bourgeoisie and its subsequent anglicisation and incorporation into the British ruling class. It was only with the emergence of the imperialist era, the development of a native petit-bourgeoisie and an increased awareness of Wales' susceptibility to the vagaries of capitalist imperialism, largely due to the failure of the British state to develop secondary industries in Wales, that Wales saw the development of a national movement. For

---

[186] William James Rees, 'Rhagymadrodd' in *Y Maniffesto Cominwyddol* (Cardiff, 1948), pp. 16–18.
[187] Idris Cox, *The Fight for Socialism in Wales 1848–1948* (Cardiff, 1948), pp. 4–19.

Thomson, Wales' development was similar to that of the colonies, although the situation in Wales was complicated by the bourgeoisie's incorporation into British imperialism, thus leading to the leadership of the national movement been handed to the petit-bourgeoisie.[188] One of the more positive aspects of this pattern of development was the emergence of a proletarian culture within Wales, following its abandonment by the anglicised bourgeoisie, a culture, Thomson argued, that the party should be at the forefront in defending.[189] For Thomson, the national question was something the party could not ignore and he urged the party to assume leadership on the issue within the labour movement to combat the potentially divisive role of the nationalist parties. Noting that the national movement in Wales was underdeveloped compared to that in Scotland, in particular in relation to the involvement of the labour movement, Thomson argued that the Welsh party had an ideal opportunity to do this. In light of this, Thomson recommended that the Welsh party establish a National Convention similar to that seen in Scotland, while also proposing that the party centre establish a Welsh Cultural Committee that would be responsible for working out a programme for the Welsh language in schools, universities and in the party's own propaganda, as well as making a commitment to self-government in its next general election programme.[190]

Rees's report to the Welsh Committee, like Thomson's, also offered a historical analysis of the development of the national question in Wales, and like Thomson attributed it to uneven development. Identifying the roots of Wales' underdevelopment to the persistence of a tribal society until the English conquest of 1282, Rees, in line with Thomson, identified the weakness of the Welsh bourgeoisie, its anglicisation and dependency on English capital, as the main reason for the failure of a national movement to develop, a process exacerbated by the Tudor accession. Indeed, for Rees, the Act of Union 'simply legalised the status quo', rubber-stamping the

---

[188] George Thomson, 'Report on the National Question in Scotland and Wales', pp. 1–6, 1949, Bert Pearce Papers WN 1/1, NLW.

[189] Thomson, 'Report on the National Question in Scotland and Wales', p. 8.

[190] Thomson, 'Report on the National Question in Scotland and Wales', pp. 9–10.

incorporation of the Welsh ruling class into the British state.[191] For Rees, it was the development of the Methodist movement in the eighteenth century that finally saw the emergence of an embryonic national movement character-ised by an increasing identity of interests between the rural tenantry and the industrial bourgeoisie. This class alliance was to find its full expression in the form of Welsh Liberalism and saw the emergence of the first Welsh national movement in the form of Cymru Fydd. While Rees acknowledged the progressive role played by the liberal bourgeoisie in the nine-teenth century, he noted that with the emergence of imperialism their role had been largely negative and reac-tionary. Rees noted that Wales had both benefited and paid for this bourgeois dominance, for while Wales was trans-formed by the development of industrial capitalism, in more recent years it had paid a heavy price for this development through the misery of the inter-war years. The main reason for Wales paying such a heavy price was the failure of the British state to recognise it as a national unit, leading to a crisis in both industry and agriculture, the failure to recog-nise Wales as a national unit identified as being due to exploitation of the Welsh economy in the interests of the British bourgeoisie rather than those of the Welsh nation.[192]

In the cultural sphere, Rees noted that the depopulation of rural areas was immensely damaging to the Welsh language and while acknowledging the advances made through the growth of key Welsh institutions such as the University of Wales, the National Library and the National Museum, Rees argued that these advances obscured the fact that without legal status for the language, Welsh culture was becoming more anglicised, constituting a fundamental threat to the existence of the Welsh language.

> Underneath this attractive surface the Anglicisation of economic and social life in Wales has during this same period, taken immense strides. Only in parts of rural Wales does the Welsh language retain any dignity in daily affairs. Nowhere does it possess any status in legal and purely

[191] William Rees, 'The Problem of Welsh Nationality and the Communist Solution', [1950], pp. 1–2, Bert Pearce Papers, WN 1/1, NLW.
[192] Rees, 'The Problem of Welsh Nationality and the Communist Solution', pp. 4–5.

business transactions. Even in the schools where the status of the language is highest it is used as a medium of instruction only in a few cases, and its status is usually that of a foreign rather than an active language. Yet it is on the vitality of the language in the daily affairs of the people, rather than on the brilliance of individual literary productions, that the vitality of a people's culture depends. Welsh culture today, therefore, characterised though it is by one-sided advance, is undermined by more general decay and disintegration. While, the Welsh language is taught in most schools, while Welsh cultural institutions multiply, and while Welsh writers and poets flourish as never before, the language is becoming more and more divorced from the daily life of the people; the cultural institutions acquire more and more an artificially Welsh character, and Welsh literature assumes more and more a parasitic existence. In short, the future of the cultural and literary heritage of the Welsh people is more in doubt today than at any other time in their long and troubled history.[193]

Rees' analysis on this issue was particularly advanced for communist commentators, reflecting a tendency, also evident in Humphrey's contribution, to recognise the depth of the threat to the Welsh language.

Rees' solution to the national problem placed him squarely on the federalist wing of the party, recommending 'the establishment of a Welsh autonomous state within a British Federal Union', which would have responsibility for justice, health, education, roads, internal trade, light industry and agriculture, the British Parliament retaining responsibility for defence, foreign affairs and trade, heavy industry and the railways. In addition, Rees called for the replacement of the House of Lords with a House of Nationalities, with equal representation for Wales, Scotland and England, as well as for Wales to be given the right to secede 'if and when it desired to do so'. In the economic field Rees, arguing that 'revolutionary constitutional changes would be merely a fraud and a deception of the people if they were not also vehicles of revolutionary social changes', called for an extensive programme of nationalisation and for the establishment of a Welsh Economic Planning Board to lead the reconstruction of Welsh industry based on the development of light industries across Wales. In particular, Rees stressed that this

[193] Rees, 'The Problem of Welsh Nationality and the Communist Solution', p. 6.

reconstruction of industry should be carried out 'in a manner which will remove the concentration of industry and population from the two counties of Monmouthshire and Glamorganshire', and 'remove the disparity of living standards between rural and industrial Wales'. On the cultural level, Rees called for Welsh to be granted equal legal status, backing the party's demands for Welsh to be taught in all schools, for Welsh to be the main language of schools in Welsh-speaking areas, for the establishment of a Welsh Broadcasting Corporation and for better support to be given to Welsh institutions.

Rees's report on the national question represented the most wide-ranging contribution to the debate yet offered to the Welsh Committee, in particular in its analysis of the nature of Wales' historical development and of the threat to the Welsh language. However, while Thomson's recommendation to the Welsh party that it should form a national convention were partly taken on board, the party agreeing to Undeb Cymru Fydd's proposal that it join the Parliament for Wales Campaign at the 1950 Welsh Congress, Rees's paper was ultimately shelved, after meeting with strong opposition from the Welsh Committee.[194] That Rees' main proposals bore a distinct similarity to those proposed by the Welsh Committee itself in 1946, suggests that those opposed to federalism were now in the ascendancy on the Welsh Committee. As we shall see in the next chapter, the removal of Idris Cox, identified as an arch-federalist in 1946, as Secretary of the Welsh party amidst charges of 'bourgeois nationalist deviation' in 1951 offers further proof that this was the case.

The party's engagement with the national question between 1943 and 1950 is best viewed in the context of reconstruction and as a means of preventing Wales from slipping back to its fate during the inter-war years. In this it was focused less on cultural issues and concerned more with issues related to constructing an effective national plan for Wales. In turn, this led the party to think more about the form of self-government that it wanted to see implemented. It was this that was to lead to serious divisions amongst the

---

[194] Davies, 'Heading for the Rocks', p. 10.

party leadership on the issue, which had been complicated by the formation of the NUM, a realisation of one of the major demands of south Wales' miners since *The Miners' Next Step*. In addition, as with the late 1930s, the national question was, as far as the evidence goes, met with indifference by a large proportion of the party membership, despite the fact that Congress voted in favour of measures of devolution throughout the period. Reflecting the tendency towards economism that was often attributed to the party in Wales, the Welsh Committee failed in its attempt to enthuse the party membership over the issue. They had, however, succeeded in manoeuvring party policy a considerable distance with its commitment not only in support of a Welsh Parliament, but also in adding a distinctively Welsh dimension to how the party thought about the problems Wales faced, not least in viewing Wales as a national economic unit.

Conclusion: A National Consciousness Awakened?

The period between 1936 and 1950 marked a sea change in the way the Communist Party thought about the national question in Wales. While the break between the two periods was somewhat artificial, forced upon the party by the new political priorities of the Second World War, it is still possible to note a number of distinctive features in the evolution of the party's policy on the national question that differentiate its pre-war and post-war attitudes to the national question. These distinctive features owed much to the circumstances in which they emerged. The initial change of attitude owed much to the emergence of the Popular Front. At the international level the major factor that brought about a more meaningful engagement with the national question was a realisation that in order to build a popular national anti-fascist movement, the communist parties had to present themselves as national parties that were not aloof from national sentiment and concerns. Broadening the communist parties appeal meant moving away from a strictly Marxist-Leninist position at times and embracing more mainstream modes of politics as well as occupying political spaces previously seen as belonging to the bourgeois and right-wing parties. In practical terms, the example of France had shown that the use of national symbols and of patriotic rhetoric could produce significant results in broadening a party's appeal. Equally important was the realisation that the use of national symbols by fascism had to be countered. Communists were aware of the use made by fascism of national symbols in attracting working-class and middle-class support and realised that to counter this merely with internationalist arguments would be futile. The communists also saw that nationalism held potent political capital and the creation of a communist form of nationalism/patriotism was seen as a key component in combating the rise of fascism.

At the British level, the desire to make the party less alien and more British was crucial. This is not only evident from the discussion over the need to broaden the appeal of the party's propaganda, but also in the organisational change within the party from factory cells to branches, a change that was designed to make the party fit in with the organisational structures of the mainstream political parties. This desire to broaden the appeal of the party can also be seen in the calls for the language used by communists also to be popularised and made more readily understandable to the workers. The decision taken to start publishing in Welsh was the most literal example of this, and it needs to be noted that this decision was initially taken at the party centre rather than within the South Wales District.

In Wales, the initial engagement with the national question can be seen as a logical extension of the Popular Front, the nationalists, viewed as the representative of a definite section of the Welsh population – the Welsh-speaking petit-bourgeoisie – seen as a useful component to add to the broader movement. In particular, the progressive views of many rank-and-file nationalists were seen as fruitful territory to explore in this regard. However, the seeming emergence of nationalism as a political force following Penyberth also played a role. Although the Nationalists failed to gain the political capital they expected from this event, the heightened publicity given to the party around this time certainly alerted many communists to the need for the party to engage with the issues related to the national question. Within the communist ranks in Wales it was discussions between nation-alist and communist students and the formation of the small North Wales District that provided the impetus for its engage-ment with the issue, without which these issues may have taken longer to rise to the surface. With the formation of the North Wales District, in particular, the party was forced to confront these issues, now that there was a district based in the heartland of the Nationalist's support base. In addition, the issues that affected the anglicised industrial south were different to the Welsh-speaking rural North, and thus opened up communist politics in Wales to these broader themes leading to a move away from the economism that to a certain extent dogged the politics of the party in south Wales.

In the post-war period, the party's engagement with the national question was tied both to the experiences of the war and to the general mood of change and the sense that a new world with new possibilities was on the verge of being created. As Humphreys notes in his article for *Labour Monthly*, the war had made people think about the birth and rebirth of nations. These new national aspirations were given added impetus by the plans formulated by the government for national reconstruction, which defined Wales as an economic unit for the first time, and the administrative changes that had taken place during the war, which had given a similar impetus to calls for a Secretary for State and other devolu-tionary measures within the Labour Party during the war years.[195] In addition, a decisive shift in the nature of commu-nist politics from the revolutionary disavowal of the possibilities of bourgeois democratic politics to an accommo-dation with it, and recognition that change was now achievable through a reformed parliamentary system, was equally important. Crucially, as the post-war party came to view socialism as achievable through parliamentary means, the party also committed itself to supporting broad demo-cratic reforms, of which Welsh and Scottish Parliaments were only a component. The roots of this shift can be found in the Popular Front era and the party's commitment to the defence of the gains made under bourgeois democracy, while the

---

[195] Jones and Jones, 'Labour and the Nation', p. 248.

party's flirtation with the political mainstream during the Second World War had also contributed to this shift. In Wales the experience of the inter-war years was also a major factor in post-war support for Welsh self-government. Welsh self-government was seen by its supporters within the party as a means of preventing such a calamity from happening again by allowing Wales to plan for its specific needs. At the heart of this was a recognition that Wales had been treated poorly by the British state, and that as a nation it had the right to be treated differently than a region of England.

Different circumstances produce different perspectives and it is notable that both periods also had a different emphasis in the approach to the national question. Unavoidably the post-war period saw the party place more emphasis on the development of practical proposals for the type of government to be put in place – and especially on economic planning for Wales as a single national economic unit. In contrast, during the inter-war years the party had been reluctant to admit that Wales was an economic unit, and ultimately backed away from supporting a Welsh parliament, instead fudging the issue and opting to support the immediate demand for a Secretary of State. However, that this was due to intervention from the party centre remains a distinct possibility. More consistent was the party's policy for the Welsh language, which remained consistently progressive throughout. The party maintained a commitment to granting equal status to Welsh and advanced proposals for the better provision of Welsh-language education in schools in both periods, although it was not until the post-war period that the nature of the threat to the language was fully recognised. The other significant constant was the party's commitment to solving the national question within a British context, reflecting the party's overriding commitment to the unity of the British working class.

Engagement with the national question, however, had also led to conflict, both within the party in Wales, and with the party centre. The role of the party centre was at times contradictory, for while the initiative for the party's initial engagement with the issue, according to Roose Williams, came at least partly from the party centre, with the commissioning of *Llwybr Rhyddid y Werin*, it is probable that it was the party centre that played the key role in pulling the party back from supporting a Welsh parliament in the late 1930s. Unfortunately, the exact details remain obscure. Its post-war role is more positive, with the impression given that the party centre was supportive of those on the Welsh Committee who favoured engagement with the national question. This was, however, complicated by conflict within the Executive Committee over the issue, as seen at the party's 17th Congress. That it was Pollitt who was opposed to a Welsh parliament is perhaps telling, for it was Horner, from a similar trade union background, who became its most visible opponent in Wales. Much of Horner's opposition was rooted in the same desire not to break the unity of the working class in Britain that had led the supporters of self-government to federalism. For Horner and other communist activists within the newly formed NUM, the turn towards federalism was totally contradictory to their long struggle to form a central-ised miners' union.

The evidence also suggests that despite the efforts of the party's leadership in Wales to get the rank and file to engage more meaningfully with the national question, by and large, they were met with indifference over the issue. Party members, while willing to support these measures at congress, were less willing to engage with the national ques-tion in their day-to-day political work. This can be partly explained by a tendency to economism within the party in Wales, a feature of the party that had been noted since its inception. However, the recurrent reminders in the party's propaganda on the issue that engagement with the national question did not mean advocating separatism or supporting the policies of the Welsh Nationalists suggests not only a level of confusion over the issue, but also a belief, at least within sections of the party, that these were issues that were not the preserve of the party but the nationalists.

However, by the 1940s the party had made significant strides in its approach to the national question. This was largely due to the influence of significant sections of the party leadership and, during the 1930s, the influence of the North Wales District, which, while small, was key in developing party policy on this issue. The impetus for the party's engagement with the issue thus came from the top down, and it is within the party leadership that we first see the development of a national consciousness. That there was a degree of instrumentality to the party's decision to engage with the issue is undeniable, the party viewing the national question as means of building the Popular Front in the 1930s and of allowing it to win support within the previously untapped Welsh-speaking rural areas. However, the commitment of men like John Roose Williams to the issue was clearly genuine. Ultimately, while they had failed in enthusing the general party membership over the issue of the national question, they had succeeded in transforming the party's policy on the national question. More importantly, compared to its early years, the party, by the 1940s, was now a distinctly Welsh party, which was much more aware of Welsh issues and had a policy programme that encompassed the whole of Wales. It is here that the real value of the agitation over the national question can be seen. Welsh communists, whether supportive of engagement with the national question or not, had adopted a distinct Welsh perspective. It is in this sense that we can talk of an awakening of a national consciousness within the party. For those on the Welsh Committee most committed to developing a distinct communist approach to the national question the period to come would be frustrating, for while the party was now committed to supporting a Welsh Parliament and was to become part of the Parliament for Wales Campaign, active mobilisation over the issue was soon to be restricted to a ritualistic expression of support at the annual party Congress, with the issue dropping off the party's radar until the upsurge of nationalism in the mid-1960s. In addition, a key supporter of Welsh self-government, Idris Cox, was removed from the party leadership, ostensibly over the party's failure at the 1951 General Election, but also amid accusations of 'bourgeois nationalist deviation'. In the next chapter we will examine the party's role in the Parliament for Wales Campaign, the party's turn away from the national question and its re-engagement with the issue following Plaid Cymru's emergence as a political force in the mid-1960s.

3

PRAXIS, NEGLECT AND RENEWAL, 1950–1969

Communist politics between 1950 and 1969 were dominated by international events, with the party's response to Khrushchev's 'secret speech' and to the Soviet invasion of Hungary in 1956, and to the Soviet invasion of Czechoslovakia in 1968, illustrative of changing attitudes within the party. Despite its optimism following the publication of a new party programme, *The British Road to Socialism* (*BRS*), in 1951, the following two decades were to be among the most difficult in the CPGB's history, the party undergoing its most serious crisis yet following Khrushchev's revelations at the 20th Congress of the CPSU and the Soviet invasion of Hungary. For many in the British party the impact of Khrushchev's revelations and the failure of the party leadership to deal adequately with the questions they raised, coupled with its support for the Soviet invasion, led to disillusionment with the party's politics, with over a quarter of the membership leaving the party.[1] Much of the following period was spent regaining this lost membership, which the party had succeeded in doing by 1964. However, its image had been badly damaged, its unflinching support of the Soviet line doing little to bolster its claims to being a supporter of national independence. In contrast, the EC's condemnation of the Soviet invasion of Czechoslovakia, while leading to serious dispute with Stalinist die-hards like Dutt, did not lead to a mass exodus and was a sign that the party was now willing to show independent judgement in relation to the Soviet Union. The publication of the *BRS* also saw a significant shift in the party's politics, committing the party to a parliamentary road to socialism, abandoning the commitment to the revolutionary takeover of power contained in its previous

---

[1] Steve Parsons, '1956: What Happened Inside the CPGB' in *The Communist Party and 1956: Speeches at the Conference* (London, 1993), p. 26. The actual figure was 9,447, or 28 per cent of the party membership.

party programme, *For Soviet Britain*, published in 1935. This new commitment to parliamentary politics did not, however, translate into electoral support, with the party's electoral performance being consistently poor in each of the general elections between 1950 and 1969, its failure to make an electoral breakthrough leading, by the 1960s, to serious debate as to where the party's priorities should lie – in its electoral work or in its industrial work.

By the late 1960s, the party's industrial work had undergone something of a revival, overcoming difficulties brought by the onset of the Cold War in the late 1940s and early 1950s, by the events of 1956, and by the effects of a particularly damaging vote-rigging scandal within the communist-controlled Electrical Trades Union (ETU) in 1961. This had led to a switch to a Broad Left strategy within the trade unions, that saw the CPGB work more openly and in alliance with its allies on the left, supporting both communist and non-communist candidates in elections for official positions. By the late 1960s the party could point to its leading role in the formation of the Liaison Committee for the Defence of Trade Unions (LCDTU), and the election of non-communist Broad Left candidates such as Hugh Scanlon (AEU) and Jack Jones (TGWU) to top union positions as a sign of the strategy's success. In terms of its extra-parliamentary politics the party was at the forefront in campaigns against racism, for colonial freedom and for peace, the party's role within the Campaign for Nuclear Disarmament (CND), once it abandoned its commitment to multilateral nuclear disarmament in 1960, showing its continued relevance to the politics of the day. However, by the late 1960s, with the emergence of radical student politics, the party's position as the pre-eminent Marxist organisation was under threat as alternatives emerged in the form of the New Left and Trotskyite organisations.

In Wales, the party had entered the 1950s in a state of turmoil, its membership receding and faced, by 1951, with a serious crisis of leadership. A quick turnover in leadership, following the removal of Idris Cox in 1951 and the retirement of Alun Thomas in 1953, led to a more stable period under Bill Alexander from 1953 until 1959, before Bert

Pearce took over as District Secretary. While the party had begun to regain some of its membership by 1956, much of this was lost in the aftermath of that years events, some 300 members leaving the party in Wales following the invasion of Hungary. While it took until 1961 to recover the lost ground, party membership began to slowly increase, reaching the 2,000 mark in 1964 and consequently maintaining this level until 1969. In electoral terms the party's performance, as in the rest of Britain, was on the whole disappointing, and, despite some success in the local elections, the Welsh party failed to make the electoral breakthrough it imagined it could. The party in Wales could, however, point to greater success in the labour movement, with Will Paynter elected President of the South Wales Area NUM in 1951, and Dai Dan Evans, elected Vice President. Evans was subsequently elected its General Secretary in 1958, to be followed in that position by Dai Francis in 1963. The party was thus able to maintain a significant presence within the South Wales Area NUM throughout this period.

The CPGB's attitude to the national question in Wales was also shaped by events. While the party in Wales had begun the 1950s taking a proactive role on the issue, most notably through its support for the Parliament for Wales Campaign, the party's interest in the national question had begun to wane by the mid-1950s. Despite an abortive attempt to re-engage with the issue during 1956 and 1957, the party did not pick up the baton again until the early 1960s when it put forward proposals for a Welsh Parliament as part of its recommendations for the reform of local government. The national question, however, was not to become a main issue for the party until the resurgence of Welsh nationalism from 1966 onwards, following the election of Gwynfor Evans, the Plaid Cymru president, as MP for Carmarthen, and close calls for the nationalists at both Rhondda West and Caerphilly the following year. Faced with an increasingly popular Plaid Cymru and an increasingly vocal language movement in the form of the Welsh Language Society (CYIG), the CPGB was forced into a rearguard action, which put the national question back on to the forefront of the party's political agenda, this time at both the Welsh and British level.

THE REMOVAL OF IDRIS COX, THE PARLIAMENT FOR WALES CAMPAIGN AND *THE BRITISH ROAD TO SOCIALISM*, 1950–1956

The publication of the *BRS* in 1951 marked a significant change in the CPGB's politics, the party formally adopting a parliamentary road to socialism; the British parliament, alongside the creation of a broad extra-parliamentary move-ment, now seen as the main vehicle through which socialism in Britain would ultimately be achieved, abandoning its earlier commitment of achieving revolutionary power through soviets and workers' councils. In doing this, the party signalled a move away from a strictly Leninist form of politics and towards a reformist outlook that accommodated itself within the system of British parliamentary democracy, despite maintaining the use of Leninist rhetoric. While Stalin played a significant role in the drafting of the programme's first edition,[2] over the subsequent two editions, published in 1958 and 1968 respectively, the party formulated its own brand of radical reformist politics based on large-scale nationalisation, socialist economic planning, the eradication of monopoly capitalism, British neutrality, national inde-pendence, the end of empire, peace, nuclear disarmament and the reform of the parliamentary system at home. Unfortunately for the party its conversion to electoral politics in 1951 coincided with the beginning of its decline in terms of electoral support, and raised questions by the 1960s as to where the party's political priorities lay, with the primacy given to electoral politics a significant source of friction within the party. By 1954, the party had also begun to offer its own in-depth analysis of the British political system and the British state, offering arguments in favour of the decentrali-sation of power and the need for electoral and parliamentary reform. This analysis, coupled with the party's commitment to democratic politics and Britain's 'national independence', was to have important implications for the development of the party's attitude to the national question in Wales and

---

[2] George Matthews, 'Stalin's British Road?', *Changes*, 23, 1991 (Supplement), pp. 1–3.

Scotland. By the late 1960s, the party's focus on democratic and constitutional reform had helped make the call for Welsh and Scottish parliaments a live issue once again. Arguably, the party had been moving towards an accommodation with parliamentary politics since the adoption of the Popular Front in 1935, with its exhortation to defend the democratic gains made under bourgeois democracy. A more explicit commitment to parliamentary politics was contained in the party's post-war policy proposals, *Britain for the People*, which called for a broad programme of electoral reform, reform of the machinery of local and central government and an extensive devolution of power, including the setting up of Welsh and Scottish parliaments.[3] The notion of a specific British road to socialism had been first mooted by Stalin to a Labour Party delegation to Moscow in 1946, with Stalin arguing that 'there were two roads to socialism ... the Russian way and the British way ... The Russian road was shorter but more difficult, and had involved bloodshed ... the parliamentary method involved no bloodshed, but was a longer process.'[4] This idea of a 'British Road' was further developed by Pollitt in his book, *Looking Ahead*, published in 1947, while the emergence of a progressive consensus in Britain and in the international sphere was viewed as allowing for a peaceful transition to socialism in Britain, through a radical democratic transformation of the British state and a programme of socialist nationalisation.[5]

However, while the party was moving towards the development of a particular British road to socialism, it was the intervention of Stalin that played the major role in its development. The idea of producing a long-term party programme emerged from conversations between Stalin and Pollitt in May 1950, during which Pollitt was presented with a list of recommendations outlining the direction the party should take. Following a number of drafts by high-level party functionaries, such as Dutt and George Matthews, a further intervention from Stalin in October 1950, once again

[3] *Britain for the People*, pp. 20–1.
[4] Matthews, 'Stalin's British Road?', p. 1.
[5] Harry Pollitt, *Looking Ahead* (London, 1947), pp. 85–97.

through Pollitt, saw most of Stalin's policy formulations included in the final draft.[6]

The party's new programme revolved around four major themes – the democratic road to socialism; the national independence of Britain and the colonies; the need for socialist nationalisation; and for rapprochement between East and West. The party's main aim was now to win the return of a parliamentary majority of Communist and Labour MPs which would, in turn, lead to the setting up of a 'People's Government' and a radical reformation of the British parliamentary system and the machinery of government. This parliamentary majority was predicated on the formation of a broad extra-parliamentary movement made up of the organised working class, professionals, farmers and the progressive middle class, but with the organised working class taking the leading role. Its aim would be to win the electorate over to progressive policies prior to winning a parliamentary majority and once a People's Government had been established, to provide it with a support base that would allow it to push through the reform of the parliamentary system and machinery of the state in the face of opposition from the interests of monopoly capital.[7] Explicitly rejecting soviet power, the party dismissed accusations that it would seek to abolish Parliament if it won a parliamentary majority as a 'slanderous misrepresentation of our policy'.[8] Instead, arguing that 'democracy under present conditions is restricted for the majority of the people by the privilege and power of the wealthy few and their agents', the party sought to implement a programme of electoral reform based on the introduction of proportional representation, the lowering of the voting age to eighteen, and the abolition of the House of Lords and the monarchy, alongside a purge of the civil and diplomatic services, the judiciary and the armed forces and the dismantling of media monopolies.[9]

The party's analysis of the British state and parliamentary system was further advanced in two books published by the

---

[6] Mathews, 'Stalin's British Road', pp. 1–3.
[7] *The British Road to Socialism* (London, 1951), pp. 12–17.
[8] *The British Road to Socialism*, p. 14.
[9] *The British Road to Socialism*, pp. 14–16.

party during the mid- to late 1950s, one by John Gollan and the other by Noreen Branson and Roger Simon. Gollan had previously come out in support of a Scottish Parliament,[10] but did not touch on this issue directly in his analysis of the British political system, instead noting a tendency towards centralisation that was damaging to British democracy. For Gollan, the political system in Britain was archaic, dominated by monopoly capital and by the big landowners, who were able to exert their power through both the direct and indirect control of the levers of power, via their control of the state machine, and by the successful dissemination of capitalist ideology through the education system and the mass media.[11] For Gollan, the two-party system was geared towards maintaining the stable rule of capital whilst excluding those who questioned the capitalist system by means of an unfair electoral system. Gollan was highly critical of the notion of a 'loyal opposition' that failed to challenge the fundamentals of the political system, instead conspiring to prop it up, and argued that the ruling class' aim had been to assimilate the working-class movement into this system, 'to catch up the Labour movement and working-class representatives in the British constitutional net'.[12] Central to Gollan's concerns was a tendency towards the curtailment of democracy, characterised by the trend towards government by cabinet and the bypassing of parliament, and the increasing centralisation and expansion of the machinery of state.[13] Building on Gollan's analysis, Branson and Simon also identified a tendency towards the centralisation of power, increasingly evident in the field of local government, where central government was curtailing the power of local authorities for its own benefit. Branson and Simon viewed this as an attempt by central government to put a break on the activities of progressive local authorities and argued for the reform of local government as part of a broader policy of

[10] John Gollan, *Scottish Prospect: A Social, Economic and Administrative Survey* (Glasgow, 1948), pp. 210–28.

[11] John Gollan, *The British Political System* (London, 1954), p. 13.

[12] Gollan, *The British Political System,* pp. 18–19.

[13] Gollan, *The British Political System,* pp. 104–16.

decentralisation,[14] with decentralisation viewed as a crucial component in the transformation to socialism.[15] From the late 1950s, the national question was increasingly viewed in these terms, discussed in the context of both broadening democracy and decentralising power from Westminster.

However, in the first edition of the *BRS* the national question in Wales and Scotland was viewed in the context of Britain's national independence. For the CPGB, Britain was increasingly coming under the dominance of American imperialism, its economic interests and its military subordinated to the interests of American big business and foreign policy. Accusing the Conservatives and the Labour Party of a 'betrayal of the British people' and of being 'spokesmen of a foreign power', the *BRS* argued that Britain had lost 'for the first time in history ... its independence and freedom of action'.[16] The CPGB's defence of British national independence was clearly guided by Cold War sensibilities, the restoration of Britain's national independence through its withdrawal from the North Atlantic Treaty and the Brussels Pact a means of striking a blow to the US's emerging Cold War alliances, and thus serving the interests of the communist movement. The threat to Britain's national independence was also given a cultural dimension, focused on the increasing influence of American popular culture, the party warning against such baleful influences as the American comic-book and the influx of American films, and later, of rock 'n' roll.[17] In response to this cultural imperialism, the party set up a National Cultural Committee (NCC) in 1947 whose main focus by the early 1950s was what it termed 'the American threat to British culture'.[18] For Sam Aaronovitch, secretary of the NCC, the influx of American popular culture was 'cynically devised for the debasement of man', while for George

[14] James Harvey and Katherine Hood, *The British State* (London, 1958), pp. 241–3. Branson and Simon were writing under pseudonyms.

[15] Harvey and Hood, *The British State,* p. 258.

[16] *British Road to Socialism,* 1951, pp. 9–10.

[17] For examples, see Patrick Goldring, 'The Menace of the Comic Strip', *World New and Views,* April 14, 1951, p. 171; David Platt, 'Force and Violence in American Films', *Communist Review,* October 1950, pp. 311–13.

[18] John Callaghan, *Cold War, Crisis and Conflict: The CPGB 1951–68* (London, 2003), p. 87

Thomson, echoing Zhdanov, Britain's cultural heritage needed to be protected from a 'bourgeois culture that increasingly tended to the decadent, reactionary and cosmopolitan'.[19] While these attacks on American culture betrayed a distinctly puritan streak at the heart of the CPGB's cultural thought, focused as much of the discussion was on the prevalence of sex and violence in American popular culture, it also reflected genuine fears not only regarding Britain's moral welfare, but also regarding the threat to Britain's cultural industries, such as its film industry, and the use made by the CIA and other US agencies, of art and culture in Cold War politics. Responding to Andrei Zhdanov's dictum that culture should be in touch with the people, the NCC and the party championed aspects of British cultural heritage, which it viewed as more representative of the cultural proclivities of the working people, most notably championing folk music over American-influenced music, which had helped spark a folk revival through communist-inspired artists such as Ewan MacColl by the mid-1950s. In line with this commitment to Britain's cultural heritage, the party also held up the eisteddfod as an inspirational form of cultural activity, with Aaronovitch singling out the South Wales Area NUM's Miners' Eisteddfod, established largely through the efforts of Dai Dan Evans, for praise.[20] Despite this, in Wales, apart from Evans' role in establishing the Miners' Eisteddfod, this cultural dimension does not seem to have played a major part in the party's politics in the 1950s, with the party's presence at the National Eisteddfod, for example, diminishing in comparison to the immediate post-war era.[21]

By focusing the argument on Britain's national independence, the party was able to turn the accusations so often used against the CPGB on to the mainstream parties. The *BRS* was thus able to portray the party as 'true patriots' whose aim was a 'Britain, free, strong and independent' which would 'be

[19] Callaghan, *Cold War, Crisis and Conflict*, pp. 87–8.
[20] Sam Aaronovitch, 'Culture and the People', *World News and Views*, 2 February 1952, p. 54.
[21] Enoch Collins, 'Importance of Progressive Nationalism', *World News*, 2 February 1957, p. 77.

subordinate and subservient to no foreign power' standing 'in friendly association and equal alliance with all powers that recognise and respect Britain's national interests'.[22] The party now declared that it rejected 'all theories which declare national sovereignty to be out of date, arguing that 'Real international co-operation can be based only on the sovereign freedom and equal rights of all nations, great and small.'[23] For the party, Britain's national independence was thus bound to that of the colonies, with Dutt in particular arguing that Britain's loss of national independence and its subservience to America was inextricably linked to Britain's crisis of empire, now only capable of being maintained with American backing due to Britain's fading role in the world system.[24] For Dutt, empire had distorted national feeling in Britain, and he argued that it was now vital that the party reclaimed patriotism and national sentiment for the left, pointing, in particular, to the contempt Welsh and Scottish national feeling had been held due to the overriding narrative of empire and the form of Britishness associated with it.

> The fact that Britain has been for centuries an aggressive, conquering, colony-owning Power, and still controls the largest world colonial empire, is one of the factors which helps to obscure from view the national subjection of the British people to American domination. All the traditional sentiments of national pride and patriotism have been crushed and distorted by the ruling class in order to establish in their place jingoism, contempt for 'inferior' races, and the pride of painting the map red, so that the very conception of 'patriotism' has become traditionally suspect to the Left … This conscious suppression of national feeling by the ruling class in the interests of imperialism has been illustrated, not only in the deletion of such terms as 'England' and 'the English' from the official imperialist vocabulary, but also in the parallel contemptuous blindness to Scottish national feeling or Welsh national feeling.[25]

The *BRS* itself recognised Welsh and Scottish national feeling maintaining that 'there must be recognition of the

---

[22] *British Road to Socialism*, p. 10.

[23] *British Road to Socialism*, p. 11.

[24] For Dutt's analysis, see R. Palme Dutt, *The Crisis of Britain and the British Empire* (London, 1953).

[25] R. Palme Dutt, 'The Fight for British Independence', *Communist Review*, February 1951, p. 45.

national claims of the Scottish and Welsh people, to be settled according to the wishes of these peoples'.[26] However, while it recognised Wales' right to self-determination it stepped back from explicitly supporting a Welsh parliament, a provision supported in the drafts prepared by Dutt, Emile Burns and George Matthews for the Political Committee prior to Stalin's second intervention.[27] While this raises tantalising questions as to Stalin's views on the national question in Britain, the decision to opt for such a general statement of principles rather than a bolder statement in favour of the establishment of Welsh and Scottish Parliaments shows that some trepidation may have remained within the higher echelons of the party regarding the exact nature of its policy vis-à-vis the national question in both Wales and Scotland, although the inclusion of a more general statement of principle may have been viewed as better suited for a long-term party programme.

The immediate post-war era had seen a flurry of activity from the Welsh Committee on the national question as the party sought to define its position on the issue and formulate its policy. Much of the responsibility for this activity was down to the Welsh District Secretary, Idris Cox, who, along with other Welsh Committee members, such as John Roose Williams and Cyran Lloyd Humphreys, had helped develop party policy on the issue of Welsh self-government. However, as we saw in the previous chapter, the focus placed on the national question and on federalism had also led to significant opposition within the party and on the Welsh Committee, largely it seems from party members within the NUM, who found it difficult to reconcile the call for self-government on a federal basis with their hard-fought battle to build a centralised miners' union. For these opponents of federalism, self-government would inevitably lead to separation and the break-up of the British working-class movement. Despite the decision of the Welsh Congress to accept Undeb Cymru Fydd's invitation to join the Parliament for Wales Campaign (PWC) in June 1950, the sidelining of William

[26] *British Road to Socialism*, 1951, p. 11.
[27] Matthews, 'Stalin's British Road?', p. 2.

Rees' proposals by referral to a party commission suggests that disagreement on the national question had reached breaking point.[28] The tide, it seems, was turning against the devolutionists within the CPGB leadership in Wales, and the removal of Idris Cox as District Secretary in April 1951 was, according to some historians, related to his stance on the national question.

Brian Davies, writing in 1982, noted that Cox 'was transferred from Wales to the International Department in London, amid accusations of "bourgeois nationalist deviation"', while Gwyn Alf Williams notes that 'after Idris Cox, on the instructions of the Welsh Congress, had joined the Parliament for Wales Committee, he was displaced from his office, appointed to the International Department and sent to Iraq', after which, with regards to the national question, 'The Communist Party fell in line with Labour'. [29] For both historians, therefore, Cox's stance on the national question was central to his removal as District Secretary. Both Davies and Williams' arguments were based on rumours abound in the party that Cox's removal was related to the national question, but, unfortunately, neither historian offers any solid evidence for this assertion. Indeed, in a later interview Davies conceded that 'these decidedly muddy waters were never really cleared up', noting Cox's evasiveness on the issue.[30] Others closer to Cox argue that the national question had little to do with his removal as District Secretary, while Cox's autobiography puts his removal down to dissatisfaction with the party's poor showing in the 1950 General Election.[31] Nina Fishman, on the other hand, links Cox's removal to his support for the NUM South Wales Area Executive's opposition to an unofficial dispute at the Wern Tarw colliery in the Garw Valley, contrary to the wishes of the party centre. Fishman notes that he was also considered 'too headstrong

[28] Davies, 'Heading for the Rocks?', p. 10; 'Welsh District Report to the Political Committee for the Period May 1950 to April 1951', p. 3, 1951, Bert Pearce Papers WD 1/4, NLW.

[29] Davies, 'Heading for the Rocks?', p. 10; Williams, *When Was Wales?*, p. 275.

[30] Quoted in Lyndon White, 'The CPGB and the National Question in Post-war Wales: the Case of Idris Cox', p. 17.

[31] Interview with Dr John Cox, September 20, 2008; Cox, 'Story of a Welsh Rebel', pp. 81–2.

and certain of his opinion to be a reliable apparatchik'.[32] The matter therefore remains somewhat controversial.

The decision to remove Cox as District Secretary was taken by the Political Committee in April 1951, ostensibly due to its disappointment with the election results and with the organisational weakness of the Welsh District under Cox's leadership. There is little doubt that by this time the party found itself once again facing a serious organisational crisis. Party membership had declined rapidly in Wales since the end of the war, falling from 2,724 in 1944 to 1,248 by April 1951, amounting to a loss of over half the party's membership.[33] In addition, by April 1951 it had only three functioning Area Committees – in West Wales, Rhondda and Cardiff – and while the Mid-Glamorgan Area Committee continued to meet on an irregular basis, the Monmouthshire, East Glamorgan and North Glamorgan Area Committees were moribund. The realities of maintaining a Welsh Committee were also beginning to prove strenuous for the party, with the party office in Cardiff having some difficulty in maintaining regular contact with the North Wales Area, an attempt to share some of the responsibility for the area with the Lancashire District proving unworkable in practice.[34]

In his unpublished autobiography, Cox notes that a special commission of the Political Committee (PC) had met with the Welsh Committee in December 1950 to discuss the poor election results and that this was followed by a special District Congress 'at which there was severe criticism and self-criticism on this situation'.[35] In April 1951, a highly critical Welsh Committee report to the PC noted a failure of collective leadership in Wales, which had led to situation where Welsh Committee decisions were not being carried out in some Areas. A dwindling number of active party cadres and a small full-time staff meant that those party leaders that were taking responsibility were finding it difficult to cope with the workload. Cox himself was singled out for failing to provide

[32] Fishman, *Arthur Horner: A Political Biography*, Vol. 2, pp. 812–13.
[33] Newton, *The Sociology of British Communism*, p. 178; 'Report to the Political Committee, April 1951', p. 6.
[34] 'Report to the Political Committee, April 1951', pp. 6–7.
[35] Cox, 'Story of a Welsh Rebel', p. 81.

adequate political leadership and failing to make 'the fullest use of his key position in the broad movement that is growing in Wales', although in mitigation this was linked to the overwhelming technical and organisational duties he had to undertake due to the small size of the party's full-time staff.[36] Cox was removed as Welsh party leader by the PC later that month with most of the available evidence pointing to Cox's removal due to organisational and leadership matters. Certainly, Cox himself makes no reference to the national question as a cause for his removal; indeed, he states that he had 'felt for some time that a change would be for the better', noting that he had proposed the appointment of a new District Secretary in 1949, following criticism from the PC – a proposition rejected by the Welsh Committee.[37] This view is reinforced by his assertion in a letter to Pollitt that he had felt 'hampered by organisational and routine tasks for the past 12 years'.[38] Despite this, Cox also expressed some dissatisfaction with the manner of his removal, noting that the Welsh party's electoral performance had differed little to that elsewhere in Britain and that the change of leadership did little to change the party's situation in Wales, a situation that 'was a mirror of the serious problem facing the party as a whole'.[39]

Such comments suggest that other factors, such as the national question or personal differences, may also have played a part in his removal. While no accusations of 'bourgeois nationalist deviation' are present in the limited number of documents available,[40] it remains plausible that such accusations may have been used against him by his opponents on the Welsh Committee in addition to the more serious accusations regarding his leadership of the DPC, his removal coinciding with the campaign against the 'bourgeois

[36] 'Report to the Political Committee, April 1951', pp. 8–9.

[37] Cox, 'Story of a Welsh Rebel', p. 82.

[38] CPGB Archive, Idris Cox to Harry Pollitt, 31st May, 1951, CP/CENT/PERS/2/1 (LHASC).

[39] Cox, 'Story of a Welsh Rebel', p. 82.

[40] No record exists, for instance, of the PC meeting that led to his removal or of the Welsh Committee meeting that saw him removed, or of Cox's personal statement to the PC in response to its decision. Cox's autobiography deals only perfunctorily with the debate on the Welsh Committee, see 'Story of a Welsh Rebel', p. 81.

nationalist deviations' of Titoism. Reporting on attitudes to the PWC, the Welsh Committee in its 1951 report to the PC, noted significant apathy and even opposition within the party to the Campaign, including opposition amongst the party leadership;

> The Party membership as a whole is largely indifferent to this move-
> ment. Some are even hostile, and there is a lack of conviction among
> even many leading members. This seems to be due to three main
> reasons: (a) fear that the Party will 'contaminate' itself with middle-
> class and religious elements, (b) the erroneous idea that a Parliament
> for Wales means economic and political separation and (c) that we
> shall neglect the class fight and our Socialist aims.[41]

Given Cox's prominent position on the central committee of the Campaign, such fears of bourgeois 'contamination' of the party and neglect of the class struggle would have easily been translated into accusations of 'bourgeois nationalist deviation' from his opponents on the Welsh Committee and elsewhere within the party, once the opportunity was provided by the PC's broader concerns regarding the party's organisation and political leadership in Wales.

However, that organisational and leadership matters were the central issue in Cox's removal is evident from the Welsh Committee's 1952 report to the PC, which concentrated solely on these issues in its analysis of the PC's decision, noting that the 'Party in Wales had got in a groove' attributing this to 'weaknesses in the leadership' and 'insufficient criticism and self-criticism'.[42] Despite claims in the same report that the party had turned a corner following Cox's removal, the reality was somewhat different. While the Welsh Committee could point to an increased membership by September 1952, up from 1,248 to 1,415, and was also claiming eight functioning Area Committees, the report also noted that 'There are big political and organisational weaknesses to overcome in most of the Areas.' Tellingly, there were only full-time organisers in the three Area Committees

---

[41] 'Report to the Political Committee, April 1951', pp. 3–4.
[42] 'Report of Welsh District to Political Committee, September 1952', Bert Pearce Papers WD 1/4, NLW.

that were fully functional in 1951 – West Wales, Rhondda and Cardiff. In addition, the Young Communist League (YCL) remained stagnant, with membership up from 106 in April 1951 to 110 by September 1952, whilst the party continued to have difficulty in forming pit and factory branches, the main focus of party's industrial organisation by the early 1950s.[43] By the following year, the party had experienced a further downturn in its fortunes with membership falling to 1,305, the YCL in disarray, losing contact with most of its 85 members due to personnel problems, and the number of factory and pit branches drastically reduced from 19 to 4.[44]

While the role of the national question in Cox's removal remains somewhat nebulous, it is incontrovertible that following Cox's removal the party's focus on the national question diminished. While the national question had been given prominence in the Welsh Committee's 1951 report, it is noticeable that the issue received much less prominence from the Welsh Committee in its reports in the years that followed, meriting only a paragraph in the 1952 report and completely absent from the report by 1955.[45] Concerns regarding the party's attitude to the national question were also voiced by those party members who maintained an interest in the issue. At the 1952 Welsh Congress while Alun Thomas, the new District Secretary, had declared that the party gave its 'maximum support for the National liberation movements of the colonial people, and play our part in the campaign for a Welsh Parliament', linking the Welsh national struggle to that of the national liberation struggles abroad, both John Roose Williams and Bryn Daniels, a delegate from Ammanford, expressed concern that the party was neglecting the issue.[46] Daniels noted 'the need of concentrating much more attention on the Welsh language and the culture and heritage of Wales', while Williams 'raised the importance of

---

[43] 'Report of Welsh District to Political Committee, September 1952', pp. 7–8; 'Report to the Political Committee, April 1951', pp. 6–7.
[44] 'Report to Political Committee on the Work of the Communist Party in Wales, 26 January 1954', pp. 11–14, Bert Pearce Papers WD 1/4, NLW.
[45] 'Report to the Political Committee, September 1952', p. 10; 'Report to Political Committee from Welsh Committee of Communist Party, April 1955', Bert Pearce Papers WD 1/4, NLW.
[46] *Party News*, October 1952, p. 3.

paying far more attention to the fight for a Welsh Parliament'.[47] Similar complaints were also expressed by Enoch Collins, a Llanelli communist dissatisfied with the party's lacklustre attitude to the national question;

> A serious weakness in our Party's work is the slowing down of national demands for 'small nations'. In Wales we find very little effort or enthusiasm for the campaign for a Parliament for Wales. Theoretically we agree, but in practice we are idle and allow the Nationalists to carry on in a confused way.
>
> Also we find reluctance inside our Party to champion the Workers' Parliament for Wales – a Welsh Trades Union Congress. Wales is the only small nation inside Great Britain without a TUC, in a country where we find a real trade union record. Some comrades talk about it as separating the unions from the others inside Great Britain. Such is not the case, since the Scottish and Irish TUC's are in addition to the British TUC.[48]

Collins' concerns regarding support for a Welsh TUC proved justified, the PC, in consultation with the Welsh Committee, recommending in June 1954 that the immediate demand for a Welsh TUC should be dropped for the time being, despite the positive benefits accrued for the CPGB from the formation of a Scottish TUC. For the PC, 'The situation in Wales ... shows that the proposal for a Welsh TUC, although we favour it in principle, cannot be posed as an immediate issue around which a campaign can be organised by the Party.' Instead, the party was to focus its energies in this field on trying to make the TUC Advisory Council and trade union district committees in Wales more effective bodies; 'This, rather than an abstract campaign for a Welsh TUC, will be the surest way of eventually achieving one.'[49] Clearly, by 1954 the party's interest in some aspects of the national question was on the wane.

On the other hand, the party continued to play a role in the PWC, the decision to join the campaign taken at the 1950 Welsh Congress, following an invitation from Undeb Cymru Fydd, the non-partisan body responsible for organising the

---

[47] *Party News*, October 1952, p. 8.
[48] *World News*, March 6, 1954, p. 196.
[49] 'Political Committee to the Welsh Committee, June 4, 1954', Bert Pearce Papers WD 1/5, NLW.

campaign. Inspired by the success of John McCormick's Scottish Covenant Association, the campaign revolved around the presentation of a petition in support of a Welsh Parliament to the government, which it was hoped would lead to some action at Westminster.[50] As we saw in the previous chapter, the CPGB had also been thinking along the lines of organising a broad movement in favour of a Welsh Parliament, with George Thomson having explicitly recommended this course of action to the Welsh Committee in his report on the national question in 1949, calling on it 'to consider what action can be taken with a view to calling a National Convention such as was first summoned in Scotland in 1924'.[51] From the very beginning, however, the PWC faced significant opposition from the Labour Party, with Cliff Prothero, secretary of the Welsh Regional Council of Labour (WRCL) dismissing the campaign as a 'small number of people who represent no serious body of opinion in Wales', describing the demand for a Welsh Parliament as 'frivolous'. Prothero's position was endorsed at the 1950 WRCL Annual Conference which urged 'the whole of the Labour Movement to have nothing to do' with the campaign.[52] Labour's vocal opposition was to hamper the campaign from its inauguration, despite the support of five rebel Welsh Labour MPs, S. O. Davies, T. W. Jones, Cledwyn Hughes, Tudor Watkins and Goronwy Roberts.

The CPGB's decision to take part in the campaign marked its first step into practical activity related to the national question, the campaign seen as a means of enabling 'the party to reach out to wider circles and to demonstrate its serious concern with the problems of Wales as a special aspect of the

[50] For an account of the campaign see John Graham Jones, 'The Parliament for Wales Campaign, 1950–1956', *Welsh History Review* 6 (2), 1992; Elwyn Roberts, 'Ymgyrch Senedd i Gymru' in John Davies (ed.), *Cymru'n Deffro: Hanes y Blaid Genedlaethol 1925–75* (Talybont, 1981). For a more analytical approach to the campaign, see Emily Charette, 'Framing Wales: The Parliament for Wales Campaign, 1950–1956' in T. Robin Chapman (ed.), *The Idiom of Dissent: Protest and Propaganda in Wales* (Llandysul, 2006); for the campaign's aims, see *Parliament for Wales* (Aberystwyth, 1953).

[51] George Thomson, 'Report on the National Question in Scotland and Wales', p. 10.

[52] Jones 'Parliament for Wales Campaign', p. 212.

problems of the British people as a whole'.[53] Reflecting the importance placed on the campaign by the Welsh Committee, the party was represented by Idris Cox, then District Secretary, at its inaugural conference at Llandrindod Wells. Cox was elected on to the campaign's committee and also appointed to its working group, which brought him into a working relationship with a number of leading Welsh nationalists, including Gwynfor Evans, J. R. Jones, Dr Gwenan Jones and Dafydd Jenkins.[54] In his speech to conference Cox, stressing the importance of the campaign remaining a non-partisan affair, nevertheless sought to link the CPGB's support for the campaign to broader communist policy, arguing that the campaign should express its support for wage increases, as a means of winning working-class support, and linking the right of self-government to the CPGB's campaigns against the wars in Korea and Malaya. Cox, however, offered the CPGB's full support for the campaign, declaring 'Let the people of every country in the world have their right of self-government and freedom. We Communists will support this movement to the hilt.'[55]

Cox's insistence that the campaign should remain non-partisan reflected concerns as to the negative reaction among the party membership to such an open alliance with Plaid Cymru. This is evident from the *Daily Worker*'s report from the conference, which, over the course of three different reports in that day's three editions, studiously failed to mention any involvement by the nationalists in the campaign, only noting the speeches made by Cox, Megan Lloyd George and S. O. Davies. Such concern was merited, for, as noted earlier, the campaign failed to inspire a substantial number of the party rank and file, as well as a number of the party's leading members during the first ten months of the PWC's existence. While the Welsh Committee put this down to fears of bourgeois and nationalist contamination of the party, a tendency to see self-government as separation from the rest of Britain, and a fear that the class struggle was

[53] 'Report to the Political Committee, April 1951', p. 3.
[54] Minutes of the Central Committee of the Parliament for Wales Campaign, 9 December 1950, Undeb Cymru Fydd Papers 202, NLW.
[55] *Daily Worker*, 3 July 1950, p. 3; *Y Faner*, 5 July 1950, p. 5.

being neglected, party members must also have been under-whelmed by the inauspicious start made by the campaign following the Llandrindod conference. The PWC took some time to get up and running, the campaign not appointing a secretary until November 1950 or a full-time organiser until the next year.[56] Its working group was only established in December 1950, while the campaign itself was not formally launched until August 1951 at the Llanrwst National Eisteddfod and then re-launched at the 1953 Rhyl National Eisteddfod following further difficulties. By September 1952, the campaign's weaknesses were recognised by the Welsh Committee which noted 'There is less enthusiasm about this campaign than when it started and it certainly hasn't caused a ripple in the Broad Labour Movement in South Wales.'[57] In addition to this, the economism that had been a feature of communist politics in Wales was evident, the party also having difficulty in mobilising its members around the campaign to form Peace Committees in Wales, amongst the party's highest priorities during the early 1950s, leading to attempts to form a Welsh National Peace Council based on this movement being abandoned by 1957.[58] Despite this, the Welsh Committee continued to see some value in main-taining contact with the PWC, especially in drawing non-communists to the party's own campaigns, noting that 'In linking up the fight for a Welsh Parliament with the fight for peace, British Independence and colonial liberation we are able to get our message over to a section of the popula-tion we don't normally touch.'[59]

As we have seen, however, concerns at the level of the party's involvement had already been aired, both in the Welsh Committee's report to the PC in April 1951 and by John Roose Williams at the Welsh Congress in October 1952. While some party activists such as Roose Williams, who was working alongside Ambrose Bebb on the Bangor PWC

[56] Jones, 'Parliament for Wales Campaign', p. 214; Roberts, 'Ymgyrch Senedd i Gymru' p. 101.

[57] 'Report to the Political Committee, September 1952', p. 10.

[58] See the Welsh Committee's reports to the Political Committee for 1951–1957, Bert Pearce Papers, WD 1/4, NLW.

[59] 'Report to the Political Committee, September 1952', p. 10.

committee, Hywel Davy Williams at Rhigos and Enoch Collins at Llanelli were active in the PWC, the majority of party members it seems remained indifferent.[60] Cox himself was to maintain his position on the campaign committee until November 1952, although he had not attended regular meetings since around June 1951, and despite an agreement to allow for his replacement on the committee, no such replacement was put forward by the party.[61] Despite this, the party leadership maintained contact with the PWC, with Alun Thomas, the new District Secretary, speaking at a large campaign meeting at Ammanford.[62] However, its failure to keep a seat on the campaign's executive body seriously curtailed its influence over the campaign. By early 1954, new concerns regarding the PWC and the party's attitude to the national question were being raised. Whilst noting the successful relaunch of the campaign, the Welsh Committee expressed concern that Plaid Cymru were attempting to take it over, a response to the secondment of Plaid Cymru's Elwyn Roberts into the role of national organiser. Reviewing its attitude to the campaign and to the national question in general, the party noted that it had made 'twin errors' in its approach:

> On the one hand work has been inadequate so that reactionary ideas have increasingly come to the fore in the movement and we have been unable to harness the national aspirations towards a British Road to Socialism. On the other hand some elements in the Welsh party elevate the national question out of its place and think of solutions without a British People's Democracy. We must do two things (a) get clarity and unity in the party on a number of the problems arising, (b) be more active on the national problem, winning allies in the fight for Peace and Socialism.[63]

While the Welsh Committee's concerns again reflected a lack of meaningful activity on the part of the party

[60] For John Roose Williams's activity on the Bangor PWC Committee, see the Minute Book for the Bangor Committee of the Parliament for Wales Campaign 1952–1956, Elwyn Roberts Papers 31, NLW; for Hywel Davy Williams, see his letter to Y Cymro, 31 March 1966, p. 3.

[61] No replacement for Cox from the CPGB is listed in those attending Central Committee meetings from November 1952 onwards, see Undeb Cymru Fydd Papers 202 and Elwyn Roberts Papers 30, NLW.

[62] 'Report to the Political Committee, September 1952', p. 10.

[63] 'Report to the Political Committee on the Work of the Communist Party in Wales, 26 January 1954', Bert Pearce Papers WD 1/4, NLW, p. 10.

membership, now viewed as particularly damaging in having allowed the 'reactionary ideas' of Plaid Cymru to take control of the PWC, it also reflected concerns that some party members were coming too close to 'bourgeois nationalist' positions. That the question was now viewed as becoming increasingly divisive is reflected in the Welsh Committee's call for greater unity and clarity on the national question, while the insistence that solutions to the national question must be within the context of the setting up of a People's Democracy, stressed once again the primacy to be given to the class struggle and the victory of socialism. Despite the Welsh Committee's call for greater activity over the national question, its relegation to an issue that could only truly be dealt with following the ultimate victory of socialism in Britain, could only lead to the conclusion for many communists that it was an issue which held little urgency in the general scheme of the party's aims. Significantly, the importance of the PWC and the national question as far as the Welsh Committee was concerned was now purely instrumental; they were now simply a means of broadening the party's own support base.

The party's most significant role in the PWC was, however, still to come in the form of the attempt to win the support of the South Wales Area NUM for a Welsh Parliament. The question of a Welsh Parliament had first been raised within the South Wales Area NUM at its 1953 Annual Conference, at which time the debate had been curtailed following the intervention of the South Wales Area president, Will Paynter, who deferred the debate for six months to allow for further consideration of the issues, and to seek the views of both the PWC and the WRCL. Due to some foot-dragging over the issue by the WRCL, the debate was again deferred at a subsequent NUM Area Conference until the 1954 Annual Conference.[64] In preparation for the debate copies of the PWC pamphlet, *Parliament for Wales*, were distributed to all NUM lodges in south Wales, as was a CPGB statement in favour of a Welsh Parliament and one in opposition by the

---

[64] *NUM (South Wales Area) Annual Report of the Executive Council 1953–54* (Cardiff, 1954), pp. 85–6.

WRCL.[65] Lacking the support of the WRCL, the PWC held great stall in winning the South Wales Area NUM over to the campaign, viewing it as crucial if it was to make a breakthrough within the broader Welsh labour movement. The WRCL viewed the upcoming debate with some trepidation, fearing that the miners would vote in support of a Welsh Parliament without resolute action on their part. In particular, Cliff Prothero feared that Communist influence on the issue could lead to large numbers of miners being won over to the campaign's position.[66] Reacting to these fears, the WRCL used its influence within the south Wales NUM to win speakers' rights for three anti-campaign MPs, Jim Griffiths, D. R. Grenfell and D. J. Williams, all influential miners' MPs.[67] In contrast, the Executive Council of the South Wales NUM refused similar speakers rights to PWC representatives, including S. O. Davies, despite the presence of a number of communists at the meeting, arguing that having distributed literature for all parties concerned to the lodges, PWC representation at conference served 'no good purpose'.[68] These machinations, along with a negative press campaign against the PWC's proposals, helped tilt the odds in the WRCL's favour.

The refusal to let PWC representatives speak at conference left much of the onus of the pro-devolution camp on the CPGB. In its statement released prior the debate, the party had been somewhat equivocal in its support for a Welsh Parliament. While arguing that a Welsh Parliament was the party's long-term goal, in keeping with the analysis of the national question presented to the PC that January, it argued that this would only be possible within the context of a People's Government at Westminster. Linking the fight for a

[65] Minutes of Parliament for Wales Central Committee Meeting, 7 November 1953, Elwyn Roberts Papers 30; NUM (South Wales Area) Minutes of Executive Council Meeting, April 27, 1954, p. 401, SWCC/MNA/NUM/3/1/3, South Wales Coalfield Collection, University of Swansea.

[66] Jones, 'Parliament for Wales Campaign', p. 217.

[67] *Western Mail*, 10 May 1954.

[68] NUM (South Wales Area) Minutes of Executive Council Meeting, 27 April 1954, p. 401. Among the Communists present at this meeting were Will Paynter (president), Dai Dan Evans (secretary), Dai Francis and Jack Jones; Robert Griffiths, *S. O. Davies: A Socialist Faith* (Llandysul, 1983), p. 181.

Welsh Parliament with the party's broader campaigns, the Welsh Committee urged greater activity in the day-to-day struggles for better living standards and against the Tory Government.

> The Communist Party says the Welsh people must be given their full freedom to develop their economic, social and cultural resources, and welcomes the growing determination of the people to have a greater say in the running of the affairs of our country. A Parliament for Wales alone can ensure the full development of the Welsh People.
>
> But the guarantee of the future of the Welsh people; the final solution of their problems can only be achieved by a radical break with present policies, and the formation of a People's Government determined to build a Socialist Britain. Only such a Government can fully recognise and satisfy the national claims of the Welsh people.
>
> The struggle, then, for the future of Wales, for a Parliament for Wales, must be seen in its present day position: the movement for peace, higher wages, a decent life and to get rid of the Tory Government. When Welsh people are drawn into activity for these immediate decisive issues they will see the need for a Welsh Parliament and acquire the political strength to win it. There can be no future for Wales without Peace and Socialism.

This focus on immediate issues was also echoed in the statement's call for the appointment of a Secretary of State and of under-secretaries in charge of Welsh departments for Agriculture, Trade, Labour, Health, Education and Housing, the establishment of a Welsh National Planning Commission and regular meetings of Welsh MPs and representatives from the local authorities, trade unions and political parties to discuss Welsh affairs. Despite ending the statement with the assurance that 'The Communist Party in Wales works for a Parliament for Wales, for the satisfaction of the national aspirations of our people', the presentation of the Welsh Parliament as a long-term goal and the focus on the immediate demand for a Secretary of State was hardly a ringing endorsement of the campaign's aims.[69] The focus on immediate demands coincided with the arrival of a new district secretary, Bill Alexander, in April 1953. He replaced Alun

[69] 'Communist Statement on the Future of Wales', April 1954, Bert Pearce Papers WN 1/1, NLW.

Thomas, who had been forced to resign due to ill-health.[70] Alexander, a former commander of the British Battalion of the International Brigade, had been brought in from Birmingham to help resolve the Welsh District's continuing problems. In June, the Welsh Committee, whilst warning of the danger of central Wales turning into 'a human desert – an area of pine forests and water catchments for English cities', argued for devolution in much the same terms, focusing on the immediate demands as the vital step needed in moving towards a Welsh Parliament.[71] Similarly, it was under Alexander that the Welsh Committee took a step back from calling for the formation of a Welsh TUC.

Despite this, it was CPGB members who put forward the resolution at conference in support of 'the now widespread demand for a Parliament for Wales', with Cyril Parry, chairman of the Morlais Lodge, moving the resolution, and Hywel Davy Williams, of the Rhigos Lodge, seconding it.[72] The Morlais Lodge had come out in support of a Welsh Parliament in September 1953, following a unanimous vote in its favour at a general lodge meeting,[73] with both Parry and the lodge secretary delegates to a PWC meeting that December.[74] At conference Parry, Williams and their supporters, Dick Beamish, a Labour Party member close to the CPGB, and Gwyn Phillips were opposed by two of the three Labour MPs granted speaking rights, Jim Griffiths and D. R. Grenfell, as well as Glyn Williams, a member of the South Wales Area NUM executive. The deployment of such high-profile speakers in opposition to the resolution by both the WRCL and the NUM executive reflected the concerns expressed earlier by Prothero that the vote could

[70] *Party News,* April 1953, p. 1.
[71] 'Press Statement by Welsh Communist Party on the Council for Wales and Monmouthshire Second Memorandum, 22nd July 1953', Bert Pearce Papers WD 1/4, NLW.
[72] *NUM (South Wales Area) Minutes of Area Annual Conference held at the Pavilion, Porthcawl, on 10th, 11th, 12th and 15th May 1954* (Cardiff, 1954), p. 455, 450–2, SWCC/MNA/NUM/3/1/3/4, South Wales Coalfield Collection, University of Swansea.
[73] General Lodge Meeting, 26 September 1953, Morlais Lodge Minute Book, SWCC/MNB/NUM/1/D/5, South Wales Coalfield Collection, University of Swansea.
[74] Lodge Committee Meeting, 20 December 1953, Morlais Lodge Minute Book.

go either way. It also reflects a NUM executive in South Wales still dominated by Labour Party supporters, despite having communists elected to its leading positions. Having effectively banned high-profile PWC speakers, such as S. O. Davies, from addressing conference, the South Wales Area executive, had, in connivance with the WRCL, done everything in their power to ensure a rejection of the resolution. Pitted against such high-profile speakers, those arguing in favour of the resolution faced an uphill struggle from the outset.

Moving the resolution, Parry offered no specific plan for devolution, instead basing his argument on the principle of supporting self-government. At the outset, Parry stressed that support for a Welsh Parliament came from across the political spectrum, noting that it was not a party political issue for his Lodge, distancing it from Plaid Cymru. For Parry, the main argument in favour of a Welsh Parliament lay in the inability of the House of Commons to deal adequately with Welsh affairs. Rejecting the Welsh Day as incapable of doing justice to Welsh issues at Parliament, Parry argued that a Welsh Parliament would be better placed to deal with problems associated with health, education, unemployment and the transport links between north and south Wales, while bringing about a closer relationship between the Welsh people and their elected leaders. Allaying fears regarding separatism and the fate of the NUM and the trade union movement following the formation of a Welsh Parliament, Parry argued that separatism would be an absurd proposition, noting that 'Ties that had been established over centuries could not be severed very easily.' Rejecting the need for the Welsh miners to secede from the NUM, for Parry, a Welsh Parliament, if anything, would lead to more effective links between the trade union movement and government, and to greater trade union influence over political affairs, noting that a Welsh Parliament would, in effect, mean a socialist government in Wales. Such trade union influence would allow the South Wales Area to exert greater influence within the NUM, not less. Noting the economic disparity between England and Wales, Parry argued that a Welsh Parliament would be able to more effectively plan the

Welsh economy and the coal industry in particular, whilst arguing that a Welsh Parliament would ultimately, through socialism, be of benefit to all, 'A socialist Government in Wales would be the means of improving considerably the standard of life of the people and would develop the cultural and the particular characteristic of the Welsh people.'[75]

Hywel Williams, seconding the resolution, approached the demand from a different angle, viewing the establishment of a Welsh Parliament as a potentially unifying force, which would go some way in integrating rural and industrial Wales. In particular, Williams argued that a Welsh Parliament would be able to better protect 'the Welsh way of life', which was now restricted to rural Wales. However, as with Parry, the crux of the issue lay in a point of political principle – whether or not the Welsh miners supported the right to self-determination. Appealing to the miners' internationalist instincts, Williams linked the Welsh people's right to self-determination to that of the colonial peoples, noting, 'What was good for the Malayans, the people of Indo-China and the people of British Guiana was also good for the Welsh people.'[76] Beamish, arguing in favour of 'the necessity for the decentralisation of political power in the form of a Welsh Parliament', focused on the support given to such proposals in the past by the labour movement in Wales, quoting from Regional Council of Labour documents in favour of self-determination for Wales, and noting both Keir Hardie and Arthur Henderson's support for Welsh devolution.[77]

Opposing the resolution, Glyn Williams, noting a disparity of views within the PWC on the proposed parliament's powers and functions, argued that the miners should trust the decision of the WRCL to oppose a Welsh Parliament and the PWC. For D. R. Grenfell, Westminster already provided ample opportunity for the discussion of Welsh affairs on both Welsh Day and in committee, a privilege not accorded to either England or Scotland. Expressing his loyalty to the Westminster Parliament, Grenfell declared, 'I claim on

---

[75] *Minutes of Area Annual Conference, 1954*, pp. 449–51.
[76] *Minutes of Area Annual Conference, 1954*, pp. 451–2.
[77] *Minutes of Area Annual Conference, 1954*, p. 453.

behalf of the Parliament in Westminster, to which we send the representation, that we represent democracy in Wales as no other part of Britain.'[78] The most substantial speech in opposition, however, came from Jim Griffiths. Now viewed as the great facilitator of Welsh constitutional change within the Labour Party during the 1950s and 1960s, Griffiths at conference was staunchly opposed to the demand for a Welsh Parliament. For Griffiths, the main issue was whether the miners wanted a federal system of government in Britain. In opposing this proposal, Griffiths argued that a Welsh Parliament would, in effect, mean the separation of both the Welsh economy and its social services from the rest of Britain – a factor that had led the WRCL to reject a Welsh Parliament. Such a step, he argued, would leave Wales at a grave disadvantage to the rest of Britain and threaten its way of life, noting that only within the context of the unitary state could Wales' best interests be secured.[79]

Thus, Griffiths linked opposition to a Welsh Parliament to fears that such a step would lead not only to separatism, but also to the loss of the gains made under Labour between 1945 and 1951. For Griffiths, the Westminster Parliament would remain the machinery through which social change for Wales could be most effectively achieved.

Despite the efforts of the resolution's proponents, conference rejected supporting a Welsh Parliament by 121 votes to 34.[80] While this effectively ended the PWC's attempts to win over the labour movement to its cause, it was also a blow to the CPGB's own attempts to rally the labour movement to supporting Welsh national rights, its main focus in relation to the national question since it first engaged with the issue in the 1930s. Nevertheless, communists continued to support the campaign with Dai Francis speaking at a PWC meeting at the Miners' Hall in Ystradgynlais during the National Eisteddfod in August 1954.[81] At the 1954 Welsh Congress, Bill Alexander called on the party to initiate a broad campaign for the 'Future of Wales', which was to be centred

---

[78] *Minutes of Area Annual Conference, 1954,* p. 452.
[79] *Minutes of Area Annual Conference, 1954,* pp. 453–4.
[80] *Western Mail,* 12 May 1954, p. 3.
[81] Roberts, 'Ymgyrch Senedd i Gymru', p. 114.

on the campaign for peace, a campaign for the national independence of Britain and for the 'satisfaction of the national
aspirations of the Welsh people'.[82] During the final push for
signatures 'a number of branches helped canvass for the
Parliament for Wales Petition',[83] however, the party's enthusiasm for the campaign seems to have waned significantly by
1955, with no comment by the Welsh Committee on the
party's involvement in the campaign in that year's report to
the PC.[84] Considering the failure to win over the section of
the labour movement where it held most influence, and the
further blow suffered by the campaign following the defeat
of S. O. Davies's Government for Wales Bill, this loss of enthusiasm was perhaps understandable.[85]

The CPGB's relationship with the PWC ended with failure,
the defeat at the South Wales NUM's annual conference
dealing a heavy blow to the hopes of those communists who
wanted to win the working class over to lead the struggle for
Welsh national rights. The party's relationship with the PWC
had also caused friction within the party, with the leadership
once again faced with opposition from within its own ranks
and a membership that was largely indifferent, if not hostile,
to the cause, viewing the PWC as a distraction from the
CPGB's own campaigns on day-to-day economic and social
issues. From 1953 onwards, the leadership itself had begun
to question its role in supporting the PWC, expressing fears
that it was in the process of being wholly taken over by Plaid
Cymru, a situation aided by its own lack of activity, and abandonment of an executive position in the movement following
the resignation of Idris Cox from the campaign committee in
November 1952. The party had not been helped by a quick
turnover in its own leadership, with Alun Thomas replacing
Cox in April 1951 and Bill Alexander replacing Thomas in
April 1953, Cox's removal, in particular, proving the most
damaging to the priority given to the national question by

[82] *Party News,* October 1954, p. 1.
[83] 'Report of the Work of the Welsh Committee 1955/57', p. 2, Bert Pearce
Papers WD 1/4, NLW.
[84] 'Report to the Political Committee, April 1955'.
[85] On S. O Davies's Government for Wales Bill see John Graham Jones, 'S. O.
Davies and the Government for Wales Bill, 1955', *Llafur,* 8 (3), 2002, pp. 67–77.

the Welsh party. For Cox, the party's lack of activity was the great weakness in regards to its role in the PWC:

> I don't think anyone would claim that it succeeded in creating a mass movement in favour [of a Welsh Parliament]. I frankly admit Plaid Cymru was far more active than the Communist Party in this campaign, and one needs to be self-critical of the weakness of the Communist Party in this respect.[86]

To an extent, the party's support for the PWC was also damaging to the campaign itself, with the Labour Party even less likely to sign up to the campaign in the knowledge that it had Communist support. Robert Griffiths notes that following the Llandrindod conference, a number of newspapers accused the campaign of being a communist front, while Elwyn Roberts, the campaign's national organiser from 1953 onwards, later argued that Communist support proved a real hindrance in winning the support of local Labour parties.[87] However, the party also provided the PWC with an important bridge into the NUM which helped facilitate the 1954 debate over a Welsh Parliament. It also provided the PWC with a number of petitioners, admittedly in limited numbers, in the key battleground of industrial south Wales, although claims apparently made by Gwynfor Evans that CPGB members collected some 90 per cent of the signatures collected in the industrial south seem wide of the mark.[88] For the CPGB, its support for the PWC showed that its support for Welsh national rights extended to practical action for the cause, however limited in nature that practical action was, and for the time being it could claim to be the only party representing the industrial working class that openly supported a Welsh Parliament.

NEGLECT AND RENEWAL – THE CPGB AND THE NATIONAL QUESTION, 1956–1964

Much of the CPGB's energies between 1956 and 1964 were spent dealing with, and recovering from, the effects of the

---

[86] Idris Cox, 'Socialism and the National Question', *Planet* 37/38, May 1977, p. 93.

[87] Griffiths, *S. O. Davies*, p. 171; Roberts, 'Ymgyrch Senedd i Gymru', p. 112.

[88] Interview with Dr John Cox, 20 September 2008.

crises of 1956. Party membership fell from 34,117 in June 1956 to 24,670 by February 1958, a loss of over a quarter of the party membership, the YCL losing almost half of its members.[89] The party did not fully recover these lost members until 1964, its membership reaching 34,281, only to begin a steady decline from 1965 onwards that continued until the end of the 1960s and to the party's dissolution in 1991.[90] This period also saw a change of leadership and a change in policy, with John Gollan taking over as party secretary in 1956 after Pollitt had to step down due to ill-health, although he remained party chairman until his death in 1960. More significantly, by the mid-1960s all of the old guard, who had been running the party since the 1920s, had made way for a new generation of party leaders, with Dutt the last to leave office in 1965. The change in leadership marked a further move towards a post-Leninist form of politics, the party by the early 1960s taking its role as a mainstream political party more seriously, presenting evidence to a number of government inquires and commissions, while adopting a more serious attitude towards elections. The publication of a new edition of the *BRS* in 1958 saw the party further develop its programme in a reformist direction, this time free from interventions from Moscow. The seeds of a new outlook were also visible in the aftermath of a damaging vote-rigging scandal in the communist-controlled ETU in 1961. This scandal, while dealing another blow to the CPGB's democratic credentials, led to a significant change in its industrial strategy, based on the abandonment of the culture of secrecy that had surrounded its trade union politics and a move towards a more open form of industrial politics centred on the formation of alliances with the left of the trade union movement – a strategic change that facilitated the emergence of the Broad Left movement from 1965 onwards. The party was able to regain a significant number of members through its association with CND, in which it had become a major player by the mid-1960s, its role within it providing

---

[89] Parsons, '1956: What Happened Inside the CPGB', p. 26. YCL membership dropped from 2,540 to 1,387.

[90] Thompson, *The Good Old Cause*, p. 218.

access to a new generation of political activists boosting, in particular, the membership of the YCL. The campaign against the bomb became one of the main focuses of the party's politics during this period, along with campaigns against racism, for colonial freedom, for the raising of living standards and against proposals for an incomes policy.

The events of 1956 had been a traumatic experience for many communists, for whom the revelations of Khrushchev's 'secret speech' and the subsequent invasion of Hungary had led to a serious reassessment of the political commitment they had made to the communist movement.[91] For many communists, drawn to the movement by a humanitarian commitment to the bringing about of a better society, Khrushchev's revelations came as a profound shock, bringing into question the meaning, in some cases, of their whole life's work. The extent of this shock can be gauged from the furious response to Dutt's assertion that Stalin's crimes amounted to little more than 'spots on the sun', following which he issued a rare apology.[92] To some of these communists, Khrushchev's revelations, coupled with the Soviet invasion and the dishonesty of the party leadership in dealing with the issues raised by these events, led quickly to disillusionment and exodus from the party. For others, the aim was to stay within the party and attempt to change it from within, a course of action frustrated by the party leadership and a lack of internal party democracy, leading again to disillusionment and exodus for many. Three-quarters of the membership, however, chose to remain within the party; for some leaving the party was not an option, a commitment to defending the Soviet Union remaining paramount in their thoughts, for others there was an outright refusal to face up to the crimes

---

[91] For its impact on the party, see the papers collected in *The Communist Party and 1956: Speeches at the Conference* ; for a vivid account of the mental turmoil created by the events of 1956, see Alice McLeod, *The Death of Uncle Joe* (Woodbridge, 1997); for accounts by leading party dissidents, see John Saville, 'The Twentieth Congress and the British Communist Party', *The Socialist Register,* 13, 1976, pp. 6–21 and Malcolm McEwen 'The Day the Party Had to Stop', *The Socialist Register,* 13, 1976, pp. 29–30; for Khrushchev's speech, see Nikita Khrushchev, *The Dethronement of Stalin: Full Text of Khrushchev's Speech* (Manchester, 1956).

[92] 'Notes of the Month', *Labour Monthly,* May 1956, p. 194; 'Notes of the Month', *Labour Monthly,* June 1956, pp. 247–9.

committed under Stalinism, while for still others the decision to stay was based on a refusal to abandon the movement which they had dedicated their lives to, despite broadly agreeing with much of what the dissidents had said.

The impact of 1956 was also to have a direct effect on the development of the party's policy both for Wales and the national question. Having made significant gains prior to the Hungarian invasion, the Welsh party, claiming a membership of 1,517 in October 1956, up from 1,292 in March 1955, had, by November 1957, lost some 20 per cent of its membership, falling back to 1,220. The effect on the YCL was catastrophic, with membership falling by 82 per cent, from 92 in 1956 to 17 by January 1958.[93] Amongst the party leadership five members of the Welsh Committee resigned their posts or left the party, including Jack Maunder, the West Wales Area Secretary.[94] Maunder, in a letter to Bill Alexander, expressed his sense of bewilderment and shock following the events of 1956 noting,

> The Hungarian Events, plus the revelations at the 20th Congress, came as a tremendous shock to me, but I tried to reconcile them with my fundamental beliefs and endeavoured to keep going, hoping that the faith and great enthusiasm I have always had for the Communist Party would at least be partially recaptured during discussions and activities. But instead of recapturing that feeling I find the contrary taking place, and I am growing depressed as a result. I find the strain of trying to explain events, which I was previously prepared to defend so fiercely, too much for me.[95]

Publicly, the party's leading industrial figures expressed loyalty to the party, but while Horner initially stuck to the party line, Paynter was more equivocal arguing that while the suppression of 'right-wing extremists' in Hungary had been necessary, the Soviet intervention had been a mistake.[96]

---

[93] 'Report of the Work of the Welsh Committee 1955/57', Bert Pearce Papers WD 1/4, NLW, pp. 2–3; 'Report to Political Committee of Activity in Wales September 1958', Bert Pearce Papers WD 1/4, NLW, p. 14.

[94] 'Report of the Work of the Welsh Committee 1955/57', p. 4.

[95] Jack Maunder to Bill Alexander, 8 January 1957, Bert Pearce Papers WT/5, NLW.

[96] *Western Mail,* 19 November 1956, p. 1 and 3. Horner was nevertheless repulsed by the repression and killing of Hungarian workers by the invading Soviet army and was to speak out against the execution of Imre Nagy in 1958, see Fishman, *Arthur Horner: A Political Biography* Vol. 2, pp. 910–14 and pp. 926–8.

Privately however, both had 'serious misgivings' about the Soviet intervention.[97]

Assessing the impact of the events of 1956 on the Welsh party, Bill Alexander noted that they had 'brought to the surface serious doubts and lack of faith in our fundamental positions'. These doubts had been fuelled by the pressure exerted by the increased economic prosperity in Britain during the 1950s, which had brought an air of unreality to the party's prediction of an imminent general crisis of capitalism.[98] Noting that the number of active party cadres had fallen since 1956, the party 'trying to do too much with too few members', and recognising that the party was now experiencing severe financial difficulties, forcing it to cut its already meagre full-time staff, Alexander relayed the impression of a thoroughly demoralised party. Significantly, in relation to the national question, Alexander acknowledged that it was now finding itself unable to develop its policy for Wales and on the national question due to these difficulties noting, 'The Welsh Committee comments on most important Welsh affairs either by press statements or in meetings but we certainly have not got the initiative or very developed policy on many National questions such as language, rural problems etc. We have tried to develop national policy but progress has been very slow. At the moment we cannot afford to devote more time and cadres to this.'[99] This effectively signalled an end to the Welsh party's efforts in the 1950s to develop its Welsh policy programme.

In reality, the party's Welsh policy programme had been left undeveloped since the publication of *Wales in the New World* in 1944, and by the mid-1950s calls for its review and further development were increasing. In particular, in the run-up to the 1957 Welsh Congress, the Welsh Committee had come under pressure from sections of the party to develop a specific policy programme for Wales and to deal with the national question, with the Welsh Committee conceding that these issues demanded 'greater attention on

---

[97] Parsons, '1956: What Happened Inside the CPGB', p. 32.
[98] 'Report to the Political Committee 1958', p. 9.
[99] 'Report to the Political Committee 1958', pp. 11–13.

our part'.[100] At Congress, the Treherbert branch moved a successful resolution urging the party to 'work out an economic and cultural policy for Wales, and put it into pamphlet form as soon as possible'.[101] Hywel Williams also urged the party to do more, linking the national struggle in Wales to the 'national awakening all over the world' and arguing that 'The Communist Party should not only concentrate on the industrial areas but pay very much more attention to all the national problems in Wales.'[102] In his speech to Congress, Alexander conceded that more work needed to be done in this area, but noted that any solution to Welsh problems was predicated on the victory of socialism in Britain as a whole.

> We are a Welsh Communist Party. Because we are a national party we have the responsibility to develop and apply general principles to our national conditions. We welcome and accept the criticisms that we must work out in more detail our policy on specific Welsh questions. The new Welsh Committee must tackle this work.
>
> But it is necessary to warn there can be no major progress in Wales without a solution of the British problems. No major advance is possible for the Welsh people under capitalism. The Welsh capitalists are as bad as the English or any other capitalist.[103]

For Alexander, the party, while continuing to stand for a Welsh Parliament, needed to campaign more actively for it, arguing that it was 'not enough to leave it as a slogan – it is essential to campaign for more say in the running of Welsh affairs now'. Viewing the proposal for a Secretary of State as a step in the right direction, Alexander also called for the development of the party's policy on language issues, noting, however, that while they were 'often given great prominence … they are not decisive'.[104]

Throughout 1957, however, the party had not made much of its commitment to supporting a Welsh Parliament, instead stressing its support for the lesser goal of a Secretary of State. Accusations that the party were by 1957 merely following

[100] *Party News,* May 1957, p. 1.
[101] 'Branch Resolutions', June 1957, Bert Pearce Papers WC/1, NLW.
[102] *Party News,* June 1957, p. 3.
[103] 'Report to the Welsh Congress, June 1957', Bert Pearce Papers WC/1, p. 17.
[104] 'Report to the Welsh Congress, June 1957', pp. 19–20.

Labour's lead on the issue are thus given some credence in the cautious welcome given by the party to the Council for Wales and Monmouth's recommendation of a Secretary of State as part of its memorandum on the administration of Wales. Noting that a Secretary of State had formed a part of the party's policy for some time, Annie Powell called for the appointment of more under-secretaries, the creation of a Welsh National Planning Commission and a regular meeting of Welsh MPs and the local authorities to discuss Wales' problems. Noting that 'Real power ... would still remain with the House of Commons in London', Powell argued that it would nevertheless allow the Welsh people better access to the civil servants that ran Wales. However, Powell's report on the memorandum saw the party under Alexander, once again, reluctant to call for a Welsh Parliament, for despite locating the real power in Westminster, no attempt was made by Powell to argue for a Welsh parliament, instead merely calling for more pressure to be exerted 'to ensure that adequate time is allocated for discussion of Welsh affairs in Parliament'.[105] A similar stand was taken by the party on the appointment of a Minister for Wales by the Conservative Government in December 1957. The party, while dismissing the appointment of the new minister as 'a travesty of democracy and contrary to the expressed opinions of the Welsh people' who would hold 'trifling powers, inadequate to cope with the sharpening and complex needs of Wales', once again made no mention of the need for a Welsh Parliament, preferring to reiterate its short-term goal of a Secretary of State.[106]

Pressure for the development of party policy on the national question was also evident in the pre-Congress discussion for the 25th Party Congress, held in April 1957, with Enoch Collins once again calling on the party to do more on the issue. Collins was highly critical of the Welsh Party's attitude to the national question, arguing that little had been done since the 1940s, comparing the party unfavourably with Plaid Cymru, whilst arguing that the CPGB showed a

---

[105] *Party News*, February, 1957, p. 5.
[106] 'Press Statement, 15 December, 1957', Bert Pearce Papers WD 1/4, NLW.

tendency to follow Labour Party policy on issues such as a Welsh Parliament and Wales TUC. Collins, in particular, highlighted the party's failure to offer a lead on the proposed flooding of Capel Celyn to create the Tryweryn Reservoir, instead leaving the path clear for Plaid Cymru to play the lead role. Looking back at the party's role in the PWC, Collins argued that it was its failure to campaign more actively on this issue that had brought about the miners' rejection of the resolution in favour of supporting a Welsh Parliament in 1954. For Collins, the party needed to give greater attention to the national question in Wales, standing for a Welsh Parliament and Welsh TUC, actively participating in Welsh cultural life, and publishing pamphlets on Welsh issues, urging the Welsh party to 'personify our nation and its life'.[107] Similar complaints were aired by Sid Jones, a party member from Barry, who in an article lamenting the failure of the Welsh party to engage with Welsh cultural life, noted that for many Welsh communists there was a tendency to dogmatism in their approach to the national question, 'The old dogmatic Marxism seems to mould too many Welsh Communists' thoughts, e.g. "internationalism" excludes "nationalism", so although the Communist Party stands for a Welsh Parliament, they will not work for it.'[108]

The national question was also evident in the debate on the new draft of the *BRS*, which had left the wording on the party's attitude to the national question in Wales and Scotland unchanged from the first edition. Honor Arundel, a Scottish party member, noted that the unchanged wording reflected the party's general lack of interest in the issue, which she attributed to too many party members viewing Welsh and Scottish self-government as 'mere trimming upon the socialist cake and that to take part now in campaigning for national rights is diverting strength from the main struggle for socialism'. For Arundel, therefore, it was vital that the new edition of the *BRS* offer a broader assessment of the national question in Wales and Scotland that would encompass a commitment to Welsh and Scottish parliaments,

---

[107] Enoch Collins, 'Importance of Progressive Nationalism', pp. 77–8.
[108] Sid Jones, 'Welsh and English Poetry', *World News*, 8 September 1956, p. 578.

a statement of the party's attitudes to the national minorities in both countries, and a promise to encourage and protect the Welsh and Gaelic languages and all aspects of Welsh and Scottish national cultures.[109] Arundel's stance was backed by Desmond Greaves, later the biographer of James Connolly, who complained that the *BRS* was too Anglocentric considering it was meant to be the joint programme of communists from England, Wales and Scotland. A general statement that the party supported the national claims of Wales and Scotland was not enough, with Greaves arguing that the party should state its preference for the resolution of the national question on a federal basis, its commitment to protecting Welsh and Gaelic and its commitment to planning on a national basis in both countries.[110] In the event, this pressure wore off, the wording in the *BRS* altered to encompass the party's commitment to Welsh and Scottish parliaments.[111] Significantly, the national question was now featured under the section on 'Socialist Democracy' reflecting a shift in emphasis within the party programme from a focus on Britain's national independence to a broader focus on the extension of democratic rights.

Interest in the national question had also come from an unexpected source, the CPGB Linguists' Group, who in late 1955 were concentrating their efforts on minority languages. Its secretary, William Lockwood, had taken a particular interest in the fate of the Welsh language, presenting the Communist position on the language to a Plaid Cymru Study Circle at Birmingham in April 1955.[112] Lockwood had written to Alexander requesting any recent party material on the Welsh language and national question, material the party had tellingly been unable to provide.[113] In an article originally intended for the party's short-lived journal, *Marxist Quarterly*, Lockwood argued that it was imperative that the

[109] Honor Arundel, 'National Aspirations', *World News*, 16 February 1957, p. 108.
[110] C. Desmond Greaves, 'The National Question in Britain', *World News*, 20 April 1957, pp. 251–2.
[111] *Draft Revised of the British Road to Socialism* (London, 1957), p. 17; *The British Road to Socialism* (London, 1958), p. 24.
[112] *Y Faner,* 13 April 1955, p. 2.
[113] William Lockwood to Bill Alexander, 28 November 1955, Bert Pearce Papers WT/5, NLW.

party took a more robust position on the Welsh language, arguing that 'Platitudes of the sort "We desire the preservation of the Welsh language and culture" are quite inadequate', noting that similar positions were also being taken by the Conservatives.[114] For Lockwood, the Act of Union and the subsequent anglicisation and assimilation of the native population of Wales, had led, by the 1950s, to the Welsh language facing a serious threat to its existence.[115] These were the tactics of imperialism, with Lockwood linking the language policies used in Wales to those being used in the colonies, each geared to impose English as the dominant language in order to assimilate the native population to better suit the needs of empire.[116]

Lockwood, while conceding that the language question may not have been a live issue in the anglicised areas of industrial Wales, urged the party to make an unequivocal stance over giving Welsh official status as a language, noting that for those in the Welsh-speaking areas 'the struggle for the right to use this language is ... part of the wider struggle against tutelage from above and for democratic rights'.[117] For Lockwood, it was the Soviet Union that provided the model on how to best deal with the language question, noting approvingly the language policies of the Soviet Bloc, which gave official status to minority languages and encouraged the development of both a national press and of the written language, under which Welsh, Lockwood argued, would be thriving, in stark contrast to its position under the British state.[118] The Linguists' Group, however, had some difficulty getting this article published. Emile Burns, editor of the *Marxist Quarterly*, rejected it, leaving the Linguists' Group both 'disappointed' and 'annoyed', with Lockwood noting, 'The language question is the main cultural question of every area in the British Empire which is not naturally English-speaking. It seems to me a reproach that the Party has not

[114] W. B. Lockwood, 'Languages and the National and Colonial Question', Bert Pearce Papers WN 2/1, NLW, p. 2.
[115] Lockwood, 'Languages and the National and Colonial Question', pp. 1–2.
[116] Lockwood, 'Languages and the National and Colonial Question', p. 6.
[117] Lockwood, 'Languages and the National and Colonial Question', p. 2.
[118] Lockwood, 'Languages and the National and Colonial Question', pp. 3–4.

considered this matter in our journals.'[119] When it was finally published in *World News*, all mention of the language issue in Wales had been expunged, the article concentrating solely on the language issue in the colonies.[120] Lockwood would again return to the issue of the party's engagement with the national question in April 1956, urging the party in Wales, in a letter to Alexander, to start formulating its policy on the issue.[121]

Some tentative steps had, in fact, been taken by the Welsh Committee to further develop the Welsh party's position on the national question with a party day school on the issue held in September 1956. Announcing the day school in the party press, Edgar Evans admitted that 'The Communist Party is not sufficiently conversant with the many problems which cause so much controversy among large sections of the Welsh people', a stark admission considering its very public support for the PWC. Noting that Wales was a 'stable and historically distinct community of people, possessing a common territory, a common language and a common tradition', Evans argued that 'no party will succeed to win over the people of Wales unless it is able to formulate a National policy that will fit in with the interests of the Welsh people'. For Evans, the Labour Party had chosen to ignore the issue, 'satisfied with the process of "devolution" which has been operating more or less during the past few years', while Plaid Cymru had been able to capitalise on the issue with what was essentially a reactionary policy based on the interests of the middle class. It was thus vital for the CPGB to develop a policy that could link up 'The social and economic struggles of the Welsh people with their national aspirations to be able to give a "Welsh" or "National Slant" in our approach to problems.'[122]

Following the 1957 Welsh Congress, the Welsh Committee began a consultation within the party on aspects of the

---

[119] William Lockwood to Bill Alexander, 28 November 1955.
[120] W. B. Lockwood, 'Languages and the Colonial Question', *World News*, 19 May 1956, pp. 315, 318; *World News*, 26 May 1956, pp. 336–7.
[121] William Lockwood to Bill Alexander, 18 April 1956, Bert Pearce Papers WT/5, NLW.
[122] *Party News*, August 1956, p. 2.

national question, in particular on its position on the Welsh language. A questionnaire on the Welsh language sent out by the Welsh Committee received answers from a handful of party members, all with a prior interest in these matters.[123] On the whole, the respondents were positive in regards to the language, supporting its right to official status and the compulsory teaching of Welsh in schools and for an extension of Welsh-language education to the whole of the education system, including the universities. The respondents also agreed with greater democratic control of the BBC in Wales, whilst backing the creation of 'a genuine Welsh National Press' to counter the domination of the *Western Mail.* For all the respondents, the language was a crucial factor in the debate on national rights, with Gwen Harries, in particular, viewing the use and development of the language as 'important for destroying the remains of a sense of inferiority among the Welsh People'. Hywel Williams, linking the decline of the language to imperialism, argued that a greater focus on language issues would help the party make gains in rural areas.[124] There was, however, concern among the respondents that the Party was doing too little over the language question and the national question as a whole, with Tom Hopkins and Williams calling for the party to publish party literature in both languages and to make an effort to target some of the party's literature specifically at Welsh-speakers.

For Williams, the party's most important task was 'to prove to the people of Wales, both Welsh and English-speaking, that it stands for the best in the Welsh tradition, the Party must impress upon them that its first allegiance is to its own compatriots and not to any foreign power'.[125] The party was also urged to do more to foster Welsh culture within party branches, with Sid Jones calling on party members to better

[123] 'Welsh Language', [*c.*September 1957], Bert Pearce Papers WN 2/1, NLW; Tom Hopkins to Bill Alexander, 29 September 1957; Sid Jones to Bill Alexander, 22 October 1957, Gwen Harries to Bill Alexander, [*c.*January 1958], Hywel D. Williams to Bill Alexander, [*c.*September 1957], Bert Pearce Papers WN 2/1, NLW; William Lockwood to Bill Alexander, 23 March 1957, Bert Pearce Papers WT/5, NLW.

[124] 'Questionnaire on the Welsh Language', [*c.*January 1958], Bert Pearce Papers WN 2/1, NLW.

[125] 'Questionnaire on the Welsh Language', [*c.*January 1958], pp. 1–3.

familiarise themselves with Welsh literature, song and music, so that branch life would develop a distinctly Welsh character. Criticism was also levelled at the party for having failed to make any significant contribution to the protests over Tryweryn, urging greater co-operation with Plaid Cymru on such issues.[126] Further discussion on the issue within the Welsh Committee led to the release of a statement on the Welsh language by the party later in 1958, but efforts to develop other aspects of Welsh policy were slow and had effectively petered out by September 1958. A renewed effort to develop such a policy was not embarked upon until the appointment of Bert Pearce as District Secretary in November 1959.

Pearce had been born in Pembroke Dock in 1919 but had moved to Birmingham in 1938 where he joined the CPGB, holding a number of responsible positions before becoming Birmingham party secretary in 1952.[127] Pearce took over as district secretary just as the party was making a modest recovery from its setback following the events of 1956, with party membership having risen from 1,249 in February 1958 to 1,452 by November 1959. The YCL had also made a modest recovery although membership remained worryingly low at 59.[128] On his return to Wales, Pearce's main aim was to revitalise the party and develop its Welsh policy programme. In his report to the 1960 Welsh Congress, Pearce emphasised the need for the party to develop its policy for Wales, calling on the party to speed up its work on a Welsh programme, so that it could be published in pamphlet form. The Welsh party programme was to be based around the need for a national economic development plan; the development of social services; the protection and development of the Welsh language and culture; and the reform of government, both at a national and local level, with Pearce reiterating the party's support for a Welsh Parliament.[129]

[126] 'Questionnaire on the Welsh Language', [c.January 1958], p. 3.
[127] *Party News*, November 1959.
[128] 'Report of the Work of the Welsh Committee, July 1957–January 1960', p. 3, Bert Pearce Papers WC/3, NLW.
[129] 'Political Report to Welsh Congress March 19, 1960', pp. 13–15, Bert Pearce Papers WC/3, NLW.

The establishment of the Commission on Local Government in Wales in 1961, to which the party was to give evidence, provided a catalyst for the development of the party's policy on government reform. It was in this context that the party found itself in a position to bring up the question of a Welsh Parliament once again, the party's evidence to the Commission calling for its remit to be expanded to deal with the question of devolution on a national level. The party, proposing a sweeping reform of local government based on the creation of five large local authorities, covering East Wales, West Wales, South Wales, Central Wales and North Wales, argued that 'The first boundary change should be to recognise Wales as a Nation and that is why we propose that there should be an elected Parliament for Wales.'[130] For the party, it was only through the ability to run its own affairs that Wales could advance and local government be truly responsive to the needs of the Welsh people.

> Wales is a nation. Its people have a distinct history, heritage and culture. Today Wales has special problems and special opportunities to develop as a country offering its people an assured economic and social future. These aspirations and hopes can only be met, the Welsh people can only grow to full stature if they have a decisive say in running the affairs of Wales. Only a Parliament for Wales can give our people the full democratic control over their own affairs and bring with it the vigorous functioning of local government at all levels.[131]

The call for a Welsh Parliament was made the 'keystone' of the party's proposals, a parliament seen as the only body that would be able to 'combine such a scale of planning with full democratic control'.[132] While the party still called for a Secretary of State as an immediate demand, the placing of a Welsh Parliament as the lynchpin of the party's proposals was significant, marking a move away from the primary focus on immediate demands that had been characteristic of the party's stance on the national question since the mid-1950s.

[130] 'Local Government Commission for Wales: Statement to Cardiff Conference, November 29, 1961', Bert Pearce Papers WM/3, p. 3 NLW.
[131] 'Memorandum of Evidence to the Commission on Local Government in Wales', [c.1961], Bert Pearce Papers WM/4, p. 1, NLW.
[132] 'Second Memorandum of Evidence to the Local Government Commission of Wales, July 24, 1961', Bert Pearce Papers, WM/4, p. 3, NLW.

Efforts by the Welsh Committee to develop a policy programme for Wales continued throughout 1960 and 1961, with Alistair Wilson presenting a first draft of the party's new policy document to both the Welsh Committee and Secretariat in January 1962, in preparation for a special session at the Welsh Congress that April.[133] The document presented to the Welsh Committee reflected a growing concern for the national question, giving considerable space to the growth of national consciousness and the need for it to be harnessed to the working-class struggle. Whilst arguing for the continued need for a united British working class as the only guarantor of social change in Wales, and arguing against 'the sterile fantasy of the separation', Wilson noted that the historical trajectory of the growth of the modern national movement and the working-class movement in Wales had been similar. For Wilson, the growth of national consciousness in Wales was linked to the growth of industry and communications, to struggles against imperialism and colonialism abroad, the experience of the inter-war years, and the development of the capitalist state in Britain, with national consciousness in modern Wales developing most in the era of monopoly capital.[134]

Whilst acknowledging that social and economic conditions in Wales had improved during the post-war boom, Wilson nevertheless identified a number of policy areas, such as employment, health, education, housing and social services, where Wales was falling behind England. Similarly, the rationalisation of the coal industry, the concentration of industry on the southern seaboard and the programme of railway closures initiated by the Conservative Government were all seen as having a negative effect both on employment and on the continued migration from rural and industrial areas.[135] To counter these problems, Wilson recommended a sweeping programme of reform, centred on a proposal for the establishment of a Welsh Parliament, seen as the key to changing Wales' fortunes. Central to the party's proposals

[133] 'Welsh Committee and Secretariat Proposed Agendas', 1962, Bert Pearce Papers WM/3, NLW.
[134] 'Policy for Wales', January 1962, p. 1, Bert Pearce Papers WC/4, NLW.
[135] 'Policy for Wales', January 1962, pp. 2–3.

was the development of an all-Wales economic plan, based on the nationalisation of the major industries, the development of a more diverse industrial sector and of the agricultural sector; the reform of the education system; a large-scale programme of slum clearances and house building; the reform of the health service; and the improvement of transport links. Welsh culture was to be developed through the allocation of larger grants for cultural activities, the establishment of a national theatre, drama school and orchestra, the establishment of more Welsh schools and of a council to promote the production of Welsh-language films, books and magazines. In particular, the introduction of comprehensive education was viewed as key to fostering the Welsh language, giving teachers more time and space in their curriculums to allow Welsh to be taught in all schools.[136] However, the establishment of a Welsh Parliament was the prerequisite to such a sweeping programme of reform with Wilson noting, 'we emphasise that the all-round satisfaction of the needs of Wales requires the establishment of a Welsh Parliament'.[137] The Welsh Parliament itself was to be a unicameral legislature, elected by proportional representation with powers to legislate for agriculture, forestry, fisheries, industry, transport, labour, social services, housing and education and with the power to plan economically for the whole of Wales. However, the parliament remained a long-term goal for the party, part of the party's broader programme for a socialist Britain. Wilson, in the interim, reiterated the party's proposals for a Secretary of State, a broadened Council for Wales and regular meetings of Welsh MPs in Cardiff.[138]

Gaining approval from the Welsh Committee, the party's new programme was put before Congress in April 1962, with a special session dedicated to discussing Welsh policy. For the party leadership, the new programme was viewed as 'Linking all ... [immediate] demands and the fulfilment of the national aspirations of the Welsh people with the aim of a

---

[136] 'Policy for Wales', January 1962, pp. 4–9.
[137] 'Policy for Wales', January 1962, p. 4.
[138] 'Policy for Wales', January 1962, p. 4.

Socialist Britain and the broad alliance of the British people' while 'Expressing the role of the working class, the Labour Movement, Trade Unions and Communist Party as the leadership of the Welsh people in their struggle both for the satisfaction of their national aspirations and the achievement of Socialism.'[139] Gaining Congress' approval, the final version of the party's programme was published as *The New Way for Wales* in 1964, ready for that year's general election. However, less emphasis was placed on the national question in the final version, with much of the focus in Wilson's draft on the need to combine the national struggle with the struggle for socialism expunged and peace issues and the struggle for socialism given greater prominence. Despite this, a Welsh Parliament was still viewed as the only way to ensure social and economic progress as part of a broader socialist programme for Britain.[140]

For the party leadership in London, as well as in Wales, the 1964 election was seen as crucial, with Britain viewed as standing at a political crossroads. For John Gollan, the election was 'a momentous, decisive election' and a chance for the party to make the long-hoped for electoral breakthrough, while for the Welsh Committee the elections were 'an essential step on the road to serious electoral work'.[141] The party, Gollan later admitted, had not begun to take the general elections seriously until the 1960s, the conversion to electoral politics in the *BRS* taking some time to bed in. For many party members, electoral failure merely served to highlight the party's weaknesses in a way that its industrial work did not, and were useful only for propaganda purposes. However, as the party formulated its own approach to electoral politics in new editions of the *BRS*, so the party took elections more seriously, although an Electoral Department was not set up until the 1966 election.[142]

In Wales, the party's participation in parliamentary elections had been minimal, the party only contesting the Rhondda East constituency in the 1951 and 1955 general

---

[139] 'Draft Political Report March 1962', p. 9, Bert Pearce Papers WM/4, NLW.
[140] *The New Way for Wales* (Cardiff, [1964]).
[141] Callaghan, *Cold War, Crisis and Conflict*, p. 188; 'Draft Political Report Welsh District Congress, 13 December 1964, p. 2, Bert Pearce Papers, NLW.
[142] Callaghan, *Cold War, Crisis and Conflict*, p. 188.

elections, with Neath added to the list in 1959. For the 1964 election, the British party put up 35 candidates, double the number that stood for the party in 1959, but failed to increase its proportion of the vote. In Wales, the party contested five seats, Aberavon, Llanelli, Neath, Pontypool and Rhondda East, where Annie Powell won the largest Communist vote in the whole of Britain, coming second in the poll with 3,385 votes, 11 per cent of the votes cast. However, Powell's vote had in fact dropped from 4,580 at the 1959 election, a fact viewed as a 'real disappointment' by the Welsh Committee, although the party took some solace in heading off the challenge of Plaid Cymru. Overall, the five Communist candidates in Wales won a combined vote of 9,377, an increase on its previous total at the 1959 elections, however, the party had only contested two seats in 1959 and in reality the average vote for each candidate had dropped from 3,271 in 1959 to 1,875 in 1964.[143] Reflecting the negative attitudes of some members towards the party's electoral work, the Welsh Committee expressed disappointment that the party had 'only convinced and mobilised a small part of our membership' in the electoral campaign.[144] The election of a Labour Government was welcomed by the Welsh Committee, as was the decision to grant Wales a Secretary of State, despite criticism that the powers granted were inadequate to deal with the level of economic and social planning needed in Wales.[145] For the party, the main advantage of the creation of the new office was that it would provide a focus and "stimulate demand for much more radical attacks on the backwardness of housing, health and welfare in Wales".[146]

The period from the mid-1950s to the mid-1960s had seen the party attempt to reformulate its policy for Wales. In the immediate period following the end of the PWC, the party's attempts to formulate a policy programme floundered, largely due to the impact of 1956 on the party, while its

---

[143] 'Political Report Welsh District Congress, December 13, 1964', pp. 15–19, Bert Pearce Papers WD 1/12, NLW; General Election results from Beti Jones, *Etholiadau'r Ganrif 1885–1997*: Talybont, 1999, pp. 103–5 for 1959 and pp. 107–10 for 1964.

[144] 'Political Report Welsh District Congress, December 13, 1964', p. 17.

[145] 'Political Report Welsh District Congress, December 13, 1964'; 'Draft Political Report, 1964 Welsh Congress', p. 7.

[146] 'Draft Political Report 1964 Welsh Congress', p. 7.

attitude to the national question had increasingly focused on the immediate demand for a Secretary of State rather than on the long-term goal of a Welsh Parliament. In doing this the party had, as Enoch Collins and, later, Gwyn Alf Williams noted, moved towards aping Labour Party policy on the issue. However, when a new party programme was developed it placed the national question back to the centre of the party's policy, the call for a Welsh Parliament providing the key pivot on which the social and economic development of Wales was to be based in a socialist Britain. To an extent, however, the party's position remained underdeveloped with much of its policy on the national question and for Wales not dissimilar to that developed during the 1940s. What was different was the greater focus on the expansion of demo-cratic rights evident in the new edition of the *BRS*, with the party developing its own brand of 'Socialist Democracy' a conscious effort to dissociate the party from the negative associations that the People's Democracies held after 1956. In Wales, the creation of a new party programme in the early 1960s provided it with a solid policy programme with which it could fight elections, whilst in terms of the national question it allowed the party to distance itself from the Labour Party. The party now hoped that armed with a new policy programme it could make an electoral impact, but the modest increase in its vote in 1964 must have led to concerns that the party was not making the impact it felt it should in Wales. However, the party could still find solace in with-standing the challenge of Plaid Cymru in the seats that it contested, but a political transformation was imminent that would bring a very different political reality to Wales than the one the CPGB hoped to see.

THE CPGB AND THE RESPONSE TO A RESURGENT WELSH NATIONALISM, 1965–1969

The emergence of Plaid Cymru as a political force in the mid- and late 1960s, coupled with the formation of the Welsh Language Society (CYIG) in 1963, in the wake of Saunders Lewis' Tynged yr Iaith (Fate of the Language) BBC lecture, had brought the national question back to prominence in

Welsh politics by the second half of the decade. As with much of the working-class movement, the CPGB was caught off-guard by the nationalist breakthrough and its response was characterised by a prolonged effort between 1966 and 1969 to re-examine and reformulate its approach to the national question and the priority given to it in party policy. Plaid Cymru's electoral breakthrough was a particularly bitter pill to swallow as the nationalists made the breakthrough that the party had laid such stall in achieving themselves, exposing serious organisational weaknesses within the party while raising concerns about its aging demographic and the loss of a younger generation of political activists to nationalism. Faced with a new political reality, the party's attitude towards Plaid Cymru also mellowed somewhat, although tensions remained beneath the surface for some communists.

The communist politics of this period were dominated by the Soviet invasion of Czechoslovakia, which crushed the attempt by the Czechoslovak Communist Party (KSČ) to pursue its own road to socialism outside the confines of the Soviet model. The dispute within the party over the Czechoslovak crisis was a role reversal of the situation in 1956 with the party leadership condemning the Soviet interven-tion and the dissidents supporting it. The party leadership had been sympathetic, despite pressure from the Soviet embassy, to Alexander Dubček's attempts to reform the KSČ and the Czechoslovak state,[147] and issued a statement condemning the Soviet intervention, which precipitated a split amongst the membership. The majority supported the EC, the YCL describing the Soviet action as an invasion, while opposition to the EC coalesced around Dutt and the 'Stalin of Suburbia', Sid French, the hard-line secretary of the Surrey District.[148] As in 1956, the debate that followed consumed the party over the next year, the EC eventually securing the support of most of the Districts, including

[147] Reuben Falber, *The 1968 Czechoslovak Crisis: Inside the British Communist Party* (London, [1996]), pp. 5–10.

[148] Mike Waite, 'Sex 'n' Drugs 'n; Rock 'n' Roll (and Communism) in the 1960s', in Geoff Andrews et al. (eds), *Opening the Books,* pp. 220–1; Falber, *Czechoslovak Crisis,* p. 26.

Wales,[149] as well as that of the 31st Congress, where the EC's position was carried by 292 votes to 118.[150] While the dissidents had been defeated in the short term, the consequences of the split over the Czechoslovak crisis were to have a profound effect on the future course of the party. The leadership's decision to condemn the invasion played an important part in keeping many of the party's young activists in the party, many of whom would go on to develop the Gramscian perspectives that helped push the party towards Eurocommunism in the 1970s and 1980s. On the other hand, unlike in 1956, the defeated dissidents chose to remain within the party, forming a 'permanent opposition' and providing the rump of the opponents to the move towards Eurocommunism.[151] The debates of 1968 thus played a significant role in the evolution and eventual dissolution of the party.[152] The CPGB's decision to condemn the Soviet action, in the face of the opposition of Soviet loyalists within the party, was not only a turning point in terms of the party's 'Soviet complex', the party condemning the Soviet Union for the first time on a major issue, and its internal politics; it also had profound implications for its stance on the national question.[153] In contrast to 1956, when the party's support for the Soviet intervention in Hungary had undermined its commitment to self-determination in Wales, its decision to oppose the Soviet invasion in 1968, and to back the Czechoslovak right to self-determination, gave the party significant credibility as it declared its support for parliaments in Wales and Scotland in 1969.

In some respects, the Welsh party was in a better position to respond positively to the upsurge of nationalism in the mid-1960s having put a Welsh Parliament and language rights back at the centre of its policy agenda during the early

[149] 'Minutes of Welsh Committee September 29, 1968', Bert Pearce Papers WM/10, NLW; Falber, *Czechoslovak Crisis*, p. 25. Only Surrey, Hampshire and Dorset, and North East England voted against.

[150] Falber, *Czechoslovak Crisis*, p. 33.

[151] Falber, *Czechoslovak Crisis*, p. 34.

[152] Geoff Andrews, *Endgames and New Times: The Final Years of British Communism 1964–1991* (London, 2004), p. 95.

[153] The term 'Soviet Complex' is borrowed from John Callaghan; see *Cold War, Crisis and Conflict*, p. 50.

1960s. However, these still remained somewhat abstract concerns for the time being, the party largely focused on electoral work between 1964 and 1966, as it fought two general elections; on the threat to the Welsh economy from the government's spending plans; and on the campaign against the Vietnam War.[154] The party had, however, not been completely oblivious to the emergence of the language movement, an article published in the party's theoretical journal, *Marxism Today*, highlighting the language issue in both Wales and Scotland, and drawing attention to Saunders Lewis' warnings on the dire situation of the language. Almost a decade after Lockwood's unsuccessful attempt to raise the issue in the party press, the article by Tim Enright warned that 'Anglo-American capitalism is unconcerned with the survival of Gaelic or Welsh. On the contrary, they form a barrier in the path of a uniform advertisement-conditioned English speaking market.'[155] Linking the language's decline in the twentieth century to the depopulation of the rural areas during the inter-war years, in which emigration had been directed out of Wales rather than to the industrial south, and to the anglicising influences of the mass media and advertising, Enright warned the language could disappear within a generation if action was not taken immediately to protect it.[156] Pointing, like Lockwood, to the example of the Soviet Union and stressing Welsh's position as an essentially plebeian language, Enright urged the party to take the lead and galvanise the labour movement in support of the language issue, noting that it was not just an issue for the Welsh but for the whole of the British people – who would lose the rich literary tradition associated with Welsh if it was to die out.[157]

The language issue was raised again in December 1965, this time leading to some controversy, in an article by Hywel Williams, who welcomed a report recommending granting

[154] 'Report of the Work of the Welsh Committee from December 1964 to October 1966', pp. 1–2, Bert Pearce Papers WC/6, NLW.
[155] Tim Enright, 'Britain's Minority Languages', *Marxism Today*, August 1964, p. 247.
[156] Enright, 'Britain's Minority Languages', pp. 248–9.
[157] Enright, 'Britain's Minority Languages', p. 253.

Welsh official status. For Williams, while Welsh remained under threat, especially with the decline of the chapels and the Welsh societies associated with them, it was also undergoing somewhat of a revitalisation through the Welsh schools movement, a growth in academic journals and periodicals and through the publication of a new Welsh dictionary by the University of Wales.[158] Williams' optimistic prognosis was met with an attack on the language by Benn Everest, a Welsh Committee member from Swansea, who argued that Williams' appeal to preserve the language reflected a 'predilection for anything "folksy"' amongst British Marxists, a character trait that, for Everest, the CPGB would be better without. Contending that the language had been 'nurtured by the Welsh Nationalist Party' and was viewed by many in Wales 'as merely the instrument for building a nation within a nation', Everest argued that Welsh was not the language of the labour movement, and unable to sustain a daily newspaper had no place in the modern world, dismissing it as 'about as useful as hand-weaving'. For Everest, 'a movement that looks to the "new", "that which is developing not which is dying away"' should allow the Welsh language to wither away.[159]

Everest's intervention was met with universal disapproval by party members from Wales and outside of Wales within the pages of *Comment*, with Everest accused of 'Great English chauvinism' by Royston Green, the Welsh-speaking Cornish secretary of the Celtic Union.[160] For Edgar Evans, Everest's comments betrayed a simple lack of knowledge regarding Wales, and he expressed surprise that a resident of the Swansea Valley would consider Welsh a dead language. While Welsh may not have been the language of the higher echelons of the labour movement, Evans argued that it remained the language of a large section of the rank and file. Noting that the language had survived 'in spite of the efforts that have been made to drive it into oblivion', Evans dismissed the assertion that it was an instrument of the nationalists.

[158] Hywel D. Williams, 'Has the Welsh Language a Future?', *Comment*, 11 December 1965, pp. 797–8.
[159] *Comment*, 1 January 1966, p. 6.
[160] *Comment*, 15 January 1966, p. 45.

The fact that the Welsh Nationalist Movement uses it as a powerful
weapon in their armoury is no argument against its existence. This is
not a Marxist approach to the problem ... The Welsh language is still a
powerful medium of communications. Its songs, poetry and literature
give pleasure to Welsh-speaking and English-speaking Welshmen.
Should the people of Wales be deprived of this heritage? No. We
should encourage and support every effort to place the Welsh
language on at least an equal basis with English.[161]

Hywel Williams, responding to Everest, argued that Welsh
was relevant to the modern world, pointing to the publication of journals such as *Y Gwyddonydd* as an example of its
modernity. Williams, like Evans, also refuted Everest's claim
that the language was merely a tool of the nationalists, noting
'Many zealous Welshmen, whilst campaigning for the
language, sharply disagree with the official line of the Welsh
Nationalist Party.' Another leading Welsh communist, Dai
Dan Evans, also condemned Everest's comments, arguing
that man had the right to enjoy the culture of his nation in
any language he saw fit, a factor that was even truer in the
modern age as he found himself with more time on his
hands. Evans, reminding Everest that in the Soviet Union
and China minority languages were respected and not made
to succumb to the majority culture, noted, 'This is not the
time to denude our language wardrobes but to extend them
in every way possible.'[162]
Everest was thus rebuked for his comments, with leading
communists such as Edgar Evans and Dai Dan Evans leading
the assault, but his views no doubt reflected those of some
communists and of some sections of the wider labour movement. That Everest, a member of the Welsh Committee,
made such forthright views on the language public reflected
at least some dissatisfaction with the party's language policies
within the higher echelons of the Welsh party. His views,
however, were not those of the majority, the party's main
power base, outside the Rhondda, now lying in the valleys of
west Wales, largely Welsh-speaking areas. For men like Dai
Dan Evans, Edgar Evans and Hywel Williams, who all

---

[161] *Comment,* 5 February 1966, p. 95.
[162] *Comment,* 26 February 1966, p. 139.

stemmed from Welsh-speaking backgrounds, Everest's views were clearly untenable, as they were for the majority of the party leadership.

While debate in the party press focused on the Welsh language, the Welsh party was firmly focused on the upcoming general election. The 1966 election, like that of 1964, was viewed as crucial in terms of the party's electoral work, with an Electoral Department set up at King Street, the CPGB's central office, and 57 candidates put up by the party. In Wales the party contested eight seats, Aberavon, Aberdare, Llanelli, Neath, Pontypool, Rhondda East, Rhondda West and Swansea East, the highest number it had ever contested in Wales. The party's campaign was focused on the failure of the Labour Party's policy in Wales, especially the absence of an effective economic plan for the whole of Wales and the increase in pit and railway closures and depopulation. For the party, the Welsh working class's loyalty to Labour had been betrayed with Labour pandering to the needs of monopoly capital rather than those of the Welsh people.[163]

The centrepiece of the party's manifesto was a call for an All-Wales Plan, based on the nationalisation of the key industries, the development of technical education and innovation in Welsh industry, and greater investment in social services, health and housing. The manifesto reiterated its commitment to a Welsh Parliament, which was linked a broader commitment to democratic control in local government and the nationalised industries.[164] In the event, the election results were a disappointment for the party both at the British level and in Wales, the CPGB winning 62,112 votes in the British poll. In Wales, the party's results were mixed, for while the overall vote had increased to 12,769, a further fall in its vote at Rhondda East, the party's electoral stronghold, was a cause of serious concern not just for the Welsh party, but also at King Street. These results were compounded by the party's failure to withstand the nationalist challenge in a number of the constituencies, with Alistair Wilson, Bob Hitchon, Arthur True and W. R. Jones all finishing behind the Plaid Cymru

[163] 'Go One Better For Wales', 1966, p. 2, Bert Pearce Papers WM/8, NLW.
[164] 'Go One Better For Wales', pp. 3–7.

candidate. Even in Rhondda East, where both the CPGB and Plaid Cymru vote had fallen, the gap between the two parties had been reduced to 261 votes.[165]

The extent of the nationalist challenge was made clear following the election of Gwynfor Evans as MP for Carmarthenshire in July 1966 and Vic Davies's close call at Rhondda West in March 1967. Both by-election results were viewed by the party as a reaction by the electorate to the failure of right-wing Labour policy, the electorate's turn to Plaid Cymru seen as an indication that they were eager for change. That Plaid had been successful in mounting a serious challenge to Labour did not come as a total surprise to the party, the Welsh Committee having warned from the late 1950s onwards that the levels of inactivity, apathy and corruption within the Labour Party were turning the electorate against it and allowing Plaid to gain a foothold, while Labour's failure to advance socialist policies was also seen as encouraging the nationalists.[166] The initial reaction to the Carmarthen by-election was cautious, with Bert Pearce noting that while the by-election had been 'a massive rejection of Mr Harold Wilson's policy', Plaid Cymru policy did not offer the solutions to Wales' problems and that 'Carmarthen is a powerful challenge which only a revived and united Left movement can answer.'[167] Other communists were more enthusiastic, John Cox arguing that Pearce had been overly negative in his assessment of Plaid's victory and calling for it to be viewed as an opportunity to build a broader progressive movement rather than as a challenge.

> Prominent Welsh Liberals and Socialists have been quicker to appreciate the positive features of the Nationalist triumph and have been engagingly magnanimous in defeat. There can be little doubt that Welsh (and Scottish) affairs will receive far more Government attention in the future and that such attention can only be to the benefit of the working people of the two nations. The pity is that the Communist

[165] The Plaid Cymru vote was 2,088, compared to 2,349 for Annie Powell, the Communist candidate; at the 1964 General Election, Powell had been 1,024 votes ahead of the Plaid Cymru candidate, Beti Jones, *Etholiadau'r Ganrif 1885–1997*, pp. 111–14.
[166] 'Report to the Political Committee 1958', pp. 6–7; 'Draft Discussion Statement 1964 Welsh Congress', p. 1, Bert Pearce Papers WM/6, NLW.
[167] *Morning Star*, 16 July 1966, p. 5.

Party has not led the fight on the national issues. The election of Gwynfor Evans is not an isolated event. Votes and support for Nationalist parties have increased steadily for some years now while Communist votes have decreased. More attention to genuine local and national grievances might avoid this decline in Communist support. Also to be welcomed is the nature of the Welsh Nationalist Party's general policy. The party is more Socialist than the Welsh Labour Party and has taken part in many Peace demonstrations. It is to be hoped that it will take part in the activities of the united Left, desired by Communists, Socialists and many Nationalists. But this is unlikely to be achieved by statements such as, 'Carmarthen is a powerful challenge which only a revived and united Left movement can answer'.[168]

Cox's letter received a mixed reception, with a number of Welsh communists arguing that while there were progressive elements in Plaid's policy, it was not a socialist party.

For Julian Tudor Hart, who admitted that Evans's victory 'gave me a bit of a kick', Plaid, while taking a progressive stance on some issues, had 'no consistent principles at all' and tended to adopt 'positions of absurdly exaggerated nationalism' that would split the British working class.[169] Pearce himself offered a more measured response to the by-election result in an article in the *Morning Star*, conceding that Evans's victory had 'struck a chord in many Welsh hearts of all political persuasion' and that it 'expressed the widespread desire for an end to the neglect and wasted opportunities which Wales … has suffered through 20 postwar years'. For Pearce, it had illustrated the clear need for the labour movement and the left in Wales to declare itself in favour of a Welsh Parliament and to form the nucleus of a movement for such devolutionary change, made up of socialists, nationalists and other progressives. The Welsh party, Pearce declared, despite opposition to elements of Plaid Cymru policy, was willing to work with Plaid and other nationalists on campaigns in which they shared common interests.[170]

---

[168] *Morning Star,* 20 July 1966, p. 2.
[169] *Morning Star,* 25 July 1966, p. 2.
[170] *Morning Star,* 29 July 1966, p. 2.

The Carmarthen by-election also led the party to begin reassessing its approach to the national question, initiating a debate within the Welsh Committee which saw the party begin to formulate a new policy document on the national question.[171] The party had, in fact, made some progress on the issue prior to the July by-election, the Welsh Committee approving a resolution in favour of a Welsh TUC in June.[172] Carmarthen, however, provided added impetus to the debate prior to the Welsh Congress held that October. A number of resolutions to Congress expressed a concern that the party was not doing enough to get its policy programme over to the Welsh electorate. The Glyncorrwg branch urged the Welsh Committee to publish a pamphlet explaining the party's long-term policy programme for Wales, whilst the Aberdare branch called on the Welsh Committee to publish a policy statement on its proposals for a Welsh Parliament and local government reform. The Welsh Committee itself put forward a number of resolutions related to the national question, in favour of a Welsh TUC, an All-Wales Plan and condemning the failure to halt depopulation and the rundown of areas in south and mid Wales, developments viewed as particularly damaging to Welsh life.[173] At Congress, the party's main innovation was to call for a 'National Convention' of all civil society organisations – political, economic, industrial, social and religious – to draw up an effective programme in order 'to beat back the disaster threatening Wales'.[174] Reiterating its support for a Welsh Parliament, Congress offered support to the 'courageous efforts of our people fighting for equal status for the Welsh language', a clear reference to CYIG's activities while linking the decline of the language to economic issues and migration;

> We make an especial call to the young people of Wales – stay and fight for a career here. Refuse to be driven from Wales. In fighting for your

---

[171] 'Minutes of Secretariat', 30 October 1966, Bert Pearce Papers WM/8, NLW.

[172] 'Minutes of Welsh Committee', 19 June 1966, Bert Pearce Papers WM/8, NLW.

[173] 'Resolutions submitted to Congress, 1966', Bert Pearce Papers WC/6, NLW.

[174] 'Fight the Freeze – To Save Wales: A Declaration of Policy issued by the Welsh Congress of the Communist Party, October 1966', p. 2, Bert Pearce Papers WM/8, NLW.

right to work in your own country you are winning the national future
of your own people. We are for the living future of Welsh life, culture
and language ... Above all the survival of Welsh life and language
depends upon people – people with jobs, and communities with
security.[175]

While Carmarthen had led the party to begin reassessing
its position on the national question, it was Rhondda West
that confirmed the emergence of a new political reality in
Wales. This time a Communist candidate, Arthur True, had
also been standing against the Plaid Cymru candidate and
the party had held great hopes that it would be able to make
significant gains due to the unpopularity of the Labour
Government, but it was to Plaid, rather than the CPGB, that
the electorate turned to express their dissatisfaction. That it
was the Rhondda that had turned to the nationalists was also
a psychological blow to the party, although in reality it was in
Rhondda East that the party had always been strongest electorally, the party contesting Rhondda West for the first time
in the post-war period in 1964. For King Street, the increase
in Plaid's vote signalled that it was now time for the CPGB
and the broader labour movement to realise that it had 'not
only to recognise in words the rights of people to run their
own affairs, but must work to help achieve this aim'.[176]

Similar conclusions were drawn by the Welsh Party, but
Rhondda West had also exposed deeper weaknesses within
the party, its report on the by-election campaign admitting
that Plaid had run a superior campaign, in stark contrast to
the CPGB's which had lacked both funds and bodies on the
ground.[177] The influx of young people to the Rhondda Valley
to canvass support for Plaid drew particular attention, the
report noting that the party had been overreliant on its older
members to do its campaigning and canvassing.[178] The YCL
had been a cause of concern for the party since the early
1950s with membership reaching its nadir in the aftermath
of 1956. The YCL had made a modest recovery in Wales

[175] 'Fight the Freeze – To Save Wales: A Declaration of Policy issued by the Welsh
Congress of the Communist Party, October 1966', p. 4.
[176] *Morning Star*, 13 March 1967, p. 3.
[177] 'Rhondda West By-election', 1967, p. 2, Bert Pearce Papers WM/9, NLW.
[178] 'Rhondda West By-election', p. 3.

during the 1960s with membership up to 178 by September 1962, rising to 203 by June 1967. While this was a significant improvement on the YCL's fate in the 1950s, reflecting a period of overall growth across Britain, the party was becoming increasingly concerned that the new generation of political activists were being won over to nationalism rather than socialism, the Secretariat noting in August 1969 that nationalism remained 'a significant diversion and attraction' to the youth of Wales.[179] Just as ominous for the party's electoral fortunes, and a reflection of their increasing marginality in electoral contests, was the admission by some communist supporters that were going to vote for Plaid in the by-election as they viewed a vote for the nationalists as a more effective protest vote than one for the CPGB.[180] The Welsh party was, however, able to draw some crumbs of comfort from the fact that its vote had not collapsed in the face of the nationalist challenge, with True polling 1,723 votes, only slightly down from the 1966 General Election, but its vote had not risen either and the party had remained on the periphery of the electoral contest, unable to make the breakthrough it had hoped.[181]

Rhondda West had, however, provided a new urgency to the debate on the national question within the party's higher echelons with the issue coming under discussion at the PC in April 1967 and at the EC in July. Serious discussion of the issue on the Welsh Committee had begun in December 1966, with a Secretariat meeting early that month dedicated to the national question in preparation for the upcoming meetings with the party centre, with Bert Pearce, Allan Baker, Joe Berry and Alistair Wilson present. The Secretariat debate was broad, covering the historical and theoretical background of the national question whilst raising questions as to the party's approach to the issue following the Carmarthen by-election. Wilson, introducing the historical background to the national movement, noted that the labour movement had

[179] *Party News*, September 1962, p. 2; CPGB Archive, 'Appendix Minutes of Welsh Committee, June 18, 1967', CP/CENT/ORG/11/01 (LHASC); 'Minutes of Secretariat, August 27, 1969', Bert Pearce Papers WM 11, NLW.
[180] 'Rhondda West By-election', p. 2.
[181] 'Rhondda West By-election', p. 1.

neglected the issue for much of the twentieth century, while the CPGB had itself not begun to engage with the issue until the 1930s and had thus allowed Plaid Cymru to take the national movement out of the hands of the labour movement. Pearce was critical of the party's engagement with the national question in the 1940s, arguing that it had focused too much on history and theoretical issues, which, while helpful, had not answered the practical question facing the party. In turn, the debate in the early 1960s had been hampered by confusion over the scope of a Welsh Parliament, party members unsure whether it meant self-government or separation, with Pearce noting that references to the national question in the *BRS* were unhelpfully short. Debate within the party, Pearce noted, had also been stifled by the perception that the national question was not a major issue and that to place undue emphasis on it would be a diversion from the class struggle and lead to divisions within the ranks of the working-class movement. For Pearce, however, it was now vital that the party engage with the issue and that the most important part of the debate would be how to link the national question to everyday party politics.

Despite this, theoretical debate remained important, the Secretariat defining the nation in terms of Stalin's formula and the right of self-determination. For the Secretariat, the main theoretical questions facing the party in the light of the nationalist upsurge were the need to identify its basic approach to the national question, and the relation of the national struggle to that of socialism, in particular its position on federalism, the scope to be given the Welsh Parliament, Wales' status as a nation, the importance of the national question and why it had emerged as a political force in the 1960s. On a more practical level, the Secretariat identified a number of questions that the Welsh party needed to deal with focusing on the need to better understand Plaid policy and formulate its approach to that party, whether there should be separate political parties for Wales and a trade union movement in the form of a Welsh TUC, what form self-government should take and what specific powers should be granted to a Welsh parliament.[182]

---

[182] 'Staff Study, December 6, 1966', Bert Pearce Papers WM/8, NLW.

The Secretariat's debate laid the basis for discussion that took place on the Welsh Committee in January as it formulated a policy document to put in front of the PC and EC in April and July.[183] The discussion document put before the Welsh Committee argued that national consciousness was growing and would continue to grow in Wales, Plaid's success only one illustration of its growing importance to Welsh politics. It attributed the growth of national consciousness in the post-war era to the impact of national liberation struggles; the continued economic and social exploitation of Wales; disillusionment with right-wing Labour Party policies; and the growth of Plaid Cymru. Plaid's growth was identified as a particular problem for both the party and the labour movement, its policy platform viewed as a mixture of progressive policies on peace, nuclear weapons, Vietnam, economic planning, railway and pit closures and the Welsh language, but essentially reactionary in relation to the class struggle.[184] Noting that the national dimension of Welsh politics was now here to stay, the party and the labour movement were urged to develop their policy and offer their leadership on the national question, whilst endeavouring to bring the national and working-class movements under one united left-wing leadership.[185] The party itself had to develop its own policy in relation to the powers and functions of a Welsh parliament and its relationship with the rest of Britain; the particulars of a Welsh economic plan; the language question; and its approach to raising the national question within the labour movement.[186]

Following further discussion on the national question on the Secretariat in May, the Welsh Committee endorsed a paper outlining its position on the issue at its April meeting in preparation for the PC debate on the national question

[183] 'Minutes of Welsh Committee January 22, 1967', Bert Pearce Papers WM/9, NLW.
[184] 'Brief Notes for Discussion on Problems of Welsh National Development Today', January 1967, pp. 2–3, Bert Pearce Papers WN 2/1, NLW.
[185] 'Brief Notes for Discussion on Problems of Welsh National Development Today', pp. 3–4.
[186] 'Brief Notes for Discussion on Problems of Welsh National Development Today', p. 4.

that month.[187] Encompassing much of what had been included in the January discussion document, the Welsh Committee reiterated that it was vital for the party to engage with the national question and related the growth of nationalism to the crisis of imperialism in Britain and the growth of monopoly capital, which had precipitated economic and social decline in Wales.[188] In particular, the Welsh Committee argued that monopoly capital had had a negative impact on Welsh-language culture, noting that demands for Welsh-language rights while 'real and justifiable' were in conflict 'with the restrictions of capitalist commercialism and the anglicisation which accompanies it'. For the Welsh Committee, the Plaid Cymru near-miss at Rhondda West was a 'protest against economic as well as cultural exploitation', the 'basic element of any national movement' and that any 'attempt to separate the causes of such a "protest vote" into "purely economic" and "purely national"' would lead to a misreading of the development of national consciousness in Wales.[189] Combined with the Labour Party's failure to adequately address Wales' problems, characterised by 'complacency, careerism, nepotism and the worst features of reformism', the electorate was now demanding real political change.

In particular, the Welsh Committee pointed to the Labour Party's lethargy and indifference to the national question, arguing that since 1945 it had largely ignored the issue, retreating from its pre-war positions on home rule, only reluctantly implementing measures such as a Secretary of State and the Welsh Economic Council. The CPGB's own attitude was also criticised, the party having 'done too little to launch any serious campaign to win national demands, or in particular to win the Labour Movement for active support of them'. This failure stemmed from two causes – a tendency amongst party members, contrary to party policy, to think

---

[187] 'Minutes of Welsh Committee, April 16, 1967', Bert Pearce Papers, WM/9, NLW.
[188] 'Communist Policy and Problems of Welsh National Development To-day', 1967, p. 1 & 3, Bert Pearce Papers WN 1/3, NLW.
[189] 'Communist Policy and Problems of Welsh National Development To-day', p. 3.

that self-government was impracticable under capitalism, and to view any struggle for national rights in Wales as diversionary and divisive for the working-class movement.[190] For the Welsh Committee, these attitudes were also 'at the root of the dominant attitude in the movement in England, which is not so much hostile, as indifferent and lacking appreciation of the national question as a matter of any serious, practical significance', a state of affairs encouraged by the failure of the labour movement in Wales to engage meaningfully with the national question and thus challenge these prevailing attitudes.[191]

These were attitudes that had to be overcome; for the Welsh Committee it was only through the united action of the British working class that a Welsh parliament could be achieved while ensuring that the national movement did not become a tool of reaction. The Welsh Committee stressed that a Welsh parliament was now achievable under capitalism, and argued that the real danger of splits and division would emerge 'if the Party and the working-class movement neglects to lead on the national issues and thus leaves them in the hands of sections whose political basis is petty bourgeois and non-socialist ... Ignoring the national question will not cause it to disappear.' This course of action held two dangers: first, the emergence of a non-socialist national movement, which had the potential to penetrate the labour movement and raised the possibility of splits within the trade unions on national lines. Second, the possibility that the national movement itself, without the support of the working class, would become ineffective, giving the British ruling class a free hand in implementing its own brand of reforms.[192]

Thus, for the Welsh Committee, the only solution lay in the formation of a broad national movement comprised of the CPGB, the labour movement, Plaid Cymru and all other organisations willing to co-operate, centred around the

[190] 'Communist Policy and Problems of Welsh National Development To-day', p. 6.
[191] 'Communist Policy and Problems of Welsh National Development To-day', pp. 6–7.
[192] 'Communist Policy and Problems of Welsh National Development To-day', p. 7.

working-class movement and under united left leadership. Co-operation with Plaid Cymru was viewed as crucial, the Welsh Committee noting that 'the wide body of sympathisers with the Welsh nationalist aspirations are voters for Plaid candidates, including some of the best and most youthful sections, many of whom have strongly socialist and communist convictions. The utmost friendly discussion and co-operation with them is vital for the future of Wales and the socialist movement.'[193] Such a movement also held the potential to provide the impetus for building a broader anti-monopoly alliance serving 'as an important new stage in rallying the widest forces against the monopolies, exposing the real ruling class and enabling the struggle for socialism to be carried on in a new way most effectively linked with the struggle for Welsh national fulfilment'.[194]

The Welsh Committee proposed that the party follow three main political lines: first, that the party's recognition of the need for a Welsh Parliament be given a prominent position in the party's policy; second, that it should aim to win the support of the labour movement in order to pressurise the Labour Government into producing proposals on devolution; third, that the campaign be focused on the general principle of national rights to allow the party to develop its detailed position on the issues related to self-government and the national question. In terms of party policy, the Welsh Committee urged the party to recognise the Welsh people's right to decide their own fate, including the right to secession, to support the call for an All-Wales plan and for the preservation and development of the Welsh language.[195] The Welsh Committee also declared its support for a quasi-federal system, based on separate parliaments in Wales and Scotland and a British parliament at Westminster, structured 'to guarantee the rights of the smaller nations … against being overborne by a numerical majority on matters of vital

[193] 'Communist Policy and Problems of Welsh National Development To-day', p. 13.
[194] 'Communist Policy and Problems of Welsh National Development To-day', pp. 7–8.
[195] 'Communist Policy and Problems of Welsh National Development To-day', pp. 8–10.

concern to them'.[196] Central to the Welsh Committee's proposals on federation was a belief that Wales' economic problems could only be solved by access to the economic resources of the whole of Britain used in conjunction with socialist planning. For the Welsh Committee, however, this union had to be voluntary, recognising that the forced union under capitalism had been damaging to the interests of Wales.[197] Turning to the party itself, the Welsh Committee urged the publication of a pamphlet on the party's Welsh policy programme. Furthermore, it stressed the need for the Welsh party to publish its own material in both Welsh and English and for the national question to become an issue for the British party as a whole. Most significantly, the Welsh Committee called for a rule change to allow the Welsh and Scottish parties to be given national rather than district status.[198] This, along with the Welsh Committee's declaration that a Welsh parliament was possible under capitalism, were the most ground-breaking elements of its proposals. The insistence that a Welsh parliament was viable under capitalism, in particular, was a breakthrough, for the party's previous declarations had either explicitly stated that a Welsh parliament was only achievable following the victory of socialism or implied this. It was this formulation that had allowed the party in the 1950s to focus on immediate demands rather than on that of a Welsh parliament, and had given those party members who opposed such a measure a convenient fallback position.

The reaction of the PC to the Welsh Committee's proposals was, however, disappointing with Pearce declaring himself 'taken aback' by its response. For Gordon McLennan, the debate offered nothing new and he declared himself unwilling to put forward an amendment to the party's rules that would allow Wales and Scotland to be given national status. McLennan, instead, argued that for him three main

---

[196] 'Communist Policy and Problems of Welsh National Development To-day', p. 9.
[197] 'Communist Policy and Problems of Welsh National Development To-day', pp. 5–6.
[198] 'Communist Policy and Problems of Welsh National Development To-day', p. 13.

points emerged that needed to be explored further. First, the need to clarify the party's position vis-à-vis the nationalist parties; second, noting that both the Labour Party and TUC were opposed to parliaments in Wales and Scotland, the need to clarify the attitude of the labour movement to the national question, arguing in favour of launching a campaign for a Welsh TUC first; and third, the need to develop the party's public presentation of its case and to increase party education on the issue. Bert Ramelson was more negative arguing that the party had been stampeded into acting on the issue by the Rhondda West and Glasgow Pollock by-elections. For Ramelson, the level of national consciousness had been overstated and while arguing that there was some logic to complete separation, the proposals put forward were 'half-baked', 'glib' and 'superficial', with Ramelson questioning whether plans for separate social and economic planning were compatible with a united labour movement.[199]

Despite this underwhelming response, a joint statement on the 'National Future of Scotland and Wales' received a better reception from the EC in July.[200] Covering much the same territory as the paper delivered to the PC in April, the establishment of parliaments in both countries was now presented as 'a matter of urgency' – a call for the widest possible popular movement, with the labour movement at its heart, to 'be roused to break down the Government opposition and delay on this key issue'.[201] With support apparently growing across Britain, their establishment was now considered an achievable goal as a 'democratic reform long overdue' and 'a major step in uniting the progressive people in those countries in the struggle against the social system which is the main obstacle to their national development'.[202] The new statement also offered some detail as to the

[199] CPGB Archive, Notes of Political Committee, 27 April 1967, CP/CENT/PC/09/16 (LHASC); Bert Pearce's notes of Political Committee, 27 April 1967 [undated] , grouped together with Staff Study notes, Bert Pearce Papers, WM/8, NLW.

[200] CPGB Archive, Notes of Executive Committee Meeting, 8–9 July 1967, CP/CENT/EC/12/02 (LHASC)

[201] CPGB Archive, 'For the National Future of Scotland and Wales', July 1967, p. 3, CP/CENT/EC/12/02 (LHASC).

[202] CPGB Archive, 'For the National Future of Scotland and Wales', p. 4.

composition of these new parliaments calling for single-chamber assemblies elected by proportional representation with sufficient financial resources to allow them to act independently and on their own initiative. Both parliaments were to have responsibility over trade, industry, agriculture, housing, planning, land, fisheries, forestry, education, health, social services, transport, broadcasting, utilities and research and development, with their establishment linked to a broader concern with democratic reform.[203] This statement formed the basis of the EC statement on the national question released in October 1967 which, highlighting the 'distorted and unstable economy' evident in both Wales and Scotland, reiterated the call for the formation of a broad national movement for Welsh and Scottish parliaments.[204] The Labour Party's intransigence on the issue was now identified as the main challenge to the British labour movement in this regard.[205] For some, however, the party's decision to give the national question greater prominence came too late.

For Bill Bowen, a party member from the Rhondda, the statement had certainly come too late with Bowen having left the party and joined Plaid Cymru just prior to the Rhondda West by-election. Bowen, in a letter to Bert Pearce congratulating the party on its new policy pronouncement, noted that he had left the party due to the opprobrium heaped on him by some party members for his stance on the national question. Bowen noted that he had 'been labelled fascist and reactionary by members of the CP because of these views', the breaking point coming with the party's local election committee's declaration that 'people who held the view or sympathised with the cause of Welsh Home Rule were either fools or knaves'.[206] Things had got worse for Bowen once he was elected as a Plaid county councillor, with Cliff True declaring him an 'enemy of the people' in the council

---

[203] CPGB Archive, 'For the National Future of Scotland and Wales', pp. 3–4.

[204] 'The National Future of Scotland and Wales', *Comment,* 21 October 1967, p. 663.

[205] 'The National Future of Scotland and Wales', *Comment,* 21 October 1967, p. 665.

[206] Bill Bowen to Bert Pearce, 17 October 1967, Bert Pearce Papers WD 1/15, NLW.

chamber.[207] Bowen's case, while an isolated incident, is informative as it offers some insight into the negative reaction of some party members to both the national question and Plaid Cymru. Pearce himself was quick to condemn these actions, declaring them out of kilter with party policy, and noted that as it reassessed its attitude to the national question, the party needed members like Bowen within its ranks.[208] While animosity towards Plaid continued to emanate from some party members, there were signs that the party's attitude to the nationalists was mellowing somewhat with Gwynfor Evans given space to put forward the nationalist case in both the *Morning Star* and *Labour Monthly*; Evans paying the CPGB a significant compliment on its stance on the national question noting, 'In contrast to the record of the Labour Party towards self-government stands the honourable record of the Communist Party which for many years has advocated a form of Welsh political autonomy. The Communist policy in this respect avoids undue centralism and is based upon the necessity for the active participation of the people.'[209]

The EC's statement was endorsed at the 30th Party Congress held in November 1967. In the run-up to Congress, debate on the national question focused on federalism and the new draft of the *BRS*, its section on the national question remaining, as Bert Pearce had commented some months earlier in regards to the 1958 edition, unhelpfully short, comprising all of two sentences.[210] On federalism, Idris Cox argued that the party's failure to deal with the issue of an English parliament was a serious omission, while Alan Jones, a party member from Brecon, called on the party itself to adopt a federal structure, in light of its support for Welsh and Scottish parliaments.[211] On the *BRS*, the space given to the national question was criticised as inadequate, its

[207] Bill Bowen to Bert Pearce, undated [c.October 1967], Bert Pearce Papers WD 1/15.
[208] Bert Pearce to Bill Bowen, 19 October 1967, Bert Pearce Papers WD 1/15, NLW.
[209] Gwynfor Evans, 'The Case for Welsh Nationalism', *Labour Monthly*, December 1967, p. 560; *Morning Star*, 6 February 1968, p. 2.
[210] *Draft of the British Road to Socialism* (London, 1967), p. 22.
[211] *Comment*, Congress Discussion Supplement, 18 November 1967.

formulations 'not good enough' according to one Scottish party member who noted that 'the political problems and circumstances are more acute and have always been quite different in each of the four countries concerned, with different backgrounds of history, psychology, culture and language. Our Party claims to have always stood for self-determination and independence for each country; then why does it not act as though it was sincere?'[212] For another, it was 'the neglect and lack of understanding of the national question in Britain which is holding up our advance to socialism'.[213]

Significantly, more space was given to the national question in the published edition, the national claims of Wales and Scotland given their own section, a reflection of the issue's growing prominence. The establishment of a Welsh parliament was now viewed as 'one of the most urgent steps in any real extension of democracy in Britain' with 'National history, democratic right and modern development' combining 'to make this an essential act of justice, which the entire British labour and working class movement will be the foremost to support'.[214] The extension of democratic rights was placed at the centre of the struggle for socialism with 'Every step that extends the people's control over the affairs of the country' viewed as weakening the power of monopoly capital.[215] However, there was less clarity regarding the party's preferred constitutional set-up, the new edition only noting that 'radical constitutional reform is not only necessary for the national development of Scotland and Wales; it is in line with the urgent need for increased popular control and democratic effectiveness in the whole structure of government in England as well'.[216]

Concerns as to the nature of the constitutional set-up the party should endorse were at the heart of the debate that ensued on the national question in the pages of *Marxism Today* following Congress. Initiating the debate, Bert Pearce noted that 'new approaches to the problems of state power

---

[212] *Comment,* Congress Discussion Supplement, 28 October 1967.
[213] *Comment,* Congress Discussion Supplement, 11 November 1967.
[214] *The British Road to Socialism* (London, 1968), p. 41.
[215] *The British Road to Socialism,* p. 39.
[216] *The British Road to Socialism,* p. 42.

and local government, regional democracy and planning' were emerging and that in Wales these developments were 'bound to take on national forms'. Pearce, while supporting the establishment of a Welsh parliament, argued in favour of maintaining the unitary British state 'in some form', while recognising that Wales' experience under it had been negative.[217] For Idris Cox, the main weakness of the party's position was its failure to deal adequately with England, drawing attention to the need to make the issue relevant to English workers if it was to win the support of the British labour movement as a whole.

> To win the demand for separate Parliaments for Wales and Scotland presupposes overwhelming support in England. It is most unlikely this demand can ever be achieved unless it becomes an all-British issue. At the moment England has no stake in the fight for separate Parliaments in Wales and Scotland, unless the aim is also set for a separate English Parliament, and a federal system of government for the whole of Britain.[218]
>
> … It seems to me that there is no solution to the problem except by means of a federal system for Britain in which there is a separate Parliament for England, as well as for Scotland and Wales. In my view this is extremely important, for it is my belief there will never be separate Parliaments for Scotland and Wales unless England gives its backing. Otherwise, the national problem in Britain is contracted out to Wales and Scotland, doomed to linger on as a special minority issue in relation to Britain as a whole, without any hope of a solution.

Cox raised a salient point – the party's approach to federalism and to the implications of devolution for England remained underdeveloped. Cox's argument for an English dimension to the party's plans for federation won the support of a number of other contributors as did his call for the Welsh and Scottish Districts to be granted national status in light of the party's recognition of Welsh and Scottish national rights.[219] However, Cox was on shakier ground as he sought to accommodate Wales into Stalin's definition of a nation,

[217] Bert Pearce, 'The National Future of Scotland and Wales', *Marxism Today*, November 1967, p. 345.
[218] Idris Cox, 'The National Problem in Britain', *Marxism Today*, June 1968, p. 190.
[219] Cox, 'The National Problem in Britain', p. 192.

arguing that as it had never developed a community of economic life,[220] it was better classed as a 'nationality' that was in the process of becoming a nation.[221] Cox was, as another contributor noted, confusing the nation with the state.[222] Cox use of Stalin's definition was striking, however, with Cox himself admitting that Stalin's works had become unfashionable since his death in 1953. However, arguing that a distinction had to be made between Stalin's writings and his actions, Cox noted that his work on the national question, which had won the approval of Lenin and the Bolsheviks, contained 'much that is extremely valuable for a basic analysis of the national problem in Britain today'.[223] Nevertheless, for Pearce, the return to concentrating on Wales' status as a nation was frustrating, 'a stumbling block' which he pointedly related to a tendency within the party to stick to overly rigid definitions of the nation.[224] Nevertheless, the debate in *Marxism Today*, which continued until April 1969, had, for the first time, given prolonged coverage to the debate on the national question in Wales and Scotland in the party press, highlighting the prominence now given to the issue following the nationalist upsurge. The debate had also proved inconclusive, the party's approach to the constitutional changes related to federalism, in particular, remaining unresolved.

While the debate continued in *Marxism Today* during 1968, the party in Wales prepared for the debate on the national question at that year's Welsh Congress. In February, the party had held a day school on the national question.[225] In September, following the Free Wales Army's bombing of the Temple of Peace in Cardiff, the party, responding to George Thomas' call for a cross-party meeting to discuss the

---

[220] Cox, 'The National Problem in Britain', pp. 188–9.

[221] Idris Cox, 'More on the National Problem in Britain', *Marxism Today*, April 1969, p. 124.

[222] B. Ruhemann, 'The National Problem in Britain', *Marxism Today*, August 1968, pp. 251–252.

[223] Cox, 'The National Problem in Britain', p. 189.

[224] Bert Pearce, 'The National Problem in Britain: A Reply to Some Points in Discussion', *Marxism Today*, December 1968, p. 362.

[225] 'One-Day School on Welsh National Problems and Socialism, February 25, 1968', Bert Pearce Papers WM/10, NLW.

bombings, while condemning the violence, argued that it would be more fruitful to organise a meeting of all parties to discuss Wales' economic problems and self-government, arguing that it was 'high time the Government showed some initiative in discussing the practical steps which need to be taken'.[226] However, it was the Welsh Committee's own failure to organise such a meeting which drew the attention of the Welsh Congress, the Glyncorrwg branch reproaching the outgoing Welsh Committee for failing to call the National Convention that had been at the centre of the 1966 Congress' resolution.[227] At Congress, the party called for the establishment of a Welsh parliament, a Welsh TUC and for immediate steps to be taken to solve Wales' economic crisis in the form of an All-Wales Plan,[228] while criticising the labour movement for its failure to engage with the national question.[229] In a further reflection of the prominence of national issues, amongst the branch resolutions adopted at Congress were ones condemning the Investiture and calling for the EC to set up a committee to draw up proposals on a new constitutional settlement.[230] Reviewing the decisions of the Welsh Congress, the Welsh Secretariat agreed to propose to the Welsh Committee that amongst the main campaigns for 1969 would be one 'for a united National Movement for a Parliament for Wales', whilst also giving the go-ahead to the publication of a new theoretical journal for Wales, *Cyffro*.[231] The decision to publish a new journal was significant, the reduction of the party's publishing output since the heyday of the 1940s had been a sign of the party's decline, and was viewed by many party members as having hampered its ability to reach out to the Welsh people. A new journal was viewed

---

[226] 'Press Release, September 15, 1968', Bert Pearce Papers WM/10, NLW.

[227] 'Branch and Emergency Resolutions Welsh Party Congress 1968', Bert Pearce Papers WC/7, NLW.

[228] 'Draft Resolution on the National Future of Wales: Welsh Congress November 1968', pp. 2–4, Bert Pearce Papers, WM/10, NLW.

[229] 'Unity of the Left – The Way Ahead for Wales Draft Resolution for the Welsh Congress of the Communist Party, November 9–10, 1968', pp. 2–3, Bert Pearce Papers WC/7, NLW.

[230] 'Branch and Emergency Resolutions', p. 1; *Morning Star*, 11 November 1968, p. 3.

[231] 'Minutes of Secretariat, 27 November 1968, Bert Pearce Papers WM/10, NLW.

as essential to filling this gap, providing the Welsh party with an important, bilingual forum for debate and a means of disseminating communist policy for Wales to the masses. By the 1970s, *Cyffro* had become an important part of the party's armoury, providing a forum for debate not only between party members but also with others on the left, from within the labour movement, the Labour Party and the nationalist movement.

Following the Welsh Congress the focus on the national question moved to the party's 31st Congress, the Welsh and Scottish Committees in conjunction with the PC developing a major resolution on the issue.[232] The resolution put before Congress was the culmination of three years of debate and discussion within the party and represented the most far-reaching assessment of its position on the national question so far. Welcoming the growth of national consciousness in both Wales and Scotland the resolution linked this to the continued economic exploitation of both countries by monopoly capital, the failure of successive governments to deal with these issues and to 'the worldwide advance of national consciousness and liberation'. While the exploitation of Wales and Scotland was viewed as similar to that suffered in underdeveloped areas of England, the status of Wales and Scotland as nations meant that this exploitation undermined 'the social and cultural existence of nations already suffering from a long history of restrictions on their national rights, institutions and languages'. Significantly, the resolution insisted that a Welsh Parliament was not only achievable under capitalism, but also urgently needed to allow the Welsh people to gain more effective democratic control and allow for more effective planning. Rejecting separatism, Wales and Scotland were to remain part of a unified but federalised state to allow both countries to reap the benefits of the combined resources of all three countries, the Welsh Parliament envisioned as providing the Welsh

---

[232] CPGB Archive, 'Political Committee Agenda, May 22, 1969, CP/CENT/ PC/11/02; Political Committee Agenda, 12 June 1969', CP/CENT/PC/11/03; 'Political Committee Agenda, 17 July, 1969', CP/CENT/PC/11/04; 'Political Committee Agenda, 28 August, 1969', CP/CENT/PC/11/05; 'Political Committee Agenda, 4 September, 1969' CP/CENT/PC/11/06 (LHASC).

people with a stronger, more united voice in a federal British parliament.

The precise details of the powers and functions of the new parliaments were, however, left to be decided at a later date, as was the precise nature of the constitutional relationship between England, Scotland, and Wales. The resolution did, however, offer a broad overview of the powers and functions to be given to both parliaments with powers to be granted over trade, industry, transport, agriculture, social services, health, education, research and development and the media. Ministries were to be set up in both countries and, significantly, both parliaments were to be given finance and tax-raising powers. The Welsh language would be given equal status and the establishment of a Welsh TUC supported. Predicating the establishment of both parliaments on the establishment of a broad popular movement made up of Communists, the Labour Party, nationalists, trade unions and any other civil society organisations willing to co-operate, the party, reflecting the more accommodating brand of Broad Left politics that had emerged within the CPGB by the late 1960s and its move away from the Leninist conception of the vanguard party, did not claim leadership of this movement, instead promising to play 'its full part in helping to develop this campaign throughout the country'. Reflecting the party's commitment to a united British working-class movement, the resolution argued that a campaign must also be developed amongst the English workers in support of these proposals, to be based on arguments related to justice and the struggle for devolution as a new front in the battle against monopoly capital.[233]

Much of the resolution was by now familiar, offering an extension of the statement released by the EC in October 1967 and endorsed at that year's Congress. The Welsh Committee was also vindicated, the resolution supporting many of the recommendations put forward in the position paper presented to the PC in April 1967. The inclusion of tax-raising powers for the Welsh parliament was an important addition offering a solution to the vexed question of

---

[233] *Comment,* 6 December 1969, pp. 780–1.

how these new parliaments were to be funded. However, a failure to delineate the precise powers and functions of the new parliaments reflected the work that the party still needed to do in preparation for the newly established Royal Commission on the Constitution, which had been given a cautious welcome by the party the previous November.[234] The issue of the constitutional relationship between England, Scotland and Wales also remained unresolved, the defeat of an amendment in favour of an English parliament leaving the party's position on federalism underdeveloped.

The debate on the Congress floor was, at times, heated with those opposed to the resolution condemning it as diversionary and a distraction from the class struggle. For John MacDonald, a delegate from Worksop, the party had to be 'ultra-careful' in giving the impression that it supported constitutional change under capitalism as a solution to Wales and Scotland's problems, noting, 'Under the capitalist system, every constitution that has been designed has divided and exploited. International working class solidarity is more important than borders, and that is what we have got to keep in mind.' For other opponents, the establishment of the new parliaments would do little to solve Wales and Scotland's special problems, which could only be solved under socialism. For those in favour, however, for the party to neglect the issue would be suicidal, with Bert Pearce noting that to do so would 'hand the national movement over lock, stock and barrel to reactionary, non-working class leadership. Anyone who cannot see the genuine national feelings which are aroused among thousands of young people in Scotland and Wales today is not a Marxist. He is myopic.'[235] In the event, the resolution was passed with only 11 votes against and 12 abstentions, as was an amendment to the party's rules that gave the Welsh and Scottish parties' national status. Significantly, this amendment was not restricted to a mere titular change but also gave the Welsh and Scottish parties extra powers to develop Welsh and Scottish policy within the broad outlines of the party's general policy – recognising the

---

[234] *Morning Star,* 1 November 1968, p. 1.
[235] *Morning Star,* 19 November 1969, p. 5.

direction the relationship between these sections of the party and the party centre had been heading for much of the post-war period.

The emergence of Welsh nationalism as a serious political force in the late 1960s had forced the party to reassess the priority given to the national question in its politics. By 1969, the party had formulated a concrete policy on the issue and, more importantly, had given the national question consider-able prominence in the party's programme. While much of the new policy had its roots in the pioneering efforts of men like Idris Cox and John Roose Williams in the 1940s, with Pearce himself noting that the conclusions arrived at by the Welsh Committee were 'not radically different from those over 20 years ago',[236] there were significant new dimensions added to the party's policy by the late 1960s. Most significant was the insistence that a Welsh parliament was achievable under capitalism, giving the issue a new prominence in party policy that it had lacked in the period before the late 1960s. The party's abandonment of its insistence on taking the lead role in any national movement was also significant, as, in theory, it made the formation of a broad popular movement easier. Support for giving a Welsh parliament tax-raising powers also gave the party's proposals more credibility, answering the concerns of those within and without the party who questioned how such a parliament would be funded. However, fundamental issues remained unresolved, most notably the form of federalism to be adopted and the details of the power and functions of the new parliaments. As it entered the 1970s and prepared to give its evidence to the Royal Commission, plenty of work remained to be done.

CONCLUSION

The record of the party's engagement with the national ques-tion between 1950 and 1969 was chequered. While the party had begun and finished the period giving some prominence to the issue, during the intervening years the party's interest in the national question had been intermittent. The party

---

[236] 'Staff Study Notes'.

had begun the 1950s by taking, for the first time, a proactive role in the national movement, voting to join the PWC in 1950, but the removal of Idris Cox and the South Wales Area NUM's rejection of a Welsh parliament in 1954 had led to a loss of interest in the issue. While some effort had been made in the late 1950s to devise a policy programme for Wales and to re-engage with the national question, this had been abandoned due to the impact of 1956 on the Welsh party. The main characteristic of the party's approach from 1954 onwards had been its focus on the immediate short-term goal of a Secretary of State, with the party, to a considerable degree, aping Labour Party policy, despite maintaining a commitment to a Welsh parliament in its party programme. The arrival of Bert Pearce saw a more concerted effort to develop a new Welsh policy programme, with the long-term goal of a Welsh parliament given greater prominence in the party's policy on the national question, but it remained a side-issue until the resurgence of nationalism in the mid-1960s. It was only following Carmarthen and Rhondda West that the party once again gave the national question prominence in its party programme, not only in Wales but also at the British level. In this, the party had once again acted reactively in relation to its engagement with the national question, in effect missing the opportunity, as a number of communist commentators noted, to harness national consciousness for the labour movement.

Despite missing this particular bus, the party had, during this period, taken some important steps in its approach to the national question. The most significant was its insistence from the mid-1960s onwards that a Welsh parliament was achievable under capitalism. The party's previous assertion that a Welsh parliament would have to wait until the transition to socialism had been a key factor in dampening down the support for its establishment amongst party members, providing those opposed to the measure a convenient fall-back position, making the national question seem an irrelevant issue in immediate terms and allowing the party to focus on short-term goals in the aftermath of the failure of the PWC. The abandonment of this position and the increasing insistence that the fight for a Welsh parliament and national rights was now a key factor in the immediate fight for socialism and against monopoly capital was key to returning the issue to prominence in the late 1960s. This return to prominence was also helped by the party's increasing focus on the extension of democratic rights, precipitated by the publication of the new party programme in 1951. As the party further developed its programme in subsequent editions and began taking parliamentary politics more seriously, it also began to take the reform of the British political system and British state more seriously. The change of emphasis in the *BRS* in relation to the national question in Wales from a Cold War focus on British national independence to a broader commitment to the extension of democratic rights in the editions of 1958 and 1968 is evidence of this. By the 1968 edition the considerable coverage given to the issue in the party programme was a reflection of the importance placed on the issue. This process was also symptomatic of the party's move towards an increasingly post-Leninist form of politics that now took the parliamentary road and parliamentary reform seriously.

Weaknesses, however, remained in the party's engagement with the national question. The failure to adequately deal with the constitutional implications of devolution for Wales, Scotland and England remained a major flaw, the party having some difficulty in formulating its approach to federalism in the UK. However, this was a problem that was not specific to the CPGB and it is an issue that has remained a problem for all the unionist parties since devolution. In addition, the party's insistence that any constitutional change was reliant on the support of a united British working-class movement was also problematic. As the party acknowledged at times, the labour movement in England and at the British level remained indifferent, if not hostile, to the question of Wales's national rights, and Cox was surely right to suggest that to ensure their support the party had to give them a stake in the devolutionary process. Finally, the party, despite its admirable commitment to Welsh-language rights, had allowed its own internal commitment to bilingualism to falter, especially in terms of its publishing output in the Welsh language, which amounted to precisely nothing. While this was largely attributable to the party's dire financial situation throughout the period, the Welsh party failing to publish many pamphlets in English as well, comparison with the immediate post-war period, when the party made a concerted effort to become central to Welsh cultural life, leaves the party in the 1950s and 1960s fairing badly. It was only at the end of the 1960s with the publication of *Cyffro* that the party began to rectify this situation. Despite these weaknesses, the Welsh party entered the 1970s with the national question again at the centre of its policy programme. The basis laid down first by the pioneers on the national question in the 1940s and then by the efforts of the late 1960s allowed the party to take an active role in the battles over devolution in the 1970s and 1980s. The party would further develop its attitude to constitutional change as it gave evidence to the Royal Commission and campaigned in favour of a Welsh Assembly in the 1979 referendum. The party was also to play a key role in the formation of a Wales TUC in 1974. The development of Eurocommunism and of Gramscian perspectives within the party would also impact on the national question, especially in terms of the party's relationship with the nationalist movement. By the 1980s, while the party became increasingly marginalised as it fought an internal battle that would lead to its eventual dissolution, party members were prominent on the Campaign for a Welsh Assembly. The foundations for this next stage had, however, been laid in the 1940s and late 1960s.

4

DEVOLUTION, DEFEAT AND DISSOLUTION, 1970–1991

The final two decades of the CPGB's existence were marked by an increasingly bitter internal party conflict whose roots lay in the decisions taken by the party over Czechoslovakia in 1968 and in the emergence of Eurocommunism within the leading Western European communist parties. Within the CPGB, the Eurocommunist wing of the party, heavily influenced by the work of Antonio Gramsci and associated with the party's theoretical journal *Marxism Today*, had, by the late 1970s, gained significant political ground. This shift was evident in the new edition of the *BRS*, published in 1978, which adopted a number of key Eurocommunist positions. By the mid-1980s the party's EC, seeking a new means to counter Thatcherism and the rise of the New Right, had been won over to Eurocommunist positions. However, the publication of the *BRS* had led to the first of two splits from the party, with the formation of the New Communist Party (NCP) in 1977, under the leadership of Sid French. A second, more serious split emerged in the 1980s between the leadership and the Communist Campaign Group (CCG), organised around the *Morning Star*, which led to the loss of the party paper and the formation of the rival Communist Party of Britain (CPB). The disintegration of the party during the 1980s was in stark contrast to the relatively influential position in which the party had found itself during the first half of the 1970s, its involvement in the industrial struggles of the early 1970s, arguably its most influential period since the anti-fascist struggles of the 1930s. However, the party failed to capitalise on this period of industrial militancy, party membership remaining stagnant between 1970 and 1974, followed by a period of significant decline – between 1975 and 1979 party membership dropped from 28,519 to 20,599, a pattern that was to be replicated during the 1980s.[1]

[1] Thompson, *The Good Old Cause*, p. 218.

Nevertheless, during the 1980s the party remained a significant presence on the left, playing an important role in a number of domestic and international campaigns. Electorally, the party's share of the vote continued to decline in both general and local elections, while the YCL was disbanded due to a lack of members. As the party imploded, the only real success the party could point to was *Marxism Today*, which had, by the early 1980s, transformed itself into a significant forum for theoretical and strategic debate on the left, increasingly influential in its analysis of Thatcherism. Along with the annual Communist University of London this pointed to a new direction for the party as a facilitator and initiator of discussion on the left, a role it sought to fully embrace on its dissolution into the Democratic Left in 1991. By the late 1980s, the party had formally rejected Marxism-Leninism, its final party programme *Manifesto for New Times* making the case for a new form of post-Fordist politics.[2] International events had, however, overtaken the party, the collapse of communism in the Eastern Bloc leading to a further period of reassessment. Faced with a dwindling membership – down to 7,615 by 1989 and to 4,742 by July 1991[3] – and a new political reality following the fall of communism, what remained of the party voted to transform itself into the Democratic Left at its final Congress in November 1991.

In Wales, the party was to play a significant role in the industrial struggles of the period, as well as in a number of domestic and international campaigns. Despite this, the 1970s and 1980s were characterised by serious financial and organisational difficulties, marked by a dwindling membership and stagnant or inactive branches. The publication of the Welsh party's journal, *Cyffro*, allowed it to make some inroads into the broader political sphere, becoming an important forum for debate on the left in Wales. However, its infrequent publication pointed to the deeper financial and organisational problems afflicting the party. While some pride and psychological respite was to be found in the

[2] *Manifesto for New Times: A Strategy for the 1990s* (London, 1990).
[3] Thompson, *The Good Old Cause*, p. 218.

election of Annie Powell as mayor of the Rhondda in 1979, electorally, as in the rest of Britain, the Welsh party's efforts were a tale of dwindling returns, although it could at least lay claim to some relative success in the continued election of Communist councillors at the local elections up until the party's dissolution in 1991. The 1980s were to witness two changes of leadership, with Dave Richards replacing Bert Pearce as Welsh secretary in 1984, and Richards himself replaced by Les Skeats in 1990. Despite some disagreement over the new edition of the *BRS*, the party in Wales largely accepted the change of direction undertaken by the party under Eurocommunist leadership. During the two splits, in 1977 and the mid-1980s, the party membership, as a whole, remained loyal to the leadership, with only a handful of Welsh party members joining the NCP and the CPB. The Welsh party, unlike the party in Scotland, largely acquiesced in its dissolution, although differing perspectives as to the direction the party should take were also evident in Wales.

The Welsh party remained engaged with the national question for much of the period, becoming an active participant in the extended devolution debate of the 1970s, putting forward its own recommendations to the Royal Commission on the Constitution, maintaining a critical commentary at the various stages of the debate, and affiliating to the Wales for the Assembly Campaign in the run-up to the 1979 Referendum. Party members also played an important role in the formation of the Wales TUC in 1974, while the party sought to initiate a broader level of discussion on the national question through the pages of *Cyffro* and through the organisation of cross-party conferences. Despite this, relations between the Welsh party and Plaid Cymru were at times strained, a situation partly remedied by the leftward turn within Plaid and within the broader nationalist movement following the referendum defeat, and by the new perspective of the broad democratic alliance (BDA) adopted by the CPGB from 1977 onwards. Preoccupied with the impact of Thatcherism on Wales, the national question disappeared from view as a major issue for the Welsh party during much of the 1980s, although it maintained a commitment to a Welsh assembly with legislative powers throughout. Real interest in the issue was only reignited in 1987 when it became part of the Campaign for a Welsh Assembly. This was to be its last significant contribution on the national question.

'KILBRANDON'S TIME BOMB': THE CPGB AND THE DEVOLUTION DEBATE IN WALES, 1970–1979

The 1970s were to witness, with the emergence of Eurocommunism, a significant realignment within the international communist movement. A set of common principles rather than a common programme, Eurocommunism emerged as a significant force within the PCI, the Spanish Communist Party (PCE) and the PCF during this period, the PCI under Enrico Berlinguer its driving force. Each of these parties in a set of joint declarations released in 1975 and 1977, committed themselves to three key principles. First, a commitment to achieving the transition to socialism through peaceful, gradual and democratic means. Second, a commitment to the absolute independence of communist parties. Third, a commitment to an independent Europe that was free from either American or Soviet influence.[4] The focus placed on democratisation by the three parties inevitably added a fourth dimension, the need to democratise the communist parties themselves. Rejecting the Leninist revolutionary model, for the Eurocommunist parties, revolutionary change was envisaged as a gradual process to be achieved through the democratisation of state structures and of society. Central to this strategy was the decentralisation of power and the building of broad alliances and popular movements, best illustrated by the PCI's 'historic compromise',[5]

---

[4] 'Joint Declaration of the Italian and Spanish Communist Party, July 12 1975' in Peter Lange and Maurizio Vannicelli (eds), *The Communist Parties of Italy, France and Spain: Postwar Change and Continuity* (London, 1981), pp. 357–8; 'Joint Declaration of the French and Italian Communist Parties, November 15, 1975' in ibid., pp. 358–60; 'Joint Declaration by the PCE, PCF and PCI, March 3, 1977' in ibid., pp. 360–1. On Eurocommunism, see Santiago Carrillo, *'Eurocommunism' and the State* (London, 1977); for a sympathetic yet critical analysis, see Fernando Claudin, *Eurocommunism and Socialism* (London, 1978); for a more hostile analysis, see Ernest Mandel, *From Stalinism to Eurocommunism* (London, 1978).

[5] On the historic compromise see Enrico Berlinguer, 'Reflections After the Events in Chile', *Marxism Today*, February 1974, pp. 39–50.

with greater democratic control viewed as both a central component of socialism and the means by which society could be mobilised for a transition to socialism. This commitment to a democratic road to socialism was a concerted attempt by these parties to break with the last vestiges of Stalinism evident in the invasion of Czechoslovakia, to distance themselves from the negative, authoritarian connotations linked to Soviet-style communism, whilst offering an alternative form of communism that was better suited to western European conditions. This necessarily entailed an acceptance of, and accommodation with, the bourgeois democratic structures and institutions of the liberal-democratic western European state.

As we saw in the previous chapter, the focus on democracy found in Eurocommunism had also been an increasingly important factor in the CPGB's propaganda and political strategy during the 1950s and 1960s. The publication of an EC statement on 'Questions of Ideology and Culture', drawn up by the party's Cultural Committee in 1967, had been another significant step in this direction, the party coming out in favour of scientific, artistic and religious freedom, rejecting dogmatic approaches to ideological and cultural issues and reiterating its commitment to a democratic road to socialism.[6] Support for Eurocommunist positions within the CPGB came largely from a group of increasingly influential party intellectuals that were representative of an emergent British Gramscian tradition and whose reading of Gramsci coincided with a number of the positions taken up by the PCI and PCE, Gramsci having a 'prolonged, deep and diversified' influence on the British Marxist tradition from the 1970s onwards.[7] The publication of a new edition of the BRS in 1978 marked a significant, if qualified, victory for this group of party intellectuals. For this group the CPGB's strategy was overly economistic, focused too heavily on the industrial sphere, whilst ignoring other important dimensions of politics such as ideology and culture and

---

[6] 'Questions of Ideology and Culture: Statement from the Executive Committee of the Communist Party of Great Britain', *Marxism Today,* May 1967, pp. 134–8.

[7] David Forgacs, 'Gramsci and Marxism in Britain', *New Left Review,* 176, July–August 1989, p. 70.

underestimating the role of non-class actors such as the emergent social movements, including the Welsh and Scottish national movements. The common defining feature of these disparate groupings was viewed as lying in their pursuit of greater democratic rights. The new edition of the *BRS* was a significant advance for these party intellectuals, placing a number of their key ideas at the centre of the party's strategy. Amongst these key concepts was an acceptance of a broader definition of the working class,[8] of the role that consent played in maintaining class rule,[9] and the inclusion of the concept of the BDA, the main vehicle, along with a Labour Government of a new type, through which the new party programme envisioned the transition towards a socialist society taking place. However, while this advance marked a significant change in the party's strategy, the new *BRS* was also a compromise document, introducing a number of the Gramscians' key strategic concepts while maintaining a level of continuity with previous editions of the *BRS*.[10]

Recognising the need to transcend the sectionalism and defensive posture of the working-class movement and noting the failure of the industrial militancy of the early 1970s to bring about any tangible progress in political terms, the new *BRS* argued that the working class had to seek broader alliances that would allow it to build a movement strong enough to challenge capital, develop an alternative policy and broaden the arena of struggle. In contrast to the anti-monopoly alliance put forward in previous editions of the *BRS*, the alliance proposed in the new edition was to be based on uniting those forces who were seeking an extension of democratic rights. For the *BRS*, this was the 'common thread' running through the various struggles engaged in by the working-class movement, the CPGB and the new social movements, which, if unified, could mount a significant challenge to capitalism.[11] Explicit in the BDA was a recognition that not all forms of oppression could be reduced to class oppression

---

[8]   *The British Road to Socialism* (London, 1978), pp. 18–19.
[9]   *The British Road to Socialism*, pp. 8–9.
[10]   Andrews, *Endgames and New Times*, p. 165; Forgacs, 'Gramsci and Marxism in Britain', pp. 80–1.
[11]   *The British Road to Socialism* (4th edition), p. 17.

and that the party had to pursue alliances with those social forces and movements that did not belong to a particular class or which spanned several classes.[12] The new strategy also stressed the need for the working-class movement to broaden its outlook to encompass the arenas of ideology and culture.[13] With revolutionary change viewed as a gradual, 'complex, difficult and many sided process',[14] the BDA was viewed as the key component in the transition to socialism. This was not only in terms of building a mass movement that could put forward alternative policies and help push the Labour Party and future Labour governments leftwards, but also as the arena in which new forms of participatory democracy could be developed through new forms of popular organisation. This in turn would help democratise political power, in combination with efforts by successive left governments to democratise and devolve the power of the state.[15]

Thus, the BDA, with its theoretical roots located in Gramsci's concepts of hegemony and the hegemonic bloc, as well as in the type of alliances advocated by the Eurocommunist parties, marked a significant development and change of focus for the party. The BDA was also controversial, open to a number of interpretations. For its Gramscian advocates, the adoption of a new strategy of alliances was a vital contribution to the renewal of the left and a change sorely needed in view of the changes in British society, in particular in terms of class structure, the emergence of new social movements and the strains evident within Britain's political system, exemplified by the emergence of minority parties, such as the nationalists, as significant political forces.[16] For its opponents, it was viewed as devaluing both the party's industrial work and class politics, effectively abandoning the concept of working class leadership.[17] These

---

[12] *The British Road to Socialism,* p. 29.
[13] *The British Road to Socialism,* p. 10.
[14] *The British Road to Socialism,* p. 37.
[15] *The British Road to Socialism,* pp. 45–6.
[16] Dave Cook, 'The British Road to Socialism and the Communist Party', *Marxism Today,* December 1978, pp. 370–1.
[17] Mick Costello, 'The Working Class and the Broad Democratic Alliance', *Marxism Today,* June 1979, pp. 173–4.

issues would be at the heart of the divisions that characterised the party debate in the 1980s.

The 1970s were a difficult decade for the Welsh party. In
line with the British party, the 1970s saw a further decline in
party membership in Wales, dropping from 1,815 in 1970 to
1,336 by 1979,[18] while electorally the party's vote dropped
from 6,459 in 1970 to 4,310 in 1979.[19] The party was able to
maintain a presence in local government throughout the
decade, gaining a significant boost with the election of Annie
Powell as mayor of the Rhondda in 1979, but even here signs
of decline were evident. By November 1976, day-to-day issues
had also become a major problem, the party undergoing
serious financial difficulties and forced to relinquish one of
its three full-time party workers.[20] By October 1977, it was
struggling to even cover some of its most basic costs, unable
to pay the wages of its two remaining full-time party workers,
and forced to request financial assistance from the party
centre, Bert Pearce noting that the 'the gap between our
income and our essential needs remains huge'.[21] Continuing
to struggle with these financial woes, by 1980 the Welsh party
had been forced to reduce its full-time staff to one.[22] Despite
these difficulties, the party continued to play an active part in
Welsh politics, taking a significant role in the pivotal strikes
of the early 1970s and in the formation of the Wales TUC,
whilst maintaining an active role in the decade-long devolution debate. The party was also active in the campaigns
against the Industrial Relations Act and the Social Contract,
in campaigns against racism, for women's rights, for nuclear
disarmament, against apartheid and in solidarity with Chile,
Vietnam and other international causes. Through the publication of *Cyffro* it was also able to provide a significant forum

[18] 'Membership and Dues Report, 31st December 1970', Bert Pearce Papers WD
2/3, NLW; 'Welsh Committee Report of Work January 1979–October 1980', p. 4,
Bert Pearce Papers WC/13, NLW

[19] Beti Jones, *Etholiadau'r Ganrif 1885–1997,* pp. 115 and 127.

[20] 'The Communist Party – Welsh Committee: Report of Work, January 1975–
November 1976', p. 1, Bert Pearce Papers WC/11, NLW.

[21] CPGB Archive, Bert Pearce to Dave Cook, 1 October 1977, CP/CENT/
ORG/11/2 (LHASC).

[22] Bert Pearce and Dave Richards to Party Members, undated [c.October 1980],
Bert Pearce Papers WC/13, NLW; *The Welsh Communist,* 12 November 1980, p. 3.

for debate for the Welsh left during the 1970s, its pages open not only to party members but also to the Labour Party, Plaid Cymru, CYIG and to the left and progressive movement in general.

Within Welsh politics, devolution was to become the defining issue of the decade, the establishment of the Royal Commission on the Constitution in 1969 ensuring that it remained an ever-present issue. That this was the case was due to the slow progress of the Royal Commission itself, the Labour Government's prevarication over the issue and the tortuous path of the devolution legislation through Parliament during the latter half of the decade. Thus, the decade-long devolution debate which began with the Royal Commission was only to culminate with the referendums of 1979. Having further developed its position on the national question during the late 1960s, culminating with the 31st Congress resolution, the CPGB entered the 1970s better prepared to give evidence to the Royal Commission. The decade had, however, begun inauspiciously for the Welsh party, the 1970 General Election, fought on a platform of an extensive plan for the economic and social regeneration of Wales, the establishment of a Welsh Parliament and opposition to the Common Market, proving a significant setback for the party, its vote dropping to almost a half its 1966 figure, falling from 12,769 to 6,459.[23] Nevertheless, the party's manifesto had taken a robust position on the national question arguing, in line with a new analysis of the Welsh economy published in the previous winter's edition of Cyffro,[24] that the establishment of a Welsh Parliament, along with the nationalisation of key industries and the provision of adequate resources for redevelopment, was a prerequisite for the social and economic revival of Wales.[25] However, the only party to make a significant advance in the election in Wales had been Plaid who, despite losing its seat at Carmarthen, had increased its share of the national vote

---

[23] Jones, *Etholiadau'r Ganrif,* pp. 111 and 115.
[24] Tom Drinkwater, 'Wales Needs a New Economy', *Cyffro,* 1 (2), Winter 1969, p. 19.
[25] *Let Wales Lead the Socialist Way,* pp. 9–10.

from 4.3 per cent in 1966 to 11.5 per cent in 1970.[26] For the party, Labour's failure to deal with the national question had contributed to its drop in support.[27] Indeed, for some within the party, the election result signalled the need for the labour movement to build an alliance with the national movement, a position backed by the Welsh Committee.[28] The task now facing Welsh Communists was to convince the national movement of the merits of socialism and the labour movement of the merits of the struggle for Welsh national rights.[29]

However, the party's main focus in terms of the national question in 1970 was on the evidence it was to submit to the Royal Commission on the Constitution. The CPGB was to present three memorandums of evidence, one from the party centre, one from the Welsh Committee and one from the Scottish Committee, which were to provide the basis for the party's policy on the national question for the next two decades. Rejecting the existing constitutional settlement, the CPGB, while dismissing the Scottish and Welsh Grand Committees as inadequate and unrepresentative,[30] nevertheless argued that their mere existence was a 'recognition of the need for some special parliamentary treatment of the affairs of these countries'.[31] Similarly, the fact of Wales and Scotland's nationhood was evident not only in their distinctive history, culture and institutional presence, but also in the administrative devolution of power that had already taken place. This had led to the growth of the Welsh and Scottish Offices into powerful government departments responsible for an increasing number of policy areas. However, despite this growth of government machinery in Wales and Scotland, its failure to offer any actual degree of democratic control

[26] Jones, *Etholiadau'r Ganrif,* pp. 111 and 115.
[27] 'For Wales – Oust the Tories – Take the Socialist Road', Draft resolution for 1970 Welsh Congress, p. 4, Bert Pearce Papers, WC/8, NLW; Alistair Wilson, 'Editorial Notes', *Cyffro,* 1 (3), Summer 1970, p. 9.
[28] Wilson, 'Editorial Notes', p. 6; 'The General Election and the Way Ahead (Decisions of the Special Welsh Committee)', 6 July 1970, Bert Pearce Papers WM/12, NLW.
[29] Wilson, 'Editorial Notes', p. 9.
[30] 'Memorandum submitted by the Communist Party of Great Britain' in *Commission on the Constitution: Minutes of Evidence IV: Scotland:* London, 1971, pp. 59–60.
[31] 'Memorandum submitted by the Communist Party of Great Britain', p. 60.

and its increasingly bureaucratic nature was viewed as having only led to dissatisfaction with the existing constitutional settlement. Only by bringing this government machinery under the democratic control of Welsh and Scottish parliaments could the situation be rectified, the party centre reiterating its call for their establishment.[32] Backed up by the memorandum from the party centre, the Scottish Committee's memorandum was the shortest and least detailed of the three submitted by the party. For the Scottish Committee, a Scottish Parliament was needed on the grounds of greater democratic accountability and the uneven development of Scotland in relation to other parts of Britain, the measures of devolution already implemented having failed to quell the desire among the Scottish people for self-government.[33] The establishment of a Scottish parliament was a matter of national justice, the national dimension compounding the negative impact of uneven development.[34] Its establishment was at once a means of extending democratic rights, of providing a better platform to address Scotland's social and economic problems and of giving the Scottish people a new institutional focus. However, reflecting the party's unionist ethos, the call for a Scottish Parliament was reinforced with a commitment to the need for a united British working-class movement as a prerequisite for defeating monopoly capitalism at the British level.[35]

The Welsh Committee's submission, drawn up by Bert Pearce and Alistair Wilson,[36] was the most detailed and far-reaching of the three submissions. Arguing that constitutional matters could not be divorced from economic and social factors, the Welsh Committee sought to link devolution with the broader issues of planning and the democratic control of the economy.[37] Wales' interests were viewed as best served by

[32] 'Memorandum submitted by the Communist Party of Great Britain', pp. 60–1.
[33] 'Memorandum submitted by the Scottish Committee of the Communist Party' in *Commission on the Constitution: Minutes of Evidence IV: Scotland*, p. 63.
[34] 'Memorandum submitted by the Scottish Committee of the Communist Party', pp. 63–4.
[35] 'Memorandum submitted by the Scottish Committee of the Communist Party', p. 64.
[36] Interview with Mary and Tony Winter, 20 February 2009.
[37] 'Memorandum submitted by the Welsh Committee of the Communist Party' in *Commission on the Constitution: Minutes of Evidence V: Wales* (London, 1972), p. 159.

remaining part of the United Kingdom, both in terms of maintaining the strength of the British trade union and socialist movement, and also in terms of its own national development, a redistribution of the combined resources of the three nations and the implementation of co-ordinated socialist planning seen as the most effective means of overcoming Wales' economic and social problems.[38] However, while committing itself to the unity of the British state, the Welsh Committee included the proviso that this had to be on the grounds that Wales' national rights were recognised, the Welsh Committee endorsing both the establishment of a Wales TUC and a Welsh Parliament.[39] While Wales' problems were the result of 'the social anarchy of industrial capital', a 'radical measure of self-government' was viewed as vital to addressing Wales' specific needs and resolving the issue of national rights.[40] Recognising that the process of administrative devolution was a positive development, leading to the construction of an extensive government machinery in Wales, this process was nevertheless viewed as contradictory, leading to the creation of an 'administration divorced from popular control'. No extension of the Welsh Grand Committee would be able to adequately address this issue or those issues that were vital to Wales' social and economic life, lacking as it did any legislative function or the degree of transparency and interest that an elected Welsh Parliament would be able to muster.[41]

Its establishment, viewed at its most basic level as a recognition of Welsh nationhood, was seen as the only effective means of facilitating the process of developing a national economic and social plan that could reverse Wales' economic and social decline, the result of years of uneven development.[42] Wales' economic problems were also given a distinct

[38] 'Memorandum submitted by the Welsh Committee of the Communist Party', pp. 159–60.
[39] 'Memorandum submitted by the Welsh Committee of the Communist Party', p. 162.
[40] 'Memorandum submitted by the Welsh Committee of the Communist Party', p. 160.
[41] 'Memorandum submitted by the Welsh Committee of the Communist Party', p. 164.
[42] 'Memorandum submitted by the Welsh Committee of the Communist Party', p. 163.

cultural dimension. The Welsh Committee, while acknowledging that Wales shared some of the problems of the deprived regions of England, argued that in conjunction with 'discrimination over the centuries against our national rights and our language', Wales' underdevelopment had undermined 'a distinct national heritage and culture'. Thus, central to the party's concerns was the impact that economic and social depravation was having on Welsh culture and, in particular, on the fate of the Welsh language. If the language was 'to survive in life and not simply in the museum' then its basis in everyday life had to be secured, which was in turn dependent on securing Wales' economic growth in order to stem the tide of depopulation in Welsh-speaking areas through the creation of economically sustainable communities. For the Welsh Committee, 'no cultural revival can be deep-rooted or fruitful in the absence of the political and economic growth as a national community'.[43] Its establishment was also seen as an opportunity to create a new, more participatory, form of democracy in Wales, the Welsh Committee putting forward ambitious plans for the democratisation of the planning process as a means of wresting popular control over the process of state intervention in a way not envisioned at Westminster, of creating an 'effective democracy to suit modern needs'.[44]

The Welsh Committee proposed a 108-member single-chamber assembly, elected by proportional representation with tax-raising and extensive legislative powers. The Westminster Parliament was to maintain control over defence, foreign affairs, overseas trade, currency and electoral law, whilst also having the overall power to legislate in terms of the main objectives of general economic and social planning which would be worked out in conjunction with the Welsh and Scottish Parliaments. In turn, the Welsh Parliament was to have responsibility over drawing up and implementing an economic and social plan for Wales within the general outlines agreed at the British level, have control

[43] 'Memorandum submitted by the Welsh Committee of the Communist Party', p. 160.
[44] 'Memorandum submitted by the Welsh Committee of the Communist Party', p. 165.

over the location and direction of industry, and over the nationalised industries which were to be controlled by all-Wales boards. The Welsh Parliament, with its own executive, would take over all the responsibilities of the Welsh Office, while the Secretary of State was to be retained as the representative of the Welsh Parliament at Cabinet level with the role of representing Welsh interests and assisting in building the relationship between the two parliaments.[45] The Welsh Committee's position on the division of powers was vaguer, their delineation to be agreed in a new federal constitution. However, the very fact of the establishment of a Welsh Parliament was viewed as placing Wales in a stronger negotiating position than it was under the existing constitutional settlement, its establishment a means of institutionalising many of the tensions that were already present in the system, allowing them to be directed into more positive channels and providing an institutional focus for Welsh public opinion.[46] Conceding that the ultimate power of decision lay at Westminster, Bert Pearce noted that the Welsh parliament would retain the right of secession, should its wishes be consistently ignored at Westminster.[47] In addition, any new constitutional settlement was to be based on a reassessment and redefinition of what constituted British interests.[48] Pearce also rejected the assertion that an elected assembly would lack credibility by becoming a focus for protest votes against the incumbent at Westminster, arguing that the Welsh electorate was mature enough to vote on Welsh issues, offering an insightful analysis that tallies with the voting patterns seen at Assembly elections since devolution.[49]

The Welsh Committee's memorandum was met with a positive response, Lord Crowther, the commission's chair,

    [45] 'Memorandum submitted by the Welsh Committee of the Communist Party', pp. 167–9.
    [46] 'Memorandum submitted by the Welsh Committee of the Communist Party', p. 167.
    [47] 'Memorandum submitted by the Welsh Committee of the Communist Party', pp. 171–2.
    [48] 'Memorandum submitted by the Welsh Committee of the Communist Party', pp. 172–3.
    [49] 'Memorandum submitted by the Welsh Committee of the Communist Party', pp. 174–5.

recognising that its pursual of the middle ground between Plaid Cymru and the Welsh Council of Labour's proposals made it 'extremely interesting, and very helpful'.[50] By seeking the middle ground, the Welsh Committee believed that its proposals for a legislative Welsh Parliament within a quasi-federal governmental framework answered the deficiencies present in both those parties' submissions. Plaid's support for political independence was viewed, in practical terms, as leaving Wales economically dependent on the interests of monopoly capital, with large areas of economic policy essentially being formulated in the boardrooms of the large British and multinational companies. For the Welsh Committee, this offered in reality only a 'nominal independence', and would weaken the strength of the working-class movement at both the Welsh and British level as they divided along national lines. On the other hand, the proposals put forward by the Welsh Council of Labour were viewed as 'so minimal as not to touch the essential problem'. Its proposals for administrative devolution in the form of an elected Welsh Council were dismissed as 'so vague and fragmentary as to be totally unconvincing' and unlikely to 'satisfy the demand for more popular control over Welsh affairs, but rather to increase frustration because of its ineffectiveness'. For the Welsh Committee only its proposals, which would allow the legislative assemblies to develop a working partnership with a central British Parliament, could bring about an effective form of devolution.[51]

In its three submissions to the Royal Commission, the CPGB had put forward its most detailed proposals to date for its solution to the national question in Britain, based on both the recognition of Scottish and Welsh nationhood as well as a commitment to decentralising political and economic power and extending democratic rights. Of the three submissions, that put forward by the Welsh Committee was the most far-reaching, seeking to not only lay down its proposals for the make-up of a Welsh Parliament, but also to outline broader

---

[50] 'Memorandum submitted by the Welsh Committee of the Communist Party', p. 170.

[51] 'Memorandum submitted by the Welsh Committee of the Communist Party', p. 166.

democratic reforms that would take place under it. This was evidence of the Welsh Committee's deeper engagement with the issue, with Gordon McLennan noting that 'compared with Scotland ... Bert and the Welsh comrades are managing to deal with this difficult and demanding question'.[52] However, significant weaknesses remained in the CPGB's proposals, especially regarding the division of powers. While on the one hand, a Welsh Parliament was viewed as a bulwark to the impact of Conservative rule, providing a focus for popular mobilisation and a legislative means of challenging Tory policy, on the other the type of far-reaching economic and social planning proposed by the Welsh Committee was based on an implicit assumption of a transition to socialism. As things stood, the retention of powers over overall planning at Westminster and the granting of reserve powers to the British Parliament to ensure that the general outlines of any plan were implemented, would make it exceedingly difficult for the pursual of the type of wide-ranging planning envisioned by the Welsh Committee if governments of different hues were incumbent in Wales and at Westminster, an issue that was left unresolved. A more positive feature was the focus placed in the Welsh Committee's submission on the fate of the Welsh language, a reflection of the party's broader concern with language issues during the 1970s.

An initial focus for these concerns was the party's support for a Welsh-language television channel, the party giving evidence in its favour to the Crawford Committee on Broadcasting Coverage.[53] In more general terms, while not always agreeing with their methods, the party welcomed the upsurge in political activity related to the language movement as a positive contribution to the development of political consciousness amongst Welsh youth.[54] Similarly,

[52] CPGB Archive, Gordon McLennan to Bill Wainwright, 26 October 1970, CP/CENT/ORG/11/1, (LHASC).
[53] *Report of the Committee on Broadcasting Coverage* (London, 1974), p. 96. The Welsh Committee gave oral evidence only.
[54] 'Wales for the People', *Communist Party Welsh Congress Nov. 18–Nov. 19*, [1972], p. 13, Bert Pearce Papers WC/9, NLW; Interview with Mary and Tony Winter, 20 February 2009. The party's sympathy with the language movement is evident in the Welsh Committee's decision to protest the heavy sentences handed to Dafydd Iwan and other CYIG activists in the early 1970s, see Minutes of Welsh Committee, 18

Cyffro articles by both Mary Winter and Ann Vaughan expressed support for language activists while advocating equal status for Welsh, the compulsory teaching of Welsh in schools and the creation of a Welsh television channel.[55] Vaughan, in particular, argued that the survival of Welsh as a living language was vital for the survival of a distinct Welsh identity.[56] While the publication of Vaughan's and Winter's articles reflected a recommendation by the Welsh executive that the journal include more material on the theoretical problems of the national movement, their publication in Welsh, along with other *Cyffro* articles, reflected the journal's bilingual ethos, an ethos that had been, in practical terms, absent from the party's publications since the 1940s.[57] Despite this, the party's bilingual output, outside of the pages of *Cyffro*, remained woefully inadequate for a Welsh party. An attempt to remedy this situation later in the decade, following the adoption of a resolution calling for all party material to be published bilingually, floundered, with plans to set up a party translation group coming to nothing, largely due to financial constraints.[58]

By the end of 1970, fears were raised within the party that the Heath government would seek to close the door on constitutional change. In response to these fears the Welsh party called for the establishment of a broad campaign for the immediate establishment of a Welsh Parliament to prevent such an occurrence, declaring its readiness to 'join any meeting or movement for this aim'.[59] A similar campaign was advocated in Scotland,[60] however, neither of these campaigns was to see the light of day, with attention drawn to

January 1970, Bert Pearce Papers WM/12, NLW; Minutes of Welsh Committee, 16 May 1971, Bert Pearce Papers WM/13, NLW.

[55] Mary Winter, 'Nodiadau Golygyddol', *Cyffro*, 2(1), Summer 1971, p. 4; Ann Vaughan, 'Statws yr Iaith Gymraeg', *Cyffro*, 2 (2), Summer 1972, pp. 48–50.

[56] Vaughan, 'Statws yr Iaith Gymraeg', p. 48.

[57] Minutes of Secretariat, March 4, 1970, Bert Pearce Papers WM/12, NLW.

[58] 'The Communist Party Welsh Congress, 20–1 November 1976: Amendments and Branch Resolutions', p. 13, Bert Pearce Papers WC/11, NLW; Tim Saunders to Bert Pearce undated [December 1976]. Bert Pearce to Tim Saunders, 12 January 1977, Bert Pearce Papers WD 1/22, NLW.

[59] 'For Wales – Oust the Tories – Take the Socialist Road', pp. 6–7.

[60] Hugh Wyper, 'Some Thoughts on the Government's Approach to the National Question in Scotland', *Comment*, 7 November 1970, pp. 712–13.

this lack of activity at the CPGB's 32nd Congress, held in December 1971.[61] Further criticism of the party centre's approach to the issue was also evident at Congress, with Brian Wilkinson, a former member of the Welsh Committee and the party's parliamentary candidate for Pontypool, noting the failure of the main draft resolution to address the national question. For Wilkinson, by ignoring the decisions of the 31st Congress the resolution showed an 'obvious lack of consideration for Communists in Scotland and Wales ... by leading party members', ending up as essentially a policy programme for a 'Communist Party of England'. Linking this omission to a lingering imperialist mindset within both the party and the labour movement, Wilkinson argued that the implications of such thinking were serious, potentially hampering the party's development in both countries, leading him to put forward the case for 'serious consideration to be given to the establishment of separate Communist Parties for England, Wales and Scotland, so that each can develop in the way best suited to the political conditions in its own country'.[62]

This argument was untenable for the Welsh party leadership, with Alistair Wilson noting that 'this type of nationalism can only serve to strengthen British capitalism ... by dividing the Communist movement'.[63] Nevertheless, arguments similar to Wilkinson's, while still in a minority, would emerge later in the decade. Further dissension over the national question was evident at the 1972 Welsh Congress, this time from those opposed to the party's stance on the issue. The Swansea Central branch, influenced by the critique of the party emanating from those who had opposed the party's stance on Czechoslovakia, put forward a resolution attacking the party's support for a Welsh parliament as revisionist and of being a 'reactionary concession to the nationalists', rejecting the notion that any solution to Wales' national and

---

[61] 'Scotland and Wales', *Comment,* 18 December 1971, p. 485.
[62] *Comment,* 25 September 1971.
[63] *Comment,* 23 October 1971, p. 397. The resolution adopted at Congress did however recognise the party's policy on the national question, see *Comment,* 18 December 1970, p. 455.

cultural problems could be found under capitalism.[64] Reflecting the party's commitment to the establishment of a Welsh Parliament, the resolution was resoundingly defeated by 50 votes to 7.[65]

By 1973, the party's focus in relation to the national question had turned to the publication of the Royal Commission's report. The Commissioners, while divided on the exact form of devolution, came out in favour of changing the constitutional settlement, a majority in favour of legislative devolution for both Wales and Scotland.[66] The Kilbrandon Report was broadly welcomed by the party; for the Welsh Committee it marked 'an historic step in democratic advance in Britain'.[67] For Alex Murray, the party's Scottish Secretary, the report 'was the most comprehensive, most important, and in many respects most welcome to be produced on the issue'.[68] Bert Pearce, in a prescient warning, noted that the majority report's recommendation of legislative devolution had 'made this a realistic and unavoidable issue in political life' that meant 'a time bomb had been placed under all future governments'.[69] The party had some cause to welcome the Commission's proposals, the Welsh Committee noting that the report had granted a number of its key recommendations, including those for a legislative assembly and elections by proportional representation,[70] which for Reuben Falber, the party's assistant secretary, had also boosted the case for a more general measure of electoral reform.[71]

Despite this, the party also had significant reservations regarding the report's recommendations, most notably the

[64] *The Communist Party Welsh Congress, Nov. 18–19: Amendments and Branch Resolutions,* Bert Pearce Papers WC/9, NLW.
[65] CPGB Archive, Bert Pearce to John Gollan, 9 February 1973, CP/CENT/ORG/11/1 (LHASC).
[66] *The Report of the Royal Commission on the Constitution 1969–1973 Volume 1* (London, 1973), pp. 335–52.
[67] 'Notes on Kilbrandon and a Welsh Parliament', [1974], Bert Pearce Papers WN 1/7, NLW.
[68] *Morning Star,* 13 November 1973, p. 2.
[69] Bert Pearce, 'Parliaments and Powers (A Communist Comment on Kilbrandon)', *Cyffro,* 2 (3), Summer 1974, p. 42.
[70] 'Press Statement – The Royal Commission on the Constitution Kilbrandon Report, October 31, 1973', p. 1, Bert Pearce Papers WN 1/7, NLW.
[71] *Morning Star,* 21 November 1973, p. 2.

lack of legislative powers over economic matters and the proposal to reduce the number of Welsh MPs. For the Welsh Committee, the refusal to grant powers over the economy and over planning were a hindrance to Wales' development, which required power not only in areas such as social services, housing and health but also in those areas vital to the building of a flourishing national economy. Similarly, the proposal to reduce the number of Welsh MPs was a 'senseless and counterproductive move' that undermined the purpose of a new constitutional settlement by giving English MPs greater predominance at the British level and thus a greater say in the overall economic and planning decisions taken at that level. This was in contradiction to what the Welsh Committee viewed as the aim of devolution – to increase democratic control at both the Welsh and British levels, the proposals viewed by the Welsh Committee and the *Morning Star* as a political manoeuvre designed to bolster the prospects of the Conservative Party and nullify the influence of left-wing devolved assemblies.[72] Noting that the Sankey Commission's endorsement of nationalisation for the mines had been shelved for 25 years, the Welsh Committee demanded that the report's recommendations be acted upon immediately.[73] For the *Morning Star*, to prevent the report gathering dust it was vital that a campaign for the implementation and improvement of its recommendations was initiated by the party and the broader labour movement.[74] This position was reiterated at the CPGB's 33rd Congress, held that December, which urged 'all sections of the working class movement in Britain' to campaign for the immediate establishment of Welsh and Scottish Parliaments.[75] As with its previous calls to action on devolution this one was also to fall on deaf ears. Instead in the hands of the new Labour Government, elected in February 1974, progress on the issue was to be met with further delay as the Wilson administration began another round of consultation that June. Kilbrandon's 'time bomb' kept ticking.

[72] 'Press Statement – The Royal Commission on the Constitution', pp. 1–2; *Morning Star,* 1 November 1973, p. 1.

[73] 'Notes on Kilbrandon', p. 2.

[74] *Morning Star,* 1 November 1973, p. 1.

[75] 'The Commission on the Constitution', *Comment,* 1/15 December 1973, p. 413.

While progress stalled on the issue of a Welsh parliament, significant progress had been made on another of the Welsh party's long-standing demands, that of the formation of a Wales TUC, which, despite some equivocation over the issue during the mid-1950s, had been a feature of party policy for most of the post-war period. Writing in 1968, D. Ivor Davies, the communist secretary of the Glamorgan Federation of Trade Councils (GFTC), had put forward the case for a Wales TUC, arguing that along with a Welsh parliament the formation of a Wales TUC was vital to solving Wales' specific economic and social problems, which Labour had failed to take seriously, its approach proving totally inadequate. Noting that the Labour leadership's attitude to Wales was 'pie in the sky', Davies argued that in line with developments in the broader political sphere, a movement was emerging within the trade unions that recognised the urgent need for the creation of a Welsh TUC. For Davies, this would not only give the trade unions a greater voice in Welsh affairs and allow them to provide leadership in resolving the instability in the Welsh economy, but would also strengthen the voice of the Welsh working-class movement and allow the Welsh unions to play a more unified role within the British TUC.[76] Communist support for a Wales TUC was reiterated at both its 1970 and 1972 Welsh Congresses, the Welsh Committee arguing that its establishment was vital for 'increasing the democratic power of Welsh Trade Unionists to act as a decisive force in our National life',[77] for winning the labour movement in Wales for socialist policies, and an important component in realising 'the vast power the Welsh working class has at its disposal'.[78]

The turning point was to come following the 1972 miners' strike which had strengthened solidarity among NUM and TGWU activists while at the same time exposing the inability of the TUC's North and South Wales Regional Advisory Committees (RAC) to effectively mobilise its members in

[76] *Morning Star,* 16 February 1968, p. 2.
[77] 'For Wales – Oust the Tories – Take the Socialist Road', pp. 5–6.
[78] 'Discussion Statement on the Communist Party in Wales, Building Left Unity and the Forces for Socialism' in *Communist Party Welsh Congress Nov. 18–Nov. 19, 1972,* p. 4, Bert Pearce Papers WC/9, NLW.

support of the striking miners.[79] This point was emphasised by Dai Francis in a keynote article in support of a Wales TUC. Placing the formation of a Wales TUC within the broader context of the need for change and modernisation within the labour movement, Francis argued that in Wales a 'historic change' was vital if the Welsh trade unions were to offer an effective, unified response to the complex economic and social questions of the day, and especially if it sought to play a bigger role in Welsh political life.[80] For Francis, the RACs were no longer adequate to deal with the new challenges that faced the trade union movement in Wales, pointing, in particular, to the lack of leadership shown during the miners' strike. The formation of a Wales TUC was thus viewed as one way of countering this lack of leadership, by helping to democratise the TUC structure in Wales, enlivening its grass roots and strengthening the militancy of the TUC in the process.[81] More significantly, the formation of a Wales TUC, viewed within the context of a broader devolutionary trend within Welsh society, was seen as a means of placing the trade union movement at the centre of Welsh political life. Viewing the Wales TUC as the 'Workers' Parliament in Wales', Francis argued that through the development of policies on every aspect of Wales' economic and social life, the Wales TUC 'would be at once the most significant forum in Welsh public life' a means of providing a democratic voice to 'the largest and the most basically important body of the Welsh people'.[82] Its formation would also have a broader resonance outside the confines of the trade union movement, its establishment providing 'a powerful declaration and stimulation of the unity of Wales'.[83] For Francis, the time had come for action,

> The case for a Welsh TUC can no longer be packed up in pious resolutions, passed and pigeon-holed. The need grows from the picket lines, from the pits, depots, docks and factories where active trade unionists

---

[79] England, *The Wales TUC 1974–2004: Devolution and Industrial Politics* (Cardiff, 2004), pp. 14–15; Francis and Smith, *The Fed*, p. 480.

[80] Dai Francis, 'Needed Now – A Trade Union Congress for Wales', *Cyffro*, 2 (2), Summer 1972, pp. 8–10.

[81] Francis, 'Needed Now – A Trade Union Congress for Wales', pp. 8–9.

[82] Francis, 'Needed Now – A Trade Union Congress for Wales', p. 10.

[83] Francis, 'Needed Now – A Trade Union Congress for Wales', p. 11.

are experiencing the truth that unless our movement finds the way to stand together the Tories will destroy it. It is now a time to act … clearly much greater understanding and pressure is needed. All who see the need should join forces to spread the understanding, and to mount the pressure until every Union body in Wales is won for this historic new advance.[84]

Such pressure was not long in coming. Following the RAC's decision to ignore calls for a Wales TUC from the NUM at its annual conference in May 1972, discussions between Tom Jones, the TGWU's Welsh secretary, and Dai Francis, and then between the TGWU's Welsh Regional Committee and the South Wales Executive of the NUM, led to an unilateral declaration by the two unions, in October 1972, that they intended to create a Wales TUC, with a working party established with this goal the following month.[85] At the working party's inaugural meeting in December 1972 the decision was taken to hold a special congress at Llandrindod the following February at which its proposals for a Wales TUC were overwhelmingly adopted and its secretary, George Wright, also secretary of the TGWU in Wales following Tom Jones' retirement, given a mandate to proceed with the formation of the new body. Rejecting the TUC's own proposals for reforming its regional organisation, a second special conference was held at Aberystwyth in May 1973, following an agreement in principle between the working party and the RAC's that an all-Wales body funded by the TUC should be established, at which the new body's constitution was approved.[86]

Throughout this process the TUC General Council had been opposed to the formation of the new body with the TGWU and the NUM's unilateral action viewed as undermining the TUC's own review of its regional organisation, while raising uncertainty regarding the future relationship between the Welsh trade unions and the TUC.[87] Indeed, Vic Feather, the TUC general secretary, called for the

---

[84] Francis, 'Needed Now – A Trade Union Congress for Wales', p. 11.
[85] England, *The Wales TUC*, pp. 14–16.
[86] England, *The Wales TUC*, pp. 21–31.
[87] TUC General Council Minutes, 24 January 1973, Box 1 A1, Wales TUC Archive, Swansea University.

Llandrindod congress to be cancelled.[88] However, in Jack Jones, the TGWU general secretary, those seeking to form a Wales TUC had a strong ally who acted as their main supporter and protector on the General Council during this period.[89] Following the Llandrindod congress, the General Council refused to recognise the new body, preferring to deal only with TUC-registered organisations. Nevertheless, following the lukewarm reception given to its own proposals for regional reorganisation at a meeting with the Welsh trade unions in April 1973, the TUC leadership was forced to recognise that the RAC's were no longer adequate.[90] With the Aberystwyth congress reaffirming the determination of the Welsh unions to set up a Wales TUC, a concerted effort was now made to resolve the issue before the 1973 TUC Congress. The case for a Wales TUC was again put forward in June, this time by D. Ivor Davies, who was by now the Trade Councils' representative on the working party, at a meeting between the Welsh Trades Council Federations, the TUC Organisation Committee and the RAC's, resulting in an agreement to review the TUC's proposals for Wales. With the Organisation Committee due to report back in July, Davies, applying further pressure, urged all trades councils to inform the TUC that they rejected its proposals for reorganisation and instead backed the decisions taken at Llandrindod and Aberystwyth. The efforts put in by the TGWU, NUM and the Trades Councils were finally rewarded at the July meeting, held in Cardiff, at which the TUC delegation accepted most of the Welsh representatives' proposals, agreeing to the formation of a Wales TUC. These decisions were confirmed at the July meetings of both the TUC Organisation Committee and its General Council, with the Wales TUC's inaugural congress taking place at Aberystwyth in April 1974, at which Dai Francis was elected its first chairman.[91]

[88] Victor Feather to Affiliated Organisations, Trades Councils and Regional Advisory Committees in Wales, 24 January 1973, Dai Francis Papers C1, MNB/PP/24/C/1, South Wales Coalfield Collection, Swansea University.

[89] Interview with Hywel Francis, 27 October 2009.

[90] England, *The Wales TUC*, pp. 28–30.

[91] England, *The Wales TUC*, 32–5; for Davies's appointment to the working group. see George Wright to D. Prosser, 19 April 1973, Box 1 A1, Wales TUC Archive, Swansea University.

The CPGB had made a significant contribution to the realisation of this long-standing demand. Two of the leading figures in the process had been Communists, Dai Francis and D. Ivor Davies, who had both played key leadership roles. With party policy and trade union interests converging, both Davies and Francis had, in this instance, been able to overcome the divide, so often faced by the CPGB's industrial activists, between their party and trade union work. Bert Pearce had also played an important role, working closely with Francis in developing the strategy that led to its establishment, while also having helped develop grass-roots movements within the trade unions, amongst whose ultimate objectives was the formation of Wales TUC.[92] It was no coincidence that support for this important measure within the Welsh trade union movement came from two of the labour movement organisations in which there was a strong Communist presence, the NUM and the Trade Councils. This was testament to the success of the party's strategy within these bodies, especially the NUM, where communist activists and their counterparts on the Labour left had a good working relationship and had been able to win successive annual conferences and the executive for this policy. At the British level, the party's Broad Left strategy had also had an indirect impact, the election of Jack Jones, a firm believer in the devolving of power within the trade unions, helping to precipitate the moves towards a Wales TUC in the late 1960s and, as an influential member of the TUC General Council, giving significant protection to those involved in the unilateral moves towards creating the new national body. While it is important not to overstate the role of the party in the formation of the Wales TUC, ultimately it was the unions and not the party that had driven the process, we should also note that the party had nevertheless made an important contribution, perhaps the most important contribution the party was to make to devolution and the national question in Wales. Leading party members within the labour movement had been able to combine their union roles with party policy and were to make critical interventions at important junctures in the process, while rank and file activists had, along with their

<hr />

[92] Interview with Hywel Francis, 27 October 2009.

allies on the left, been able to maintain pressure at the grass-roots level.

The level of communist involvement did, however, mean that the formation of the Wales TUC was viewed with suspicion by some within the Labour Party in Wales, not least because of the role played by Dai Francis and the South Wales NUM.[93] In contrast, for the CPGB its formation was a welcome advance, the party coming to view it as a living example of the type of devolution it wished to see at the governmental level. For the Welsh Committee, its formation was a 'great step forward opening up new possibilities for unifying the Welsh working class', giving the trade union movement in Wales new 'prospects of exercising a decisive influence on the growth of the Left' and helping to diminish the influence of the right wing within the trade union movement in Wales.[94] In combination with the recommendations of the Kilbrandon Report, its formation, in providing for the first time a platform for debate and policy development for the Welsh working-class movement, was viewed as 'open[ing] up the possibilities of the power of the Welsh people having greater means to express themselves as ever before in our history', an opportunity that the Labour Movement had to grasp, 'and not let slip by'.[95] The Wales TUC, unwilling to let the opportunity slip by, adopted a motion, emanating from the South Wales NUM, in favour of a legislative assembly at its inaugural conference, further developing its policy on the issue in the months that followed.[96] However, the adoption of this motion drew a reprimand from the Labour Party which, committed to executive devolution, declared that neither the NUM nor the Wales TUC spoke for Labour Party in Wales.[97] Accusations by Leo Abse, the Labour MP for Pontypool, that the Wales TUC's support for legislative devolution was due to it being Communist-dominated were,

[93] Interview with Hywel Francis, 27 October 2009; England, *The Wales TUC 1974–2004,* p. 17.
[94] 'Pre-Congress Discussion Statement' in *The Communist Party Welsh Congress 1975,* p. 4, Bert Pearce Papers WC/10, NLW.
[95] 'Notes on Kilbrandon and a Welsh Parliament', p. 1.
[96] *Wales TUC First Annual Report 1974* (Cardiff, 1974), pp. 16–18.
[97] John Gilbert Evans, *Devolution in Wales: Claims and Responses 1937–1979* (Cardiff, 2006), p. 139.

however, dismissed by Bert Pearce as merely the means for Abse to gain 'a few cheap headlines' and, noting other policy areas where the Wales TUC and CPGB were in agreement, he argued that this was not the result of 'some conspiratorial brainwashing' but based on 'the common experience of Socialists in the working-class movement seeking answers to the real problems of our people'.[98] Similar accusations were to resurface during the referendum campaign, with Neil Kinnock dismissing the Wales TUC as a 'bunch of commies'.[99]

The election of a Labour Government in February 1974 set in motion the first stages of the legislative process on devolution, with the publication of a discussion paper, *Devolution within the United Kingdom*, that June and, following its re-election with a small majority in October 1974, a White Paper, *Our Changing Democracy*, setting out its own proposals for devolution, in November 1975. Both the February and October elections had seen Plaid Cymru make significant gains, winning two seats in February and another in October. For John Gollan, these gains, and those of the SNP, could be attributed directly to the Labour Party's 'complete opposition to the national problems of Scotland and Wales', the labour movement's relationship with the national movement now 'of increasing importance not only for Scotland and Wales, but for the future of United Kingdom politics as a whole'.[100] The Labour Government's initial response was, however, a disappointment, its decision to put the issue out to further consultation, on the back of the four-year Royal Commission, met with frustration by the Welsh Committee, which viewed it as another delaying tactic likely to 'lead to confusion and delay, rather than clarity and decision' and make the situation 'more intractable'.[101] For Bert Pearce, the government's failure to indicate its own preferred scheme for devolution was further testament of the Labour Party's

---

[98] *Morning Star,* 9 December 1975, p. 2.

[99] *Morning Star,* 14 March 1979, p. 4.

[100] *Morning Star,* 11 March 1974, p. 5; John Gollan, 'The General Election and the Way Forward', *Comment,* 16 November 1974, p. 355.

[101] *A Parliament with Powers for Wales: Comments Submitted by the Welsh Committee of the Communist Party to the Secretary of State for Wales on the Government Discussion Paper 'Devolution in the United Kingdom* (Cardiff, 1974), p. 1.

intrinsic conservatism on constitutional issues, its democratic vision 'limited to the present Parliamentary structure'.[102] While Labour's consultation exercise was met with frustration, it received a cautious welcome following its support for the establishment of devolved assemblies in its October manifesto. Bert Pearce, while recognising this move as a significant step, opening up the prospect of major constitutional change in the next parliamentary session, was, however, critical of the proposal to give different powers to the Welsh and Scottish Assemblies.[103] For Pearce, this decision was an 'absurdity' that reflected 'the dodgy process by which the Labour Party has been reluctantly propelled by its membership into this policy'.[104] For the Welsh Committee, while Labour's policy shift was not only a reflection of the growth of national consciousness in Welsh society, but also evidence of a realisation within the working-class movement of the value of devolution as an extension of grass-roots democracy, its support for only executive devolution was likely to 'jeopardise the whole project from the start'.[105]

The government's White Paper, *Our Changing Democracy*, which again only proposed executive devolution for Wales, was met with a similar response, the *Morning Star* noting that it read 'as if written by a hand fearful of democratic advance'. In particular, it condemned the decision not to grant legislative powers to Wales as 'outrageous' and unjustifiable, while it called for greater legislative powers to be given to both countries. For the PC, the weakness of the government's proposals and the proposed delays in implementing the legislation were likely to 'play into the hands of the nationalist parties and do great harm to the labour movement', and it called on all Labour MPs and on the labour movement to lobby the government for radical changes to the legislation.[106] For John Gollan, the government's approach had 'been the product of political opportunism, [a] belated

[102] Pearce, 'Parliaments and Powers', p. 49.
[103] Bert Pearce, 'The New Prospects for Scotland and Wales', *Comment*, 21 September 1974, pp. 296–7.
[104] Pearce, 'The New Prospects for Scotland and Wales', p. 296.
[105] *Wales Needs Communist Policy – Power to the People* (Cardiff, 1974), p. 8.
[106] *Morning Star*, 28 November 1975, p. 1.

reaction to nationalist electoral advance, instead of principle' resulting in a set of proposals that 'concedes as little as possible and creates the maximum difficulties'.[107] Similarly, for the Welsh Committee, the proposals were 'a halting halfway step' which recognised the need for the devolution of power but failed to provide the effective means for its implementation. Calling for parity with Scotland and for the extension of legislative powers to include control over economic affairs and industrial development, the Welsh Committee argued that it was 'not possible to develop the social, cultural or any other aspect of Welsh life without putting right the appalling distortion of our economic foundations, transport and communications, over the past two centuries'.[108] The main focus of the Welsh party's strategy on the national question from this point onwards was on winning the support of the labour movement and Labour MPs for radical changes to the proposed devolution legislation, whilst calling for the establishment of a broad movement for a Welsh parliament centred on an alliance between the labour and nationalist movements.

By the mid-1970s, the call for a broad campaign on devolution had become an almost ritualistic feature of Welsh party congresses. However, the party's relationship with Plaid Cymru, was at times ambiguous. Despite maintaining good grassroots relations with Plaid, the coverage given to it in the party press, in contrast to the generally positive press given to CYIG, was, on the whole, negative, while statements emanating from the party gave out distinctly mixed messages.[109] Indeed, at the 1975 Welsh Congress, while arguing that 'the national future of Wales depends upon the positive alliance of genuine national elements and the working class movement',[110] the Welsh Committee accused Plaid of pursuing 'a basically anti-labour and anti-socialist direction' and of committing itself 'to alliance with

---

[107] *Morning Star,* 2 December 1975, p. 2.

[108] 'Press Release – The White Paper "Our Changing Democracy: Devolution to Scotland and Wales", November 27, 1975', Bert Pearce Papers WN 1/12, NLW.

[109] For a typical assessment of Plaid Cymru see Alistair Wilson, 'Which Party for Wales?', *Cyffro,* 2 (2), Summer 1972, pp. 22–7, 46–8.

[110] *Morning Star,* 27 January 1975, p. 1.

reactionary forces, and to the confusion and splitting of the working class movement'.[111] As Robert Griffiths, then a leading figure on the left of Plaid, was to point out in an article in *Cyffro*, such an analysis of Plaid's position, 'in language reminiscent of Stalin's infamous "third period"', was unlikely to be conducive to building the type of 'positive alliance' the party was committed to.[112] Underlying this attitude to Plaid were a number of key factors, not least its own difficult relationship with the Labour Party, the CPGB, despite its opposition to the right-wing Labour leadership, committed in its party programme to securing the election of a Labour Government. In this light the nationalist challenge, by threatening Labour hegemony in both Wales and Scotland, had to be resisted. As a political party, Plaid, unlike CYIG, was also fighting for the same political space as the CPGB, a factor that may at least partly explain the different attitudes to Plaid and CYIG in the party press, with CYIG, as a single-issue campaign group radicalising Welsh youth, viewed in a far more favourable light. At a more basic level, there remained a deep suspicion of nationalism among sections of the CPGB's Welsh leadership, especially in its perceived vulnerability to reactionary tendencies. Similarly, the lack of any organic link between Plaid and the working class also worked against it in the eyes of the party. In addition, as for much of the labour movement in Wales, Plaid's commitment to independence was anathema to the CPGB's own strong unionist ethos, an unionism born of a concern for the unity of the British working-class movement as the only viable force that could overthrow capitalism.

Despite these difficulties, there is also evidence of a more positive relationship between the two parties. In a letter to Bert Pearce, written in January 1975, Dafydd Williams, Plaid Cymru's general secretary, recognising the CPGB's support for legislative devolution requested that the party mobilise its 'considerable influence' within the labour movement to lobby for the granting of legislative powers in parity with

---

[111] 'Pre-Congress Discussion Statement' in *The Communist Party Welsh Congress 1975*, p. 4.

[112] Robert Griffiths, 'Socialism and the National Movement', *Cyffro*, 2(4), Spring 1975, pp. 17–18.

Scotland in the forthcoming government white paper.[113] Plaid's decision to oppose continued EEC membership was welcomed by the party,[114] with both parties involved in the Wales Get Britain Out campaign during the EEC referendum,[115] leading to a 'high level of cooperation' between CPGB members and Plaid officials and the development of links with the left wing of Plaid. Significantly, relations between Plaid and CPGB members were devoid of the type of sectarianism that was a feature of relations between Plaid and Labour.[116] Mary Winter recalls that relations between the two parties were 'very positive' noting that the party was always willing to share a platform with Plaid and CYIG, the relationship proving to be one that was mutually beneficial to all parties,

> Plaid learnt to broaden its understanding of socialist thinking a lot through the connection with the Communist Party and similarly I think we gained a better understanding of national issues and how important they were and how important the language was. Because I think you shifted, you came to understand better that if you speak Welsh, if it is your first language then it's a different feeling from if you don't speak it. You came to understand that from a position where you hadn't previously [understood] how significant it was. So I think there was a cross-fertilisation of ideas.[117]

The Welsh party had made a significant contribution to this cross-fertilisation of ideas both through the opening up of the pages of *Cyffro* and through the organisation of a series of conferences, during 1976 and 1977, by the party or party members at which the national question was debated, with the general aim of providing a platform for a broad discussion and development of the left's position on the national question.[118] For Brian Davies, who was amongst those party

---

[113] Dafydd Williams to Bert Pearce, 25 January 1975, Bert Pearce Papers WM/18, NLW.

[114] 'The Communist Party Welsh Party Congress Jan. 25–26, 1975: Amendments and Branch Resolutions', p. 2, Bert Pearce Papers WC/10, NLW.

[115] Laura McAllister, *Plaid Cymru: The Emergence of a Political Party,* p. 143.

[116] Interview with Robert Griffiths, 19 December 2008.

[117] Interview with Mary and Tony Winter, 20 February 2009.

[118] 'Statement of the Aims and Organisation of the November Conference on Socialism and the National Question' [November 1977], Tŷ Cenedl Papers AIII/7, NLW.

members calling for a 'new synthesis' of nationalist and socialist discourse, these conferences, as a means of kick-starting the debate on the left on these issues, played a modest role in the development of the nationalist left by exposing them to the Marxist perspective on Welsh issues.[119] This concern for building unity between socialists and nationalists was not only restricted to the pages of *Cyffro* or the organisation of conferences, but was also a feature of the party's general engagement with the national movement, with Mary Winter, for example, at a 1976 CYIG conference, calling on the Society to build better links with the labour and trade union movement as a means of advancing its campaign over the language.[120]

On the left the party focused on the 'deplorable record of the government on the issue' and the concern that significant sections of the labour movement remained unconvinced of the 'critical importance' of devolution in broadening the struggle for socialism, with Welsh and Scottish parliaments viewed as providing new platforms for the development and implementation of socialist policies.[121] In Wales this concern was largely focused on those Labour MPs, the Gang of Six led by Leo Abse and Neil Kinnock, who opposed devolution. Pearce, while sympathetic to some aspects of their argument, especially the need to maintain the unity of the British working-class movement and the potentially divisive nature of nationalism, nevertheless rejected their conclusion that devolution had to be opposed. At the root of this opposition, according to Pearce, was a tendency 'to wrongly identify all democratic national consciousness with the "separatism" of Plaid Cymru' which had led them to 'push themselves into an untenable position as defenders of the "status quo"'.[122] By ignoring the social and economic dimensions to the growth of national consciousness, this group misread the causes of

[119]   Brian Davies, 'Towards a New Synthesis', *Planet,* 37/38, May 1977, p. 59; interview with Brian Davies, 20 February 2009.
[120]   Mary Winter, 'Yr Iaith Gymraeg a'r Mudiad Llafur', *Cyffro,* 4 (2), Summer 1976, pp. 26–9.
[121]   Gordon McLennan, 'Devolution', *Comment,* 24 January 1976, p. 23.
[122]   Bert Pearce, 'Devolution. Democracy and Socialism: Which Way for Wales Today?', *Cyffro,* 4 (1), Spring 1976, pp. 21–2.

nationalism and thus committed the labour movement to rejecting the very solutions which would allow it to harness such a political force to the broader struggle for socialism.[123] For Pearce, there was also tendency amongst this group to deny the existence of the political dimension of national feeling in Wales, with Kinnock, in particular, guilty of only acknowledging the existence of a 'cultural distinctiveness' in terms of Welsh national consciousness, a position which left 'the real core of the matter unmentioned'.[124]

In rejecting devolution its opponents on the left were, for Pearce, ducking out of an opportunity to extend democratic rights, both in government and in the industrial arena, an extension of democracy that had long formed the basis of the demands of the British labour movement.[125] More broadly, it was a matter of urgency that the whole working-class movement gain a 'much deeper understanding of the national questions and the need to fight on them', a concern that extended to the CPGB itself, with Pearce questioning whether party members 'felt the specific implications this issue has now for the crisis of the political system of British capitalism'.[126] Similar concerns were expressed by Brian Davies, who argued that the Welsh working-class movement's lack of interest in the national question was related to confusion over its national identity rooted in both the anglicisation of south Wales and in the working-class movement's desire to adopt an ideology that was the antithesis of radical Liberalism, of which a rejection of Welsh nationalism was a part. This had led to the adoption of a distorted version of internationalism that precluded Welsh nationality and which was a 'peculiarly Welsh manifestation' of the imperialist, 'Great British chauvinism', of the broader trade union movement.[127]

Despite the disappointment with its proposals, the publication of the White Paper nevertheless acted as a catalyst for further activity on the national question, the party centre

[123] *Morning Star*, 9 December 1975, p. 2.
[124] Bert Pearce, 'Let Labour Lead Now!', *Cyffro*, 2 (4), Spring 1975, p. 26.
[125] Pearce, 'Devolution, Democracy and Socialism', pp. 21–2.
[126] Pearce, 'Devolution, Democracy and Socialism', p. 17.
[127] Brian Davies, 'Towards a New Synthesis', p. 58.

and the Welsh party restating their position on the issue within the context of the White Paper in new policy statements in 1976, reiterating their support for the establishment of Welsh and Scottish parliaments, for radical changes to the government's proposals and the initiation of a broad campaign for their establishment.[128] However, the only new addition to party policy during this period came in the form of the development of the party's position on the 'English dimension' of devolution. Advocating a federal solution to the national question in Britain, for the CPGB, the English dimension was an important component of any solution to the problem. The party had expressed its disappointment that proposals for England had not been published at the same time as the Scotland and Wales Bill.[129] When a government White Paper was published in December 1976, its failure to offer any concrete proposals was criticised, the *Morning Star* declaring that 'For vagueness the government's consultative document ... takes a lot of beating.'[130]

By this time the party had been formulating its own position on the issue for a good part of a year, with a subcommission to explore the issue having been set up in January 1976.[131] Having wavered between two of the three proposals outlined in its initial report – the establishment of an English Assembly on the lines of those in Scotland and Wales, devolution to the English regions along similar lines or the proposal that English MPs within the British Parliament have sole responsibility for English affairs[132] – the final EC report on the English dimension, published in April 1977, came out in favour of two proposals, backing the latter option while expressing support for the establishment of an English assembly should a demand for one emerge from the English public.[133] Noting the lack of such a demand, Jack

---

[128] McLennan, 'Devolution' pp. 19–23; *Devolution, Democracy and Socialism: A Policy Statement by the Welsh Committee of the Communist Party* (Cardiff, 1977).

[129] *Morning Star,* 1 December 1976, p. 1.

[130] *Morning Star,* 10 December 1976, p. 1.

[131] McLennan, 'Devolution', p. 20.

[132] CPGB Archive, 'PC Sub-Commission on Constitutional Consequences for England of Devolution for Scotland and Wales 20th July 1976', pp. 1–2, CP/CENT/SUBJ/03/01 (LHASC).

[133] Jack Woddis, 'Devolutionary Politics', *Comment,* 2 April 1977, pp. 102–4.

Woddis, the subcommission's chair and the report's author, nevertheless argued that despite not having suffered from the same sort of national oppression as Wales and Scotland, the national question was also relevant to the English, who 'had their own national identity, history, culture, traditions … and need their own institutional arrangements for taking their own political decisions affecting their own specifically English questions', a factor that would become more pronounced following the establishment of assemblies in Wales and Scotland. For Woddis, however, in the absence of a resolution to the national question in Wales and Scotland, 'all talk about an English dimension is really meaningless from the point of view of political realism'.[134]

Having reiterated its policy on devolution at the 1976 Welsh Congress, despite some isolated fears on the Welsh Committee that the party's policy on the national question was a sop to the nationalists and in danger of taking the party in a diversionary direction, in general there was little opposition to the party's position on the national question.[135] The national question was absent from the debate on the new edition of the *BRS*, the debate between Welsh party members revolving around the programme's alleged revisionism, reformism and liquidationism, with the NCP on its foundation adopting a policy similar to that of the CPGB on the issue.[136] While its absence from these broader debates attests to the low priority given to the national question in the more general scheme of communist politics, the NCP's support for national rights, as with that of the CPB a decade later, shows that it remained a concern of the handful of former Welsh party members who defected to the new party. What criticism there was of the party's position came instead from those who felt that the party had not gone far enough, with the

---

[134] Woddis, 'Devolutionary Politics', p. 104.

[135] See notes of Lyn Irwin's comments, 'Special Welsh Committee Conference of Devolution, 14 December, 1975', Bert Pearce Papers, WN 1/10. NLW.

[136] For the opposite sides of the debate from a Welsh perspective, see Brian Davies's and Peter Hall's contribution, *Comment,* 5 March 1977, pp. 69–70 and Allan Baker's and Richard Spencer's response, *Comment,* 27 April 1977, pp. 107–8; for the NCP, see 'The New Communist Party, Welsh Press Release, Sunday July 17, 1977', Bert Pearce Papers, WM/19, NLW. The impact of the NCP's split on the Welsh party was negligible.

party's unionism a particular target. For Peter Hall, a Welsh Committee member, the question was whether the party should be pushing to advance the issue to one of the creation of a small socialist state in Wales.[137] Similar sentiments were expressed by Brian Wilkinson, who argued that the party should not assume a uniform response to the crises of the 1970s across the nations of Britain. Instead, Wilkinson argued 'In accepting that Wales is a nation, the Communist Party must now start to think more in national rather than supranational UK terms', asking whether, in the event of a shift to the extreme right in England (itself a reflection of the pervasive sense of imminent political crisis prevalent in 1970s British society), the party should 'press for more independence so that Wales can progress towards socialism in advance of England'.[138]

However, the most sustained critique of party policy came from Martin Gostwick, the *Morning Star*'s parliamentary correspondent, who argued that despite its formal commitment to the right of self-determination, the party was guilty of seeking to maintain the union 'at all costs' even following the transition to socialism and of rejecting the idea that independence could ever be progressive. For Gostwick, this stance essentially confined the Welsh and Scottish assemblies to a supporting role, the fundamentals of their economic and social policies still decided at Westminster.[139] This type of thinking was evidence of the 'powerful tug of … imperially founded "Britishness" or "Great-British chauvinism"' that had 'percolated deeply into the thinking of our own Party' in which there was 'only one "British" people, one "British" working class, one "British" labour movement'.[140] Such attitudes, Gostwick argued, were increasingly untenable, failing to address the very real possibility that, having been given a real measure of devolution, Wales and Scotland, in the light of different traditions, experiences and forms of

---

[137] 'Special Welsh Committee Conference of Devolution, 14 December, 1975'.

[138] Brian Wilkinson, 'Socialism and Welsh Independence: a Contribution to Discussion', *Cyffro*, 4 (2), Summer 1976, p. 62.

[139] Martin Gostwick, 'British Roads or National Roads? Hard Choices Ahead', *Marxism Today*, August 1978, pp. 263–4.

[140] Gostwick, 'British Roads or National Roads? Hard Choices Ahead', p. 265.

development, would pursue different paths to socialism.[141] For Gostwick, the concept of 'one "British" road of building one "broad democratic alliance"' had 'already been superseded by the national dimension' and it was time for the party 'to shed illusions about detaching supporters from the nationalist parties' and instead 'recognise that the national movements represent fundamentally progressive tendencies – embryonic "broad democratic alliances" under our very noses – consisting of tens and thousands of working men and women, and many people in the professional strata multiplying all the time in demanding national rights and opportunities'.[142] The option before the party was to either 'be an out-and-out, permanently Unionist party, in which case our advocacy of strong assemblies, and abstract recognition in principle of the right to independence, will be merely lip-service' or 'ourselves become a nationalist party, accepted by the peoples of Scotland and Wales as genuine champions of national rights'.[143]

While such arguments were a minority strand of opinion within the party, they show a willingness by some party members to think beyond the general parameters of party policy on the national question, to examine the party's relationship with Britishness and to recognise that the implications of devolution were not as clear-cut as the party often assumed. However, as the new edition of the *BRS* made clear, the party remained committed to both maintaining the union, albeit being based on 'the principle of voluntary co-operation between the three nations'. While the establishment of Welsh and Scottish assemblies was to remain firmly part of a 'British road', in more general terms devolution fitted in well with the general theme of the new edition, being one of 'the major steps to decentralise government and extend the involvement of the people', that would help facilitate the building of the BDA and the transition to socialism.[144]

---

[141] Gostwick, 'British Roads or National Roads? Hard Choices Ahead', p. 266.
[142] *Comment,* 28 May 1977, p. 179.
[143] Gostwick, 'British Roads or National Roads?', p. 266.
[144] *The British Road to Socialism* (4th edition), p. 56.

From late 1976 onwards, the CPGB's focus in terms of the national question was on the passage of the consecutive devolution bills through parliament and on the subsequent referendum campaign. For the party the bills, which, in line with Labour's White Paper, offered only executive devolution for Wales, were woefully inadequate, the Welsh Committee noting in relation to the Scotland and Wales Bill, that it was so 'ineffective as to invite disillusion or defeat'.[145] Similarly, for Bert Pearce, the government's proposals represented 'the least possible step toward a new structure of a voluntarily unified Britain'.[146] For the party, the main issues were the need for legislative powers for Wales, for the introduction of proportional representation in the Assembly elections, and the granting of legislative power over the economy and industry for both assemblies, the Welsh Committee committing itself to campaigning for these vital amendments.[147] The party had three major concerns with regards to the passage of the proposed legislation. First, that the implementation of executive devolution in Wales, seen as leading to the creation of only a 'powerless talking shop', would only contribute to a growing feeling of frustrated nationalism, for the Welsh Committee, a far more effective means of setting Wales on the path to separation than the granting of a legislative assembly.[148] Second, the fear that the bill would be scuppered by rebel Labour MPs, John Gollan arguing that 'It would be a tragedy if, despite its many weaknesses, any Labour MP contributed to its defeat.'[149] Third, that the government's failure to act decisively on devolution had led to 'obscurity, confusion and division' on the issue within the labour movement, despite 'the need for devolution [having] been demonstrated by life itself with glowing clarity'.[150] In light of this, the party was to focus its energies on putting pressure on Labour MPs to strengthen the bills and on winning greater

[145] 'Press Statement – Devolution Bill Must Be Changed, November 30, 1976', Bert Pearce Papers WN 1/10, NLW.
[146] *Morning Star,* 16 December 1976, p. 2.
[147] 'Devolution Bill Must Be Changed'; Bert Pearce, 'Devolution, Democracy and Socialist Advance', *Marxism Today,* December 1977, p. 366.
[148] *A Parliament with Powers for Wales,* pp. 3–4.
[149] *Morning Star,* 4 December 1976, p. 2.
[150] *Morning Star,* 1 December 1976, p. 1.

support for legislative devolution within the labour movement. In practical terms, this saw the Welsh Committee
urging party branches to establish local pro-devolution
committees, hold public meetings on devolution, lobby their
MPs and focus their attention on winning support within the
labour movement, especially by building links with trade
union committees on the issue.[151] The Welsh Committee also
established a short-lived 'Working Party on Devolution
Issues'.[152]

A number of the party's fears were confirmed following the
abandonment of the Scotland and Wales Bill in February
1977 and the concession of a referendum, a concession which
for Bert Pearce represented an abdication of leadership by
the government.[153] While laying much of the blame for the
Bill's abandonment at the door of the rebel Labour MPs, for
the party, responsibility also lay with the government which
was criticised 'not for its decision to go ahead with the Bill but
for its refusal to move with any speed and determination, its
failure to offer anything other than a half-hearted proposal
and its dogged determination to avoid stirring up a campaign
in its support'. 'If the process of devolution is torpedoed', the
Morning Star warned, 'the price Labour will be forced to pay
will be heavy indeed'.[154] For the Welsh party, opposition to
the Bill had been effective due to an underlying lack of
conviction and weakness from the government which,
treating devolution 'as an electoral manoeuvre forced on
them', had made unnecessary concessions and 'produced a
Bill lacking in fundamental conviction' which had failed not
only to 'win popular understanding of the issues but encouraged confusion and doubt'. This was confirmation, the party
argued, of the correctness of the party's own support for
more robust devolution legislation.[155] For Bert Pearce, the
most curious feature of the whole debacle was the sight of

[151] Minutes of Welsh Committee, 16 January 1977, Bert Pearce Papers WM/19,
NLW.
[152] Minutes of Welsh Committee, 20 February 1977, Bert Pearce Papers WM/19,
NLW; interview with Mary and Tony Winter, 20 February 2009; interview with Brian
Davies, 20 February 2009.
[153] *Morning Star,* 16 December 1976, p. 2.
[154] *Morning Star,* 24 February 1977.
[155] Minutes of WEC, 16 February 1977, Bert Pearce Papers WM/19, NLW. The

left-Labour MPs siding with the Conservative Party, their decision to oppose Labour Party policy, viewed as 'disastrously
and dangerously mistaken'.[156] However, the defeat of the Bill
was not 'simply a matter of Parliamentary tactics or ... a few
sectarian and short-sighted Labour MPs', but rather a
symptom of a deeper malaise, of 'the backwardness of our
Labour and working class movement generally on the
national question'",[157] a testament to the fact that it had been
caught out by the resurgence of nationalism in Wales and
Scotland.[158]

Nevertheless, at its 35th Congress the party welcomed the
introduction of separate devolution bills in November 1977,
reiterating its support for legislative devolution and the
establishment of a labour movement campaign for significant improvements to the legislation. Significantly, congress
also declared its support for a fully federal governmental
system in Britain, backing the establishment of an English
Assembly.[159] Bert Pearce also welcomed the introduction of
the Wales Bill, noting that it presented both a 'historic
second chance (or third or fourth chance if you go back in
Labour's history)' for the Labour Party to deal adequately
with the devolution issue and an 'historic challenge to tackle
the ignorance and inadequacy of the British labour movement's approach to the national question'.[160] Pearce was,
however, critical of the failure, once again, to give Wales legislative powers, arguing that it would leave the proposed
Assembly 'ineffective in practical operation and impotent in
pressing its views on Welsh affairs'.[161] This time, however, his
comments were tinged with a sense of political realism
informed by the failure of the Scotland and Wales Bill,
arguing that even a weakened bill would mark an important

section on devolution in these minutes was added following the defeat of the guil-
lotine motion on 22 February 1977.

[156] Bert Pearce, 'Devolution: The New Shape of British Politics', *Cyffro*, 4 (3),
Spring 1977, p. 50.

[157] Bert Pearce, 'Devolution, Democracy and Socialist Advance', *Marxism Today*,
December 1977, p. 360.

[158] Pearce, 'Devolution, Democracy and Socialist Advance', p. 358.

[159] 'Devolution', *Comment*, 26 November 1977, p. 453.

[160] Pearce, 'Devolution, Democracy and Socialist Advance', p. 358.

[161] Pearce, 'Devolution, Democracy and Socialist Advance', p. 366.

advance on the established constitutional set-up, representing 'a significant victory for the labour and progressive
movement in Britain' by opening up the prospect of 'new
possibilities for further democratic action and advance'.[162]
As the passage of the Wales Bill reached its final stages,
receiving royal assent in July 1978, the search for potential
allies and for the establishment of a broad campaign in preparation for the referendum had, by that June, led to the
Welsh party's affiliation to the Wales for the Assembly
Campaign (WAC).[163] Drawing attention to a lack of party
material and activity on the issue, Pearce noted that its
involvement in the campaign was the result of 'rather strenuous individual efforts'.[164] Following its inaugural all-Wales
conference, held in late June, three party members, Bert
Pearce, Dai Francis and Mary Winter, took a seat on the
campaign's executive, while all party branches were urged to
make every effort to secure support for a yes vote in both
their localities and within the labour movement.[165] The initial
focus was on maintaining unity, with Mary Winter arguing
that it was now vital that the Welsh political parties overcame
their differences in order to 'ensure that the devolution issue
does not become a secondary issue',[166] hopes that were to
suffer a significant blow following the Labour Party and
Wales TUC's decision to go it alone during the referendum
campaign.
   Nevertheless, for the party, the referendum campaign still
held considerable potential as a means of not only developing links with the Labour Party and the Plaid Cymru left,
but also of giving the Welsh party and its policies a higher

[162] Pearce, 'Devolution, Democracy and Socialist Advance', pp. 365–6.
[163] For the politics surrounding 1979 referendum campaign, see the essays in
Foulkes et al. (eds), *The Welsh Veto;* for the Labour Party perspective, see Evans,
Devolution in Wales, pp. 136–201; for the attitude of the Labour Party leadership,
see Andrew Edwards, '"Te Parti Mwncïod"? Rhwyg, Anghytgord a Datblygiad Polisi
Llafur ar Ddatganoli, 1966–1979', *Cof Cenedl XXIV,* 2009, pp. 161–89.
[164] CPGB Archive, 'Report of Progress on Main Issues of Work' [undated, *c.*June
1978], CP/CENT/ORG/11/2 (LHASC).
[165] Minutes for WAC Executive Committee Meetings, Wales for the Assembly
Campaign Papers, 9 (Group 2), NLW; 'Communist Party Welsh Congress 1979:
Draft Resolutions, Branch Amendments, Resolutions', p. 13, Bert Pearce Papers
WC/12, NLW.
[166] 'Editorial Notes', *Cyffro,* 4 (4), Summer 1978, p. 6.

profile, with particular stress placed on the importance of the party's campaign work as a means of increasing its presence within local communities and ultimately drawing people to the Communist perspective. In the longer term, the campaign was also viewed as a platform for building a broader movement that would campaign for left-wing and socialist policies, in line with the strategy outlined in the *BRS*.[167] The party's affiliation to WAC had, however, meant a significant shift in position, hinted at in Pearce's comments on the Wales Bill, for while the party maintained its commitment to legislative devolution, the party now accepted the limitations of the Wales Act, depicting the proposed assembly not as a 'powerless talking-shop' but as 'the first step toward the democratisation of Welsh society', a focus for political mobilisation and a forum for public debate on the decisions taken at Westminster.[168]

The main focus of the party's campaigning was on winning the support of working-class voters, especially trade unionists, with devolution presented not only as a vital democratic reform but as the only means of dealing with Wales' economic problems. In doing this the party linked devolution to issues of job creation and economic and industrial development. Similarly, particular focus was placed on Conservative opposition to devolution and on the disloyalty of the rebel Welsh Labour MPs, while the party's pamphlet for the campaign sought, in an echo of the Popular Front era, to link devolution with Wales' progressive tradition and its history of working-class militancy, as well as to issues of democratic control and the left's alternative economic strategy.[169] For Bert Pearce, an Assembly was 'most urgently needed to focus public energy and public funds in tackling the long-standing disease of the Welsh economy', which, had it already been established, would have allowed for the better protection of Welsh jobs.[170] For Dai Francis, there was a clear class dimension to the devolution campaign, the opponents of devolution depicted as 'our traditional class enemies', the

---

[167] 'Devolution and the Welsh Assembly', pp. 1–2.
[168] 'Devolution and the Welsh Assembly', p. 1.
[169] *Welsh Communists Say Vote Yes on Thurs. March 1st – Work for Wales:* Cardiff, 1979.
[170] *Morning Star,* 9 February 1979, p. 4.

campaign as one of 'Wales Against the Tories'.[171] The exception to this was the rebel Labour MPs, whose attitude to devolution Francis found difficult to fathom, rejecting their argument that the legislation was a sop to the nationalists:

> If they believe that sort of tripe they've got no faith in the labour movement because the Labour Party was talking about an Assembly for Wales long before the Plaid came into existence. I cannot understand the attitude of Kinnock and that crowd – they believe in a Welsh rugby team, a Welsh soccer team, a Welsh Labour Party, a Welsh Communist Party and a Welsh Liberal Party. Why not a Welsh Assembly?[172]

Strong support for the campaign was also evident in the party press with the *Morning Star*, in particular, giving prominent coverage to the campaigns both in Wales and Scotland, publishing a week-long set of features in support of the devolution in the final week of campaigning with contributions from across the political spectrum. While absent from the arguments put forward in favour of devolution, also present in the party press were intimations that the establishment of Scottish and Welsh assemblies heralded the end of empire.[173]

While the party was now focused on a particular strategy and despite all branches being urged 'without exception' to make contact with their local WAC committees and to mobilise in support of the campaign,[174] concerns were raised by February 1979 regarding the level of the branches activity in the campaign.[175] Anecdotal evidence suggests that the level of party activity was varied, its involvement hampered by a decline in the number of active party members and branches. For Julian Tudor Hart, a Glyncorrwg communist and Welsh Committee member, it was often a case of 'all chiefs and no Indians'. John Osmond, a leading figure in WAC, recalls that despite the active role of party leaders such as Bert Pearce and Dai Francis, who as chair of the South Glamorgan WAC

---

[171] Dai Francis, 'Devolution D-Day ... It's Wales Against the Tories', *The Miner*, February/March 1979, p. 4.

[172] *Morning Star*, 7 February 1979, p. 2.

[173] See the cover of *Comment*, 17 February 1979 and a similar, but earlier, cartoon in *Cyffro*, 4 (3), Spring 1977, p. 30.

[174] Minutes of WEC, 31 January 1979, Bert Pearce Papers WM/21, NLW.

[175] Minutes of WEC, 7 February 1979, Bert Pearce Papers WM/21, NLW.

spoke at numerous public meetings, the party's involvement in the campaign was hampered by both a lack of bodies on the ground and the lack of an effective national organisation, in contrast to Plaid Cymru whose members carried out the majority of the campaigning for WAC.[176] In other areas, however, party branches were active in the campaign; in the Dulais Valley, where Hywel Francis was chairman of the party branch, much of the canvassing was left to CPGB and Plaid Cymru members. Such was the lack of support for devolution from within the local Labour Party that Francis was asked to chair a Labour Party meeting in support of the referendum, the local Labour Party unable to find anyone within the party who was willing to take the chair.[177] Similarly, the Aberdare branch was also active in its local WAC, helping to organise public meetings in support of a yes vote.[178] In north Wales, the party's involvement in the campaign had, according to its secretary Manny Cohen, 'promoted the small Communist organisation into the political mainstream'.[179] Thus, anecdotal evidence points to only sporadic involvement from party branches in the campaign, a result not of a lack of support for devolution but of significant organisational difficulties and a decline in active membership of the party. At a more general level, the party's main role in the campaign was as a conduit into the labour movement, the campaign seeking to use the party leadership's strong links with the labour movement to win its support for the campaign.[180] The Welsh Committee's own assessment was that its activity had been 'uneven' but that some party branches had played a significant role in initiating WAC groups in their areas.[181]

While the defeat of the Wales Act at the referendum had not been wholly unexpected, the extent of the defeat was a deep disappointment for the party, the resounding no vote making it clear that the efforts of the CPGB, Labour Party

[176] Interview with Julian Tudor Hart, 5 December 2008; interview with John Osmond, 11 November 2009.

[177] Interview with Hywel Francis, 27 October 2009.

[178] Interview with Mary and Tony Winter, 20 February 2009.

[179] *Morning Star*, 20 February 1979, p. 2.

[180] Interview with John Osmond, 11 November 2009.

[181] 'Welsh Committee Report of Work, January 1979–October 1980', Bert Pearce Papers WC/13, NLW.

and Wales TUC had failed to win over the mass of those organised in the labour movement for devolution. The defeat was a particular disappointment for leading party figures prominent in the campaign, such as Dai Francis, to whom the extent of the defeat came as a real shock, leaving him depressed and particularly angry at the role played by Neil Kinnock and the rebel Labour MPs.[182] Despite this the party's initial response was defiant, the *Morning Star* calling on Parliament to abandon the 40 per cent clause and give Scotland its parliament. For the paper, despite the referendum setbacks devolution remained a live issue,

> The Welsh and Scottish nations are a fact. The problems which face Welsh and Scottish people day by day are a fact. Facts are stubborn things, and they can only be coped with by facing up to the need to extend democracy through devolution. For this reason the fight for the Assemblies must continue.[183]

Similarly for the Welsh Committee, the referendum marked 'not an end but a new stage. It has brought the argument out of parliament and to the minds of many people for the first time. The case for a Welsh Assembly will grow and come again.'[184]

In the EC's report on the referenda, Gordon McLennan placed the main responsibility for the defeats at the door of the Labour Government and the rebel Labour MPs.[185] However, McLennan was also critical of the party's own approach to the campaign, arguing that it had failed to put forward the arguments for devolution 'with anything like sufficient determination and consistency' within the labour movement. McLennan pointed specifically to the contribution of the Welsh and Scottish parties, arguing that in the period since 1969 neither party had 'campaigned as they should have done for the establishment of Assemblies. Devolution has been seen as one of a number of issues, not the critical and central feature of all our work'. This was a situation that had to change, 'This it must become. Apart

---

[182] Interview with Hywel Francis, 27 October 2009.
[183] *Morning Star*, 3 March 1979, p. 1.
[184] 'The Referendum, March 1, 1979', Bert Pearce Papers WN 1/10, NLW.
[185] 'Devolution Referenda and After', p. 3, Bert Pearce Papers, WN 1/15, NLW.

from all the great democratic, economic and national questions involved, it is also clear that the building of our Party as
a decisive force in Scotland and Wales will be determined by
how we deal with this.'[186] For the Welsh Committee, while the
no vote was 'a severe setback for democratic progress in
Wales', in reality it was the particular form of devolution
proposed in the Wales Act that had been rejected and not
devolution itself, the referendum campaign having shown
how deeply rooted the issue was in Welsh political life.[187] At
the root of the referendum defeat was the 'feeble' Wales Act
which, pleasing nobody, 'was a peg which the No campaigners
could hang all their fearsome bogeys, while its actual powers
for Wales were so limited as to rouse little enthusiasm
amongst the most ardent supporters of devolution'.[188] The
government's culpability had been further compounded by
its failure to adequately explain the Act to the public, instead
offering only a misplaced appeal to Labour loyalty at a time
of increasing government unpopularity, and by its failure to
face down Labour opponents of devolution at an earlier
stage.[189] However, while much of the blame lay with the inadequacy of both the Wales Act and the Labour Government,
the party also recognised that its own campaign had failed to
win the argument amongst the rank and file of the labour
movement, with 'far too little … done, both by our party and
others, to carry the arguments in detail to the people and to
the basic organisations of the movement'.[190]

Reeling from the impact of the referendum defeat the
party was dealt a further blow in the form of the election of
the first Thatcher government in May 1979, an election
victory which marked the end of the political consensus
which had dominated British politics since the end of the
Second World War. The CPGB was to be at the heart of the

[186] 'Devolution Referenda and After', pp. 5–6. Bert Pearce's copy of the report,
however, has a question mark over the section where the lack of activity by the Welsh
party on devolution is discussed, suggesting he disagreed with McLennan's interpretation of the party's work on devolution.
[187] 'Devolution Buried but is it Dead?', c.March 1979, p. 2, Bert Pearce Papers
WN 1/4, NLW.
[188] 'Devolution Buried but is it Dead?', p. 5.
[189] 'Devolution Buried but is it Dead?', pp. 4–5.
[190] 'Devolution Buried but is it Dead?', p. 6.

debate that engulfed the left as it sought a new strategy with which to combat Thatcherism and the New Right with much of the period that followed seeing the party, when not engaged in internecine warfare, seeking to build new alliances around which a counter-hegemonic movement could be built. For some Welsh party members, the best hope for building such a movement in Wales lay in a continuation of the campaign for devolution. Speaking at a conference at Aberystwyth in late 1979, Alistair Wilson argued the case for the foundation of a broad movement for democratic rights in Wales centred on the demand for devolution, the dormant possibilities of the referendum campaign and on the emergence of a plethora of community groups and social movements, each concerned at their heart with the extension of democratic rights and community control. For Wilson, each of these groups shared a common political impulse, 'they are all actively working for more say in the school or health centre, the village, town, city, and also more say in factory or pit, more power over the right to work, to better education, and health, better conditions of work, and more say in the way in which the economic and social life of Wales is being conducted'. This impulse, Wilson argued, was one that could be linked to support for a Welsh Assembly,

> What they are all saying is 'We want more say about the way in which we run our lives, in industry as well as in the Community'. Is not the movement for a Welsh Assembly with legislative and financial powers an extension of this demand? Is not an increasing section of Welsh people saying – 'We want more say in the way Wales is run'?[191]

However, such hopes were for the time being to prove unrealistic, the extent of the referendum defeat seemingly killing off any possibility that a broad popular movement could be built around devolution, despite the party's determination to keep devolution a live issue. The period that was to follow was to be one of crisis and renewal for the left. In Wales, the election of a Conservative government with a drastically improved vote, following on from the referendum

---

[191] Alistair Wilson, 'National Consciousness and Class Consciousness, [1979]' p. 13, Bert Pearce Papers WN 1/5, NLW.

defeat, compounded the sense of crisis on the left, leading some party members to question the existence of a Welsh nation, the Welsh seemingly abandoning their own distinctive national and political traditions. The search for a way out of this impasse was to become the main feature of the party's politics during the next decade.

Defeat, Renewal and Dissolution, 1980–1991

Having lost over a quarter of its membership between 1975 and 1979, the 1980s were to witness the final, terminal decline of the CPGB. The party, riven with splits for much of the decade and faced with the continuing decline of both its membership and its core industrial base and natural political constituency, was unable to escape the long shadow of the collapse of communism in both Eastern Europe and the Soviet Union, despite its significant ideological shift away from Marxism-Leninism. Despite this, during the early 1980s the party was still able to make an important contribution to the politics of the day, taking an active, organisational role in mobilising against unemployment through the People's March for Jobs, and remaining a significant force in the campaigns against apartheid, for women's rights and within CND. Most significant, and most controversial, for the party, however, was the success of its theoretical journal, *Marxism Today*, which, under the editorship of Martin Jacques, had by the mid-1980s become one of the few success stories, not only for the CPGB, ensuring that it remained a significant political actor on the left, but for the left in general. The journal provided an important forum of debate for the left as well as offering an influential analysis of Thatcherism and the future of the left in Britain rooted in the Gramscian analysis of British society developed within the party during the 1970s and in the strategy of the BDA. The success of *Marxism Today* had helped the Eurocommunists win back their position of influence within the party sparking a backlash from those, especially among its industrial activists, who opposed their interpretation of the BDA, their critique of the labour movement, and the implications of their analysis of both Thatcherism and the future of the left. This led directly to the damaging split within the party that was to dominate its internal politics for much of the decade.

The Eurocommunists, and their allies, questioned the party's and the left's overriding focus on the labour movement which, according to a highly critical assessment developed from the mid-1970s onwards, had entered a period of significant decline, failing to adapt to changes in British society, while engaging in increasingly sectional and economistic forms of militancy.[192] The left's fortunes had been compounded by the rise of Thatcherism which, according to *Marxism Today*'s influential analysis, represented a new form of Conservatism, a right-wing hegemonic project which, by building a hegemonic bloc based on themes of anti-collectivism, anti-statism, law and order and an emergent jingoistic British nationalism, had engineered a rightward shift in British politics. In doing this it had emerged victorious from an organic and hegemonic crisis that had developed in British society since the mid-1960s as the post-war social-democratic consensus had collapsed.[193] For the Eurocommunists, the solution lay in the radical realignment of the left, based on broadening the outlook of both the labour movement and the left and building links with the broader social forces and movements that had emerged during the 1970s, with labourism in both its left and right-wing forms identified as a political dead-end in the changed circumstances of 1980s British society. Amongst those groups pinpointed by the Gramscians was the nationalist movement, whose emergence as an electoral force in the 1974 General Elections was viewed as exemplifying the 'wider process of fragmentation, erosion and realignment' associated with the hegemonic crisis of the 1970s.[194] For those opposed to this

---

[192] See, in particular, Bill Warren and Mike Prior, *Advanced Capitalism and Backward Socialism* (Nottingham, 1975); Mike Prior and David Purdy, *Out of the Ghetto* (Nottingham, 1979); and Eric Hobsbawm, *The Forward March of Labour Halted?* (London, 1981).

[193] Stuart Hall, 'The Great Moving Right Show', *Marxism Today*, January 1979, pp. 14–20. For a revised version of this article and others presenting the Thatcherism thesis, see Martin Jacques and Stuart Hall (eds), *The Politics of Thatcherism* (London, 1983).

[194] Martin Jacques, 'Thatcherism: Breaking Out of the Impasse' in Jacques and Hall (eds), *The Politics of Thatcherism*, pp. 48–9.

analysis, the main points of contention were rooted in class politics. The analysis of Thatcherism as a qualitatively different form of Conservatism was rejected as placing too much emphasis on Thatcherism and not enough on the underlying continuity of capitalist class rule, while the focus on the BDA was viewed as an effective abandonment the central role of class and class struggle in Marxist analysis. In addition, the notion of a labour movement in decline was rejected as a misreading of the actual situation, while the critical nature of *Marxism Today*'s coverage of the Soviet Union was viewed as anti-Soviet.[195]

As a result of this split, by 1985 the party had lost control of the *Morning Star* along with a good proportion of its industrial militants with a large number of party dissidents purged, the leadership, by this time allied with the reformers within the party, turning to democratic centralism to discipline its errant members. The impact of the split, especially the loss of the party paper hampered its ability to offer a fully effective national response to the miners' strike of 1984–85, although it was able to play a significant role within the NUM in both Wales and Scotland. By 1988, many of these party dissidents had found a new home in the CPB, while their defeat had, by the late 1980s, led to a significant ideological shift within the CPGB, a process boosted by Gorbachev's attempt to reform communism in the Soviet Union. This process culminated in the drafting of a new party programme, *Manifesto for New Times*, published in 1990.

In line with much of the thinking developed in the pages of *Marxism Today*, the main theme of the *Manifesto* was the need to develop a socialist strategy that was relevant to the conditions that had emerged following a decade of Thatcherism, a period which, the *Manifesto* argued, had witnessed the emergence of a post-Fordist society.[196] Noting

---

[195] For a full exposition of this position, see Ben Fine, Laurence Harris, Marjorie Mayo, Angela Weir and Elizabeth Wilson, *Class Politics: an Answer to its Critics* (London, 1984); for a rebuttal, see Eric Hobsbawm, 'The Retreat into Extremism', *Marxism Today*, April 1985, pp. 7–12.

[196] On post-Fordism, see Robin Murray, 'Fordism and Post-Fordism' in Stuart Hall and Martin Jacques (eds), *New Times: The Changing Face of Politics in the 1990s* (London, 1989), pp. 38–53.

the failure of both the post-war settlement to meet the aspirations of a diverse number of groups in society and of the left
to adequately respond to this failure,[197] the *Manifesto*, identifying Thatcherism as both a hegemonic project[198] and a form
of 'conservative modernisation',[199] put forward an alternative
programme for a self-managing socialist society. This was to
be based on sustainability, decentralisation, greater democratic control, constitutional reform, new forms of social
ownership and a feminist, anti-racist and green agenda. The
Manifesto repudiated Marxism-Leninism, rejecting it as a
'tarnished socialism, in which the individual and civil society
were subordinated to the state and the party', while the
communist states were viewed as having 'sought to justify
their authoritarian and repressive nature by developing a
rigid and dogmatic ideology which borrowed the language of
Marxism, while distorting its essence'.[200] Other basic tenets
of the party's politics were also questioned, notably the
primacy of class, the importance of class identities as 'a strong
point of common identity, commitment and purpose' viewed
as having diminished, the issue of identity becoming more
complex, with gender and race now equally likely to deter-
mine life chances. Similarly, moving away from labourist,
top-down, state-based solutions to Britain's economic and
social problems, the *Manifesto* advocated the devolving of
economic and political power through new forms of social
ownership and planning combined with market mechanisms
as an alternative to large-scale nationalisation.[201]

The *Manifesto* retained the CPGB's commitment to the
establishment of devolved assemblies and a federal Britain,
the denial of national rights to Wales and Scotland viewed as
one of the components of the failed post-war settlement that
had led to its collapse during the 1970s.[202] Welsh and Scottish
nationalism were viewed as being among those currents
offering an alternative path in British politics, presenting 'a

[197] *Manifesto for New Times*, pp. 19–22.
[198] *Manifesto for New Times*, pp. 27–32.
[199] *Manifesto for New Times*, p. 25.
[200] *Manifesto for New Times*, pp. 13–14.
[201] *Manifesto for New Times*, pp. 74–84.
[202] *Manifesto for New Times*, p. 21.

fundamental challenge to the character of the British state, insisting it be remade democratically' whilst also challenging Thatcherism's 'British-bulldog nationalism'.[203] Their resurgence during the 1980s, especially in Scotland, was viewed as a critical component of the reaction to Thatcherism's restructuring of British society and its economy, a response stemming from the 'disproportionate costs of restructuring' that both countries had borne.[204] In particular, the Scottish Constitutional Convention was viewed as an archetypical example of the type of broad alliance that could successfully challenge Thatcherism.[205]

Support for devolution was also linked to a more general growth in national consciousness across the world, associated with the growth of localisation alongside, and in response to, globalisation,[206] while support for Welsh and Scottish assemblies was also linked to the emerging perspective of a Europe of the regions. The devolved assemblies, as a vital extension of democracy and forum for the decentralisation of power, would have important roles to play in solving both Britain's constitutional crisis and in helping regulate the British economy, ensuring greater democratic control over the regulatory process.[207] Alongside support for devolved assemblies and a federal Britain, the *Manifesto* was also critical of the attitude of the Labour Party and the labour movement to constitutional change, accusing both of being constitutionally conservative. The Labour Party was criticised for being overly committed to 'the supremacy of parliamentary politics, to the central state and the British union',[208] while the labour movement was criticised for seeking 'to occupy the state when the state needs to be transformed', retaining its commitment to the British union and opposing electoral reform and a bill of rights.[209] If Britain was to be modernised in a more humane, sustainable and democratic way,

[203] *Manifesto for New Times*, p. 10.
[204] *Manifesto for New Times*, p. 25.
[205] *Manifesto for New Times*, pp. 38–9.
[206] *Manifesto for New Times*, p. 67.
[207] *Manifesto for New Times*, p. 80.
[208] *Manifesto for New Times*, p. 41.
[209] *Manifesto for New Times*, p. 49.

devolution was to be one of the key components of this modernisation.

By this time, however, the party had undergone a further decade of decline, party membership falling from 20,599 in 1979 to 4,742 by 1991, the party haemorrhaging some 10,000 members as it fought out its internal battles in the mid-1980s.[210] Similarly, its electoral results continued their downward trajectory, falling to 11,606 in 1983 to 6,078 in 1987.[211] At its 41st Congress, held in November 1989, the party initiated the process that would lead to its dissolution in 1991, Congress calling on the new EC to review and launch a discussion on the party's future. Events were, however, to overtake the party's transformation, the collapse of communism in Eastern Europe bringing debates regarding the party's future to a head, an emergency resolution at Congress welcoming the changes taking place in Eastern Europe, calling for the speedy implementation of political reforms and democratisation.[212] Much of the party's hopes in relation to the changes in Eastern Europe lay in a vision of a more democratic version of socialism emerging from the ruins of the Eastern Bloc regimes. However, with this failing to emerge, the changes in Eastern Europe amounting to a rejection, at least in the short term, of socialism per se, the party found itself firmly, as Willie Thompson notes, on the wrong side of history.[213]

In the opening speech to Congress, Martin Jacques made the implications of the changes in Eastern Europe clear: 'It is the end of the road for the communist system as we have known it: the central plan, the authoritarian state, the single-party system, the subjugated civil society. Stalinism is dead and Leninism – its theory of state, its concept of the party, the absence of civil society, its notion of revolution – has also had its day.'[214] For Jacques, it was impossible for the party to avoid transforming itself under such circumstances, the party

---

[210] Thompson, *The Good Old Cause*, p. 218. Party membership had dropped to 10,350 by 1987 and to 7,615 by 1989.

[211] Craig, *British Electoral Facts 1832–1987*, pp. 48 and 50.

[212] *News and Views*, December 1989, p. 2.

[213] Thompson, *The Good Old Cause*, pp. 204–5.

[214] Martin Jacques, 'After Communism', *Marxism Today*, January 1990, p. 37.

having 'moved intellectually' had failed to move on as an organisation, 'its culture, habits, sense of hierarchy, and sheer conservatism' remaining 'determinately stuck in history', the gap between its intellectual direction and its party culture a 'yawning chasm'. What was now required was 'the most open discussion' on the party's future with 'no hold barred, no forbidden territory, no heresies … we have no future as we are'.[215]

Proposals for the party's transformation were presented to the EC by Nina Temple in January. Temple's report, noting that the party's decline was 'inexorable' and rejecting the Leninist party as 'no longer appropriate or desirable', put forward three proposals: modernising and democratising the existing party; transforming into a loose political association; or, Temple's own preferred option, adopting a twin-track approach that would combine the two, modernising the party while setting up a political association that would create a broader political network outside of the party.[216] Despite opposition from significant sections of the party, most notably the Scottish party, which by this time had the largest membership, and the remnants of the Straight Left faction, the party chose the latter option at its 42nd Special Congress held in December 1990. However, the proposals put forward by the EC in March 1991 were, in essence, proposals for a political association, which were nevertheless accepted by the party at its final 43rd Congress, held in November 1991, the party transforming itself into the Democratic Left, revelations regarding the continuation of Soviet funding of the CPGB up until 1979 providing the final nail in the party's coffin.[217]

In Wales, the party's decline continued during the 1980s, its membership falling from 1,284 in 1980 to only 277 by 1991,[218] while electorally the party's vote fell from 2,015 in the 1983 General Election to 869 in 1987.[219] The 1980s also

---

[215] Jacques, 'After Communism', p. 38.

[216] *7 Days*, 20 January 1990, p. 6.

[217] *Changes*, 16–29 November 1991, p. 2.

[218] 'Welsh Committee Report of Work, January 1979–October 1980', p. 4; 'Report of Work July 1990–June 1991', p. 1, Bert Pearce Papers WC/18, NLW.

[219] Jones, *Etholiadau'r Ganrif 1885–1997*, pp. 131–5, 137–40. In 1987, the party only contested one seat compared to three in 1983.

saw two changes in party leadership, with Dave Richards replacing Bert Pearce as Welsh secretary in 1984 and Les Skeats replacing Richards in 1990. Party membership did not, however, drop under a thousand until 1985, following the defeat of the miners, the party's rapid decline thereafter mirroring the rapid disappearance of the mining industry in south Wales.[220] The party's dependence on the mining communities and its failure to expand into different industries and communities was a problem recognised by the party leadership,

> The Welsh Party has been so heavily involved in the mining industry that this was to a large extent its political base in Wales ... With the shrinking of the coalfield and the closure of the pits, we witnessed a shrinking of the Party's size and influence. There was, and still continues to be, a failure to build the Party in the 'new' industries, and also in the newer communities, where we have no, or very little branch activity and membership.[221]

Such was the CPGB's predicament by the mid-1980s that even the Welsh party's modest achievement of maintaining its membership at a consistent level between 1982 and 1984 was praised by Dave Cook, the party's national organiser, at the 1984 Welsh Congress.[222] Despite this, the Welsh party leadership were fully aware of the predicament that now faced the party with only two functioning Area Committees, Rhondda and North Wales, in existence by the end of that year, those in Cardiff and West Wales having to be re-established and aggregate meetings held in other areas to start new area committees from scratch.[223] Similar difficulties were also evident at branch level with Congress resolutions

---

[220] Party membership dropped from 1,236 in 1981 to 1,044 in 1982, and hovered around the thousand mark until 1985 when it dropped to 765, beginning a sustained period of decline that continued until the party's dissolution: see Welsh Committee 'Report of Work, January 1981–October 1982', p. 4, Bert Pearce Papers, WC/14, NLW; 'Report of Work December 1982–November 1984' p. 3, Bert Pearce Papers WC/15, NLW; 'Report of Work of Welsh Committee 1985–86', p. 5, Bert Pearce Papers WC/16, NLW.

[221] 'Communist Party: Welsh Congress' [1984], p. 8, Bert Pearce Papers WC/15, NLW.

[222] 'Text of speech delivered by Dave Cook to the 1984 Welsh Congress', Bert Pearce Papers WC/15, NLW.

[223] 'Communist Party: Welsh Congress' [1984], p. 11.

throughout the 1980s bemoaning the poverty of branch life and activity, its hampering of the party's attempts to build a BDA and its serious effect on the party's finances.

With party branches viewed as the core element in the building of a BDA rooted in community activism, their decline was a serious issue for the Welsh Committee,[224] which noted in late 1980 that it was 'still too much of a party of devoted individuals, rather than a party firmly based in functioning workplace branches and local branches'.[225] Two years later, the Welsh Committee was again commenting on the small size of the party and the decline in branch life, noting that it was hampering the party's ability to fully engage with the labour movement let alone 'fulfil our potential role of campaigning for a revolutionary change in society'.[226] In 1984 the Welsh Committee, recognising the party's 'very long term problem' in this regard, again noted the unevenness and inadequacy of the party's organisation, noting that 'although some branches are successful in some respects' most branches met 'infrequently or not at all' while workplace organisation was 'almost non-existent'.[227] These difficulties were compounded by serious financial problems, the Welsh party, by 1987, forced to raise party dues and approach a group of party members for extra donations in order to cover basic costs, being unable to cover the wages of its one full-time party worker,[228] a matter that was still not fully resolved by 1990 despite the establishment of a Finance Review Group.[229] The party's organisational problems were, ultimately, to prove insurmountable, with Les Skeats noting in 1991 that the party's organisational structure had 'almost collapsed' with only 'a few branches' remaining that worked

---

[224] 'Communist Party Welsh Congress: The Communist Party as a Campaigning Force to Defeat the Tories to Save the Future for Wales' [1980], p. 6.
[225] 'Communist Party Welsh Congress: The Communist Party as a Campaigning Force to Defeat the Tories to Save the Future for Wales', p. 12.
[226] 'Communist Party Welsh Congress: The People in Action – The Way Ahead for Wales', [1982], p. 8.
[227] 'Communist Party Welsh Congress' [1984], p. 8.
[228] Minutes of Welsh Committee, 19 October 1987, Bert Pearce Papers WM/29, NLW.
[229] Minutes of WEC, 10 January 1990, Bert Pearce Papers WM/31, NLW; Minutes of Welsh Committee, 26 January 1989, Bert Pearce Papers WM/30, NLW.

effectively.[230] Nevertheless, despite these difficulties the party was still able to make a significant, if diminishing, contribution to Welsh politics during the 1980s, especially in the early to mid-1980s, organising a Welsh People's March for Jobs in 1981 and 1982, playing a prominent role within CND Cymru and in the Welsh Anti-Apartheid Movement, and, most significantly, as part of the Wales Congress in Support of Mining Communities (WCSMC) during the miners' strike of 1984–85. By the late 1980s and early 1990s, however, the party's contribution to these movements was increasingly on the basis of individual initiative, rather than the result of the broad activity of the party as a whole.

Despite its continued commitment to the establishment of a Welsh Assembly, the party's practical engagement with the national question during this period was limited to its involvement in the Campaign for a Welsh Assembly in the late 1980s and early 1990s. In part, this can be explained by the more pressing need to respond to the devastating impact of Thatcherism on Wales and the Welsh economy, the Thatcherite programme of economic restructuring leading to the decimation ~of the country's core industries, coal and steel, and to serious cutbacks in the public sector, the country's largest employer. For the CPGB, the election of a Conservative government was disastrous for Wales, not only causing 'untold anxiety and hardship' in the present but having grave implications for Wales' future development, not only by undermining Wales' economic base,[231] but also by launching an unprecedented attack on the social values that had sustained Welsh society.[232] Invoking memories of the inter-war years, for the Welsh Committee, the impact of Thatcherism would be even more damaging to the Welsh economy than the inter-war depression, with Thatcherite economic restructuring identified as a programme of

[230] *Eye on Wales: The Death of the Old Communist Party in South Wales,* 14 April 1991, BBC Radio Wales, Screen and Sound Archive D/RM 1272/6, NLW.

[231] 'Communist Party Welsh Congress: The Communist Party a Campaigning Force to Defeat the Tories and Save the Future for Wales' [1980], p. 3, Bert Pearce Papers WC/13, NLW.

[232] 'Communist Party Welsh Congress: The Communist Party a Campaigning Force to Defeat the Tories and Save the Future for Wales', p. 4.

deindustrialisation that brought into question 'the survival of Wales as an industrial nation',[233] with Wales viewed as being particularly vulnerable due to the central role played by the nationalised industries and the public sector in the Welsh economy.[234]

It can also be partly explained, at least in the early 1980s, as a response to the failure of the devolution referendum of 1979, a defeat which left the national movement reeling and the prospects for any type of measure of self-government for Wales looking decidedly grim. With its political strategy, in line with the *BRS*, centred on building a BDA, initial hopes that such an alliance could be built out of what remained of the WAC were dashed. Instead, the party focused its energies on other issues that had the potential around which to build the BDA – unemployment, nuclear disarmament, the future of coalmining communities and the threatened privatisation of the NHS – only to return to devolution following the Conservative Party's electoral setback in Wales in the 1987 General Election, which brought into stark relief the extent of the democratic deficit at the heart of the British constitutional settlement. Despite this, devolution remained an important component of the Welsh party's analysis and critique of Thatcherism throughout the 1980s, while the national movement remained a central component of any BDA that was to be built in Wales.

The prospect of such an alliance being built was greatly improved following a significant leftward shift within the national movement during the early 1980s. Entering the 1980s both the left and the national movement were in disarray, the referendum defeat compounded by the election of a Conservative government, which having gained three seats at the 1979 election was to win a further three at the 1983 election. With a total of 14 seats it won its largest ever number of MPs in Wales, and seemingly threatened, for the first time, Labour's hegemony. In a grim assessment of the implications of this double blow, Gwyn Alf Williams, then a

---

[233] 'Communist Party Welsh Congress: The People in Action – The Way Ahead for Wales', [1982] p. 3, Bert Pearce Papers WC/14, NLW.
[234] 'Defend and Extend People's Rights – A Working Democracy for Wales', [1984], p. 1, Bert Pearce Papers WN 1/7, NLW.

member of the CPGB and one of the leading Welsh Marxist intellectuals of the period, reflected the sense of crisis pervading Welsh politics, noting,

> In 1979, the Welsh electorate wrote finis to two hundred years of Welsh history. They rejected every tradition to which the modern Welsh had committed themselves. They drove into bankruptcy every political creed which modern Wales had embraced … 'Welsh politics' ceased to exist, the Welsh had finally disappeared into Britain. First of the British, they looked like being the last.[235]

For Williams, Wales was undergoing an existential crisis, the restructuring of the Welsh economy radically transforming Wales' distinct industrial and political identity, leading to the transformation of working-class communities in the south Wales valleys into 'commuter beds of atomised individuals', while in north and west Wales communities struggled to cope with the impact of English migration.[236] Complementing this structural crisis was a crisis of political representation, characterised by an increasingly ineffective Labour Party and Wales TUC, and a divided socialist movement, unable to come fully to terms with the national movement, its resistance to Thatcherism classed as 'puny'.[237] In the social sphere, Williams detected an increasing, 'viciously destructive', cleavage between Welsh- and English-speaking communities, linked to the success of the 'heroic and dedicated crusade' of the language movement and a subsequent backlash from those English-speakers, especially amongst the working class, who felt excluded from its gains.[238] For Williams, the solution to overcoming these divisions, and for the regeneration of the Welsh left, lay in the Welsh socialist movement redefining its approach to Wales and Welshness, abandoning the constitutional conservatism and negative attitudes to Wales evident within parts of the movement, and asserting the Welsh identity of the English-speaking Welsh, while making the campaigns for the Welsh

---

[235] Gwyn A. Williams, 'Mother Wales Get Off Me Back?', *Marxism Today,* December 1981, p. 14.
[236] Williams, 'Mother Wales', p. 18.
[237] Williams, 'Mother Wales', p. 19.
[238] Williams, 'Mother Wales', p. 20.

258 DEVOLUTION, DEFEAT AND DISSOLUTION, 1970–1991

language and for national rights part of the broader socialist struggle.[239]

Williams had also noted the changes afoot within the national movement, which were characterised by the growth of its Marxist wing.[240] The extent of the referendum defeat had left an ideological and political vacuum at the heart of a deeply demoralised Plaid Cymru which the left was able to fill, while CYIG was also to adopt a socialist strategy by 1982.[241] Within Plaid Cymru two separate Marxist strands can be detected, the orthodox Marxism-Leninism of the Faner Goch grouping and the Gramsci-influenced Marxism of the National Left. The Faner Goch grouping's Marxism-Leninism found its fullest expression in the pamphlet *Sosialaeth i'r Cymry*,[242] which, published shortly after the referendum defeat, formed the basis for the short-lived Welsh Socialist Republican Movement (WSRM). In arguing that the struggle for national liberation had to be based on the working class, and that socialists had to recognise the centrality of the national question to its struggle against capitalism, *Sosialaeth i'r Cymry*, written by Robert Griffiths and Gareth Miles, reflected significant elements of the CPGB's position on the national question, the authors drawing partly on the work of Communists such as John Roose Williams and Brian Davies.[243] However, other elements, most notably its call for an independent Welsh Socialist Republic, were anathema to the mainstream thought on the national question within the party and there was little contact between the CPGB and the WSRM.[244]

[239] Gwyn A. Williams, 'Land of our Fathers', *Marxism Today*, August 1982, pp. 29–30.
[240] Williams, 'Mother Wales', p. 19.
[241] For the ideological shift in Plaid Cymru, see Richard Wyn Jones, *Rhoi Cymru'n Gyntaf: Syniadaeth Plaid Cymru Cyfrol 1*, pp. 186–226; for the shift within CYIG, see Dylan Phillips, *Trwy Dulliau Chwyldro? Hanes Cymdeithas yr Iaith Gymraeg 1962–1992* (Llandysul, 1998), pp. 155–76.
[242] Robert Griffiths and Gareth Miles, *Sosialaeth i'r Cymry* (Cardiff, 1979); this was also published in a revised English-language edition as *Socialism for the Welsh People* (Cardiff, 1979).
[243] For John Roose Williams, see Griffiths and Miles, *Sosialaeth i'r Cymry*, p. 24; for Brian Davies, see Griffiths and Miles, *Sosialaeth i'r Cymry*, pp. 30–1.
[244] Griffiths and Miles, *Sosialaeth i'r Cymry*, p. 32. Interview with Robert Griffiths, 19 December 2008. For the WSRM, see Robert Griffiths, 'Resolving Contradictions

Of more significance for the prospects of building of a BDA was the ascension of the National Left within Plaid Cymru. Formed at a fringe meeting at the 1980 Plaid Cymru Conference,[245] its leading figures, Dafydd Elis Thomas and Emyr Wyn Williams, in a trenchant critique of the report by Plaid Cymru's Commission of Inquiry into the party's direction following the referendum defeat, called for a reformulation of the national question based on class and Marxist theory. In particular, Thomas and Williams emphasised the need for Plaid to unite the national struggle with that of the working class, calling on the party to position itself 'as a party at the service of that class. And through that class at the service of a new national and international economic and political order.'[246] Committed to a programme of decentralised socialism, by 1981 the National Left had succeeded in securing support from the party conference for the establishment of a decentralised socialist state. Despite its early focus on class, the thinking of the National Left was to develop along similar lines to that of the Eurocommunists within the CPGB, its foundational political statement, written by Emyr Wyn Williams, rejecting the solutions of both labourism and the traditional revolutionary left. This reflected a broader intellectual trait evident within the National Left that refused to be tied down by a dogmatic approach to socialist politics and which was willing to combine a number of different political influences in its political philosophy, [247] a modus operandi similar to that adopted by the Eurocommunists grouped around *Marxism Today*. While initially focused on building an alliance with the working class, by the mid-1980s the National Left had, for all intents and purposes, adopted the position of the BDA with Phil Cooke, another leading figure in the movement,

Between Class and Nation' in John Osmond, *The National Question Again: Welsh Political Identity in the 1980s* (Llandysul, 1985), pp. 194–7; John Osmond, *Police Conspiracy?* (Talybont, 1984); Ioan Roberts, *Achos y Bomiau Bach* (Llanrwst, 2001); John Davies, Lord Gifford and Tony Richards, *Political Policing in Wales* (Cardiff, 1984).
[245] McAllister, *Plaid Cymru*, p. 174.
[246] Emyr Wyn Williams and Dafydd Elis Thomas, 'Commissioning National Liberation', *Bulletin of Scottish Politics*, 1981, pp. 153–5.
[247] Wyn Jones, *Rhoi Cymru'n Gyntaf*, p. 214.

explicitly arguing for an alliance to be built around the working class, women, ethnic minorities, the professional middle class and the self-employed, whilst noting 'the demise of class politics'.[248] This further shift in position had received an added impetus from the entry of Gwyn Alf Williams into Plaid Cymru in 1983, who brought with him a distinct Eurocommunist and Gramscian perspective.[249] Williams's exit from the CPGB, frustrated at the failure to get plans for an ambitious historical and theoretical party journal to replace *Cyffro* off the ground, at the lack of support for the second Communist University of Wales and at the general conservatism of the Welsh party,[250] was a significant loss for the CPGB, leading to a situation where the most thorough-going Gramscian analysis of Welsh society was emanating not from the CPGB but from within Plaid Cymru.[251] Ironically, Williams's exit from the CPGB coincided with the entry of both Robert Griffiths and Gareth Miles into the party, whose commitment to Marxism-Leninism would see both ousted from a rapidly reforming CPGB by 1986.[252]

A similar shift to the left was also evident within CYIG, which had since the mid-1970s sought to develop its own left-leaning political philosophy, cymdeithasiaeth, based on participatory democracy, co-operation and social rather than market values, which was anti-capitalist and communitarian in nature.[253] For CYIG, the election of the Thatcher government had come as a significant blow, raising fears regarding the damage that its laissez-faire attitude to the language would have on language policy, especially the impact of proposed cuts to public services. These fears were confirmed following the government's decision to backtrack on a promise to establish a Welsh-language fourth television

---

[248] Phil Cooke, 'Decentralism, Socialism and Democracy', *Radical Wales*, 5, Winter 1984, p. 19.

[249] Wyn Jones, *Rhoi Cymru'n Gyntaf*, pp. 220–1.

[250] ' ... And Why I Joined', *Radical Wales*, 1, Winter 1983, pp. 6–7. For Williams's ambitious plans for a new Welsh party journal, *Y Gweithiwr*, see 'Proposal for a new Communist Party Theoretical-Historical journal', [*c.*1980], Bert Pearce Papers WP 3/4, NLW.

[251] See, in particular, Gwyn A. Williams, 'Sardinian Marxist and Welsh Predicament', *Radical Wales*, 7, Summer 1985, pp. 18–21.

[252] 'Why I Left Plaid Cymru ...', *Radical Wales*, 1, Winter 1983, pp. 4–5.

[253] Phillips, *Trwy Dulliau Chwyldro?*, pp. 162–3.

channel. By 1981, having dissipated its energies on the campaign for a fourth channel, the Society was increasingly rudderless, a situation that led to a major reassessment of its politics, the publication of its 1982 manifesto seeing the Society take a definitive leftward shift, declaring itself a socialist organisation.[254] Significantly, like the National Left and the Eurocommunists, CYIG called for the formation of a 'broad front' of political movements and organisations that were seeking to change the Welsh society, such a coalition viewed as the 'common sense' solution to encompassing the broad political terrain that CYIG was proposing to cover in its own activities.[255]

Throughout this early period the national question remained an important part of party policy, viewed as one of the issues around which a BDA could be built. The 1980 Welsh Congress welcomed efforts to re-establish the WAC,[256] and called for the immediate establishment of both a Welsh Assembly and a Welsh Economic Development Council under its control,[257] while noting the negative impact of the erosion of Wales' economic base on the future of the language.[258] For the Welsh Committee, an elected assembly would have been a vital bulwark against Thatcherism, providing an important focus for resistance to Thatcherite policies and a forum for the development of alternative policies with 'life itself', in the period since the referendum defeat, bringing into stark relief the need for devolution:

> We declared after the Referendum that events must raise again the basic issues of the devolution debate. The economic crisis now engulfing Wales, and the indiscriminate destruction of our industries, and our social life, confirms how urgent it is for the people of Wales to have those extensions. We will work now to see that these fundamental democratic demands are not lost sight of by the Labour Party, and the

---

[254] Phillips, *Trwy Dulliau Chwyldro?*, pp. 164–71; Cymdeithas yr Iaith Gymraeg, *Maniffesto '82* (Aberystwyth, 1982), p. 7.

[255] *Maniffesto '82*, p. 50.

[256] 'Communist Party Welsh Congress: The Communist Party as a Campaigning Force to Defeat the Tories to Save the Future for Wales' [1980], p. 15.

[257] 'Communist Party Welsh Congress: The Communist Party as a Campaigning Force to Defeat the Tories to Save the Future for Wales', p. 11.

[258] 'Communist Party Welsh Congress: The Communist Party as a Campaigning Force to Defeat the Tories to Save the Future for Wales', p. 14.

Trade Union Movement, but are seen as a key necessity in the battle for jobs, and for a secure future.[259]

This perspective, that Thatcherism made devolution more of a necessity, was reiterated at both the 1982 and 1984 Welsh Congresses, while the resolution adopted on devolution at the 37th Congress, held in November 1981, stressed that Thatcherism's 'consequences for the survival of the Welsh and Scottish nations need special consideration'.[260] With the Welsh Congress of 1980 welcoming the efforts to revive the WAC, the Welsh Committee sought to further develop its strategy in regards to the national question, a paper by Welsh Committee member Kath Edwards stressing the need for the party to take a long-term perspective as it approached the issue. For Edwards, the party's future devolution strategy had to be rooted in learning from the failures of the referendum campaign. The key to any successful new campaign on devolution lay in a longer-term strategy of raising political awareness of devolution by linking it to day-to-day issues and healing the geographical and linguistic schisms exposed during the referendum campaign by promoting a broader conception of Welshness that recognised the validity of the Welsh identity of all the communities in Wales.[261] A similar perspective was evident at the 1982 Welsh Congress, the resolution on devolution stressing the necessity of winning greater understanding for the need for a Welsh Assembly within the context of increasing democratic control over Welsh affairs, while declaring its support for the establishment of a movement for a Welsh Assembly.[262]

The same Congress had also seen a significant recognition of the emergence of the National Left within Plaid Cymru, an amendment from the Aberystwyth branch, accepted by the party's Resolutions Committee, arguing that 'The

[259] 'Communist Party Welsh Congress: The Communist Party as a Campaigning Force to Defeat the Tories to Save the Future for Wales', p. 14. On the concept of 'Life Itself', see Nina Fishman, *The British Communist Party and the Trade Unions, 1933–45* (Aldershot, 1995), p. 12.

[260] 'The National Question', *Comment*, 5 December 1981, p. 28. The resolution was moved by Welsh Committee member Allan Baker.

[261] Kath Edwards, 'Devolution Lives', 1980, Bert Pearce Papers WJ/14, NLW.

[262] 'Communist Party Welsh Congress: The People in Action – The Way Ahead for Wales', [1982], p. 16.

continuing split on the left over Welsh nationalism is a major problem which Communists must face up to', while noting that 'Any broad democratic alliance would be gravely weakened without their participation.' Building unity between the left and the national movement was now an 'important strategic aim for the party', the main barrier to which lay 'in the deep running sectarianism, present in both the Labour Party and Plaid Cymru'.[263] In a similar vein, Gareth Rees, later a member of the Welsh Committee, argued that the National Left 'should have a secure and important place' in any broad alliance that was to be built in Wales.[264] By the 1984 Welsh Congress, the party's position had shifted once again, a successful composite amendment from the Cardiff East and Rhyl branches calling on the party 'to increase our contacts at all levels, not only with the "National Left" but with local Plaid branches and individual members'.[265]

For Robert Griffiths, the leftward shift within the nationalist movement was one of a number of important factors that made the establishment of a new campaign for an Assembly a viable prospect. Responding to the return of devolution to the Welsh Labour Party's agenda at its 1984 conference, Griffiths argued that five years of the Thatcher government had led to a position where the issue could once again be raised with confidence. In particular, Griffiths pointed to not only the emergence of a leftward shift within Plaid, but also to the left's adoption of the issue of local autonomy in relation to the Liverpool, South Yorkshire and Greater London councils; the important gains made by the left within the Labour Party and the trade union movement; and the Thatcher government's attack on democratic rights. In this light, Griffiths argued that the case for a Welsh Assembly could be presented in a new light,

> Not as a dry, constitutional and half-hearted reform – but as a vigorous expression, defence and renewal of Progressive Wales. Not merely an arrangement of bricks, a charter of functions and a collection of bodies – but a progressive people's Assembly, one which could

---

[263] 'Amendments to resolutions', [1982], p. 6, Bert Pearce Papers WC/14, NLW.
[264] Gareth Rees, 'Plaid Cymru: a Political Paradox', *Moving Left in Wales*, 3, Summer 1984, p. 17.
[265] 'Resolution 1', Bert Pearce Papers WC/15, NLW.

intervene in social and economic affairs, would clear patronage and unaccountability from the corridors and committee rooms, would act as a rallying point for peace, and which would take a lead in the fight for women's emancipation, racial equality and cultural variety.[266]

Griffiths's calls for the establishment of a new campaign for an assembly were echoed in the main resolution adopted at the 1984 Welsh Congress,[267] which sought to put forward an outline of a 'Charter of Democratic Rights for Wales' as the basis for a broader discussion on the creation of a broad movement for democratic rights in Wales.[268] Calling for the extension and protection of democratic rights in areas such as the workplace, the home, local government, the trade unions, the media and in relation to race and the disabled, the party also called for greater rights for the Welsh language and for the establishment of a Welsh Assembly. On the language, the party called for an 'end to discrimination against the Welsh language', for the development of a bilingual language policy throughout Wales and the right to be taught through the medium of Welsh at all levels of the education system.[269] Backing a legislative assembly to be elected by proportional representation, the party argued that it would be a powerful bulwark against the impact of Thatcherism, providing a focus of resistance to attacks on the Welsh economy and society and giving Wales a stronger voice in relation to Westminster, and a means of developing polices and a more effective plan for the development of Wales.[270]

Despite these continued calls for the establishment for a new campaign on devolution, the party's direct campaigning on the issue during this period had been limited. Indeed, its energies and quest for unity on the left were focused on other issues such as unemployment, primarily through the People's March for Jobs, through the peace movement and the Wales Anti-Apartheid Movement. While these campaigns had some success in drawing the disparate forces of the left together, hopes of building a BDA were not fully realised

[266] Robert Griffiths, 'The Spectre Returns', *Moving Left in Wales*, 3, Summer 1984.
[267] 'Defend and Extend People's Rights – A Working Democracy for Wales', p. 6.
[268] 'Defend and Extend People's Rights – A Working Democracy for Wales', p. 2.
[269] 'Defend and Extend People's Rights – A Working Democracy for Wales', p. 3.
[270] 'Defend and Extend People's Rights – A Working Democracy for Wales', p. 6.

until the onset of the 1984–85 miners' strike and the formation in the late summer of 1984 of the WCSMC.[271] Distracted
by its own internal conflicts and having lost control of its
daily newspaper, the CPGB, despite its members and
branches playing an active role in the dispute on a par with
that played in the 1920s, was, at the British level, unable to
offer an effective leadership role during the strike, in spite of
the presence of significant party figures such as Mick
McGahey within the NUM leadership. In particular, differences between Arthur Scargill and the party leadership,
which was critical of Scargill's tactics, had led to the emergence of a strained relationship between the party and the
NUM leader.[272] In south Wales, where the party's organic
links with the local NUM leadership and the mining communities remained strong, party activists, both within and
outside the NUM, were, alongside other non-communist
activists and the South Wales Area NUM leadership, able to
develop a different, less isolationist strategy that in many ways
reflected the more practical and realistic outlook of past
Welsh communist miners' leaders such as Horner, Paynter
and Francis. Significantly, it was also from south Wales that
the most vocal criticisms of Scargill's tactics from within the
NUM emanated, often from party activists, and it was the
South Wales Area NUM, in an attempt to save the union, that
took the difficult decision to call the miners back to work.

The Welsh party was particularly active during the strike,
its Mining and Energy Advisory meeting weekly to co-ordinate the party's activities and party branches playing a central
role in organising support groups.[273] In the party press, the
Welsh party sought to put forward the case for coal as a safe

[271] For an incisive account of the strike, see Martin Adeney and John Lloyd, *The Miners' Strike 1984–85: Loss Without Limit* (London, 1988). For the strike in Wales, see Hywel Francis, *History On Our Side: Wales and the 1984–85 Miners' Strike* (Ferryside, 2009); Hywel Francis and Gareth Rees, 'No Surrender in the Valleys: The 1984–85 Miners' Strike in South Wales', *Llafur,* 5 (2), 1989, pp. 41–71; David Howell, 'The 1984–85 Miners' Strike in North Wales', *Contemporary Wales,* 4, 1991, pp. 67–97; Steffan Morgan, '"Stand By Your Man": Wives, Women and Feminism During the Miners' Strike 1984–85', *Llafur,* 9 (2), 2005, pp. 59–71.

[272] Francis Beckett, *The Enemy Within: The Rise and Fall of the British Communist Party* (London, 1998), pp. 204–10; Thompson, *The Good Old Cause,* pp. 191–2.

[273] 'Report of Work – December 1982–November 1984', p. 1, Bert Pearce Papers WC/15, NLW; interview with Hywel Francis, 27 October 2009.

energy in opposition to nuclear power, whilst stressing the impact of pit closures on whole communities and portraying the miners as representing the frontline in the battle to save British industry, as fighting not only for themselves but for the nation.[274] The strike was characterised by the emergence of a broad support network for the miners, most notably in the form of the women's support groups that emerged within the mining communities, but also from other disparate groups such as ethnic minorities, the churches and gay and lesbian groups. For the CPGB, it was through developing this broad support network into a broader alliance for political support for the miners, and ultimately as a broader platform of opposition to Thatcherism, that the strike could be won. Party activists, within and outside the NUM, were critical of Scargill's isolationism and focus on tactics such as mass picketing, the tried and tested tactics of industrial politics of the 1970s viewed as ineffective against the full force of the state machine utilised by the Thatcher government. In particular the NUM leadership were criticised by some party activists for failing to recognise the new political phenomenon, Thatcherism, that faced the strikers, and for adopting a quasi-syndicalist attitude to the strike that ignored its broader political dimensions.[275]

That much of the criticism of the NUM's strategy had come from party activists in south Wales, such as Hywel Francis, Allan Baker and Kim Howells, reflected the fundamentally different approach taken by the local NUM leadership in its conducting of the strike. South Wales was the only NUM area to actively tap into the groundswell of public support behind the miners to build a broad popular campaign in support of the miners, indeed the Welsh experience was singled out the for praise at the party's 39th

[274] For an example, see Allan Baker, 'Why the Miners' Fight is for the Industrial Survival of Britain', *Moving Left in Wales*, 3, Summer 1984, pp. 11–13.

[275] See, in particular, Allan Baker's contributions in 'Strike to the Finish: A Roundtable Discussion', *Marxism Today*, September 1984, pp. 10–15 , and 'The Miners' Strike: A Balance Sheet', *Marxism Today*, April 1985, pp. 21–7; Hywel Francis, 'NUM United: A Team in Disarray', *Marxism Today*, April 1985, pp. 28–34; Pete Carter, 'Striking the Right Note', *Marxism Today*, March 1985, pp. 28–31; and the section on the strike in the *Communist Party 39th Congress Report* (London, 1985), pp. 11–12.

Congress as showing the 'potential for the creation of broadly-based campaign movements within local communities'.[276] However, the real significance of the creation of the WCSMC was its success in building a national movement in Wales that not only drew together the disparate groups that supported the miners' cause, but also linked up the communities of the rural north and west with those of the industrial south through the twinning of towns and villages with their counterparts in the coalfield. The creation of the WCSMC also helped reinvigorate a sense of nation in the south Wales coalfield, helping to begin the process of healing the rifts so successfully exploited during the devolution referendum. As Kim Howells noted shortly after the strike, 'In South Wales we also discovered something else: that we are a part of a real nation which extends northwards beyond the coalfield into the mountains of Powys, Dyfed and Gwynedd. For the first time since the industrial revolution the two halves of the nation came together in mutual support.'[277]

The formation of the WCSMC owed much to the developments within the nationalist movement and within the CPGB which had taken place during the late 1970s and early 1980s, in particular the support for building broad alliances, and in CYIG's case its increasing engagement with issues not directly linked to the language. Certainly, for the CPGB, it became an archetypical example of the BDA in action, and, as Hywel Francis noted at the 1984 Welsh Congress, the WCSMC 'expressed the themes of the party's programme'.[278] However, its formation was largely spontaneous, a 'common sense' reaction to the direction the strike had taken in Wales by August 1984, following the sequestration of the South Wales Area NUM's funds and the increasing focus on fund-raising and food collection within the coalfield. Its establishment was the result of initiatives from below, initially from CYIG, CPGB and NUM activists, rather than the result of any initiative from the CPGB leadership, whether in London or in Cardiff. Indeed, Hywel Francis, the Wales Congress' chair,

---

[276] *Communist Party 39th Congress Report*, p. 11.
[277] Kim Howells, 'Stopping Out: The Birth of a New Kind of Politics' in Huw Beynon (ed.), *Digging Deeper: Issues in the Miners' Strike* (London, 1985), p. 147.
[278] *Morning Star*, 27 November 1984, p. 3.

notes that in the WCSMC, 'We were carrying forward on this strategy ahead of the Communist Party', party activists within the NUM and on the Mining and Energy Advisory proceeding with the initial discussions to set the new body without seeking the go-ahead of the party leadership. The creation of the WCSMC had its immediate roots in the activity in support of the miners at the 1984 Lampeter National Eisteddfod, where CYIG and NUPE had played a prominent role in raising funds for the miners, and which led to leading CYIG activists approaching the NUM asking how the Society could do more to involve themselves in the dispute. Following further discussion between representatives from the CPGB, Plaid, the Labour Party and CYIG, as well as from groups such as the Welsh Council of Churches, the decision was taken to form a permanent national body in support of the miners, leading to a formal request from the South Wales Area NUM by the late summer that such a body be established, the Wales Congress' inaugural conference taking place at Cardiff City Hall in October 1984.[279]

While evoking comparison with the struggles of the 1920s and 1930s, in particular of the Popular Front era,[280] the WCSMC was a body unique to twentieth-century Welsh politics drawing together the Labour Party, Plaid Cymru, the CPGB, the women's movement, the peace movement, language activists, farmers' groups, the churches and gay and lesbian groups, amongst others, into a broad coalition. Initially a means of better co-ordinating the efforts of support groups and of putting forward the case for coal, it transformed, as the strike developed, into an attempt to create a broad anti-Thatcher alliance. Organising conferences in support of the miners across Wales the Congress had, by December, begun to emerge as a national movement with local Congresses organised in north Wales and the Rhondda.[281] Playing an important role in keeping the NUM in south Wales from becoming isolated, the WCSMC was able to counter some of the negative media focus placed on the

---

[279] Interview with Hywel Francis, 27 October 2009; Hywel Francis, 'Mining the Popular Front', *Marxism Today*, February 1985, p. 12.
[280] Francis, 'Mining the Popular Front', p. 13.
[281] Francis, 'Mining the Popular Front', p. 15.

strike. Most significantly, it was able to construct an impressive 'alternative welfare system' that played an important role in sustaining the miners and their families, which the Congress sought to link to broader democratic issues, its first pamphlet arguing that it pointed the way to the means of creating a 'more participatory society'. From the outset, the WCSMC's focus was on the threat that pit closures held not only to jobs but to whole communities, an argument that resonated amongst broad sections of the Welsh population, and which in portraying the strike as one against a National Coal Board that saw itself as 'the "judge and jury" in deciding the future of industry and its communities' was also linked to fundamental democratic issues related to the control of communities.[282]

There was also a concerted attempt to link these issues to a broader critique of Thatcherism, the WCSMC linking the proposed pit closures to the government's broader economic strategy, to privatisation, and to a 'wider strategy to transform Britain in the interests of a privileged minority', arguing that 'The miners and their communities are being sacrificed for Thatcher's political dogma.'[283] For Hywel Francis, these concerns were at the root of the WCSMC's success in building such a broad alliance, arguing towards the end of the strike that 'The Congress was born of a realisation by large sections of the Welsh people that the miners were struggling for the future of Wales. If Thatcherism could defeat the miners, then all Welsh communities were in danger.'[284]

The decision to continue with the Congress' activities following the end of the strike, while clearly motivated by a desire to support the mining communities as they faced their most desperate hour, was also partly linked to hopes that a more long-lasting anti-Thatcher alliance could develop from the Congress. Certainly for CPGB activists such as Francis, the WCSMC remained 'pregnant with possibilities', the new alliances created during the strike in Wales 'point[ing]

---

[282] Wales Congress in Support of Mining Communities, *Wales and the Miners' Strike*, [1984] p. 4.

[283] Wales Congress in Support of Mining Communities, *Democracy, Thatcherism and the Miners Strike*, [1985].

[284] Francis, 'Mining the Popular Front', p. 15.

towards a genuine broadly based anti-Thatcher alliance with hopefully a trade union movement willing to engage in struggle at the core of it'.[285] These hopes, at least in the short term, were to be dashed. Relaunched at a conference held at Maesteg in June 1985, tensions between Plaid Cymru and Labour, initially linked to the Brecon and Radnor by-election, had already begun to emerge within the coalition. These tensions were further exacerbated by an article in *Radical Wales*, the journal linked to the National Left, which, with some justification, accused Labour of seeking to sabotage the Congress, leading to unsuccessful discussions between Dafydd Elis Thomas, Dave Richards and Hywel Francis that sought to dissuade Plaid from attacking Labour in the interests of maintaining unity.[286] Despite a successful rally at the 1985 Rhyl National Eisteddfod, in the face of these tensions, and the rapid disappearance of pits in south Wales, which was matched by a correspondent reduction in the number of support groups, the WCSMC had itself folded by 1986.[287]

Despite the WCSMC ending in some acrimony, for some of its leading figures, such as Hywel Francis and Dafydd Elis Thomas, in the long term the experience of the strike and the unity achieved during it began the political process that was to lead to the establishment of the Welsh Assembly fourteen years later. Indeed Thomas, recalling the period in late 2008, noted 'that was when it all began'.[288] While Francis acknowledges that the link between the two events can be viewed as a tenuous one, there can be little doubt that the experience of the WCSMC showed the possibilities that could be achieved with such unity, not least in demonstrating, through the creation of an alternative welfare system, the practical possibilities of self-government and of an

---

[285] Francis, 'NUM United: A Team in Disarray', p. 33.

[286] Interview with Hywel Francis, 27 October 2009. The article in question was Phil Cooke, Sian Edwards, Gerald Howells and Dafydd Elis Thomas, 'Congress at the Crossroads', *Radical Wales*, 7, Summer 1985, pp. 14–15.

[287] Francis, *History on Our Side*, p. 70. The workforce in the south Wales coalfield had almost halved between October 1985 and October 1986, dropping from 21,500 to 11,943; Francis, *History on Our Side*, pp. 76–7.

[288] Quoted in Francis, *History on Our Side*, p. 55. This is also the main argument of Francis's book on the strike.

alternative to Thatcherism. Certainly, the WCSMC represented, as it was portrayed at the time and as it has been since,
the emergence of a new politics that was in line with that
envisaged in the *BRS*. As Gareth Rees noted following the
end of the strike, the WCSMC had shown at least part of the
way forward, in particular through its replacement of the
electoralism of the Labour Party with a more participatory
form of politics. For Rees, this form of participatory politics,
cutting across party lines, represented a 'cultural change
which has seen the emergence of new social forces in the
peace movement, women's organisations, Welsh-language
activism and elsewhere' on which the creation of an 'alternative vision of society' depended. [289]

While the return to the surface of the underlying tension
between the Labour Party and Plaid Cymru reflected the
limitations of this unity, marking a return to the more
mundane reality of Welsh political life, the experience of the
WCSMC also helped foster long-lasting links between disparate groups and communities that had been involved in the
strike. Of more direct consequence for the national question, the strike, as noted above, had also begun the process of
healing the rifts that had been exploited during the 1979
referendum campaign. For Hywel Francis, the formation of
the WCSMC represented the creation of the type of coalition
that the CPGB had hoped would emerge during the 1979
referendum, the strike bringing about the creation of a new
sense of 'Welsh unity and identity, overcoming language and
geographical differences'.[290] The extent of this change was
evident in the short shrift given to comments made by the
Rhondda's Labour MP, Allan Rogers, who, in an echo of the
1970s devolution debate, sought to portray the WCSMC as a
'Commie and Nats plot', although this view retained some
currency within sections of the Labour Party.[291] The strike
had also brought into stark relief the impact Thatcherism
was having on Wales, helping to bring issues of the democratic control of communities to the fore, the rapid loss of its

[289] Gareth Rees, 'A New Politics', *Planet*, 53, October/November 1985, p. 17.
[290] Francis, 'Mining the Popular Front', p. 15.
[291] Francis, 'Mining the Popular Front', p. 15; Cooke et al., 'Congress at the
Crossroads, pp. 14–15.

mining industry in the aftermath of the strike playing a part in the electoral reversal that the Conservatives were to experience in Wales at the 1987 General Election, their parliamentary representation, at eight MPs, reduced to its 1974 level. This electoral setback, further highlighting the democratic deficit in Wales, helped put devolution back on to the political agenda.

While the strike had initially provided a boost for the Welsh party, helping to reinvigorate dormant branches and leading to the recruitment of 55 new members by November 1984,[292] in the longer term the demise of the coal industry in south Wales was also to herald the final stage of the Welsh party's decline. By late 1985, party membership had fallen to 756, dropping to 620 by 1988.[293] A further decline in 1990 to 377 and in 1991 to 277, this time linked to the party's organisational and ideological transition, confirmed the party as a spent force, its involvement in the miners' strike representing its last major contribution to Welsh politics.[294] The strike had also exacerbated tensions between the two wings of the party, the criticism of Scargill emanating from the party leadership and the Eurocommunists leading to accusations of betrayal. The internal conflict over the *Morning Star* and the party's ideological direction had continued unabated during the strike, reaching its conclusion in 1985 with the 39th Special Party Congress, the split in the party formalised with the formation of the CPB in 1988. The impact of the split in Wales, as in 1977, was limited, with only a handful of party members, among them Bob Jones, a member of the Welsh Committee, and Robert Griffiths, expelled from the party for their activity as part of the CCG, with Jones the most senior party figure in Wales to be disciplined.[295] On the whole, however, the Welsh party remained loyal to the party leadership, the CPB on its formation in 1988 having to build

[292] 'Report of Work – December 1982–November 1984', pp. 1 and 3.

[293] 'Report of Work of Welsh Committee 1985–86', p. 5; 'Report of Work/Factual Information' [1988], p. 1, Bert Pearce Papers WC/17, NLW.

[294] 'Report of Work July 1990–July 1991', p. 1, Bert Pearce Papers WC/18, NLW.

[295] 'Report of Work of Welsh Committee 1985–86', p. 5; Correspondence between Robert Griffiths and Dave Richards, Bert Pearce Papers WD 1/22, NLW; Bob Jones to Dave Richards, October 16, [1985], Bert Pearce Papers WD 1/22, NLW.

the new party from scratch in Wales.[296] The Welsh party adopted a series of more explicitly Eurocommunist positions from the mid-1980s onwards, the Welsh Committee, by 1986, arguing that the CPGB's role was to find a 'third way' between the right wing and the 'left sectarian' thinking within the labour movement.[297] One rare issue on which there was little disagreement between the CPGB and the CPB was that of devolution, with the CPB in its inaugural Welsh Congress declaring its support for a legislative assembly, an economic development plan for Wales and for Welsh-language rights, echoing the CPGB's position.[298]

The CPGB's own focus with regards to the national question during the late 1980s and early 1990s was linked to its involvement in the Campaign for a Welsh Assembly (CWA), established in 1987. While support for legislative devolution remained a central part of the party's Welsh policy programme, the party reaffirming its commitment to a Welsh Assembly at its 1986 Congress, its focus on the national question as an immediate campaigning issue had declined. Indeed for some party members in the heat of struggle during the miners' strike the issue seemed a throwback to the debates of the 1970s, with Gareth Rees noting that his initial reaction to seeing an advertisement for a conference on the national question at Coleg Harlech was one of disbelief that 'serious people could devote their time and energies to the consideration of issues of such mind-blowing irrelevance'.[299] While such sentiments were not shared by the Welsh Committee, its own lethargy over the issue is evident from its failure to act on proposals made in February 1985 to set up an advisory on the national question and in the absence of campaigning on devolution from the party's main lines of work adopted at the 1986 Welsh Congress.[300] Indeed, it was not until 1987 that a working group on devolution was

[296] Interview with Robert Griffiths, 19 December 2008.
[297] 'Discussion Statement and Proposals for Main Lines of Work', [1986], p. 5.
[298] 'Draft Resolutions from the Welsh Committee, Communist Party of Britain, Communist Party Welsh Congress '88', pp. 7–11.
[299] Rees, 'A New Politics?', p. 13.
[300] Minutes of Welsh Committee, 17 February 1985, Bert Pearce Papers WM/27, NLW; 'Main Lines of Work Adopted by Welsh Congress of the Communist Party 1986', Bert Pearce Papers WM/28, NLW.

established by the Welsh Committee. That the party did refocus some of its activities on the national question in 1987 was partly due to the intervention of the party centre, renewed discussion on devolution during the election campaign in Wales and the emergence of the CWA. In a report delivered to the EC in January, Ian McKay, the party's national organiser, noted that amongst the main priorities for the Welsh and Scottish parties was 'to confront the challenge that they face in a developing political situation in which the national question is re-emerging in a new and important way'.[301] While this focus on the re-emergence of the national question largely reflected developments in Scotland, where a Campaign for a Scottish Assembly was building the momentum that would lead to the foundation of the Scottish Constitutional Convention in 1988, it also held some resonance for Wales.

That February, Mary Winter noted that while there had been little interest in devolution in the years following the referendum defeat, things had begun to change by 1987, with Plaid Cymru raising the issue in the run up to the election and the impact of Thatcherism on Wales reopening the devolution debate. For Winter, devolution had not been seen as a major issue due to 'the traditional economism of British political debate', an approach that had to be transcended by linking devolution to other issues,

> Devolution is seen as a separate issue, and unless and until people can understand how an issue like devolution affects their daily lives they will not see it as an issue at all. Devolution and greater political democracy need to be portrayed as something that is closely connected to and can be of benefit to matters like employment prospects or the health service. It is essential that it becomes a part of the working class movement's programme for social advance.[302]

While these sentiments echoed those of Kath Edwards seven years earlier, Winter also noted the difficulties that any campaign for devolution faced under Thatcherism, especially in light of the success of its ideological focus on less

[301] CPGB Archive, 'Review and Estimate of Districts, Scottish and Welsh Congresses 1986', p. 1, CP/CENT/EC/23/01 (LHASC).
[302] Mary Winter, 'Breaking the Bureaucratic Bonds', 7 Days, 7 February 1987, p. 6.

government and a smaller state, suggesting that focus should be placed on the Assembly as a democratic counterweight to the appointed bureaucratic bodies that were running public services in Wales. It was also vital that the CPGB, the Labour Party, and the left more generally recognise the importance of the national question, Winter arguing 'The left needs to learn to look further than its economic nose. Areas like Wales remain deprived partly because they have no political leverage, and special regional aid programmes or industrial grants and loans cannot solve the problems long-term without an associated devolution of political power.'[303]

For the CPGB, the 1987 election results confirmed the need for a Welsh Assembly, the EC's report on the election arguing that the decisive vote against the Conservative Party in both Wales and Scotland gave 'overwhelming support to the demand for an elected assembly'.[304] For Bert Pearce, the fact that the Thatcher government only had the support of a quarter of the Welsh electorate reflected the 'urgent need to debate the structure and democratic nature of the present United Kingdom'.[305] At its 40th Congress, held in November 1987, the party again noted the democratic deficit evident in Wales and Scotland's rejection of the Conservatives, reiterating its support for the establishment of legislative assemblies in both countries. Welcoming the emergence of the broad campaign in Scotland, identified as a nascent BDA, the party pledged itself to campaign for assemblies in both countries 'as a prerequisite to extending democracy and solving the British national question'.[306] By this time, the Welsh party had already begun to make some progress on the issue, having set up a working group on devolution policy in July, whose aim was 'to develop our thinking and assess our existing policy', and setting in motion plans to organise a broad conference, 'Devolution Alive', on the issue. In addition, the Welsh party's Trade Union Advisory was to approach the Wales TUC and the individual trade unions to discuss their approach to, and position on, devolution. The party

[303] Winter, 'Breaking the Bureaucratic Bonds', p. 7.
[304] 'Unite and Fight – The Way to Win', *7 Days,* 20 June 1987, p. 3.
[305] Bert Pearce, 'Wales', *7 Days,* 28 November 1988.
[306] *News and Views,* December 1987, p. 19.

had also by this stage become involved in the preliminary meetings that were to lead to the foundation of the CWA.[307]

Progress was slow, however, especially in terms of developing the party's policy on devolution, the Welsh executive again agreeing to consider setting up a team that would work on updating and republishing the party's Kilbrandon submission in March 1988, although this does not appear to have happened.[308] Instead, the party's main focus in terms of the national question was by now its involvement in the CWA on whose Campaign Council four CPGB members, Bert Pearce, Mary Winter, John Cox and Maureen Lewis, sat.[309] Launched in November 1988, but in gestation since 1987, the CWA sought to build in Wales an organisation similar to the Scottish Constitutional Convention that would win the broad support of all political parties in Wales and would be able to develop a 'realistic and constructive programme' for devolution in Wales.[310] Despite the inclusion of representatives of all the opposition parties in its leadership the CWA, in the absence of official support from either the Labour Party or Plaid Cymru and in the face of the continued hostility between the two main opposition parties, was unable to emulate the kind of broad popular movement that had emerged in Scotland. Despite this, it was able to play some part in shifting attitudes towards devolution within the Labour Party, helping to move the issue up that party's political agenda.[311]

The establishment of the CWA was welcomed by the party, a resolution put forward by the Cardiff East branch at the 1988 Welsh Congress, held in December, calling on all party branches to affiliate to the campaign and to participate in the activities of its local groups.[312] For Dave Richards, its establishment was 'an example of us, the people of Wales,

[307] Minutes of Welsh Committee, July 1987, Bert Pearce Papers, WM/29, NLW.
[308] Minutes of WEC, [30 March 1988], Bert Pearce Papers WM/30, NLW.
[309] 'Report of Work/Factual Information', [1988], p. 2; Campaign for a Welsh Assembly, *Agreeing an Assembly for the 1990s* (Cardiff, 1989), p. 1.
[310] *Agreeing an Assembly for the 1990s*, p. 9.
[311] Laura McAllister, 'The Road to Cardiff Bay: The Process of Establishing the National Assembly of Wales', *Parliamentary Affairs*, October 1999, p. 638.
[312] 'Branch Resolutions Welsh Congress Communist Party 1988', p. 4, Bert Pearce Papers WC/17, NLW.

setting the political agenda, an example of us demanding an extension of our democratic rights, instead of being on the defensive, as we have to a large extent over the last ten years, trying to defend and maintain what little democratic voice we have'.[313] Viewing the campaign as a potential BDA in the making, the Welsh Committee took its involvement in the campaign seriously, setting up a Welsh Assembly Campaign Advisory in January 1989.[314] However, in the face of a declining membership and an organisational structure that was rapidly withering away, its contribution to the campaign, at least as an organised political force, was limited. Despite this, individual party members involved in the campaign were able to make a significant contribution, with Bert Pearce, in particular, providing a conduit into the Labour Party and labour movement, as the CWA sought to win the support from both for devolution.[315] In terms of its own activity, the party again declared its support for a Welsh Assembly at its 1988 Welsh Congress,[316] while in October 1991 the Welsh Committee called on David Hunt, the Secretary of State, to include devolution in the government's consultation on local government. However, by this time, and indeed from the end of 1989 onwards for what remained of the party in Wales the main focus was on its own future.[317]

The period from the 41st Congress in November 1989 to the 43rd Congress in November 1991 saw the party in Wales, as elsewhere, engaged in the debate over the party's future and its transformation into the Democratic Left. Postponing the 1990 Welsh Congress to allow for proper preparation for the 42nd Party Congress in December, the Welsh party was largely acquiescent in the decisions taken at that Congress, engaging in a further period of debate over a new constitution, including a Welsh conference on the party's transformation held in Cardiff in May 1991. While there was

---

[313] Untitled speech by Dave Richards at the Pontypridd By-election Open Forum, [c.February 1989], Bert Pearce Papers WD 1/23, NLW.

[314] Minutes of Welsh Committee, 26 January 1989, Bert Pearce Papers WM/30, NLW.

[315] Interview with John Osmond, 11 November 2009.

[316] Welsh Congress Discussion Statement, [1988], p. 1, Bert Pearce Papers WC/17, NLW.

[317] Les Skeats to David Hunt, October 28, 1991, Bert Pearce Papers WN 1/7, NLW.

recognition within the Welsh party for the need for radical transformation, the Welsh Committee initially urged caution. Dave Richards, in the initial debate on the proposals to change the party at the January 1990 EC meeting, while backing the need for change, rejected the transformation of the party into a loose political association as 'leading to the dispersal of the 'collective intellectual' of the Communist Party', arguing that there was 'still a need for a political party based on Marxism, enriched by feminism, by greenery and that is essentially democratic'.[318] Similarly, for Bert Pearce it was vital that the party did not abandon Marxism altogether, urging the party to recognise its own domestic pre- and post-1917 heritage, which it should now to seek to tap into as it sought to escape the last strictures of its association with Marxism-Leninism.[319] By March, however, under new leadership and in the light of the events in Eastern Europe, the party leadership was more outspoken on the need for change, with Les Skeats declaring the end of the Leninist party as a relevant or useful form of political organisation while calling for a political organisation that was 'quite distinct from social-democratic politics'.[320] Welcoming the decision to follow the twin-track approach taken at the 42nd Congress, Skeats argued that the right choice had been made, rejecting the option to renew the CPGB as a political party as 'mere tinkering' that would not have resolved the root causes of the party's decline and the need for change.[321]

The final stage of the debate came with the publication of the draft Democratic Left constitution in early 1991, the constitution committing the new organisation to a politics based on 'creative Marxism', feminism, anti-racism and environmentalism whilst proposing a federalist organisational structure that gave its Welsh and Scottish sections full autonomy over their policies, organisational structure and officials, within the context of the organisation's broad set of aims and values.[322] Committed to a thorough democratic reform of the British political system, the draft maintained

---

[318] *News and Views*, February 1990, p. 9.
[319] *7 Days*, December 1989, p. 9.
[320] *Western Mail*, 23 August 1990.
[321] *Western Mail*, 12 December 1990.
[322] *Democratic Left Draft Constitution* (London, 1991), p. 16.

the CPGB's support for the establishment of Welsh and Scottish assemblies.[323] The Welsh party broadly welcomed the draft, the majority of the Welsh contributions on the debate in the party press proving positive.[324] There were, however, dissenting voices, such as that of Charlie Swain, the veteran Cardiff communist, who called on

> the present usurpers ... to go ahead and run their course of dismemberment and de-teething of the party. Then the principled ones who are left might come together again and reform the Communist Party of Great Britain, with branches and district committees, based on Marxism, having learned from the trauma of recent events and ready to campaign for socialism and against capitalism.[325]

While such views were in a minority, the whole transformation process heralded a further decline in party membership between 1990 and 1991, the Welsh Committee noting that the loss of some 100 members was directly linked to the party's transformation, a combination of disaffection at the pace of change or the belief that such a change was not necessary.[326]

The Welsh party agreed to transform itself into the Democratic Left at its final Welsh Congress in September 1991, the Welsh Committee declaring its abandonment of Leninism, arguing that the Leninist party was now obsolete having dogmatised Marxism, 'corrupted the nature of the socialist party itself' and being, with its centralised structure and adoption of a 'command philosophy', unsuited to a period where fundamental democratic change was a prerequisite.[327] Unlike in Scotland which, retaining a relatively large membership and remaining active in broad campaigns such as the Constitutional Convention, saw a significant breakaway to form the Communist Party of Scotland, such a development was never a realistic proposition in Wales due

---

[323] *Democratic Left Draft Constitution*, p. 5.
[324] See, for example, the contributions of Bert Pearce and Richard Spencer, *Changes,* 26 October–8 November 1991, Supplement pp. 1–3 and that of Les Skeats, *Changes,* 9–22 November, Supplement, p. 1.
[325] *Changes,* 22 June–5 July 1991, Supplement, p. 3.
[326] 'Report of Work July 1990–July 1991', p. 1.
[327] 'Welsh Congress CPGB: Congress Documents', [1991], p. 5, Bert Pearce Papers WC/18, NLW.

to its small membership and inactive branch structure. Instead the Welsh party drew up its own draft principles for the Welsh Democratic Left, adding a commitment to a Welsh Assembly and the equality of the Welsh language to its core aims and values.[328] Acquiescing in the decisions taken at the 43rd Congress, Democratic Left Wales held its inaugural Welsh Conference in October 1992, amongst its main resolutions, in the continuation of at least one Communist tradition, a call for the establishment of a Welsh Assembly.

CONCLUSION

The 1970s and 1980s had not only witnessed the final, terminal decline of the CPGB but also its final transformation from a Leninist party into a political formation that would have been unrecognisable to its founding members, the culmination of a process that can be traced back to its adoption of a parliamentary road to socialism in 1951. In Wales, the 1970s had also witnessed a highpoint in the party's engagement with the national question, most significantly, in its role in the formation of the Wales TUC, but also evident in its contribution to the devolution debate of the period and in the development of its policy, at least in the early 1970s. Clearly, there were also serious limitations to the party's engagement with the issue. Despite repeated, almost ritualistic, exhortations at party Congresses calling for the establishment of a broad movement to campaign for a Welsh Assembly, it proved unable to initiate such a movement under its own auspices, and while it was able to make a contribution in winning official trade union support for a Welsh Assembly, it proved unable, along with the rest of the organised trade union movement, to win the support of its rank and file for such a measure, as the 1979 referendum defeat showed. Despite initial hopes in the early 1980s that a broad democratic alliance could still be built around a campaign for a Welsh assembly, the party, without completely abandoning these hopes, temporarily revived with the formation of the CWA in 1987, sought unity through its engagement

---

[328] 'Welsh Congress CPGB: Congress Documents', p. 6.

with other, more politically relevant issues during the initial stage of Thatcherism. Similarly, the party's failure to further develop its policy on the issue from the mid-1970s onwards, best exemplified in the repeated attempts to set up advisories on the issue, efforts which either floundered or failed to produce anything tangible, reflected its disengagement from the issue, the party's policy still based on its Kilbrandon submission and its 1976 Congress resolution in 1988.

This situation was only rectified with the partial reformulation of the party's position on the national question in the *Manifesto for New Times*, which replaced the formulation of the 1970 Kilbrandon submission with a concept of Welsh devolution that was firmly in a European, globalised context, in which nationalisation and planning was replaced by a democratically controlled mixed economy, and which also questioned the labour movement's devotion to the unitary state. On the whole, however, the party's engagement with the national question, as with other issues was severely hampered in the 1980s by the party's inexorable decline. Nevertheless, the party had succeeded in further developing some aspects of its policy on the national question, most notably on the English dimension to devolution, by the late 1970s supporting a fully federalist solution to the national question that backed the establishment of an English Assembly. By opting for this solution, however, the CPGB reiterated its commitment to the maintenance of the union. Significantly, the intermittent criticism of the party's unionist ethos, evident from a minority within the party that sensed that the implications of devolution would be more profound than the party leadership assumed, remained a voice in the wilderness, the party inexorably entwined in a left-wing British patriotism, rooted in the party's commitment to the British labour movement.

That the party's main contribution to Welsh devolution came in the industrial sphere, with the formation of the Wales TUC, is not surprising. It was in this sphere that the party exercised its greatest influence, especially within the South Wales Area NUM, its rapid decline following the demise of the mining industry clear evidence of this organic link between party and industry, but also a sign of its failure, despite repeated attempts, to expand into newer industries and different communities. Nevertheless, despite these difficulties, the party was able to offer a consistent set of policies and a principled stand on the national question, its propagation of a third way in between Plaid Cymru and the Labour Party offering a plausible left-wing alternative to both parties' positions. The party had also maintained a principled stand on the language question, remaining committed to bilingualism and to equal rights for Welsh speakers, even if the implementation of its own internal language policy left much to be desired. The party's warnings as to the dire consequences of Labour's foot-dragging over devolution during the 1970s proved prescient, while its arguments for devolution in the 1980s – as being able to provide a vital bulwark to Thatcherite polices – rang true.

In terms of the internal party split, in one sense the national question transcended the debate, being one of the few issues on which both wings of the party could agree, with the CPGB, the NCP and the CPB supporting the creation of a Welsh Assembly, a reflection perhaps of the low priority placed on the issue by these parties, at least at the British level. On the other hand, with its focus on the extension of democratic rights, on decentralisation and on the formation of a broad popular movement involving new social forces such as the national movement, the Welsh party's engagement with the national question in some senses prefigured the positions taken by the Eurocommunists. While its central concern lay in winning over the labour movement for devolution, an important part of the Welsh party's strategy during this period was to establish better links with the nationalist movement. Certainly, there were also difficulties here, the party's immersion in the culture of the Welsh labour movement leading to an ambiguous approach from the party leadership, a combination of calls to unity and distinctly negative attacks on Plaid Cymru in particular. Despite this, it is also evident that there was, at the grass-roots level and also amongst the party leadership, a refreshing absence of the sectarian attitudes to the national movement, and especially Plaid Cymru, so evident in the Labour Party. The concerted efforts by the party to bring socialists and nationalists together, from the mid-1970s onwards, boosted by the adoption of the perspective of the BDA, led to the emergence of important links between Communists and nationalists, most fruitfully during the miners' strike, and a significant cross-fertilisation of ideas, that contributed to the emergence of the left within the national movement, its adoption of the Gramscian ideas and of the perspective of broad alliances reflecting the influence of communist thinking.

Its initial hopes of building a broad alliance out of the remnants of the 1979 referendum campaign dashed, the party adopted a longer-term strategy that reflected the failures of the referendum campaign identified by the Welsh Committee and the EC. While maintaining its commitment to devolution, its energies were understandably directed elsewhere as the party sought to pursue unity through other more immediate issues. When unity came in the form of the WCSMC, the Welsh party, despite its internal difficulties, was to play a significant role in the BDA that emerged during the miners' strike, making its final major contribution in a movement that can be seen as a turning point in Welsh politics, helping to begin the process of healing the divisions that had been so evident during the 1979 referendum. For the Welsh party, the CWA was also initially viewed as a potential BDA, similar to the one that had emerged in the form of the Scottish Constitutional Convention, but in reality it was more suited to the type of long-term strategy the party had sought to pursue in the early 1980s. Despite this, the party's contribution as an organised political force was now limited, the decline of the party structure and membership making it impossible for the party to make a full contribution as a political organisation. The end of the party did not, however, represent the end of the contributions made by Communists to the national question in Wales. The Democratic Left continued to support a Welsh Assembly until its dissolution in 1994, while the CPB has also maintained a commitment to the assembly receiving greater powers and has sought to build consensus between the Labour Party and Plaid Cymru.[329] Former Communists such as Bert Pearce and John

---

[329] Interview with Robert Griffiths, 19 December 2008.

Cox continued to play an important role within the CWA and in its follow-up organisation, the Parliament for Wales Campaign, while others, such as the veteran Rhondda Communist Cliff True, were active in the campaign for a Yes vote at the 1997 devolution referendum.[330] Fittingly, for the man who refocused the party's energies on the national question in the early 1960s, and who had remained a dedicated campaigner for devolution since that time, Bert Pearce, despite the onset of serious illness, was present at City Hall, Cardiff to witness the announcement of the referendum result that paved the way to Wales becoming a devolved nation.

[330] *A Celebration of the Life of Cliff True: 'An Internationalist who speaks with a Welsh Accent' (1923–1999)*, July 1999, funeral oration by Hywel Francis.

CONCLUSION

Despite the significant focus placed on national and colonial questions within communist politics from the Second Comintern Congress onwards, the CPGB's engagement with the national question in Wales took some time to develop. As we have seen, up until the period of the Popular Front the national question in Wales was conspicuous by its absence in communist politics, due to a combination of factors: the party's overriding focus on building a revolutionary party in south Wales and on fighting a series of momentous industrial struggles; the absence of Wales and Scotland in the broader debate on British imperialism; the economism of the Welsh party; Welsh nationalism's association with Liberal politics; the impact of the ultra-left line of the Third Period; and a general lack of interest in an issue that was viewed as a distraction from the class struggle. It was only with the Comintern's adoption of the Popular Front that the CPGB began engaging with the national question in Wales. This process involved the interaction of both international and domestic factors. At the international level it was linked to the Comintern's response to the rise of fascism and, in particular, to Dimitrov's call for greater engagement with national sentiment in the face of fascism's appropriation of national heritage and symbols. At the British level, it was connected to the CPGB's attempt to link the party to native radical-democratic traditions. In Wales, it was connected to the party's response to the temporary upsurge in support for the Welsh Nationalist Party during the mid-1930s, the formation of a North Wales District Committee, and to the links developed between communist and nationalist students, each of which played a role in the initial development of the Welsh party's policy on the issue. While the war interrupted this process of policy development, the hopes attached to post-war reconstruction, the significant administrative changes in Wales, not least its recognition as a single economic unit, along with the new focus that the war had provided regarding the birth and rebirth of nations, helped refocus the Welsh party's energies as it developed – for the first time – a comprehensive policy programme for Wales' economic and social redevelopment, of which the granting of a Welsh parliament was to play a significant part.

By 1950 the party was, for the first time, engaged in practical action on the issue, affiliating to the PWC. However, the available evidence suggests that following the removal of Idris Cox interest in the issue waned, especially following the failure to win the support of the South Wales Area NUM for a Welsh parliament in 1954. From 1956 onwards, the party's efforts to develop its policy for Wales were also seriously hampered by increasing financial and organisational difficulties. Despite retaining a rhetorical commitment to a Welsh parliament, these factors saw the party increasingly aping Labour Party policy on the issue of self-government, choosing to focus solely on the issue of a Secretary of State from the mid- to late 1950s. This impasse in the development of the party's policy for Wales and on the national question was broken with arrival of Bert Pearce as the party's Welsh secretary, who during the early 1960s refocused the party's energies on developing its policy programme for Wales. While some progress was made during the early 1960s on the national question, not least a restatement of the party's commitment to a Welsh parliament as its long-term policy goal, it was the resurgence of the nationalist movement from the mid-1960s onwards that saw the Welsh party begin to seriously reassess its position on the national question.

In response to this the party put forward detailed proposals for the establishment of a Welsh parliament, while recognising that such a measure would be possible under capitalism. The Welsh party's efforts during the late 1960s left it better prepared to make a contribution to the decade-long devolution debate that followed during the 1970s, the party presenting evidence to the Royal Commission on the Constitution, maintaining a critical commentary during the debate that ensued, while affiliating to the WAC during the failed referendum of 1979. The 1970s also saw the party make what was its most significant contribution to the story of Welsh devolution through its important role in the establishment of the Wales TUC. By the late 1970s, however, the party had once again begun to feel the impact of organisational decline, a factor that limited its involvement in the referendum campaign, and which was to become the overriding issue as the party entered its final phase during the 1980s and early 1990s. Nevertheless, the party was able to make a contribution to Welsh politics during this period, most importantly through its involvement in the WCSMC. Its establishment had benefited from the contacts established between socialists and nationalists during the 1970s, a process in which the CPGB had played a role, and through the development of the concept of the BDA. This was to be its last major contribution to Welsh politics, and by the time of its involvement in the CWA it had, to all intents and purposes, ceased to function as an effective organised political force in Wales. The party's final dénouement came following the collapse of the Soviet Bloc, the party, despite its ideological shift away from the soviet model, unable to escape the shadow of Marxism-Leninism.

The present work has sought to offer an account of the party's engagement with the national question and to answer three key questions: First, what was the nature of the relationship between the party and the national question in Wales between 1920 and 1991? Second, what organisational arrangement existed between the British and Welsh parties and how much leeway did the Welsh party have in developing policy in relation to the national question? Third, what does the CPGB's attitude to the national question tell us about the left's approach to the national question in Wales? The answer to each of these questions lies in an exploration of a number of dimensions of the party's engagement with the national question, its specific policy programme for self-government in Wales and for the Welsh language, its broader policy programme for Wales, its relationship with both the nationalist and labour movements, and the organisational relationship between the Welsh party and the party centre.

What, then, was the nature of the CPGB's relationship with the national question between 1920 and 1991? Before turning to the party's specific policy programme on the issue, it is useful to first assess the level of influence international and domestic factors played in the party's engagement with the national question. There can be little doubt that in the initial stages of the party's engagement with the issue international factors played an important role in pushing the CPGB towards dealing with the national question in Wales. The party's initial engagement with the national question at both the British and the Welsh level can be traced directly back to the Comintern's Seventh Congress, while the impact of the Second World War, especially through the administrative changes in Wales and the hopes associated with post-war reconstruction, played a significant part in the development of party policy on Welsh self-government in the crucial immediate post-war period. However, while Comintern directives played an important role in initiating the change in party propaganda at the British level that facilitated the emergence of a national consciousness within the Welsh party, the available evidence suggests that it was domestic factors that primarily drove the party's engagement with the issue. Of most significance at the British level was the party's post-war turn towards serious engagement with parliamentary politics as a means of achieving a transition to socialism, central to which was the radical reformation of the British political system. While the resolution of the national question in Wales was initially linked to a Cold War concern with claiming back Britain's national independence from American dominance, in subsequent editions of the *BRS* the focus was increasingly on devolution as part of a broader programme of democratic and constitutional reform of which the decentralisation of power, both at the national level and within local government, was a key component. By the late 1970s, the extension of democracy had become the central theme of the party's programme. This change of direction and a consequent engagement with constitutional issues was conducive to the development of the CPGB's approach to the national question in Wales.

However, it was at the Welsh level that we find the most immediate factors that led to the party's engagement with the issue. Of most significance here was the nationalist movement around whose fortunes much of the party's engagement with the issue revolved. Certainly, the national movement played an important role in helping initiate the party's engagement with the issue in both the 1930s and the 1960s, with the impact of Penyberth along with the debates between communist and nationalist students at Cardiff University completing the interaction of international and domestic factors that initiated the party's engagement with the issue in the 1930s. Similarly, it was the resurgence of the national movement during the mid-1960s that saw the party fully re-engage with the issue, the CPGB, along with the rest of the labour movement, finding itself playing catch-up with the nationalist movement. Such events point to the reactive nature of the party's engagement with the issue. That said, any such assessment needs to be balanced with the party's proactive involvement in the establishment of the Wales TUC and in campaigns such as the PWC, WAC and CWA, although it never managed to build a broad movement for national rights under its own auspices. Similarly, other issues, such as the reform of local government, also provided a platform for the party to put forward its proposals for a new constitutional settlement. Nevertheless, it is also clear that the level of the party's interest in the national question was intermittent, despite the increasing prominence given to the establishment of a Welsh Parliament in the party's policy programme for Wales, especially from the 1960s onwards. This state of affairs can be attributed to three main factors. First, that the national question was only one of a myriad of international and domestic issues that were competing for the party's limited resources, which were primarily focused on the labour movement in Wales. Second, that the party, especially in the early period of its engagement with the national question, found it difficult to enthuse the party rank and file on the issue. Third, that the Welsh national question was a low priority in the more general scheme of communist politics, especially at the British level, where it was only rarely a major issue – in the late 1960s and the late 1970s.

In terms of the party's actual policy programme on the national question, three key dimensions can be identified. First, its support for the establishment of a Welsh parliament with legislative powers within a federal governmental system, initially as a long-term but later as its short-term goal. Second, the granting of equal status for the Welsh language and its support for the expansion of both Welsh-language education and of Welsh cultural activities. Third, the party's pursual of unity between the national and labour movements in Wales. The party's adoption of a federalist position on the national question in Wales was derived from two separate sources, from the model adopted in the USSR, which was accepted at face value by the party as a voluntary and equal amalgam of nations, and from the party's own commitment to the unity of the British working-class movement, which was viewed as a key component in achieving a transition to socialism in Britain. While the soviet model played an important role in the formation of the party's thinking on the national question, the primary motivation for opting for a federalist solution for the national question lay in the latter source. At its core, the CPGB was an unionist party whose conception of the transition to socialism, as was noted by a number of critics of the party's policy, was rooted in a single British road, which did not countenance the possibility that conditions in Wales would require a distinctly Welsh road to socialism or that independence for Wales could be in any way progressive. For the CPGB, separatism was only likely to play into the hands of British capital by leading to the fragmentation of the labour movement into competing national sections and a general weakening of the strength of the organised working-class movement. Thus, the party's unionism was rooted not so much in any adherence to the sanctity of the British state – for despite arguing that it was only through the combined resources of all three nations that their needs could be met, the party envisioned a root-and-branch reformation of the whole political system – but in a belief that capitalism could only be defeated at the British level. It was these concerns that drove both the opponents of Welsh self-government, such as Arthur Horner, to reject the establishment of a Welsh parliament, and the architects of the party's policy on the national question to embrace federalism as a viable solution that would maintain the unity of the British working class. Thus the party's federalism was ultimately derived from its unionism.

However, the party's unionism was based on the concept of a voluntary union, with the CPGB rejecting the existing constitutional settlement as having left Wales at a serious disadvantage, both economically and socially. For the party, the effects of this uneven development were heightened by Wales' status as a nation and the negative effects that such uneven development had on Wales' language and culture. Central to these concerns was the failure to develop Wales as a single economic unit, with the party arguing that the development of Welsh industry was based largely on the interests of British capital rather than on those of Wales as a nation. As we have seen, however, it was on just this issue that the party itself initially had difficulty in defining Wales as a nation within the confines of the Stalinist conception of the nation, an impasse that was only overcome by the rejection of this dogmatic approach. That said, the Stalinist definition retained significant currency for some party members through to the late 1960s. In seeking to reconcile Marxism's support for the right of national self-determination with the need to maintain the unity of the British working-class movement, by opting for an admittedly underdeveloped federalist solution the party found itself holding the centre ground between Plaid Cymru and the Labour Party on the issue.

It is also evident that party policy on the national question developed in a series of stages, which saw the party – at different times – advance and retreat on the issue. During the 1930s, despite taking some tentative steps towards the development of its policy on self-government, the major developments were on cultural issues, especially language policy. It was not until the 1940s that we see a greater focus on the development of policy on self-government and of a more general policy programme for Wales. In contrast, the 1950s, despite the party's involvement with the PWC, were in essence a period of retreat over the issue, the party increasingly focusing on the short-term goal of a Secretary of State, while the development of its Welsh policy programme ground to a halt. The 1960s were significant not only for the further development of the party's position on self-government and of its Welsh policy programme, but also for the adoption of the establishment of a Welsh parliament as its

short-term goal and its acceptance that effective self-government for Wales was possible under capitalism. During the
1970s and 1980s, the main innovation was the inclusion of
the party's approach to the national question within the
concept of the BDA and the further development of its position on federalism within the United Kingdom.

The party's policy on the national question contained a
number of strengths and weaknesses. On the plus side, the
party's insistence that a Welsh parliament be given legislative
powers was a marked improvement on the limited forms of
administrative and executive devolution proposed by the
Labour Party during this period, which recognised that for
Welsh self-government to be effective then real decision-
making powers had to be devolved from Westminster.
Similarly, the demand for powers over the economy and the
direction of industry, while linked to the party's commitment
to a broader policy based on nationalisation and large-scale
economic planning, was a recognition that Wales' economic
and social redevelopment would be best addressed through
the construction of a more balanced Welsh economy. For the
party, if Wales was to prosper it was vital that industry was not
restricted to the coastal corridors in north and south Wales
linked to Bristol, London and Liverpool, but expanded to
the whole of Wales, something successive Labour and
Conservative governments had failed to do. Only the establishment of a Welsh parliament, its energies focused solely on
Welsh issues, would be able to adequately develop Wales as a
balanced economic unit by, to paraphrase Noah Ablett, not
allowing ignorance at Westminster to sit in judgement of
knowledge in Cardiff.

Finally, the party's policies on the Welsh language were
progressive throughout this period, even if the party's own
Welsh-language output left much to be desired, supporting
equal status for the language, advocating the expansion of
Welsh-language education and offering support for the aims
of the Welsh-language movement, once it was established in
the 1960s. Similarly, the party also adopted progressive policies on Welsh cultural issues, backing greater funding for the
arts in Wales, the development and greater democratic
control of both its broadcast and print media, supporting the

establishment of bodies such as a national theatre and orchestra, while placing great emphasis on the value of Welsh cultural institutions such as the eisteddfod. In terms of the language issue, the early links made by the party between economic and social decline, unemployment, migration and the decline of the language, offered an analysis that was particularly progressive for the left in Wales and which, in some senses, prefigured the concerns of the language movement. However, as already noted, the party's Welsh-language output, apart from the concerted efforts made during the 1940s to publish Welsh-language material and the publication of *Cyffro* during the 1970s and early 1980s, was inadequate for a Welsh party. In more general terms, there was also a distinct lack of party literature on Welsh issues for large swathes of the period under discussion, especially during the 1950s and 1960s. Similarly, the party's engagement with the cultural sphere, especially during the 1950s and 1960s, was intermittent, despite the involvement of individual party members, such as T. E. Nicholas and Dai Francis, in the arts.

Three major weaknesses in the party's policy on self-government can also be identified. The first of these was the issue of the division of powers between a Welsh and British parliament which, despite reassurances regarding a redefinition and reassessment of British interests and the proposal to grant the right of secession, was never fully resolved. The balance of power remained heavily in favour of the British Parliament, which retained significant powers over the general outlines of economic and social development. A second fundamental weakness was its underdeveloped approach to federalism, the party, in particular, having some difficulty in resolving its approach to the English question, adopting for much of the period only a quasi-federal system, whereby English issues were discussed at the British parliament by English MPs. Indeed, there is little evidence that the party engaged in any prolonged discussion on the implications of federalism for Britain as a whole. In this regard the party were not unique, the implications of devolution for England remain an underdeveloped aspect of the policy of the mainstream British parties nineteen years after the

establishment of the Welsh Assembly and the Scottish
Parliament. Finally, there was a failure to recognise that the
granting of an elected Welsh parliament could have broader
devolutionary consequences – a factor linked to the party's
conception of a single British road to socialism. Within the
party, there was an underlying assumption that once given
adequate legislative powers, the Welsh parliament would be
content to leave matters as they were. As critics of party policy
pointed out during the 1970s, however, there were, in fact,
significant differences in the political, social and economic
make-up of all three countries which made it equally likely
that at some point down the line the Welsh would decide to
follow their own political path outside of the confines of the
general outlines developed at the British level.

Nevertheless, by the late 1960s the party had developed a
plausible and comprehensive policy programme for Wales
and on the national question. However, questions still
remained regarding how genuine the party's engagement
with the national question was. An accusation often thrown
at communist parties engaging with the national question
was that their interest in the issue was only skin deep, a
tactical manoeuvre to win support through appeals to
popular patriotism. This study has shown that the party's
commitment to the issue was genuine, the lifelong commitment of party members such as Idris Cox, John Roose
Williams and Bert Pearce to the issue are a clear enough illustration of this. In addition, despite some prevarication over
the issue during the 1950s, the party, on the whole, remained
committed to the establishment of a Welsh parliament at
times when such a stance proved deeply unpopular within its
natural constituency, the labour movement. However, there
was also a distinct tactical element to the party's engagement
with the national question that was evident from the 1930s
onwards. During the Popular Front period the party's
engagement with the issue was seen as broadening its appeal
to the Welsh people, a means of tapping into a previously
untapped pool of potential support that had been ignored
by the party due to its overriding focus on industrial issues.
Similarly, during the 1950s its involvement in the PWC was
viewed partly as a means of putting over the communist

perspective on a number of issues and of linking the national question to these, while in the 1970s its involvement in WAC was partly viewed in a similar manner. On a more general level, throughout the period the party retained a belief that its progressive stance on the national question would help draw members to the party from the left of the nationalist movement.

However, as this study illustrates, for much of the party's existence its relationship with the national movement was ambiguous, despite the centrality of unity between the national and labour movement to its stance on the national question. Indeed, the party only fully came to terms with the nationalist movement during the mid- to late 1970s as it shifted leftwards. While the party sought to pursue a critical, but friendly policy towards the nationalists, at times the result was the sending of distinctly mixed messages, with calls for unity with its progressive wing mixed with denunciations of the reactionary policies of the nationalist leadership and the demagogic nature of nationalism in general – a position that reflected its equally unsuccessful strategy vis-à-vis the Labour Party. This position can be traced back to the 1930s and the Welsh Nationalist Party's ambivalent stance on the Spanish Civil War, its self-depiction as a bulwark against communism and its calls for the deindustrialisation of south Wales, which were met with derision by the CPGB amid accusations of fascism. While these accusations of fascism faded with a change in Plaid Cymru's leadership, accusations regarding the demagogic nature and reactionary tendencies of Welsh nationalism persisted and remained a feature of statements emanating from the party up until the late 1970s.

Of course, such hostility was not a one-way street, the anti-communism of Plaid Cymru's early leaders only too evident, a strand of thought that remained a distinct element of the conservative stream of Welsh nationalist politics. In more general terms, Plaid Cymru remained sceptical of the CPGB's motives with regards to its stance on the national question throughout much of the post-war period. Clearly, ideological differences played a significant role in complicating the relationship between the CPGB and the nationalists, the party rejecting outright Plaid Cymru's economic position, its rejection of class struggle and its support for independence, which was viewed as divisive by the CPGB. In particular, the available evidence suggest that, especially from the 1930s through to the 1960s, many party members were suspicious of the nationalist party's petit-bourgeois character and its lack of an organic link with the working class, a trait that extended to the party leadership itself. The fate of small nations in the Soviet Union, along with events such as the invasion of Hungary, also fed into the nationalist's scepticism regarding the CPGB's engagement with the issue. The matter was further complicated by the party's immersion into the culture of the Welsh labour movement, which remained, on the whole, hostile to the national movement. In addition, its unrequited relationship with the Labour Party, based on the CPGB's programmatic commitment to the election of a Labour Government, placed it in a position where the attacks on Plaid Cymru made sense in terms of defending Labour hegemony in Wales. However, such attacks were ultimately to prove counterproductive, doing little to improve relations between the CPGB and the Labour Party while creating a further obstacle to the party's aim of building a broad movement in favour of Welsh national rights that included both the nationalist and labour movements.

Despite this, there is also evidence to show that, unlike much of the labour movement in Wales, on the whole, the CPGB also made a considerable effort to foster good relations with the nationalists. Both parties were engaged in united front activity during the 1930s, while the party's decision to affiliate to the PWC reflected a refreshing lack of sectarianism that contrasted to the Labour Party's opposition to the campaign. The party was always willing to share a platform with the nationalists, while the development of links between communists and nationalists, especially during the 1970s and 1980s, seems to have been mutually beneficial to both parties. The available evidence suggests that the cross-fertilisation of ideas between the two, and the popularisation of Gramscian ideas by the party, played a modest role in fostering the development of the nationalist left, while helping sow the seeds for the establishment of the WCSMC in the mid-1980s. Each of these developments display a

willingness on the behalf of both the CPGB and the nationalists to work with each other, although its hopes that a broad
popular movement could be built on the basis of the national
question were dashed following the failure of the 1979 referendum campaign.

While the CPGB put great store in its pursual of unity with
the nationalist movement, its primary focus with regards to
the national question was winning the support of the labour
movement for Welsh national rights, while convincing it of
the value of taking the leading role on the issue and of
forming the head of a broad national movement for them. In
doing this the CPGB offered an insightful critique of the
Welsh labour movement's attitude to the national question,
which in some ways prefigured the criticism of the economism of the labour movement that emerged within the
CPGB during the 1970s. Similarly, its warnings regarding the
Labour Party's dithering over devolution during that decade
proved prescient. However, prior to the establishment of the
Wales TUC, the party made little headway in this regard, the
defeat of the resolution in favour of a Welsh parliament at
the 1954 conference of the South Wales Area NUM having a
distinctly negative impact on the party's approach to the
issue, the party reverting for a while to aping Labour Party
policy on the national question. Appeals by the party for the
labour movement to engage with the issue continued to fall
on deaf ears throughout the 1960s and while the establishment of the Wales TUC saw the Welsh labour movement as a
corporate body come out in favour of a legislative parliament
for Wales, hopes within the CPGB that the Wales TUC would
take the lead in a broad popular campaign for devolution
were dashed as it and the Labour Party chose to organise a
separate campaign for a yes vote during the 1979 referendum. Nevertheless, while the party's efforts in this regard
were a failure, it was more successful in the sphere of the
devolution of industrial politics in Wales, playing an important role in the establishment of the Wales TUC, even if that
organisation ultimately failed to live up to the expectations
placed on it by the party.

In exploring the CPGB's organisational arrangements
within Wales and between the Welsh party and the party

centre, it is worth noting at the outset that the CPGB was amongst the first political organisations of the working class to organise itself on a national basis in Wales. Having done so it was a strong advocate of such organisation on a Welsh basis within the labour movement from the 1940s onwards. However, in reality, it remained primarily a south Wales party, although to its credit its policy programme sought to encompass the whole of Wales. That it did not succeed in building a truly national party, in terms of party organisation, can be attributed to the absence elsewhere in Wales of the particular political, economic and social conditions and political traditions bred by the development of heavy industry that were conducive to the party gaining a foothold in the south Wales coalfield. In the absence of such unique conditions and traditions elsewhere in Wales, the party struggled to make a significant impact, Marxism's appeal to the industrial proletariat making little headway in rural north and mid Wales. Nevertheless, the party did succeed in maintaining a semblance of a national organisation in Wales, the party picking up a handful of members in university towns such as Aberystwyth and Bangor, while maintaining a presence in north Wales from the mid-1930s onwards. In the context of the present study, the party's expansion to other parts of Wales was crucial in that it forced the party to deal with issues, such as the national question, that were of particular concern in areas such as north Wales. Indeed, the available evidence suggests that the small North Wales District played a pivotal role in the initial development of the party's policy on the national question in the 1930s.

While the Welsh party was to remain one of the party's largest sections throughout its lifespan, for much of the period under discussion its failure to expand significantly was a source of frustration and concern for the party leadership in Wales as well as at the party centre, a reflection of broader frustrations at the CPGB's failure to become a mass party along the lines of the PCF and PCI. In Wales, the party only really began to make progress in terms of membership following the general strike and the lockout of 1926, the south Wales party becoming the CPGB's largest district during 1927, only for these gains to be wiped out following the disastrous impact of the Third Period in Wales. These losses were recouped from the mid-1930s onwards, with party membership reaching its highpoint – at almost 3,000 members – by 1943. However, with the onset of the Cold War party membership was again to drop away rapidly a process hastened by the impact of the events of 1956, and while the party was able to recover much of this lost membership by the mid-1960s, from the 1970s onwards party membership began its final, inexorable, decline. As with the general trend at the British level, for the majority of people joining the party, membership of the CPGB was a transitory experience, the party's low membership figure belying the large number of people who passed through its ranks. A central consequence of this was that the party, while remaining a far more activist party than the Labour Party, was reliant on a smaller core of active party members to undertake much of the party's work in Wales – a factor which placed considerable strains on the party's ability to fully engage with the plethora of issues over which the party campaigned. Indeed, it is remarkable that the party was able to do as much as it did. The impact of these strains was evident in the numerous statements by the Welsh Committee bemoaning the poverty of branch life, as well as in the difficulties the party faced, especially in the post-war era, in maintaining functioning Area Committees, with several having to be reconstituted during this period. Similarly, the Welsh party's financial problems also, at times, hampered its ability to fully engage with issues such as the national question, the party's limited role in the WAC and its difficulties in developing a Welsh policy programme during the late 1950s attesting to the negative influence of both factors.

In terms of the Welsh party's relationship with the party centre, the CPGB's support for a federalist solution to the national question did not extend to the party's own internal organisation, despite the decision to grant both the Welsh and Scottish parties national, rather than district, status in 1969. This was largely the legacy of the process of Bolshevisation imposed on the party by the Comintern during the early 1920s. This was a process that severely diminished the relative freedom of action that the Welsh party

enjoyed under the CPGB's initial federalist structure – a
structure that was, however, ill-suited to the development of
an avowedly Leninist party. Nevertheless, the available
evidence suggests that within the confines of the party's
centralist dynamic, the Welsh party, especially in the post-war
era, had significant leeway in developing the details of its
general policy programme for Wales, albeit always within the
boundaries of the general outlines set by the party's British
policy programme. It was the Welsh Committee that developed the detailed proposals for an all-Wales plan for social
and economic redevelopment, and for proposals such as the
development of better transport links between the north and
south and the development of a more diverse industrial
sector in Wales. In terms of the national question and its policies on the Welsh language, the Welsh party's freedom of
action was significantly greater, with much of the CPGB's
polices on these issues developed, initially, in Wales, before
receiving the approval of the party centre. That said, the
party centre retained, and at times exercised, its considerable veto powers, the available evidence from the 1930s, for
example, suggesting that the party centre may have intervened to water down the Welsh party's tentative proposals for
self-government. Similarly, there is also evidence of intervention by the party centre on the issue of a Wales TUC in the
mid-1950s. However, for the most part the Welsh party seems
to have played the leading role in the initial development of
CPGB policy on these issues. In part, this was a recognition of
the peripheral nature of these issues to the party centre.
However, it was also a recognition that it was within the Welsh
party that the expertise on these issues existed, despite some
friction between the Welsh party and party centre over these
issues, notably in the late 1930s, the mid-1950s and late 1960s.
While the CPGB can be held up as anomaly in terms of
British political party organisation, its commitment to the
principle of democratic centralism marking it out as fundamentally different, in terms of the relationship between the
Welsh party and the party centre the CPGB, at least in terms
of policy development, largely followed the norms of the
British–Welsh relationship of the mainstream political
parties, with the details of Welsh policy developed within the

context of the broader outlines of policy developed at the British level.

The final question this study has sought to answer relates to the more general lessons that the CPGB's engagement with the national question tell us about the left's relationship with the national question in Wales. As noted at the outset of our study, this relationship has been for over a century one of the most complex in Welsh politics, characterised by periods of mutual hostility, by efforts towards reconciliation and accommodation, by periods of unity and by occasional attempts at synthesis. While the emergence of a Labour Party–Plaid Cymru coalition government at Cardiff Bay in 2007 heralded a new phase in this relationship, the soul-searching within both parties that was evident in the run-up to the signing of the coalition agreement shows that significant underlying problems remain. Much of this narrative of hostility and accommodation is focused on the relationship between the Labour Party and Plaid Cymru with too little attention paid to the alternatives also present on the left, a narrative that to an extent undervalues the breadth of the unionist left's thinking on the issue. As we have seen, the CPGB, despite the weaknesses in its approach to the issue and in elements of its policy, put considerable effort into developing a plausible and comprehensive alternative policy on devolution that offered a compromise between nationalist and Labour Party positions based on a concern with maintaining the unity of the British working-class movement. In doing this, the party was successful in putting forward a policy that was a significant advance on that proposed by the Labour Party and which showed a willingness to engage more positively with the national question and with the nationalist movement. By looking beyond the traditional narrative on the left's attitude to devolution, we find that significant alternatives were present on the unionist left.

The CPGB's policy on the issue remained, for the most part, a minority strand of opinion on the unionist left in Wales, the party, as we have seen, failing to win the support of the labour movement for legislative devolution until the 1970s, while also proving unable to change Labour Party opinion on the issue throughout the period. Clearly, this had much to do with the party's own limited ability to shift opinion within the Labour Party, despite its aspirations to do so, while it also reflects the often peripheral role the party played in Welsh politics. However, it also reflects the essentially British perspective of much of the labour movement and of the Labour Party in Wales in relation to constitutional issues, a perspective that viewed moves towards the devolution of power as threatening both the unity of that movement and the gains made by it at the British level. That the CPGB's own starting point was based on similar assumptions reflects its own immersion in the culture of the domestic labour movement. Nevertheless, it is to the CPGB's credit that while based in this perspective, in contrast to the Labour Party's begrudging and unenthusiastic approach to the national question in Wales, it made a considerable effort to develop a policy on Welsh self-government that sought an effective solution to the issue of Welsh national rights that took into consideration these concerns regarding devolution's impact on the British working-class movement, while also giving Wales real decision-making powers.

The different attitudes displayed by the CPGB and the Labour Party can be explained by a number of factors. Politically, while the Labour Party took an essentially conservative approach to constitutional matters, its incorporation into the British political establishment leading it to seek the maintenance of the status quo, the CPGB's political direction, once it had abandoned its early Leninist commitment to smashing the state and rebuilding it anew, was geared towards the radical reformation of the British state and its political system. Central to the CPGB's analysis of the British state, developed from the 1950s onwards, was a concern with the overcentralisation and bureaucratisation of state power, viewed as a central feature of state monopoly capitalism. In response to this, the party increasingly focused, in terms of its proposals for the reformation of the British political system, on the devolution of power and the extension of democratic rights as a means of empowering the population, making government more responsive to local needs and as one means of advancing the transition to socialism by chipping away at the centralised power of monopoly capital. This

focus on the extension of democratic rights was a distinct
feature of the party's politics from the 1950s onwards, as it
shifted towards accepting a parliamentary road to socialism,
which took centre stage following the turn towards
Eurocommunism in the 1970s. The focus on national rights
can also be partly attributed to the party's desire, especially
in the 1930s and in the early Cold War period, to counter
accusations that the party was an alien import into British
politics. Certainly, such concerns were part of the party's
initial motivation in engaging with the national question
during the 1930s, and are also evident in the links made by
the CPGB between Welsh self-government and British
national independence during the early 1950s. This focus on
national independence faded as the party's appeals to
popular patriotism failed to convince in the face of its own all
too obvious links to a foreign power. However, themes of
national betrayal, in particular linked to the failure of consecutive Labour and Conservative governments to address
Wales' social and economic problems, are evident in the
Welsh party's discourse on the national question in Wales
throughout the period of its engagement with the issue.
Ideologically, the party, rooted in Marxist theory, in contrast
to the Labour Party, was also better predisposed towards
taking national and colonial questions seriously and towards
recognising the progressive dimensions of the national movement in the context of the broader struggle against
capitalism. This is particularly evident in the party's persis-
tent calls for the formation of a broad national movement
for national rights, that would bring together the national
and labour movements under working-class leadership, and
in its belief that the success of such a movement in Wales
could provide a catalyst for the development of similar broad
extra-parliamentary movements at the British level. Finally,
at a personal level the genuine commitment of leading party
figures in Wales, such as Idris Cox, John Roose Williams and
Bert Pearce, to Welsh national rights, combined with a generally sympathetic British party leadership, played a crucial role
at pivotal stages in the development of party policy on the
issue. In contrast, such support from leading figures in the
Labour Party was not so forthcoming, with even a figure like

Jim Griffiths in reality only supportive of minimal measures of devolution and with the Labour leadership at the British level even less responsive. Similarly, while there was a degree of dissent within the CPGB on the issue, especially during the 1940s and early 1950s, it never became the make-or-break issue that it did become for the Labour Party in Wales.

An overall assessment of the CPGB's engagement with the national question in Wales would have to conclude that its impact was limited, its only real, tangible, contribution to the story of Welsh devolution coming with its role in the establishment of the Wales TUC. In terms of its main aim of building a broad movement in support of Welsh national rights, the party's efforts must be deemed a failure, the party proving unable to build such a movement under its own auspices, hindered by its own organisational difficulties, its ambiguous relationship with the nationalist movement and its failure to win the support of the Welsh labour movement. Considering the small size of the party in Wales it is perhaps no surprise that such a lofty goal proved impossible for the party to achieve. The achievement of such a goal was also hampered by the party's own reactive and intermittent interest in the national question in Wales, the Welsh party leadership, in particular, at least in the early stages of its engagement with the issue, having some difficulty in stimulating support within the Welsh party for Welsh national rights in the face of the general indifference of the party membership. Nevertheless, the Welsh party had begun to overcome these initial difficulties by the 1960s, the issue of Welsh self-government becoming a central component of the party's policy programme for Wales. However, this process owed much to the initial debate on the issue during the 1940s, which played a part in helping the party develop a distinctly Welsh perspective on policy. Its role in the establishment of the Wales TUC allowed it to make a lasting contribution in this area of Welsh politics. At the British level, the national question in Wales remained for the most part a peripheral issue, only emerging as an issue of particular importance for the party centre in the late 1960s and late 1970s.

Despite the party's relative failure, significant value remains in exploring its engagement with the issue. As this study has shown, the CPGB's position on the issue represented a significant strand of opinion on the left that sought to develop a coherent approach to the national question in Wales that reconciled the demands for an effective measure of devolution with the essentially British-orientated perspective of the labour movement in Wales. Without acknowledging this dimension of the unionist left's approach to the national question in Wales, the story of Welsh devolution remains incomplete. This study has sought to fill this gap by offering, for the first time, an in-depth analysis of the CPGB's engagement with the issue. While the party may not have been successful in achieving its aims on the national question, it was the organisation on the unionist left that gave the issue the greatest degree of attention and this makes its contribution, at least in terms of the development of the left's policy on devolution, significant. Indeed, we can go further, and note that in some ways the party's thinking on the national question was ahead of its time, and remains so, its proposals for extensive legislative and limited tax-raising powers remaining unfulfilled following the establishment of the Welsh Assembly. Within the context of the parties in Wales, the CPGB put forward an original position on the national question that, despite its weaknesses, sought a compromise between the positions of both Plaid Cymru and the Labour Party. In doing this, it offered a unique perspective on the issue of Welsh self-government. Finally, in terms of the study of local communisms, the present work, by looking at the party history through the prism of the national question, has also shown that while the party maintained its distinct internationalist ethos and its commitment to the British working-class movement, it also developed a distinct Welsh identity and was concerned with specifically Welsh issues for much of the post-war period; indeed, its commitment to issues such as Welsh self-government and the Welsh language allowed it to stand out on the unionist left in this regard. Alongside its commitment to internationalism and to the British working-class movement, the Welsh party also spoke with a Welsh accent.

BIBLIOGRAPHY

Archive Collections

Communist Party of Great Britain Archive, Labour History Archive and Study Centre, People's History Museum, Manchester.
Idris Cox Papers, NLW, Aberystwyth.
Jim David Papers, South Wales Coalfield Collection, Richard Burton Archives, Swansea University.
Dai Francis Papers, South Wales Coalfield Collection, Richard Burton Archives, Swansea University.
Bert Pearce (Welsh Communist Party) Papers, National Library of Wales (NLW), Aberystwyth.
Elwyn Roberts Papers, NLW, Aberystwyth.
Hywel Davy Williams Papers, South Wales Coalfield Collection, Richard Burton Archives, Swansea University.
John Roose Williams Papers, University College of North Wales, Bangor.
Undeb Cymru Fydd Papers, NLW, Aberystwyth.
Wales Congress in Support of Mining Communities Papers, South Wales Coalfield Collection, Richard Burton Archives, Swansea University.
Wales TUC Papers, NLW, Aberystwyth.
Wales TUC Papers, South Wales Coalfield Collection, Richard Burton Archives, Swansea University.

Interviews

Robin Page Arnot, 6 March 1973 (South Wales Miners Library (SWML), AUD 337)
Idris Cox, 6 June 1973 (SWML, AUD 171).
John Cox, 20 September 2008.
Brian Davies, 20 February 2009.
Edgar Evans, 30 November 1973 (SWML, AUD 210).
Edgar Evans, 9 July 1975 (SWML, AUD 212).
Glyn Evans, 5 March 1973 (SWML, AUD 346).
Hywel Francis, 27 October 2009.
Robert Griffiths, 19 December 2008.
Julian Tudor Hart, 5 December 2008.
Harry Howells, 20 January 1973 (SWML, AUD 302).

John Lane, 17 December 2008.
Len Jefferies, 12 September 1972 (SWML, AUD 271).
Len Jefferies, 20 September 1972 (SWML, AUD 272).
Len Jefferies, 11 October 1972 (SWML, AUD 273).
John Osmond, 11 November 2009.
Mel Thomas, 17 May 1973 (SWML, AUD 283).
Mary and Tony Winter, 20 February 2009.

NEWSPAPERS

7 Days
Comment
The Communist
Y Cymro
Daily Worker
Y Faner
Llais y Werin: Organ of the North Wales District of the Communist Party of Great Britain
Morning Star
Party News
The Rhondda Socialist
The Welsh Nationalist
Western Mail
Workers' Dreadnaught
World News
World News and Views

PAMPHLETS, MANIFESTOS, PUBLISHED REPORTS AND CONGRESS REPORTS

Campaign for a Welsh Assembly, *Agreeing an Assembly for the 1990s* (Cardiff, 1989).
Communist Campaign Group, *The Crisis in the Communist Party and the Way Forward* (London, 1985).
Communist Party of Great Britain, *The Battle of Ideas: Six speeches on the Centenary of the Communist Manifesto* (London, 1948).
Communist Party of Great Britain, *Britain for the People: Proposals for Post-war Policy* (London, 1944).
Communist Party of Great Britain, *The British Road to Socialism* (London, 1951).
Communist Party of Great Britain, *The British Road to Socialism* (London, 1958).
Communist Party of Great Britain, *The British Road to Socialism* (London, 1968).

Communist Party of Great Britain, *The British Road to Socialism* (London, 1978).

Communist Party of Great Britain, *Challenge Big Business – Build a New Britain* (London, 1974).

Communist Party of Great Britain, *A Charter of Democratic Rights* (London, 1979).

Communist Party of Great Britain, *Class Against Class: The General Election Programme of the Communist Party of Great Britain 1929* (London, 1929).

Communist Party of Great Britain, *The Communist Party, The Labour Party and the United Front: A Thesis Defining the Attitude of the Communist Party towards the Labour Party* (London, 1922).

Communist Party of Great Britain, *Communist Party Special 39th Congress Report* (London, 1985).

Communist Party of Great Britain, *Communist Unity Convention Official Report 1920* (London, 1920).

Communist Party of Great Britain, *For Peace and Plenty: Report of the Fifteenth Congress of the CPGB* (London, 1938).

Communist Party of Great Britain, *For Soviet Britain: The Programme of the Communist Party adopted at the XII Congress February 2nd, 1935* (London, 1935).

Communist Party of Great Britain, *It Can Be Done: Report of the Fourteenth Congress of the Communist Party of Great Britain* (London, 1937).

Communist Party of Great Britain, *The March of English History: A Message to you from the Communist Party* (London, 1936).

Communist Party of Great Britain, *Manifesto on Communist Unity* (London, 1920).

Communist Party of Great Britain, *Manifesto for New Times* (London, 1990).

Communist Party of Great Britain, 'Memorandum Submitted by the Communist Party of Great Britain' in *Commission on the Constitution: Minutes of Evidence IV: Scotland* (London, 1971).

Communist Party of Great Britain, *Our Changing Democracy: Devolution to Scotland and Wales* (London, 1975).

Communist Party of Great Britain, *Report of the Central Committee to the 15th Party Congress, September 16–19, 1938* (London, 1938).

Communist Party of Great Britain, *Report of Commission on Inner-Party Democracy* (London, 1979).

Committee on Broadcasting Coverage, *Report of the Committee on Broadcasting Coverage* (London, 1974).

Communist Party of Great Britain, *Report of the Control Commission to the Party Congress, May 1922* (London, 1922).

Communist Party of Great Britain, *Report on Organisation presented by the Party Commission to the Annual Conference of the Communist Party of Great Britain, October 7, 1922* (London, 1922).

Communist Party of Great Britain, *Victory, Peace, Security: Report of the 17th Congress of the Communist Party* (London, 1944).

Cox, Idris, *The People Can Save South Wales* (London, 1936).

Cox, Idris, *South Wales and the Bombers!* (Cardiff, 1940).

Cox, Idris, *Forward to a New Life for South Wales* (Cardiff, 1944).

Cox, Idris, *The Fight for Socialism in South Wales 1848–1948* (Cardiff, 1948).

Fine, Ben et al., *Class Politics: an Answer to its Critics* (London, 1984).

Griffiths, Robert, *Was Gramsci an Eurocommunist? A Reply to Roger Simon* (Cardiff, 1984).

Griffiths, Robert and Gareth Miles, *Sosialaeth i'r Cymry* (Cardiff, 1979).

Horner, Arthur, *Towards a Popular Front* (London, 1936).

Jones, J. E., *Satellite Parties in Wales* (Cardiff, [1960]).

Marx, Karl and Friedrich Engels, *Y Maniffesto Comiwnyddol* (Cardiff, 1948).

MacLennan, Gordon, *Quit the Market, Join the World* (London, 1975).

Miles, Gareth, *Cymru Rydd, Cymru Gymraeg, Cymru Sosialaidd* (Aberystwyth, 1972).

Pollitt, Harry, *How to Win the War* (London, 1939).

North Wales District Committee of the Communist Party of Britain, *Heddwch Ynteu Rhyfel?* (Bangor, 1939).

Parliament for Wales Campaign, *Parliament for Wales* (Aberystwyth, 1953).

Ramelson, Bert, *Social Contract: Cure-all or Con-trick?* (London, 1975).

Ramelson, Bert, *Bury the Social Contract: The Case for an Alternative Policy* (London, 1977).

Rhondda Communist Party, *South Wales in the March of History: A Message to you from the Communist Party* (Tonypandy, 1937).

Royal Commission on the Constitution, *Report of the Royal Commission on the Constitution 1969–1973, Volume 1* (London, 1974).

Samuel, Wynne, *The Political Betrayal of Wales* (Cardiff, 1945).

Scottish Committee of the Communist Party of Great Britain, *'But They Shall Be Free': Communist Party Memorandum on Scotland's Future* (Glasgow, 1953).

Scottish Committee of the Communist Party of Great Britain, 'Memorandum Submitted by the Scottish Committee of the Communist Party' in *Commission on the Constitution: Minutes of Evidence IV: Scotland.*

South Wales District Committee of the Communist Party of Britain, *A Programme of Life, Health and Work for South Wales* (Cardiff, [1937]).

South Wales District Committee of the Communist Party of Britain, *South Wales Congress Report* (Cardiff, 1939).

South Wales District Committee of the Communist Party of Britain, *The Way Forward for South Wales: Report of the South Wales Congress of the Communist Party* (Cardiff, 1943).

Unofficial Reform Committee, *Industrial Democracy for Miners* (Porth, 1919).

Wales Congress in Support of Mining Communities, *Wales and the Miners' Strike* (Cardiff, 1984).

Wales Congress in Support of Mining Communities, *Democracy, Thatcherism and the Miners' Strike* (Cardiff, 1985).

Wales TUC, *Recommendations on Devolution* (Cardiff, 1976).

Wales TUC, *Wales TUC First Annual Report 1974* (Cardiff, 1974).

Warren, Bill and Mike Prior, *Advanced Capitalism and Backward Socialism* (Nottingham, 1975).

Welsh Committee of the Communist Party of Great Britain, *Communist Policy for the People of Wales: Report of the First All-Wales Congress of the Communist Party* (Cardiff, 1945).

Welsh Committee of the Communist Party of Great Britain, *Communists and Welsh Self-Government* (Cardiff, 1944).

Welsh Committee of the Communist Party of Great Britain, *Communists Care for a Better Life for Wales* (Cardiff, 1979).

Welsh Committee of the Communist Party of Great Britain, *Devolution, Democracy and Socialism: A Policy Statement by the Welsh Committee of the Communist Party* (Cardiff, 1977).

Welsh Committee of the Communist Party of Great Britain, *A Great Welshman: A Symposium of Tributes to T. Gwynn Jones* (Cardiff, 1944).

Welsh Committee of the Communist Party of Great Britain, *Let Wales Lead the Socialist Way in 1970* (Cardiff, 1970).

Welsh Committee of the Communist Party of Great Britain, *Make 1947 a Real New Year in Wales: The Communist Plan to Save Young People and to Prevent Wales Becoming Derelict Again* (Cardiff, 1947).

Welsh Committee of the Communist Party of Great Britain, 'Memorandum Submitted by the Welsh Committee of the Communist Party' in *Commission on the Constitution: Minutes of Evidence V: Wales* (London, 1972).

Welsh Committee of the Communist Party of Great Britain, *The New Way for Wales* (Cardiff, [1964]).

Welsh Committee of the Communist Party of Great Britain, *Opportunity for Wales to Give a Lead to Britain* (Cardiff, 1974).

Welsh Committee of the Communist Party of Great Britain, *A Parliament with Powers for Wales: Comments Submitted by the Welsh Committee of the Communist Party to the Secretary of State for Wales on the Government Discussion Paper 'Devolution in the United Kingdom'* (Cardiff, 1974).

Welsh Committee of the Communist Party of Great Britain, *Report and Resolutions of the Second Welsh Congress, September 28/29, 1946* (Cardiff, 1946).

Welsh Committee of the Communist Party of Great Britain, *Wales in the New World* (Cardiff, 1944).

Welsh Committee of the Communist Party of Great Britain, *Wales Needs Communist Policy – Power to the People* (Cardiff, 1974).

Welsh Committee of the Communist Party of Great Britain, *Welsh Communists Say Vote Yes on Thurs. March 1st – Work for Wales* (Cardiff, 1979).

Welsh Committee of the Communist Party of Great Britain, '*Welsh Day' in Parliament* (Cardiff, 1944).

Williams, John Roose, *Llwybr Rhyddid y Werin* (London, [1936]).

Williams, John Roose, *The Lore of the People/Llên y Werin* (London, 1938).

Williams, John Roose, *The Flame of Welsh Freedom/Fflam Rhyddid Cymru* (Cardiff, 1944).

Winternitz, J., *Marxism and Nationality* (London, 1944).

Woddis, Jack, *Nationalism and Internationalism* (London, 1972).

Woddis, Jack, *Time to Change Course: What Britain's Communists Stand For* (London, 1973).

Theses

Williams, Sian Howys, *Bywyd a Gwaith Thomas Evan Nicholas 1879–1971*, MA Thesis, University of Wales, 1983.

Books

Aaronovitch, Sam, *The Road from Thatcherism: The Alternative Economic Strategy* (London, 1981).

Adeney, Martin and John Lloyd, *The Miners' Strike 1984–5: Loss Without Limit* (London, 1988).

Adereth, M., *The French Communist Party: A Critical History (1920–84) from Comintern to the 'Colours of France'* (Manchester, 1984).

Anderson, Kevin B., *Marx at the Margins: On Nationalism, Ethnicity and Non-Western Societies* (Chicago, 2010).

Andrews, Geoff, Nina Fishman and Kevin Morgan (eds), *Opening the Books: Essays on the Social and Cultural History of British Communism* (London, 1998).

Attfield, John and Stephen Williams, *1939: The Communist Party and the War* (London, 1984).

Beckett, Andy, *When the Lights Went Out: What Really Happened to Britain in the Seventies* (London, 2010).

Beckett, Francis, *The Rise and Fall of the British Communist Party* (London, 1999).

Bell, David, *Eurocommunism and the Spanish Communist Party* (Sussex, 1979).

Bell, D. S. and Byron Criddle, *The French Communist Party in the Fifth Republic* (Oxford, 1994).

Bell, Tom, *British Communist Party: A Short History* (London, 1937).

Bell, Tom, *John Maclean: A Fighter for Freedom* (Glasgow, 1944).

Benner, Erica, *Really Existing Nationalisms: A Post-Communist View from Marx and Engels* (Oxford, 1995).

Blaazer, David, *The Popular Front and the Progressive Tradition* (Cambridge, 1992).

Branson, Noreen, *The History of the Communist Party of Great Britain 1927–1941* (London, 1985).

Branson, Noreen, *The History of the Communist Party of Great Britain 1941–1951* (London, 1997).

Branson, Noreen and Bill Moore (eds) *Labour–Communist Relations 1920–1951: Part 1 – 1920–1935* (London, 1990).

Bukharin, Nikolai and E. Preobrazhensky, *The ABC of Communism* (London, 1969).

Byers, Seán, *Seán Murray: Marxist-Leninist and Irish Socialist Republican* (Sallins, 2015).

Callaghan, John, *Rajani Palme Dutt: A Study in British Stalinism* (London, 1993).

Callaghan, John, *Cold War, Crisis and Conflict: The History of the Communist Party of Great Britain 1951–68* (London, 2003).

Carr, E. H., *The Twilight of the Comintern 1930–1935* (London, 1986).

Carrillo, Santiago, *'Eurocommunism' and the State* (London, 1977).

Challinor, Raymond, *The Origins of British Bolshevism* (London, 1977).

Claudin, Fernando, *The Communist Movement: From Comintern to Cominform* (London, 1975).

Claudin, Fernando, *Eurocommunism and Socialism* (London, 1978).

Cope, Dave, *Bibliography of the Communist Party of Great Britain* (London, 2016).

Craig, F. W. S. (ed.), *Minor Parties at British Parliamentary Elections 1885–1975* (London, 1975).

Crick, Martin, *History of the Social Democratic Federation* (Keele, 1994).

Cymdeithas yr Iaith Gymraeg, *Maniffesto '82* (Aberystwyth, 1982).

Davies, D. Hywel, *The Welsh Nationalist Party: A Call to Nationhood* (Cardiff, 1983).

Davies, John, *The Green and the Red: Nationalism and Ideology in 20th Century Wales* (Aberystwyth, 1985).

Davies, John, *A History of Wales* (London, 1993).

Davies, John, Lord Gifford and Tony Richards, *Political Policing in Wales* (Cardiff, 1984).

Davies, Paul, *A. J. Cook* (Manchester, 1987).

Degras, Jane (ed.), *The Communist International 1919–1943: Documents Vol. 1, 1919–1922* (Oxford, 1956).

Degras, Jane (ed.), *The Communist International 1919–1943: Documents Vol. 3, 1929–1943* (Oxford, 1965).

Dimitrov, Georgi, *The Working Class Against Fascism* (London, 1935).

Dutt, R. Palme, *Fascism and Social Revolution* (London, 1934).

Dutt, R. Palme, *The Crisis of Britain and the British Empire* (London, 1953).

Eaden, James and David Renton, *The Communist Party of Great Britain since 1920* (London, 2002).

Edwards, Ness, *History of the South Wales Miners' Federation Vol. 1* (London, 1938).

England, Joe, *The Wales TUC 1974–2004: Devolution and Industrial Politics* (Cardiff, 2004).

Evans, John Gilbert, *Devolution in Wales: Claims and Responses, 1937–1979* (Cardiff, 2006).

Falber, Reuben, *The 1968 Czechoslovak Crisis: Inside the British Communist Party* (London, [1996]).

Fishman, Nina, *The British Communist Party and the Trade Unions, 1933–45* (Aldershot, 1995).

Foulkes, David, J. Barry Jones and R. A. Wilford, *The Welsh Veto: The Wales Act 1978 and the Referendum* (Cardiff, 1983).

Francis, Hywel, *Miners Against Fascism: Wales and the Spanish Civil War* (London, 1984).

Francis, Hywel, *History On Our Side: Wales and the 1984–85 Miners' Strike* (Ferryside, 2009).

Dai Smith and Francis, Hywel, *The Fed: A History of the South Wales Miners in the Twentieth Century* (Cardiff, 1998).

Gallacher, William, *Revolt on the Clyde* (London, 1978).

Gamble, Andrew, *The Free Economy and the Strong State: The Politics of Thatcherism* (London, 1994).

Gollan, John, *Scottish Prospect: A Social, Economic and Administrative Survey* (Glasgow, 1948).

Gollan, John, *The British Political System* (London, 1954).

Grant, Adrian, *Irish Socialist Republicanism 1909–36* (Dublin, 2012).

Griffiths, Robert, *S. O. Davies: A Socialist Faith* (Llandysul, 1983).

Harvey, James and Katherine Hood, *The British State* (London, 1958).

Hinton, James and Richard Hyman, *Trade Unions and Revolution: The Industrial Politics of the Early British Communist Party* (London, 1975).

Hobsbawm, Eric, *The Italian Road to Socialism* (London, 1977).

Hobsbawm, Eric, *Revolutionaries* (London, 1999).

Holton, Bob, *British Syndicalism 1900–1914* (London, 1976).

Horner, Arthur, *Incorrigible Rebel* (London, 1960).

Howell, David, *A Lost Left: Three Studies in Socialism and Nationalism* (Manchester, 1986).

Hyde, Douglas, *I Believed: The Autobiography of a Former British Communist* (London, 1951).

Jones, Beti, *Etholiadau'r Ganrif 1885–1997* (Talybont, 1999).

Jones, Richard Wyn, *Rhoi Cymru'n Gyntaf: Syniadaeth Plaid Cymru Cyfrol 1* (Cardiff, 2007).

Keating, Michael and David Bleiman, *Labour and Scottish Nationalism* (London, 1979).

Kendall, Walter, *The Revolutionary Movement in Britain 1900–21: The Origins of British Communism* (London, 1969).

Kenefick, William, *Red Scotland! The Rise and Fall of the Radical Left c.1872–1932* (Edinburgh, 2007).

King, Francis and George Matthews (eds), *About Turn: The British Communist Party and the Second World War* (London, 1990).

Klugmann, James, *History of the Communist of Great Britain Vol. 1: Formation and Early Years 1919–1924* (London, 1969).

Klugmann, James, *History of the Communist Party of Great Britain Vol. 2: The General Strike 1925–1926* (London, 1969).

Khrushchev, Nikita, *The Dethronement of Stalin: Full Text of Khrushchev's Speech* (Manchester, 1956).

Lange, Peter and Maurizio Vannicelli, *The Communist Parties of Italy, France and Spain: Postwar Change and Continuity. A Casebook* (London, 1981).

Laybourn, Keith and Dylan Murphy, *Under the Red Flag: A History of Communism in Britain* (Gloucester, 1999).

Lenin, V. I., *On Britain* (Moscow, 1958).

Lenin, V. I., *Critical Remarks on the National Question* (Moscow, 1971).

Lewis, Richard, *Leaders and Teachers: Adult Education and the Challenge of Labour in South Wales 1906–1940* (Cardiff, 1993).

Lindsay, Jack, *England, My England: A Pageant of the English People* (London, 1939).

Lindsay, Jack and Edgell Rickword (eds), *A Handbook of Freedom: A Record of English Democracy through Twelve Centuries* (London, 1939).

Linehan, Thomas, *Communism in Britain 1920–39: From the Cradle to the Grave* (Manchester, 2007).

MacFarlane, L. J., *The British Communist Party: Its Origin and Development until 1929* (London, 1966).

Macintyre, Stuart, *Little Moscows: Communism and Working Class Militancy in Inter-War Britain* (London, 1980).

Macintyre, Stuart, *A Proletarian Science: Marxism in Britain, 1917–1933* (London, 1986).

Maclean, John, *In the Rapids of Revolution* (London, 1978).

MacLeod, Alison, *The Death of Uncle Joe* (Woodbridge, 1997).

Mahon, John, *Harry Pollitt: a Biography* (London, 1976).

Mandel, Ernest, *From Stalinism and Eurocommunism* (London, 1978).

Martin, Roderick, *Communism and the British Trade Unions 1924–1933: A Study of the National Minority Movement* (Oxford, 1969).

Marx, Karl and Frederick Engels, *On the National and Colonial Questions* (New Delhi, 2001).

McAllister, Laura, *Plaid Cymru: The Emergence of a Political Party* (Bridgend, 2001).

McDermott, Kevin and Agnew, Jeremy, *The Comintern: A History of International Communism from Lenin to Stalin* (London, 1996).

McGuire, Charlie, *Roddy Connolly and the Struggle for Socialism in Ireland* (Cork, 2008).

McShane, Harry and Joan Smith, No Mean Fighter (London, 1978).

Milton, Nan, *John Maclean* (London, 1973).

Milotte, Mike, *Communism in Modern Ireland: The Pursuit of the Workers' Republic since 1916* (Dublin, 1984).

Mitchell, Alex, *Behind the Crisis in British Stalinism* (London, 1984).

Morgan, Kenneth O., *Rebirth of a Nation: Wales 1880–1980* (Oxford, 1990).

Morgan, Kevin, *Against Fascism and War: Ruptures and Continuities in British Communist Politics, 1935–41* (Manchester, 1989).

Morgan, Kevin, *Harry Pollitt* (Manchester, 1993).

Morgan, Kevin, *Labour Legends and Russian Gold* (London, 2006).

Morgan, Kevin, Gidon Cohen and Andrew Flinn (eds), *Agents of the Revolution: New Biographical Approaches to the History of International Communism in the Age of Lenin and Stalin* (Bern, 2005).

Morgan, Kevin, Gidon Cohen and Andrew Flinn, *Communists and British Society 1920–1991* (London, 2007).

Mortimer, Edward, *The Rise of the French Communist Party 1920–1947* (London, 1984).

Morton, A. L., *A People's History of England* (London, 1938).

Newton, Kenneth, *The Sociology of British Communism* (London, 1969).

Nicholas, T. Islwyn, *One Hundred Years Ago: The Story of the Montgomeryshire Chartists* (Aberystwyth, 1939).

Nicholas, T. Islwyn, *A Welsh Heretic: Dr William Price, Llantrisant* (London, 1940).

Nicholas, T. Islwyn, *Dic Penderyn: Welsh Rebel and Martyr* (London, 1944).

Nicholas, T. Islwyn, *R. J. Derfel: Welsh Rebel, Poet and Preacher* (London, 1945).

Nicholas, T. Islwyn, *Iolo Morganwg: Bard of Liberty* (London, 1945).

O'Connor, Emmet, *James Larkin* (Cork, 2002).

O'Connor, Emmet, *Reds and the Green: Ireland, Russia and the Communist Internationals 1919–43* (Dublin, 2004).

Osmond, John, *Police Conspiracy?* (Talybont, 1984).

Paynter, Will, *My Generation* (London, 1972).

Pelling, Henry, *The British Communist Party: A Historical Profile* (London, 1975).

Pimlott, Ben, *Labour and the Left in the 1930s* (London, 1986).

Pollitt, Harry, *Looking Ahead* (London, 1947).

Pollitt, Harry, *Selected Articles and Speeches, Volume 1 1919–1936* (London, 1953).

Prior, Mike and David Purdy, *Out of the Ghetto* (Nottingham, 1979).

Raymond, Gino G., *The French Communist Party During the Fifth Republic: A Crisis of Leadership and Ideology* (London, 2005).

Redfern, Neil, *Class or Nation: Communists, Imperialism and Two World Wars* (London, 2005).

Riddell, John, *Workers of the World and Oppressed Peoples, Unite: Proceedings and Documents of the Second Congress, 1920* (New York, 1991).

Ripley, B. J. and J. McHugh, *John Maclean* (Manchester, 1989).

Roberts, Ioan, *Achos y Bomiau Bach* (Llanrwst, 2001).

Sassoon, Donald, *The Strategy of the Italian Communist Party: From the Resistance to the Historic Compromise* (London, 1981).

Samuel, Raphael, *The Lost World of British Communism* (London, 2006).

Simon, Roger, *Gramsci's Political Thought: An Introduction* (London, 1982).

Stalin, Joseph, *Marxism and the National and Colonial Question* (London, 1936).

Stradling, Robert, *Wales and the Spanish Civil War: The Dragon's Dearest Cause?* (Cardiff, 2004).

Thompson, Willie, *The Good Old Cause: British Communism 1920–1991* (London, 1992).

Thompson, Willie, *The Communist Movement since 1945* (Oxford, 1998).

Thorpe, Andrew, *The British Communist Party and Moscow 1920–43* (Manchester, 2000).

Turner, Alwyn, *Crisis? What Crisis? Britain in the 1970s* (London, 2008).

Unofficial Reform Committee, *The Miners' Next Step: Being a Suggested Scheme for the Reorganisation of the Federation* (London, 1973).

Urban, Joan Barth, *Moscow and the Italian Communist Party: From Togliatti to Berlinguer* (London, 1986).

Williams, Chris, *Democratic Rhondda: Politics and Society 1885–1951* (Cardiff, 1996).

Williams, Gwyn A., *When Was Wales?* (London, 1985).

Woodhouse, Michael and Brian Pearce, *Essays on the History of Communism in Britain* (London, 1975).

Worley, Matthew, *Class Against Class: The Communist Party in Britain Between the Wars* (London, 2002).

ARTICLES AND BOOK CHAPTERS

Anon., '1926 in Aberdare', *Llafur*, 2 (2), 1977.

Anon., 'Strike to the Finish: A Roundtable Discussion', *Marxism Today*, September 1984.

Anon., 'The Miners' Strike: The Balance Sheet', *Marxism Today*, April 1985.

Aaronovitch, Sam, 'Perspectives for Class Struggle and Alliances', *Marxism Today*, March 1973.

Aaronovitch, Sam, 'The Alternative Economic Strategy: Goodbye to All That?', *Marxism Today*, February 1986.

Anderson, Paul and Kevin Davey, 'Moscow Gold? The True Story of the Kremlin British Communism and the Left', *New Statesman*, 7 April, 1995.

Anderson, Perry, 'Communist Party History' in Raphael Samuel (ed.), *People's History and Socialist Theory* (London, 1981).

Arnot, Robin Page, 'The English Tradition', *Labour Monthly*, 18 (11), 1936.

Ashton, Jack, 'After the Referendum: Scotland', *Marxism Today*, May 1979.

Azcárate, Manuel, 'What is Eurocommunism?', in G. R. Urban, *Eurocommunism: Its Roots and Future in Italy and Elsewhere* (London, 1978).

Azcárate, Manuel, 'The Present State of Eurocommunism: its Main Features, Political and Theoretical', in Kindersley (ed.), *In Search of Eurocommunism* (London, 1981).

Baker, Allan, 'Why the Miners' Fight is for the Industrial Survival of Britain', *Moving Left in Wales*, 3, Summer 1984.

Barke, James, 'The Scottish National Question', *Left Review*, 2 (14), 1936.

Berlinguer, Enrico, 'Reflections After the Events in Chile', *Marxism Today*, February 1974.

Bramley, Ted, 'Our Propaganda', *Discussion*, 2 (4), 1937.

Buchanan, Tom, 'Anti-fascism and Democracy in the 1930s', *European Historical Quarterly*, 32 (1), 2002.

Burge, Alun, 'The 1926 General Strike in Cardiff', *Llafur*, 6 (1), 1992.

Burke, David and Fred Lindop, 'Theodore Rothstein and the Origins of the British Communist Party', *Socialist History*, 15, 1999.

Callaghan, John, 'Endgame: The Communist Party of Great Britain' in David S. Bell (ed.), *Western European Communists and the Collapse of Communism* (Oxford, 1993).

Callaghan, John, 'The Communists and the Colonies: Anti Imperialism Between the Wars' in Andrews et al. (eds), *Opening the Books: Essays on the Social and Cultural History of the British Communist Party* (London, 1998).

Callaghan, John, 'Rise and Fall of the Alternative Economic Strategy: From Internationalisation of Capital to "Globalisation"', *Contemporary British History*, 14 (3), 2000.

Callaghan, John, 'The Cold War and the March of Capitalism, Socialism and Democracy', *Contemporary British History*, 15 (3), 2001.

Callaghan, John, 'Industrial Militancy, 1945–79: The Failure of the British Road to Socialism?', *Twentieth Century British History*, 15 (4), 2004.

Campbell, Alan and John McIlroy, 'A Reply to Critics', *Labour History Review*, 69 (3), 2004.

Charette, Emily, 'Framing Wales: The Parliament for Wales Campaign

1950–1956' in Chapman, T. Robin (ed.), *The Idiom of Dissent: Protest and Propaganda in Wales* (Llandysul, 2006).

Carter, Pete, 'Striking the Right Note', *Marxism Today*, March 1985.

Cohen, Gidon and Kevin Morgan, 'Stalin's Sausage Machine: British Students at the International Lenin School, 1926–37', *Twentieth Century British History*, 13 (4), 2002.

Cohen, Jack, 'Some Thoughts on the Working Class Today', *Marxism Today*, October 1973.

Cook, Dave, 'The British Road to Socialism' and the Communist Party', *Marxism Today*, December 1978.

Cook, Dave, '"Rocky Road Blues": The Communist Party and the Broad Democratic Alliance', in George Bridges and Rosalind Brunt (eds), *Silver Linings: Some Strategies for the Eighties* (London, 1981).

Cook, Dave, 'No Private Drama', *Marxism Today*, February 1985.

Cooke, Phil, 'Decentralism, Socialism and Democracy', *Radical Wales*, 5, Winter 1984.

Cooke, Phil, Sian Edwards, G. Howells and Dafydd Elis Thomas, 'Congress at the Crossroads', *Radical Wales*, Summer 1985.

Cornforth, Kitty, 'The British Road to Socialism', *Communist Review*, April 1947.

Costello, Mick, 'The Working Class and the Broad Democratic Alliance', *Marxism Today*, June 1979.

Cox, Idris, 'The National Problem in Britain', *Marxism Today*, June 1968.

Cox, Idris, 'More on the National Problem in Britain', *Marxism Today*, April 1969.

Cox, Idris, 'Socialism and the National Question', *Planet*, 37/38, May 1977.

Cox, Idris, 'Communist Strongholds in Inter-War Britain', *Marxism Today*, June 1979.

Cox, Idris, 'Early Labour Battles in Ogmore', *Llafur*, 3 (4), 1983.

Crawfurd, Helen, 'The Scottish National Movement', *Communist Review*, 5 (2), 1933.

David, Wayne, 'The Labour Party and the "Exclusion" of the Communists; the Case of the Ogmore Divisional Labour Party in the 1920's', *Llafur*, 3 (4), 1983

Davies, Brian, 'Wales – What Sort of Nation?', *Cyffro*, 4 (1), Spring 1976.

Davies, Brian, 'Towards a New Synthesis', *Planet*, 37/38, May 1977.

Davies, Brian, 'Heading for the Rocks', *Arcade*, 5 February 1982.

Davies, J. Kitchener, 'Cenedlaetholdeb Cymru a Chomiwnyddiaeth', *Heddiw*, 2 (3), 1937.

Davies, Paul, 'The Making of A. J. Cook: His Development Within the South Wales Labour Movement', *Llafur*, 2 (3), 1978.

Deery, Phillip, "The Secret Battalion': Communism in Britain during the Cold War', *Contemporary British History*, 13 (4), 1999.

Devine, Pat, 'Inflation and Marxist Theory', *Marxism Today*, March 1974.
Drinkwater, Tom, 'Wales Needs a New Economy', *Cyffro*, 1 (2), Winter 1969.
Dutt, R. Palme, 'The Fight for British Independence', *Communist Review*, February 1951.
Edwards, Andrew, 'Te Parti Mwncïod? Rhwyg, Anghytgord a Datblygiad Polisi Llafur ar Ddatganoli, 1966–1970', *Cof Cenedl XXIV*, 2009.
Egan, David, 'The Swansea Conference of the British Council of Soldiers' and Workers' Delegates, July 1917: Reactions to the Russian Revolution of February, 1917, and the Anti-War Movement in South Wales', *Llafur*, 1 (4), 1975.
Egan, David, 'Noah Ablett 1883–1935', *Llafur*, 4 (3), 1986.
Ellenstein, Jean, 'Eurocommunism and the French Communist Party', in Richard Kindersley (ed.), *In Search of Eurocommunism*.
Enright, Tim, 'Britain's Minority Languages', *Marxism Today*, August 1964.
Evans, Gwynfor, 'The Case for Welsh Nationalism', *Labour Monthly*, December 1967.
Fielding, Stephen, 'British Communism: Interesting but Irrelevant', *Labour History Review*, 60 (2), 1995.
Fishman, Nina, 'The British Road is Resurfaced for New Times: From the British Communist Party to the Democratic Left', in Martin J. Bull and Paul Heywood (eds), *West European Communist Parties After the Revolutions of 1989* (London, 1994).
Fishman, Nina, 'Horner and Hornerism', in John McIlroy, Kevin Morgan and Alan Campbell (eds), *Party People and Communist Lives: Explorations in Biography* (London, 2001).
Fishman, Nina, 'Essentialists and Realists: Reflections on the Historiography of the CPGB', *Communist History Network Newsletter*, 11, 2001.
Fishman, Nina, 'The Phoney Cold War in British Trade Unions', *Contemporary British History*, 15 (3), 2001.
Fishman, Nina, 'A First Revisionist Replies to Her Revisionists', *Labour History Review*, 69 (3), 2004.
Forgacs, David, 'Gramsci and Marxism in Britain', *New Left Review*, 176, July–August 1989.
Foster, Gavin, '"Scotsmen Stand By Ireland": John Mclean and the Irish Revolution', *History Ireland*, 16 (1), 2008.
Fowler, Carwyn, 'Nationalism and the Labour Party in Wales', *Llafur*, 8 (4), 2003.
Francis, Dai, 'Needed Now – A Trade Union Congress for Wales', *Cyffro*, 2 (2), Summer 1972.
Francis, Dai, 'Devolution D-Day ... It's Wales Against the Tories', *The Miner*, February/March 1979.

Francis, Hywel, 'Mining the Popular Front', *Marxism Today*, February 1985.

Francis, Hywel, 'Argraffiadau Cyntaf Streic y Glowyr, 1984–85' *Barn*, 267, 1985.

Francis, Hywel, NUM United: A Team in Disarray', *Marxism Today*, April 1985.

Francis, Hywel, '"Say Nothing and Leave in the Middle of the Night": The Spanish Civil War Revisited', *History Workshop Journal*, 32, 1991

Francis, Hywel and Gareth Rees, '"No Surrender in the Valleys": The 1984–85 Miners' Strike in South Wales', *Llafur*, 5 (2), 1989.

French, Sid, 'Socialist Democracy – Some Problems', *Marxism Today*, December 1976.

Fyrth, Jim, 'Introduction: In the Thirties', in Jim Fyrth (ed.), *Britain, Fascism and the Popular Front* (London, 1985).

Gealy, W. L., 'William James Rees (1914–1995)', *Efrydiau Athronyddol*, 59, 1996.

Gildart, Keith, 'Thomas Jones (Tom) (1908–90)' *in Dictionary of Labour Biography*, Vol. 11 (London, 2003).

Gollan, John, 'Socialist Democracy – Some Problems: The 20th Congress of the Communist Party of the Soviet Union in Retrospect', *Marxism Today*, January 1976.

Gostwick, Martin, 'British Roads or National Roads? Hard Choices Ahead', *Marxism Today*, August 1978.

Graham, Helen and Paul Preston, 'The Popular Front and the Struggle Against Fascism', in Helen Graham and Paul Preston (eds), *The Popular Front in Europe* (London, 1987).

Griffiths, Robert, 'Socialism and the National Movement', *Cyffro*, 2 (4), Spring 1975.

Griffiths, Robert, 'The Spectre Returns', *Moving Left in Wales*, 3, Summer 1984.

Griffiths, Robert, 'Resolving Contradictions Between Class and Nation', in John Osmond (ed.), *The National Question Again: Welsh Political Identity in the 1980s* (Llandysul, 1985).

Hall, Stuart, 'The Great Moving Right Show', *Marxism Today*, January 1979

Haslam, Jonathan, 'The Comintern and the Origins of the Popular Front 1934–1935', *Historical Journal*, 22 (3), 1979.

Haslam, Jonathan, 'The Soviet Union, the Comintern and the Demise of the Popular Front, 1936–39', in Graham and Preston (eds), *The Popular Front in Europe*.

Hauben, Ronda, 'A Pioneer in Workers' Education: Mark Starr and Workers Education in Great Britain', *Llafur*, 4 (2), 1985

Hobsbawm, Eric, 'The Forward March of Labour Halted?', *Marxism Today*, September 1978.

Hobsbawm, Eric, 'The Retreat into Extremism', *Marxism Today*, April 1985.

Hobsbawm, Eric, 'The "Moscow Line" and International Communist Policy, 1933–47', in Chris Wrigley, *Warfare, Diplomacy and Politics: Essays in Honour of A. J. P. Taylor* (London, 1986).

Hobsbawm, Eric, 'Problems of Communist History', in Hobsbawm, *Revolutionaries* (London, 1999).

Hodgson, Geoff, 'The Communist Party and Parliamentary Democracy', in *Socialism and Parliamentary Democracy* (Nottingham, 1977).

Howe, Stephen, 'Labour Patriotism 1939–83', in Raphael Samuel (ed.), *Patriotism: The Making and Unmaking of British National Identity Vol. 1: History and Politics* (London, 1989).

Howell, David, 'The 1984–85 Miners' Strike in North Wales', *Contemporary Wales*, 4, 1991.

Howells, Kim, 'Stopping Out: The Birth of a New Kind of Politics', in Beynon, Huw (ed.), *Digging Deeper: Issues in the Miners' Strike* (London, 1985).

Howkins, Alun, 'Class Against Class: The Political Culture of the Communist Party of Great Britain, 1930–35', in Frank Gloversmith, *Class, Culture and Social Change* (Sussex, 1980).

Hudson, Kate, '1956 and the Communist Party', in *The Communist Party and 1956: Speeches at the Conference* (London, 1993).

Humphreys, C. Lloyd, 'Welsh National Rights', *Labour Monthly*, 26 (11), 1944.

Hunt, Alan, 'Class Structure in Britain Today', *Marxism Today*, June 1970.

Hunt, Alan, 'Class Structure and Political Strategy', *Marxism Today*, July 1977

Jacques, Martin, 'After Communism', *Marxism Today*, January 1990.

Johnstone, Monty, 'The CPGB, the Comintern and the War, 1939–1941: Filling in the Blank Spots', *Science and Society*, 61 (1), 1997.

Jones, Glyn, 'Problems of Propaganda in South Wales', *Discussion*, 2 (7), 1938.

Jones, John Graham, 'The Parliament for Wales Campaign, 1950–1956', *Welsh Historical Review*, 6 (2), 1992.

Jones, John Graham, 'Y Blaid Lafur, Datganoli a Chymru 1900–1979', *Cof Cenedl VII*, 1992.

Jones, R. Merfyn and Ioan Rhys Jones, 'Labour and the Nation', in Duncan Tanner, Chris Williams and Deian Hopkin (eds), *The Labour Party in Wales 1900–2000* (Cardiff, 2000).

Jones, Stephen G., 'Sports Politics and the Labour Movement: The British Workers' Sports Federation, 1923–1935', *The British Journal of Sports History*, 2 (2), 1985.

Kinnock, Neil, 'Nationalism and Socialism', *Cyffro*, 2 (4), Spring 1975.

Kitchen, Martin, 'The Austrian Left and the Popular Front', in Graham and Preston (eds), *The Popular Front in Europe*.

Kozlov, Nicholas N. and Eric D. Weitz, 'Reflections on the Origins of the "Third Period": Bukharin, the Comintern and the Political Economy of Weimar Germany', *Journal of Contemporary History*, 24, 1989.

Kristjánsdóttir, Ragnheidur, 'Communists and the National Question in Scotland and Iceland, *c.*1930 to *c.*1940', *The Historical Journal*, 45 (3), 2002.

Lane, Tony, 'The Unions: Caught in the Ebb Tide', *Marxism Today*, September 1982.

LaPorte, Norman and Matthew Worley, 'Toward a Comparative History of Communism: The British and German Communist Parties to 1933', *Contemporary British History*, 22 (2), 2008.

Lawn, Martin, 'Mark Starr: Socialist Educator', *Llafur*, 4 (2), 1985.

Levy, Daniel A. L., 'The French Popular Front, 1936–37' in Graham and Preston (eds), *The Popular Front in Europe*.

Lewis, Richard, 'The South Wales Miners and the Ruskin College Strike of 1909', *Llafur*, 2 (1), 1976.

Lewis, Richard, 'Protagonist of Labour: Mark Starr, 1894–1985', *Llafur*, 4 (3), 1986.

McAllister, Laura, 'The Road to Cardiff Bay: The Process of Establishing the National Assembly of Wales', *Parliamentary Affairs*, October 1999.

Macintyre, Stuart, 'Red Strongholds Between the Wars', *Marxism Today*, March 1979.

MacLennan, R., 'The National Question in Scotland', *Communist Review*, 4 (10), 1932.

Majander, Mikko, 'The Soviet View on Social Democracy', in Tauno Saarela and Kimmo Rentola (eds), *Communism: National and International* (Helsinki, 1998).

Matthews, George, 'Stalin's British Road?', *Changes*, 23, 1991.

McAllister, Ian, 'The Labour Party in Wales: The Dynamics of One-Partyism', *Llafur*, 3 (2), 1981.

McDermott, Kevin, 'Stalin and the Comintern during the "Third Period", 1928–33', *European History Quarterly*, 25, 1995.

McDermott, Kevin, 'Bolshevisation from Above or Below? The Comintern and European Communism in the 1920s', in Saarela and Rentola, *Communism: National and International*.

McDermott, Kevin, 'The History of the Comintern in Light of New Documents', in Andrew Thorpe and Tim Rees (eds), *International Communism and the Communist International 1919–43* (Manchester, 1998).

McEwen, Malcolm, 'The Day the Party Had to Stop', *Socialist Register*, 13, 1976.

McHugh, John and B. J. Ripley, 'The Neath By-election, 1945: Trotskyists in West Wales', *Llafur*, 3 (2), 1981.

McIlroy, John, 'Notes on the Communist Party and Industrial Politics' in Alan Campbell, Nina Fishman and John McIlroy, *British Trade Unions and Industrial Politics: The High Tide of Trade Unionism 1964–79* (Aldershot, 1999).

McIlroy, John, 'Glowyr Cymru ym Mosgo: Welsh Communists at the Lenin School Between the Wars', *Llafur,* 8 (4), 2003.

McIlroy, John and Alan Campbell, 'Organising the Militants: the Liaison Committee for the Defence of Trade Unions, 1966–79', *British Journal of Industrial Relations,* 37 (1), 1999.

McIlroy, John and Alan Campbell, 'The Heresy of Arthur Horner', *Llafur,* 8 (2), 2001.

McIlroy, John and Alan Campbell, 'Histories of the British Communist Party: A Users Guide', *Labour History Review,* 68 (1), 2003.

McIlroy, John and Alan Campbell, 'Critical Reflections on British Communist Party History', *Historical Materialism,* 12 (1), 2004.

McKibbin, Ross, 'Why Was There No Marxism in Great Britain?', *English Historical Review,* 99 (391), 1984.

Miles, Andy, 'Workers Education: the Communist Party and the Plebs League in the 1920s', *History Workshop,* 18, 1984.

Miles, Gareth, 'Why I Left Plaid Cymru ...', *Radical Wales,* 1, Winter 1983.

Morgan, Kenneth O., 'Leaders and Led in the Labour Movement', *Llafur,* 6 (3), 1994.

Morgan, Kenneth O., 'Socialism and Syndicalism: The Welsh Miners' Debate 1912' in *Modern Wales: Politics, Places and People* (Cardiff, 1995).

Morgan, Kevin, 'The CPGB and the Comintern Archives', *Socialist History,* 2, 1993.

Morgan, Kevin, 'The Archives of the British Communist Party: An Historical Overview', *Twentieth Century History,* 7 (3), 1996.

Morgan, Kevin and Tauno Saarela, 'Northern Underground Revisited: Finnish Reds and the Origins of British Communism', *European History Quarterly,* 29 (2), 1999.

Morgan, Steffan, '"Stand by your Man": Wives, Women and Feminism During the Miners' Strike 1984–85', *Llafur,* 9 (2), 2005.

Morris, Dylan, 'Sosialaeth i'r Cymry: Trafodaeth yr ILP', *Llafur,* 4 (2), 1985.

Morris, Ronald, 'T. Islwyn Nicholas 1903–1980', *Llafur,* 3 (2), 1981.

Mortimer, Edward, 'Un Socialisme aux Couleurs de la France: the French Communist Party', in Paolo Fillo della Torre, Edward Mortimer and Jonathan Story (eds), *Eurocommunism: Myth or Reality* (Harmondsworth, 1979).

Murray, Robin, 'Fordism and Post-Fordism', in Stuart Hall and Martin Jacques (eds), *New Times: The Changing Face of Politics in the 1990s* (London, 1989).

Nicholas, T. E., 'Y Ddraig Goch a'r Faner Goch: Cenedlaetholdeb a Sosialaeth', *Y Geninen*, 30 (1), 1912.

O'Connor, Emmet, 'Communists, Russia and the IRA, 1920–23', *The Historical Journal*, 46 (1), 2003.

O'Connor, Emmet, 'The Age of the Red Republic: The Irish Left and Nationalism, 1909–36', *Saothar*, 30, 2005.

Parsons, Steve, '1956: What Happened Inside the CPGB', in *The Communist Party and 1956* (London, 1993).

Paynter, Will, 'The United Front in South Wales', *Labour Monthly*, 17 (4), 1935.

Pearce, Bert, 'The National Future of Scotland and Wales', *Marxism Today*, November 1967.

Pearce, Bert, 'Parliaments and Powers (A Communist Comment on Kilbrandon)', *Cyffro*, 2 (3), Summer 1974.

Pearce, Bert, 'Let Labour Lead Now!', *Cyffro*, 2 (4), Spring 1975.

Pearce, Bert, 'Devolution, Democracy and Socialism: Which Way for Wales Today?', *Cyffro*, 4 (1), Spring 1976.

Pearce, Bert, 'Devolution – The New Shape of British Politics', *Cyffro*, 4 (3), Spring 1977.

Pearce, Bert, 'Devolution, Democracy and Socialist Advance', *Marxism Today*, December 1977.

Pearce, Bert, 'A Tory 1984?', *Cyffro*, Summer 1979.

Pearce, Bert, 'The Working Class and the Broad Democratic Alliance', *Marxism Today*, November 1979.

Pitcairn, Leo, 'Crisis in British Communism: an Insider's View', *New Left Review*, 153, September/October 1985.

Pitt, Robert, 'Educator and Agitator: Charlie Gibbons, 1888–1967', *Llafur*, 5 (2), 1989.

Platt, David, 'Force and Violence in American Films', *Communist Review*, October 1950.

Preston, Paul, 'The PCE's Long Road to Democracy 1954–77', in Kindersley (ed.), *In Search of Eurocommunism*.

Pribićević, Branko, 'Eurocommunism and the New Party', in Kindersley (ed.), *In Search of Eurocommunism*.

Prior, Mike, 'Inflation and Marxist Theory', *Marxism Today*, April 1975.

Prior, Mike, 'Socialist Democracy – Some Problems', *Marxism Today*, April 1976.

Purdy, David, 'Some Thoughts on the Party's Policy Towards Prices, Wages and Incomes', *Marxism Today*, March 1974.

Rees, D. Ben, 'Sosialaeth Farcsaidd Gymraeg T. E. Nicholas', *Trafodion Anrhydeddus Gymdeithas y Cymmrodrion*, 1996.

Rees, Gareth, 'Plaid Cymru: a Political Paradox', *Moving Left in Wales*, 3, Summer 1984.

Rees, Gareth, 'A New Politics', *Planet*, 53, October/November 1985.

Rickword, Edgell, 'Stalin on the National Question', *Left Review*, 2 (14), 1936.

Roberts, Elwyn, 'Ymgyrch Senedd i Gymru', in John Davies (ed.), *Cymru'n Deffro: Hanes y Blaid Genedlaethol 1925–75* (Talybont, 1981).

Roberts, Geoffrey, 'The Limits of Popular Radicalism: British Communism and the People's War, 1941–1945', *Chronicon: an electronic history journal*, 1, 1997.

Ruhemann, Barbara, 'The National Problem in Britain', *Marxism Today*, August 1968.

Russo, Giovanni, 'Il Compromesso Storico: the Italian Communist Party from 1968 to 1978', in della Torre et al. (eds), *Eurocommunism: Myth or Reality*.

Saville, John, 'The Twentieth Congress and the British Communist Party', *Socialist Register*, 13, 1976.

Schapiro, Leonard, 'Soviet Attitudes to National Communism in Western Europe', in Howard Machin (ed.), *National Communism in Western Europe: A Third Way for Socialism?* (London, 1983).

Spence, Alan, 'The National Problem in Britain', *Marxism Today*, October 1968.

Squires, Mike, 'CPGB Membership During the Class Against Class Years', *Socialist History*, 3, 1993.

Stevens, Richard, 'Cold War Politics: Communism and Anti-Communism in the Trade Unions', in Alan Campbell, Nina Fishman and John McIlroy, *British Trade Unions and Industrial Politics: The Post War Compromise, 1945–64* (Aldershot, 1999).

Story, Jonathan, 'El Pacto Para la Libertad: the Spanish Communist Party', in della Torre et al. (eds), *Eurocommunism: Myth or Reality*.

Thatcher, Ian D., 'John Maclean: Soviet Versions', History, 77 (251).

Thompson, Willie and Sandy Hobbs, 'British Communists on the War, 1939–1941', *Oral History Journal*, 16 (2), 1988.

Thompson, Willie, 'British Communists and the Cold War, 1947–52', *Contemporary British History*, 15 (3), 2001.

Thorpe, Andrew, 'Comintern "Control" of the Communist Party of Great Britain 1920–43', *English Historical Review*, 113 (452), 1998.

Thorpe, Andrew, 'Stalinism and British Politics', *History*, 83 (272), 1998.

Thorpe, Andrew, 'The Communist International and the British Communist Party', in Thorpe and Rees (eds), *International Communism and the Communist International 1919–43*, 1998.

Thorpe, Andrew, 'The Membership of the Communist Party of Great Britain, 1920–1945', *Historical Journal*, 43 (3), 2000.

Thorpe, Andrew, 'Communist History: A Reply to Campbell and McIlroy', *Labour History Review*, 69 (3), 2004.

Togliatti, Palmiro, 'Interview with Nuovi Argomenti', in Togliatti, Palmiro, *On Gramsci and Other Writings* (London, 1979).

Togliatti, Palmiro, 'The Yalta Memorandum' in Togliatti, *On Gramsci*.

Vaughan, Ann, 'Statws yr Iaith Gymraeg', *Cyffro*, 2 (2), Summer 1972.

Waite, Mike, 'The Young Communist League and Youth Culture', *Socialist History*, 6, 1994.

Waite, Mike, 'Sex 'n' Drugs 'n' Rock 'n' Roll (and Communism) in the 1960s', in Geoff Andrews, Nina Fishman and Kevin Morgan, *Opening the Books: Essays on the Social and Cultural History of the British Communist Party* (London, 1995).

Wallis, Mick, 'Heirs to the Pageant: Mass Spectacle and the Popular Front', in Andy Croft (ed.), *A Weapon in the Struggle: The Cultural History of the Communist Party of Great Britain* (London, 1998).

White, Lyndon, 'The CPGB and the National Question in Post-war Wales: the case of Idris Cox', *Communist History Network Newsletter*, 12, 2002.

Wilkinson, Brian, 'Socialism and Welsh Independence: a Contribution to Discussion', *Cyffro*, 4 (2), Summer 1976.

Williams, Emyr Wyn, 'Commissioning National Liberation', *Bulletin of Scottish Politics*, 1981.

Williams, Gwyn A., 'Mother Wales Get Off Me Back?', *Marxism Today*, December 1981.

Williams, Gwyn A., 'Land of Our Fathers', *Marxism Today*, August 1982.

Williams, Gwyn A., ' ... And Why I Joined', *Radical Wales*, 1, Winter 1983.

Williams, Gwyn A., 'Sardinian Marxist and Welsh Predicament', *Radical Wales*, 7, Summer 1985.

Williams, Gwyn A., 'The Onward March of a Small Nation', in Hall and Jacques (eds), *New Times: The Changing Face of Politics in the 1990s*.

Williams, John Roose, 'A Social Policy for the Welsh Nationalist Party', *The Welsh Outlook*, October 1925.

Williams, John Roose, 'Comiwnyddiaeth a Chymru', *Heddiw*, 2 (1), 1937.

Williams, John Roose, 'The Welsh Nationalist Movement: Its Aims and Political Significance', *Discussion*, 3 (2), 1938.

Williams, John Roose, 'Arloeswyr Rhyddid yng Nghymru: I. Owain Glyn Dŵr', *Y Dysgedydd*, 127 (7), 1947.

Williams, John Roose, 'Arloeswyr Rhyddid yng Nghymru: II. Morgan Llwyd o Wynedd', *Y Dysgedydd*, 127 (8), 1947.

Williams, John Roose, 'Arloeswyr Rhyddid yng Nghymru: III. Griffith Jones, Llanddowror', *Y Dysgedydd*, 127 (12), 1947.

Williams, John Roose, 'Arloeswyr Rhyddid yng Nghymru: IV. Dr Richard Price, Llangeinor', *Y Dysgedydd*, 128 (1), 1948.

Williams, John Roose, 'Arloeswyr Rhyddid yng Nghymru: V. Iolo Morganwg, 'Bardd Rhyddid'', *Y Dysgedydd*, 128 (3), 1948.

Williams, John Roose, 'Arloeswyr Rhyddid yng Nghymru: VI. Jac Glanygors', *Y Dysgedydd*, 128 (4), 1948

Williams, John Roose, 'Arloeswyr Rhyddid yng Nghymru: VII. Robert Owen', *Y Dysgedydd*, 128 (8), 1948.

Willis, Fred, 'Ireland and the Social Revolution', *Communist Review*, 1 (1), 1921.

Wilson, Alistair, 'Which Party for Wales?', *Cyffro*, 2 (2), Summer 1972.

Wilson, Alistair, 'And Wales', *Marxism Today*, May 1979.

Winter, Mary, 'Rhai Syniadau ar Bamffled Gareth Miles – "Cymru Rydd, Cymru Gymraeg, Cymru Sosialaidd"', *Cyffro*, 2 (2), Summer 1972.

Winter, Mary, 'Yr Iaith Gymraeg a'r Mudiad Llafur', *Cyffro*, 4 (2), Summer 1976.

Winter, Mary, 'Devolution – What Powers for Wales?', *Cyffro*, 4 (2), Summer 1976.

Winter, Mary, 'The Open Debate – Devolution: A Step in the Right Direction', *Cyffro*, 4 (3), Spring 1977.

Worley, Matthew, 'Reflections on Recent British Communist Party History', *Historical Materialism*, 4, 1999.

Worley, Matthew, 'Left Turn: A Reassessment of the Communist Party of Great Britain in the Third Period, 1928–33', *Twentieth Century British History*, 11 (4), 2000.

Worley, Matthew, 'For a Proletarian Culture: Communist Party Culture in Britain in the Third Period, 1928–1935', *Socialist History*, 18, 2000.

Worley, Matthew, 'The Communist International, the Communist Party and Great Britain and the 'Third Period', 1928–1932', *European History Quarterly*, 30 (2), 2000.

Worley, Matthew, 'Courting Disaster? The Communist International in the Third Period', in Matthew Worley (ed.), *In Search of Revolution: International Communist Parties in the Third Period* (London, 2004).

Worley, Matthew, 'Echoes from the Dustbin of History: A Reply to Alan Campbell and John McIlroy', *Labour History Review*, 69 (3), 2004.

Young, James D, 'Marxism and the Scottish National Question', *Journal of Contemporary History*, 18, 1983.

INDEX

Aaronovitch, Sam 127
Ablett, Noah 26, 292
Abse, Leo, 224–5, 230
Alexander, Bill 121, 143–4, 147–8,
    152, 153, 154, 157, 159
Anglo-Irish Treaty (1921) 10
Arnot, Robin Page 37, 60
Arundel, Honor 156–7

Baker, Allan 178, 266
Barke, James 79
Beamish, Dick 144, 146
Bebb, Ambrose 139–40
Bell, Idris 97
Bell, Tom 23, 29
Berry, Joe 178
Borodin, Mikhail 10, 29, 34
Bowen, Bill 186–7
Branson, Noreen 126–7
Bramley, Ted 59, 62, 63, 65
British Road to Socialism (CPGB) 5,
    120, 123–5, 127–30, 150,
    156–7, 165, 179, 187–8, 197,
    199, 204–5, 233–5, 256, 271,
    288
British Socialist Party (BSP) 21, 25
British Union of Fascists (BUF) 50,
    51
Bukharin, Nikolai 36–7
Burns, Emile 130, 158

Cadwaladr, Dilys 97
Campaign for a Welsh Assembly
    (CWA) 198, 202, 255, 273,
    274, 276–7, 283, 289
Campaign for Nuclear
    Disarmament (CND) 121,
    150
Cohen, Manny 242
Collins, Enoch 136, 140, 155–6, 167

Communist Campaign Group
    (CCG) 199, 272
Communist International
    (Comintern) 7, 10, 11, 12,
    15–16, 21, 24, 28, 29, 32–3,
    36–7, 47, 52, 53–5, 56–7, 285,
    288, 299
Communist Party of Britain (CPB)
    199, 201, 248, 272–3, 282, 283
Communist Party of Great Britain
    (CPGB)
  and 1979 referendum campaign
    239–46, 256
  and Britishness 127–9, 197, 216,
    233–5, 281, 305
  and bolshevisation 28–32,
    299–300
  and English devolution 187,
    189, 194, 197, 232–3, 281
  and Eurocommunism 169, 198,
    199, 201, 202–6, 246–8,
    259–60, 272–3, 282
  and historiography of
    devolution 1–2
  and Hornerism 42–5
  and John Maclean 21–4
  and Labour Party 7–8, 33–6, 41,
    45, 48, 58, 95–6, 102–3, 149,
    167, 173, 181–3, 186, 207,
    212, 224–7, 228, 230–2,
    236–8, 268, 282, 296–7,
    301–4, 305
  and National Eisteddfod 65,
    66–8, 96, 128
  and Parliament for Wales
    Campaign 136–49, 196,
    294–5
  and Plaid Cymru 77–8, 80–1,
    82–3, 88, 89, 91, 95, 98,
    140–1, 155–6, 173–5, 177–8,

179, 181, 182–3, 207, 212,
227–9, 242, 262–3, 268, 282,
295–7, 305
and Popular Front 49, 51, 53,
57–8, 68, 81, 82, 87–8,
114–16, 118, 124, 285, 294
and Scotland 16-17, 79
and South Wales Miners'
Federation (SWMF) 8, 33, 34,
39, 41, 45, 48, 51, 68–9
and Thatcherism 199, 200, 201,
244–5, 246–50, 255–6, 261–2,
264, 268–70, 274–5
and Third Period 37–45, 48,
285, 299
and united front 33–5
and Welsh language 64–5, 67–8,
78, 80, 91, 95, 110, 111–12,
113, 135, 157–61, 164,
169–73, 176–7, 180, 181, 183,
184, 193, 197–8, 211, 215,
264, 281, 291, 292–3, 305
and Welsh Language Society
176–7, 207, 214–15, 227, 228,
229, 230, 267–8
and Welsh nationalism 77–8,
80–1, 175, 178–9
and Welsh self-government 68,
78–80, 82, 83–9, 91–4, 95, 98,
102–8, 109–13, 129–30,
178–86, 195–8, 209–14,
225–7, 236–8, 256, 261–2,
273–6, 285–7, 289–92, 293–5,
301–5
establishment 25–6
historiography of 2–3
Linguists' Group 157–9
London District Committee 52,
59
membership 28, 35, 94, 120,
122, 132, 134–5, 150, 152,
199, 200, 206, 251, 252–3,
272, 298–9
North Wales District 51, 52, 53,
67, 71–2, 73, 77, 78, 83, 86,
89, 116, 285
Scottish Committee 21, 23, 46,
79, 86–7, 91–2, 217

South Wales District 21, 31, 34,
39, 41–2, 45–6, 63, 67, 69–71,
83–7, 89, 115
support for Welsh Parliament
80, 82, 86, 91, 93, 95, 96–7,
98, 103, 105–8, 119, 124, 130,
136–49, 154–5, 156–7, 161–2,
163–4, 167, 169, 173, 179–86,
188, 189, 191, 192–5, 207,
209–12, 215–17, 218, 261–2,
264, 280–1, 289–92, 293–4
Welsh Committee 4, 51–2, 94–5,
103, 104, 105–8, 113, 118,
130, 132–3, 134, 135, 137,
138–41, 153–4, 163, 164–5,
166, 178–85, 191, 193,
209–14, 217, 218, 225, 226,
227–8, 236–7, 244, 254,
255–6, 273–4, 277, 278, 279,
299, 300
Communist Party of Ireland (CPI)
9–16, 47
Communist Party of Scotland 279
Communist Unity Group 25
Connolly, James 14, 20, 47, 157
Connolly, Roddy 14
Cook, A. J. 34, 41
Cook, Dave 253
Cooke, Phil 259–60
Cox, Idris 42, 70–1, 82, 94, 97, 99,
101, 107, 108, 109, 113, 119,
121, 130, 131–5, 138, 148–9,
187, 189–90, 194, 196, 197,
294, 303
Cox, John 174–5, 276, 283–4
Crawfurd, Helen 48, 79
Crowther, Lord 212–13
Cule, Cyril 82
Czechoslovakia, invasion of 120,
168–9, 203

Daniels, Bryn 135
Davies, Brian 131, 229–30, 231, 258
Davies, Dai Lloyd 39, 40
Davies, D. Ivor 219, 222, 223
Davies, James Kitchener 83, 102
Davies, S. O. 41, 137, 138, 142, 145

Democratic Left (DL) 200, 252,
    277, 278–80, 283
Dimitrov, Georgi 53–5, 285
Dubček, Alexander 168
Duclos, Jacques 55
Dutt, Rajani Palme 29, 37, 65, 101,
    120, 124, 129, 130, 150, 151,
    168

Edwards, Kath 262
Electrical Trades Union (ETU)
    121, 150
Enright, Tim 170
Erskine, Ruaraidh 17, 20
Evans, Dai Dan 122, 128, 172
Evans, Edgar 159, 171–2
Evans, Gwynfor 122, 138, 149, 187
Everest, Benn 171–3

Falber, Reuben 217
Faner Goch 258
Feather, Vic 221–2
Fianna Fáil 12
Fishman, Nina 131–2
Fox, Ralph 58
Francis, Ben 39
Francis, Dai 122, 147, 220–1, 222,
    223, 239, 240–2, 243, 265, 293
Francis, Hywel 242, 266, 267–8,
    269–70
Free Wales Army 190
French, Sid 168, 199

Gallacher, William 22, 28, 50, 65,
    69, 93, 101
General Strike (1926) 7, 33, 35–6,
    45
George, Megan Lloyd 138
Gilmore, George 13
Glamorgan Federation of Trade
    Councils (GFTC) 219
Goldberg, Max 39
Gollan, John 126, 150, 165, 225,
    226, 236
Gorbachev, Mikhail 248
Gostwick, Martin 234–5
Gramsci, Antonio 199, 203, 205
Greaves, Desmond 157

Green, Royston 171
Grenfell, D. R. 142, 144, 146–7
Griffiths, Jim 142, 144, 147, 303–4
Griffiths, Robert 149, 228, 258, 260,
    263–4, 272

Hall, Peter 234
Harries, Gwen 160
Hart, Julian Tudor 175, 241
Hay, William 27–8
Hewlett, William 47
Hitchon, Bob 173
Hopkins, Tom 160
Horner, Arthur 8, 34, 39, 41, 42–5,
    47, 50, 66, 69, 83, 86, 101,
    118, 152–3, 265
Howells, Kim 266, 267
Hughes, Cledwyn 137
Hungary, invasion of 120, 151–3,
    169
Hunt, David 277
Humphreys, Cyran Lloyd 92–3,
    99–101, 116, 130
Hyde, Douglas 71–2

impact of World War II 92–3, 288
Independent Labour Party (ILP)
    17, 65, 74
Industrial Democracy for Miners
    (Unofficial Reform
    Committee) 26–7
Inkpin, Albert 28
Inkpin, Harry 29
International Lenin School (ILS)
    11, 39
Irish Republican Army (IRA)
    10–13, 15, 47

Jacques Martin 246, 251–2
Jefferies, Len 39, 83, 104–5
Jones, Bob 272
Jones, D. Gwenallt 97
Jenkins, Dafydd 82, 138
Jones, Alan 187
Jones, Gwenan 138
Jones, Glyn 63–5, 83
Jones, Jack 121, 222, 223
Jones, J. R. 138

Jones, Sid 156, 160–1
Jones, T. Gwynn 97
Jones, T. W. 137
Jones, Tom 221
Jones, W. R. 173

Kinnock, Neil 225, 230, 231, 241,
    243
Khrushchev, Nikita 120, 151
Komunistická strana Československa
    (KSČ) 168

Labour Party (Èire) 10
Labour Party (Great Britain) 1,
    7–8, 33–6, 41, 45, 48, 116,
    173, 180, 181–3, 185, 186,
    187, 207, 212, 224–5, 228,
    230–2, 236–8, 239, 242–3,
    256, 257, 268, 270, 271, 276,
    282, 283, 286, 296–7, 299,
    301–4, 305
Larkin, Jim 11, 14
Larkin Jr., Jim 11
Left Book Club 50, 72
Lenin, Vladimir 22, 34, 190
Lewis, Justin 103, 104
Lewis, Maureen 276
Lewis, Saunders 167, 170
Liaison Committee for the Defence
    of Trade Unions (LCDTU)
    121
liberalism 24, 48, 80
Lindsay, Jack 60–1
Lloyd, D. Tecwyn 97
Lockwood, William 157–9, 170

MacColl, Ewen, 128
MacDonald, John 194
Maclean, John 16, 17–24
MacManus, Arthur 47
Mainwaring, W. H. 102
Malone, Lieutenant-Colonel C. J.
    21
Manifesto for New Times (CPGB)
    248–51, 281
Marx, Karl 15, 58

Marxism and the National and
    Colonial Question (Stalin) 77,
    84
Matthews, George 124, 130
Maunder, Jack 152
McCormick, John 137
McGahey, Mick 265
McLennan, Gordon 184–5, 214,
    243–4
McShane, Harry 23–4
Mellows, Liam 15
Miles, Gareth 258, 260
Miners' Eisteddfod 128
Miners' Federation of Great Britain
    26, 33
Miners' Minority Movement
    (MMM) 34
Miners' Next Step (Unofficial Reform
    Committee) 8, 26–7, 114
miners' strike (1984–85) 255,
    264–72
Murray, Alex 217
Murray, Seán 11–12, 14

National Assembly for Wales 1, 7
National Cultural Committee
    (NCC) 127
National Left 258, 259–60, 262–3,
    268
National Minority Movement
    (NMM) 36, 38
National Unemployed Workers
    Movement (NUWM) 38
National Union of Mineworkers
    (NUM) 50, 101, 102, 105,
    107, 114, 118, 221, 223, 248,
    265, 266
New Communist Party (NCP) 199,
    201, 282
Nicholas, T. E. 65, 73–5, 97, 293
Nicholas, T. Islwyn 61–2

O'Donnell, Peadar 11, 12, 13, 14
Osmond, John 241–2

Paris Peace Conference (1919) 17
Parliament for Wales Campaign
    103, 107, 113, 119, 122, 130,

131, 134, 135, 136–49, 166, 196, 286, 289, 294–5
Parti Communiste Français (PCF) 51, 52, 55–6, 202–3, 298
Partido Communista España (PCE) 202–3
Partito Comunista Italiano (PCI) 51, 202–3, 298
Papworth, Bert 50
Parry, Cyril 144, 145–6
Paynter, Will 35, 44, 83, 152–3, 265
Pearce, Bert 121–2, 161, 174, 175, 178–9, 184, 186–7, 188–9, 190, 194, 196, 201, 206, 209, 212, 225–6, 228–9, 230–1, 236, 237–8, 239, 240, 241–2, 253, 276, 277, 278, 283–4, 286, 294, 303
Penyberth 48, 52, 77–8, 115
Phillips, Gwyn 144
Phippen, George 47
Piratin, Phil 50, 102
Plaid Cymru 1, 48, 53, 72, 73, 74, 77–8, 80–1, 82–3, 88, 89, 91, 95, 98, 99, 100, 115, 119, 122, 140, 155–6, 167, 168, 171, 173–5, 177–8, 179, 180, 181, 182–3, 207, 212, 225, 227–9, 242, 258–60, 262–3, 268, 270, 271, 274, 276, 282, 283, 285, 295–7, 305
Plebs League 31
Pollitt, Harry 29, 37, 38, 55, 56, 58, 62–3, 69, 74, 101, 102, 124–5, 133, 150
Powell, Annie 155, 201
Prothero, Cliff 137, 144–5

Ramelson, Bert 185
Red International of Labour Unions (RILU) 34
Rees, Gareth 263, 271
Rees William 97, 108–9, 110–13, 130–1
Revolt on the Clyde (Gallacher) 23
Republican Congress (1934) 13
Rhys, Keidrych 97

Richards, Dave 201, 253, 270, 276–7, 278
Roberts, Elwyn 140, 149
Roberts, Goronwy 137
Robson, R. W. 58
Rogers, Allan 271
Royal Commission on the Constitution 201, 207, 208–14, 217–18, 286
Rust, William 37, 38, 42, 59, 73
Ryan, Frank 13

Saklatvala, Shapurji 38
Saor Èire 12, 15
Scanlon, Hugh 121
Scargill, Arthur 265, 272
Scotland and Wales Bill (1976) 232, 236–8
Scottish Co-operative Movement 20
Scottish Covenant Association 137
Scottish Farm Servants Union 20
Scottish Trades Union Congress (STUC) 16
Scottish Union of Dock Servants 20
Scottish Workers' Republican Party 22–3
Simon, Roger 126–7
Sinn Fèin 19
Skeats, Les 201, 253, 254–5, 278
Socialist Labour Party (SLP) 21, 25
Socialist League 65
Sosialaeth i'r Cymry (Griffiths and Miles) 258
South Wales Area NUM 122, 141–7, 196, 224, 265, 266, 267–8, 281, 286, 297
South Wales Communist Council (SWCC) 25
South Wales Miners Industrial Union (SWMIU) 68
South Wales Miners' Federation (SWMF) 8, 33, 34, 39, 41, 42, 45, 48, 50, 51, 68–9
South Wales Regional Council of Labour 69
South Wales Socialist Society (SWSS) 25, 26
Springhall, Dave 65

Stalin, Joseph 84, 123, 124–5, 130,
    151, 179, 189–90, 228
Stead, Charlie 39
Stewart, Bob 28
Swain, Charlie 279
syndicalism 8, 26–8, 31, 46

Tapsell, William 37
Temple, Nina 252
Thomas, Alun 121, 135, 140, 143–4,
    148
Thomas, Dafydd Elis 259, 270
Thomas, Mel 34–5, 44
Thomson, George 109–10, 127–8,
    137
Thorez, Maurice 55
Titoism 134
Trades Union Congress (TUC) 7,
    16, 50, 219, 220–4
Trotsky, Leon 24
True, Arthur 173, 177, 178
True, Cliff 186–7, 284

Undeb Cymru Fydd 113, 130, 136–7
Unofficial Reform Committee
    (URC) 26

Vaughan, Ann 215

Wales Bill (1977) 238–9
Wales Congress in Support of
    Mining Communities
    (WCSMC) 255, 264–5,
    267–71, 283, 286
Watkins, Tudor 137
Wales for the Assembly Campaign
    (WAC) 201, 239–42, 261, 262,
    286, 289, 294
Wales TUC 136, 144, 156, 179, 185,
    191, 198, 201, 209, 219–25,

    239, 243, 257, 281, 286, 297,
    300, 304
Welsh Language Society (CYIG)
    122, 167, 176–7, 207, 214–15,
    227, 228, 229, 230, 258,
    260–1, 267–8
Welsh Regional Council of Labour
    (WRCL) 137, 141–2,
    144–5
Welsh Socialist Republican
    Movement (WSRM) 258
Wilkinson, Brian 216, 234
Williams, D. J. 142
Williams, Dafydd 228
Williams, Emyr Wyn 259
Williams, Garfield 39, 41
Williams, Glyn 144, 146
Williams, Gwyn Alf 131, 167, 256–8,
    260
Williams, Hywel Davy 140, 144, 146,
    154, 160, 170–1, 172
Williams, John Roose 71, 72–3,
    75–7, 82–3, 85–6, 96–7, 119,
    130, 135–6, 139–40, 194, 258,
    294, 303
Wilson, Alistair 163–4, 173, 178–9,
    209, 216, 245
Wilson, Jock 39
Winter, Mary 215, 229, 230, 239,
    274–5, 276
Woddis, Jack 232–3
Workers' Socialist Federation
    (WSF) 25
Wright, George 221

Young Communist League (YCL)
    135, 150, 151, 152, 168,
    177–8, 200

Zhdanov, Andrei 128